# WHY
# MARKET
# SOCIALISM?

# WHY MARKET SOCIALISM?

## VOICES FROM

**dissent**

## Frank Roosevelt and David Belkin, Editors

*M.E. Sharpe*
Armonk, New York
London, England

**Library of Congress Cataloging-in-Publication Data**

Why market socialism? : voices from Dissent / edited by Frank Roosevelt and
David Belkin ; with a foreword by Robert Heilbroner.
p.   cm.

Includes index.
ISBN 1–56324–465–9—ISBN 1–56324–466–7 (pbk)
1. Marxian economics. 2. Socialism. 3. Capitalism.
I. Roosevelt, Frank, 1938-
II. Belkin, David, 1951-
III. Dissent.
HB97.5.W5   1994
335—dc20
94–19803
CIP

Printed in the United States of America

The paper used in this publication meets the minimum requirements of
American National Standard for Information Sciences—
Permanence of Paper for Printed Library Materials,
ANSI Z 39.48-1984.

BM (c)   10   9   8   7   6   5   4   3   2   1
BM (p)   10   9   8   7   6   5   4   3   2   1

This book is dedicated
to the memory of
IRVING HOWE

# Contents

# Contributors

**Joanne Barkan** is Executive Editor of *Dissent* and author of *Visions of Emancipation: The Italian Workers Movement Since 1945.*

**David Belkin** is an economist and fiscal policy analyst with the Office of the Manhattan Borough President, and a contributor to *Dissent.*

**Daniel Bell** is Scholar in Residence at the American Academy of Arts and Sciences. He is the author of *Marxian Socialism in the United States; The End of Ideology; The Coming of Post-Industrial Society;* and *The Cultural Contradictions of Capitalism.*

**Robert Blair** is an economist and speechwriter with an independent regulatory agency in Washington, D.C.

**Fred Block** is Professor of Sociology at the University of California, Davis, and author of *Postindustrial Possibilities: A Critique of Economic Discourse.*

**Robert Dahl** is Sterling Professor of Political Science (Emeritus) at Yale University and author of *After the Revolution? Authority in a Good Society; Polyarchy: Participation and Opposition; Who Governs? Democracy and Power in an American City; A Preface to the Theory of Economic Democracy;* and *Democracy and Its Critics.*

**Ernest Erber** is a member of the American Institute of Certified Planners and author of *Urban Planning in Transition.*

**Saul Estrin** is Lecturer at the London School of Economics and Political Science and author of *Self-management: Economic Theory and Yugoslav Practice* and (with P. Holmes) of *French Planning in Theory and Practice.* He is also coeditor (with J. Le Grand) of *Market Socialism.*

**Michael Harrington** (1928–1989) was a leader in the socialist movement and the author of sixteen books, including *The Other America; The Twilight of Capitalism; The Politics at God's Funeral;* and *Socialism: Past and Future.*

**Robert Heilbroner** is Norman Thomas Professor of Economics (Emeritus) at the New School for Social Research and author of *The Worldly Philosophers; An Inquiry into the Human Prospect; Marxism: For and Against; The Nature and Logic of Capitalism;* and *21st Century Capitalism.*

**Branko Horvat** was Professor of Economics and Director of the Institute of Economic Studies in Belgrade and is now head of the Social Democratic Union in Croatia. He is the author of *Towards a Theory of Planned Economy, An Essay on Yugoslav Society;* and *The Political Economy of Socialism: A Marxist Social Theory.*

**Irving Howe** (1920–1993) was a leading social and literary critic and was founding editor of *Dissent* from 1953 to his death in 1993. Among his books are *Politics and the Novel; World of Our Fathers; and Socialism and America.*

**Tadeusz Kowalik** is Professor of Economics and Humanities at the Polish Academy of Science in Warsaw. He is the author of several entries in J. Eatwell, M. Milgate, and P. Newman, eds., *The New Palgrave: A Dictionary of Economics.*

**David Miller** is Official Fellow in Social and Political Theory at Nuffield College, Oxford, and author of *Social Justice; Philosophy and Ideology in Hume's Political Thought; Anarchism; and Market, State, and Community: Theoretical Foundations of Market Socialism.*

**Alec Nove** (1915–1994) was Professor of Economics at the University of Glasgow and the author of *The Soviet Economic System, Was Stalin Really Necessary?* and *The Economics of Feasible Socialism.*

**Paul Ricoeur** is a leading French philosopher, best known for his development of hermeneutics. He is the author of *The Symbolism of Evil, Freud and Philosophy; The Conflict of Interpretations; The Rule of Metaphor; Hermeneutics and the Human Sciences;* and *Time and Narrative.*

**Michel Rocard** has served as Prime Minister of France and he is the author of *Par les vrais, À l'épreuve des faits, Un pays comme le nôtre,* and *Le coeur à l'ouvrage.*

**John Roemer** is Professor of Economics and Director of the Program on Economy, Justice, and Society at the University of California, Davis. He is the author of *Free to Lose: An Introduction to Marxist Economic Philosophy; A General Theory of Exploitation and Class;* and *A Future for Socialism.* He is also coeditor (with P.K. Bardhan) of *Market Socialism: The Current Debate.*

**Frank Roosevelt** is Professor of Economics at Sarah Lawrence College and a contributor to E.J. Nell, ed., *Growth, Profits and Property: Essays in the Revival of Political Economy.*

**James Tobin** is Professor of Economics (Emeritus) at Yale University. He won the Nobel Memorial Prize in Economics in 1981 and is the author of *National Economic Policy; Asset Accumulation and Economic Activity; The New Economics One Decade Older;* and *Essays in Economics: Theory and Policy.*

**Thomas E. Weisskopf** is Professor of Economics at the University of Michigan and coauthor (with Samuel Bowles and David M. Gordon) of *After the Waste Land: A Democratic Economics for the Year 2000.*

# Foreword

Irving Howe once said that socialism is the name of our desire. Today it is also the name of our disappointment and (sometimes) our despair. Socialism conjures up both states of mind because it has come to mean two things—the achievement of a transformed society in which we would all like to live, and the struggles to go beyond the limits of the society in which we do live. I shall call the first image Socialism with a capital S, and the second, socialisms with a small s at each end of the word.

These are not propitious times to speak of Socialism. The collapse of the Soviet Union, however much socialists have always distanced themselves from that regime, haunts the object of our desire, and is likely to do so for a long time. Perhaps in the end, that collapse will have a salutary effect because it teaches us that Socialism is still beyond the reach of our practical capabilities—perhaps even of our imaginations. In the shorter run, the effect is not likely to be so salutary. As we might expect, many conservatives have already drawn the conclusion that all efforts to plan an economic system are doomed to disaster, forgetting the planning that keeps capitalism off the rocks. Worse, even liberal-minded reformers tend to believe that the very idea of socialism, however small the initial letter, has died along with its grander vision.

I think that defeatist conclusion is wrong. If Socialism remains an elusive object of our desire, there is nothing elusive about the Capitalism that is the object of our concern. Socialisms of the kind with which this book is concerned represent efforts to find where boundaries can be crossed to mitigate some of the problems that affect capitalism in all its many forms—unemployment, alienation, ecological damage, cultural deformation.

Socialisms therefore constitute a kind of ongoing experiment to discover what sorts of arrangements might repair the damage wrought by the existing social order. Some of them will no doubt be easily contained within the institutional arrangements of the more progressive capitalisms, lying just across their existing borders. Others will require more far-reaching institutional changes, perhaps beyond today's reach. Still others imply social and economic rearrangements that may not come to pass without the cooperation of capitalism itself, in the form of serious malfunctions that will require "radical" remedies. In the first category I think of the democratization of political movements, and of efforts to extend various forms of flexible economic planning both at the national and at the local level; in the second category, there is the extension of popular participation in economic as well as in social life, and the gradual widening of economic rights, along with political and social ones; in the third, of experiments—no doubt at first on a small scale—with workers' ownership and control. The hope of all these socialist efforts is that they point the way for still larger transformations in the future, the nature of which we can as yet only dimly apprehend. This is a hope that is easy to deride, but not so easy to dismiss.

The distance between these dim perceptions and our immediate frustrations is what makes this an age of disappointment. How could it be anything else, when capitalism is unquestionably the order of the day, and of many many days to come? But I do not think the outlook betokens despair. Capitalism continues to be, as it always has been, the agency for its own undoing. The task of socialists is therefore not to wring their hands, but to dust off their clothes and go to work. They will not lack for an agenda. What I think they should also bear in mind is that the testing of socialist ideas with small initial letters is not only valuable in itself, but helps clear our minds about what really constitutes the Socialism of our desire.

Robert Heilbroner
January 1994

# Preface

According to traditional socialist thought, *market socialism* is a contradiction in terms. Fortunately, this has never been the view of the editors of *Dissent*—a quarterly magazine founded in 1953 and committed to the values of social inclusion, democratic participation, mutual responsibility, and cultural diversity. Beginning in the mid-1980s, the late Irving Howe, a leading critic and founding editor of *Dissent*, opened the pages of the magazine to a steady stream of articles on market socialism, initiating the series with the publication of Alec Nove's seminal essay on "Feasible Socialism" (chapter 10 in this volume).

Why market socialism? With the collapse of Communist regimes in the East and the continuing inability of capitalism to provide general economic security and a just distribution of wealth and income, there is a real need for an attractive and viable alternative that would not require centralized planning or state ownership of the means of production.

For as long as there have been socialist movements, there have been socialist thinkers who have understood the disadvantages of relying too heavily on the state to coordinate and direct the economic activities of a nation. Although markets have often been blamed for some of the more objectionable aspects of capitalism— alienation, inequality, exploitation, instability, and possessive individualism—they have also been perceived by these thinkers as making possible a dispersion of political power, decentralization of economic decision making, and efficient use of scarce resources.

Thus the essays in this book continue the efforts of a long line of writers and activists on the left who have seen the need for markets in post-capitalist society.

With the permission and encouragement of the current editors of *Dissent*—Mitchell Cohen and Michael Walzer—we bring together a selection of articles, comments, reviews, and exchanges on markets and socialism that have appeared in the magazine during the past decade. The rationale for this collection was perhaps best stated by Irving Howe in the Summer 1990 issue:

> In the past, left-wing movements under Marxist influence tended to dismiss as unhistorical [all] efforts to specify "what a socialist society would look like." . . . [T]he left used to say that the people (the workers) would take history into their own hands and then decide. Fine, but it turned out that if you didn't have a few clear ideas about what you proposed to do when history fell into your hands, you wouldn't know what to do even if it did fall into your hands. So one thing high on our agenda at *Dissent* will be a series of modest, intermittent efforts to do a little "future-painting."

We have not attempted to update any of the essays in this volume to reflect developments since their publication in *Dissent*. Instead we have included the date of original publication under the title of each chapter so that readers will be able to excuse the authors for the occasional statement rendered obsolete by the ongoing rush of events. We believe that the insights offered by the contributors will remain valuable for a considerable period of time.

We must give full credit to the editors of *Dissent,* past and present, for the high quality and readable style of the pieces reprinted in this volume. We would especially like to thank Executive Editors Joanne Barkan and Brian Morton and the magazine's Business Manager, Simone Plastrik, for the many ways in which they supported this project. We are grateful to the Harburg Foundation—and especially its president, Ernie Harburg—for underwriting the costs of preparing the manuscript and compiling the index. Our editor at M.E. Sharpe, Richard Bartel, has been most helpful with his steady support and expert advice. Finally, we wish to express our gratitude to the following individuals who, each in his or her own way, helped us to complete work on this book: Rhon Baiman, Constance Blake, Jeremy Borenstein, Martha Campbell, Nicole Fermon, Jerry Flieger, Patricia Frenz-Belkin, Jeff Gold, Suzanne Gottlieb, Barbara Kancelbaum, Steve Oliver, Kathryn Paulsen, and Jinx Roosevelt.

Frank Roosevelt and David Belkin
September 1994

# PART I

## Introduction

# Why Market Socialism? From the Critique of Political Economy to Positive Political Economy

## *David Belkin*

*If the workers in a socialist State should organize their labour in a manner convenient to themselves but detrimental to its productivity, such a one-sided policy on the part of the producers would speedily find its Nemesis. The new system would soon enter upon a path of retrogression, while the old capitalist States, existing by its side, would continue to develop their productive forces. The inevitable result would be that the workers, or at least the great part of them, in the socialist State would be worse off as consumers, in spite of the abolition of capitalist exploitation, than the workers in a capitalist society, in spite of the pressure of increasing exploitation. Sooner or later the socialist community would lose its vitality.*

Karl Kautsky (1922)[1]

The past decade has seen a remarkable flowering of ideas about market socialism. This has been prompted both by cumulative setbacks of socialist hopes and by cumulative advances in theories of social and economic organization. The setbacks have pried (most) socialists away from the naive belief that, in Alec Nove's words, a socialism is possible "in which 'society' decides" what to produce and how to distribute goods and services "without the 'detour' of market and value relations" (chapter 10). The theoretical advances have furnished powerful tools for understanding the underlying logic, necessity, and comparative advantages of both market and nonmarket "detours."

The transformed concept of market socialism that is emerging from all this appears to relinquish much of classical socialism's long-cultivated "otherness" vis-à-vis the liberal economic order; and yet, at the same time, it recovers a distinctive liberal socialist tradition whose bona fides are as old as those of the classical socialism that eclipsed it over a century ago.

The classical socialist project was in trouble from the moment socialists were given opportunities to realize it. For as Irving Howe observed in "Thinking About Socialism" (chapter 2), when state power fell into the laps of several European socialist parties at the end of the First World War, it turned out that "they often had no clear idea, no worked-out vision, of what a socialist transformation might entail." This was not only true of the German social democrats, who "began to find the idea of socialism increasingly slippery, evanescent, insubstantial" and were unable to move beyond cautious palliatives. It was equally true of the Bolsheviks, whose "aura of certainty" belied "a deep incoherence, a floundering by gifted ideologues" that led them to "veer wildly in their economic policies"—first left, then right, then left—right into Stalin's deadly embrace.

After these miscarriages of revolutionary ambitions, the argument for socialism could no longer proceed directly (if indeed it ever could) from the critique of capital. Instead, that argument became mired in seemingly endless equivocations that said more about all the ways that various socialist desiderata (public ownership, employment security, and so on) might *not* add up to genuine democratic socialism than about how they would.

The sudden collapse of Communism in the European Revolutions of 1989 stirred up democratic socialists' hopes of recovering their own voice. For a euphoric moment the toppling of false gods seemed to provide a chance to *show* what genuine socialism is, an opportunity to actually implement the ideas and models that democratic socialists had nurtured for many years, but never fully tested. The conditions seemed about right: populations in rebellion against authoritarian rule but habituated to job and income security and suspicious of competition and possessive individualism;[2] a seasoned corps of industrial planners and managers who were versed in what worked and didn't work in an administered economy; and finally the reform models themselves, schemes to retrieve the original socialist project of "politicizing the economic" by (1) placing planning under the aegis of the people ("democratizing the political") and (2) permitting some markets to operate under the aegis of the plan.

## The Rise and Fall of Simulated Market Socialism

The models favored by would-be post-Communist reformers arose out of the famous "socialist calculation" debates of the interwar period. In 1920 the Austrian economist Ludwig von Mises argued that economic calculation was not merely difficult but *impossible* in an economy without private ownership and a full set of markets (including capital markets) which, he asserted, socialism precluded by definition.[3] A decade later, a group of neoclassically trained socialist economists in England and the United States—principally Oskar Lange, Abba Lerner, H.D. Dickinson, and Evan Durbin—responded by showing that with a partial *simulation* of markets (and a few subordinate or derivative real ones), a socialist regime could retain all the putative benefits of public ownership and centralized control (equitable distribution, full employment, and rapid growth along predetermined socially optimal paths) without the excessive bureaucratization that plagued Soviet development.[4]

It is revealing that while Lange labeled his answer to Mises the "Competitive Solution," he never applied the term *market socialism* to his model. In the three-cornered debates that followed, the Competitive Solution failed to convert either sophisticated supporters of Soviet-style command planning like Maurice Dobb or sophisticated critics of all state economic planning like Friedrich Hayek, both of whom attacked it for being static and abstract.[5] Indeed, as Tadeusz Kowalik recounts in chapter 6, during the latter stages of the socialist calculation debate Lange himself began to tilt towards a mixed economy with limited state intervention in capital goods markets—only to veer back to (critical) advocacy of orthodox Soviet planning practices upon his return to Communist Poland. From the late 1940s on, "Lange's chief concern became to 'enlighten' central planners, to equip them with modern tools of analysis, forecasting, and planning" (Kowalik)—tools that did not include regulated markets.

But during the 1950s and 1960s, a circle of Eastern European reformers, including students and colleagues of Lange such as Wlodzimierz Brus, fleshed out the original idea of "central planning with regulated markets" (Brus's term) by drawing a line between production decisions that were "long-term" or "capacity-producing," and those that were "short-term" or "capacity-using." The former were to be the responsibility of politically accountable central planners, while the latter would be left to the managers of state-owned but otherwise autonomous profit-maximizing enterprises. This was the main form in which the idea of market socialism took hold in Eastern Europe, although there was also considerable interest in the Yugoslav model, which devolved more investment planning (but not ownership rights) to self-managed enterprises.

But where democratic socialist reformers wished to lead in 1989, few former Communist subjects were prepared to follow: they were simply not convinced that "central planning with regulated markets" could deliver the goods—not so much because that alternative was untested as because of the perception that enough of it *had* been tested to demonstrate that it was irreparably flawed.

The main test run took place in Hungary and lasted about two decades, from the introduction of the New Economic Mechanism (NEM) in the late 1960s until the Communist collapse. In accordance with the reform recipe, NEM rewired the circuits of state enterprise guidance by replacing quantitative targets with indirect indicators (administered prices, taxes, credits, subsidies). It turned out, however, that state enterprise managers could not or would not display the profit-maximizing flexibility and initiative expected of them when enterprise outcomes were still so dependent on variables manipulated by central planners. At the same time, those central planners could not or would not impose the requisite budget discipline on poorly managed or otherwise underperforming state enterprises. On the one hand, it was the state itself that would ultimately be held accountable for the turmoil of bankruptcy and reorganization of revenue-losing enterprises. On the other hand, the very enterprise guidance instruments that made the state accountable—the whole paraphernalia of administered prices and credits and so on—could also be used to cover (or cover up) enterprise losses and avoid such politically unpalatable reckonings. Thus planners had both the motive and the means to feed enterprises a steady diet of what János Kornai called *soft budget constraints*.[6]

In the long run, of course, the great reckoning was only postponed, because the perpetuation of soft budget constraints in the state enterprise sector sabotaged efforts to reduce waste and shortage in the Hungarian economy—and the Communist regime was finally held accountable for *that*.[7]

Kautsky's dire warning had proved prophetic. Under "central planning with regulated markets" no less than in conventionally planned economies, soft budget constraints became entitlements that allowed workers and managers to lock in underperforming investments—that is, to "organize their labour in a manner convenient to themselves but detrimental to its productivity"—and this system had indeed "found its Nemesis," if not speedily, then at least in time to discredit the reformers' claims to have designed a better noncapitalist mousetrap.[8] Brus himself came to that conclusion even before the Revolutions of '89 (see Belkin's review of Brus and Laski, chapter 7).

Contemplating Gorbachev's failed last-ditch attempt to "move from a centrally planned economy to market socialism" in the Soviet Union, David Miller concluded in 1991 that "[t]he lesson is that *the market element of market socialism must be in place prior to the socialist element*" (chapter 12, emphasis added)—the very opposite of what some observers of the Eastern European revolutions had initially hoped. What was needed, he wrote, was a setting "where working under market constraints is a familiar experience, but where many employees find themselves frustrated by the hierarchal structure of the traditional capitalist firm." That setting was in the West; but here, too, a large question mark hovered over the means and ends of the socialist project.

## The Rediscovery of the Invisible Hand

For Western socialists the end of the rainbow was, practically speaking, not behind the Bolshevik mountain, but somewhere "beyond social democracy." But as Robert Heilbroner and Joanne Barkan asked (chapter 9), just where beyond social democracy did democratic socialists want to go? Although the Competitive Solution was originally introduced and vetted in Western academic and socialist circles, resistance—or more likely indifference—toward this very cautious opening to markets persisted longer among committed democratic socialists outside the Soviet bloc than among Eastern reformers. Perhaps this was because the dilemmas of nonmarket economic administration were more remote from Western socialists than the danger of sliding down the slippery slope of social democratic reformism into what Michael Harrington called "socialist capitalism."[9] This was, after all, where the initially cautious introduction of markets into post–World War I "socialization" discussions in Germany, Austria, Sweden, and Britain had ultimately led.[10]

In any event, well into the 1970s many Western socialists who shared Lange's goal of decentralizing and democratizing social planning still leaned toward the hope that this could be done with little or no recourse to markets, perhaps by organizing the economy along something like Guild Socialist or Austro-Marxist lines, or by substituting computers and "optimal planning" techniques as the later Lange (and other giants of economics like Michal Kalecki and Leonid Kantorovich) proposed.[11] The idea that production could be directly coupled to individual and social need through democratic assemblies (or cybernetic networks) of workers and consumers was highly alluring to those who remained suspicious of the corrosive and alienating affects of any production for exchange. As Michel Rocard remarks in chapter 4, even the relatively pragmatic French Socialist Party "still partly supported a project of an administered economy in the 1970s." Among the Americans, there was only a gradual and begrudging shift toward Harrington's argument that real "socialist socialism" could join decommodification of most basic consumption with selective use of what he would later call "markets within a planning framework" (see below and chapter 3).

But by then the ground was shifting under the Western socialists' feet. As James Tobin observes in chapter 15, while the state economies of the Soviet Union and Eastern Europe slid from stagnation to collapse, Adam Smith's "invisible hand" doctrine was enjoying a remarkable renaissance almost everywhere else around the globe. From Western Europe to Latin America to East Asia, both advanced and developing nations were yielding to the pull of economic liberalization. Countries with histories of vigorous and successful state oversight of industry (Japan, South Korea) or of widespread direct state ownership (Britain, Argentina) were not immune; nor were those ruled by social democrats (Sweden), Socialists (France), and even Communists (China).

How could those in the "beyond social democracy" camp continue to prescribe squeezing private ownership and unregulated exchange down to the absolute minimum deemed necessary to prevent bureaucracy from ravaging a socialized economy, when social democracy itself remained under growing pressure to expand, not curtail, the realm of freedom from state regulation? Progressives like James Tobin could easily deflate the wildly exaggerated claims of the benefits of privatization and deregulation being bruited about by Thatcherites and Reaganauts (see chapter 15). But all this did not in itself restore the old luster of the idea that competition is fundamentally dangerous and bad. Or rather, it did not rebut the charge, powerfully reinforced by the winds of change blowing out of Eastern Europe, that "politicizing the economic" only made things worse. Michel Rocard (chapter 4) captured the problem exactly:

> And when we say [to Eastern Europeans] that they should not renounce politics, that they should preserve at least a few of the prerogatives of the state, they have the impression that we are dangerous accomplices of the Gulag. Thus it is not only the critique of the administered economy but the reality of it, too, that had blocked the social imagination. What we call the critique of totalitarianism has given rise to a vehement denunciation of political action itself.

True, in the 1990s some of the virulence of antigovernment rhetoric abated in the West (Reagan and Thatcher were gone), and the strains of the conversion to markets produced reactions across much of the former Soviet bloc. But it did not greatly help the democratic socialist cause that in the East "central planning with regulated markets" was now the preferred alternative of hardline *opponents* of reform (the same *nomenclatura* who'd earlier spurned that model when it was the reform). Nor does it bode well that the former Communists whose fortunes have been revived by popular discontent with reform can find no alternative when back in power but to stay the course of economic liberalization. Skepticism about politics remained strong everywhere, and Western socialists clinging to minimal market (or no market) blueprints seemed increasingly out of touch.

## The Forgotten Precursors of Real Market Socialism

With all the alternatives exhausted, was there any way to combine meaningful socialism with real market competition? Perhaps the first and greatest obstacle to overcome was the deep-rooted belief, shared by both critics and supporters of socialism, that this was impossible. As we saw, Lange's simulated capital market response to Mises—and the whole ensuing elaboration of models of "central planning with regulated markets"—did not fundamentally challenge the assumption that socialism *by definition* precluded real markets, or at least real capital markets.

And yet arguments linking socialism and markets—real markets— had actually been cultivated up to a century *before* Lange. Men and women within or sympathetic to the workers' movement, including Thomas Hodgskin, Pierre-Joseph Proudhon, Albert Schäffle, Richard Ely, and (above all) John Stuart Mill, prophetically catalogued the dangers lurking in the association of socialism with state-wide "conscious direction" of the economy, and argued that it was not necessary to eliminate markets in order to eliminate exploitation. Standing out from both "utopian" and "scientific" socialists, they outlined socialisms that stressed firm-wide rather than state-wide collectivization (that is, cooperative rather than societal ownership of the means of production) *and* retained competitive markets as functioning motors of economic growth and change (rather than as mere conduits of state plans and commands).

Mill, in particular, mounted a strong case that "universal association" would be inimicable both to the growth of liberty and to economic progress, which he believed were linked. Recognizing that "hitherto there has been no alternative for those who lived by their labor, but that of laboring each for himself alone, or for a master," Mill declared that "the aim of improvement should be not solely to place human beings in a condition in which they will be able to do without one another, but to enable them *to work for one another in relations not involving dependence.*"[12] Here Mill took issue not only with conservatives who overlooked the reality of patriarchal despotism (and economic backwardness) masked by the idyllic image of yeoman independence, but also with radicals who discounted the danger that a universal communistic regime would bring an "absolute dependence of each on all, and surveillance of each by all" far more invasive than anything experienced in existing society.[13]

Clearly apposite to Mill's concerns about absolute dependence was his discussion of the productivity-enhancing effects of laws furnishing productive agents with "superior security" against depredations of property—and especially against depredations by government itself.[14] This was part and parcel of Mill's more general observation that lack of "trustworthiness" added greatly to the costs of executing transactions both between and within enterprises.[15] Mill believed that profit-sharing (and eventually full worker ownership) could reduce some of the costs of securing cooperation within firm-sized associations by "connect[ing] the pecuniary interest of every person in their employment with the most efficient and most economical management of the concern."[16]

But Mill also recognized that connection of interest did not preclude conflict of interest: common ownership sacrificed a "[u]nity of authority [that] makes many things possible, which could not or would not be undertaken subject to the chance of divided councils or changes in management."[17] Thus, Mill argued (as did Hodgskin versus William Thompson, and Proudhon versus Louis Blanc), it would be critical to retain the spur of rivalry *between* cooperative associations, for "it would be difficult to induce the general assembly of an association to submit to the trouble and inconvenience of altering their habits by adopting some new and promising invention, unless their knowledge of the existence of rival associations made them apprehend that what they would not consent to do, others would, and that they would be left far behind in the race." He allowed that "competition may not be the best conceivable stimulus, but it is at present a necessary one, and no one can foresee the time when it will not be indispensable to progress."[18]

In short, what Mill and the others advocated was (although the term had not yet been invented) a proto-market socialism featuring enterprise-level collective planning in a real competitive market framework rather than simulated or regulated markets in a collective planning framework. To anticipate what the rest of this introduction will show, the essays in this volume trace out a passage from the second model, the dominant alternative to Communism and social democratic reformism in the twentieth century, to something with considerable affinities to the first.

But as will be seen, it is a passage of belated reinvention rather than rediscovery, for even in Lange's day scarcely an echo of the earlier market socialist concepts remained. During what is sometimes called the age of "classical socialism" (1890–1914), the ideas of Mill and Proudhon lost almost all their purchase in socialist circles; later pro-market *Kathedersozialisten* ("socialists of the chair") like Schäffle and Christian socialists like Ely were estranged from mainstream Second International party activity and were regarded with more or less benign contempt (or neglect) by those in that mainstream.

Within the increasingly Marxian mainstream itself it was simply given that, as Morris Hillquit typically put it, "there is no room in a socialist commonwealth for production for sale or for commerce." The familiar story was that markets were being crowded out within capitalism itself through the growth of trusts that already "demonstrated the feasibility and advantage of cooperative and planful production on a large scale." When this process progressed just a little further, it would remain only to transfer control of these trusts to the socialist state, which "with its larger powers and resources, will be able to increase the advantages of trustified production very considerably."[19] Concentration-and-centralization socialism had its critics within the Second International, but not even the most sophisticated among these—Bernstein, Vandervelde, Branting, Shaw, Bauer, and the like—could bring themselves to publicly challenge the Marxian anathema against connecting markets and socialism.[20]

It is important to understand why those attempting to communicate across the late-nineteenth century chasm between promarket liberalism and antimarket collectivism found it increasingly difficult to keep even one foot in the socialist camp in this period. Perhaps the most obvious explanation is that while proto-market socialists bridged the space between socialism and liberalism or democratic radicalism, Marxian socialism was deeply committed to sundering precisely these connections. An Albert Schäffle might have found it "remarkable, and even comforting, that all which is required to make socialism so much as a matter of practical discussion, urges it to preserve, and even intensify, the brighter elements of the liberal economic system,"[21] but the prospect of such a rapprochement utterly horrified Marx and his followers: isolation of the socialist movement from anything that smacked of "mere" reform was crucial not only to its political development (the Second International vigilantly policed incipient tendencies toward "class collaboration"), but also to sustaining its psychological allure, which was rooted in the promise that by basing all social intercourse on the principle of cooperation, socialism would (as Margaret Cole put it) "make life and living decent and beautiful instead of shameful and squalid."[22] The image of worker- or community-owned enterprises engaging in the same kind of grubby competition with one another as did capitalist enterprises did not exactly inspire this sort of eschatological rapture.[23]

## Methodological Issues in Classical Socialism's Rejection of Markets

Early arguments for market socialism also foundered on methodological weaknesses that were shared (and overlooked) by socialists and their critics. Over the years when socialist antipathy to markets became entrenched, neither of the two dominant paradigms based on critiques of classical political economy—the Marxian and the neoclassical—really had a theory of economic organization. That is, economics lacked a theory that would have identified not only when it is efficient for conscious direction (that is, democracy or hierarchy) to take over the regulation of economic exchanges from the market *but also the limits of conscious direction.*

During this period (the last third of the nineteenth century), "bourgeois" economists acquired a new set of tools for investigating the allocative and distributive properties of unsupervised voluntary exchange between autonomous agents maximizing private gains. But these tools—the marginalist theories crafted by Walras, Menger, and Jevons—did not much help explain why *some* sets of exchanges (and the agents who make them) *are* closely supervised in real market economies, or why we find, to use D.H. Robertson's later striking image, "islands of conscious power in this ocean of unconscious co-operation like lumps of butter coagulating in a pail of buttermilk."[24]

When the question of economic organization was addressed, it was supposed that firms existed to organize agents whose services complemented an indivisible productive asset (a machine, an assembly line, a plant)—that is, to exploit technical economies of scale. Yet as Yoram Barzel points out, "a large-scale *operation . . .* does not as such necessarily require a large-scale *organization*."[25] Thus the traditional theory of the firm begged the central question: why weren't agents organized to maximize scale economies through multilateral open market exchanges that preserved their status as independent contractors, even at the point of production? This was difficult to explain in a theory that barely acknowledged that the employment contract involved (on one side) a surrender of independence—indeed, a theory whose "real objective" was (as Harold Demsetz put it) precisely "to study allocation *in the absence of authority*."[26]

This was not a problem in the Marxian framework, which, as Douglass North notes, brought in "all of the elements left out of the neoclassical framework: institutions, property rights, the state, and ideology."[27] It was clear to Marx that fundamentally different principles of coordination and control supported the divisions of labor across markets and within firms. Both realms involved specialization and interdependence, but in the market, as Marx put it, "the bond between the independent labors of the cattle-breeder, the tanner, and the shoe-maker" consists of "the fact that their respective products are commodities," whereas in the firm,

> the specialized worker produces no commodities. It is only the common product of all the specialized workers that becomes a commodity. The division of labor within society is mediated through the purchase and sale of the products of different branches of industry, while the connection

between the various partial operations in a work-shop is mediated through the sale of labor-power of several workers to one capitalist, who applies it as combined labor-power.[28]

The neoclassical question of how "markets created firms" did not arise as such here. On the contrary, Marx showed that "islands of conscious power" historically preceded the "ocean of unconscious co-operation," that wealth-creation had been organized and driven by (local) hierarchies long before the enlargement of the compass of coercion and exchange had transformed (and, Marx argued, veiled) the way hierarchical authority was exercised. That the organization of production involved the "governance of people" as well as the "administration of things" was a starting point, not an afterthought, in Marx's critique of political economy.

A persuasive argument can be made that the most decisive difference between Marxian and neoclassical economics was that the former insisted that the value of labor services in production and the distribution of wealth in society were not simply a function of technology or "endowments," but were also determined by the disposition of conflicting claims and aims in the workplace. This meant that socialists were prepared, long before anyone else, to envision social welfare gains coming from more progressive "relations of production" as well as from more advanced "means of production."

But the Marxian perspective begged several central questions also—or perhaps it was really one question, asked different ways: Why, as the scale of capitalist production and organization grew, did conscious integration still envelop only certain transactions while what Marx called "unplanned anarchy" persisted among others? If a specialized producer's independence depended on whether or not his specialized product was a commodity, then what determined when a specialized product was a commodity?

Thomas Hodgskin provided the inspiration for Marx's analysis of the difference between divisions of labor within markets and firms. But perhaps Hodgskin—one of the proto-market socialists mentioned above—himself got closer to the bottom of things when he pointed to the difficulties in ascertaining "how much of [a] joint product should go to each of the individuals whose united labors produce it," which he contrasted with the relative ease another buyer will have in ascertaining the utility, and deciding what price he will consent to pay, for the "whole" product.[29] In short, Hodgskin was hinting at the idea that *some (but only some) exchanges are not commodified because of the costs of determining exactly what is being offered in the exchange*: "There is nothing on which the labourer can seize, and say, 'This is my product . . . '."[30] Here is a kernel of what, as we shall see below, we would now call a transaction cost (rather than just production cost) theory of economic organization.

And here perhaps is a key to why Hodgskin defended markets while opposing capitalism, whereas Marx, having sharply delineated the different principles of exchange across markets ("no authority other than that of competition") and within workshops ("the lifelong annexation of the worker"), heaped scorn on those who worried that "a general organization of labor in society . . . would turn the whole of society into a factory."[31] As Frank Roosevelt reminds us in chapter 5, while Marx held that *both* modes of exchange fostered an "alien attitude of men to their own product," he insisted that it would be the workshop model, writ large, that would enable "men once more [to] gain control of exchange, production, and the way they behave to one another" after ownership was socialized.[32] Hodgskin, on the other hand, appears to have had a clue that the economic advantages of conscious organization might apply—even after workers acquired control of capital—to *some* types of transactions, but not to all; evidently Marx missed (or dismissed) that clue.[33]

The ironic and tragic result of all this is that just where Marx might have been expected to equip his followers with the most profound and constructive insights—that is, on the subject of transforming "relations of production"—was where we found socialists generally contenting themselves with what can be most charitably called wishful thinking. A particularly inopportune—but alas, all too typical—instance of this was Lenin's blithe affirmation, on the eve of the Bolshevik takeover, that accounting and control in industrial economies had already been providentially "reduced to extraordinarily simple operations . . . of supervising and recording, of knowing the basic rules of arithmetic and of issuing the appropriate receipts."[34] In other words, socialist production (and hence society) would require only the "administration of things," and not the "governance of people."[35]

**From Neglect to Consideration of Agency Issues in Socialism**

The interwar socialist calculation debates were also conducted without the benefit of a coherent theory of economic organization, and the Competitive Solution camp perpetuated the unfortunate orthodox socialist tradition of neglecting the question of how socialism would cope with the "governance of people" in the economy. Lange posited transmission of social preferences through democratic politics to inform the actions of central planners, a set of rules to guide the responses of enterprise managers to the parametric prices offered by these planners, and unstinting worker fulfillment of the instructions of the managers. But he did not recognize that all this required, in effect, consummation of a long chain of *principal-agent* contracts, whose salient feature was that one party had to be motivated to take actions reflecting the interests of another. Lange glossed over the matter of what it would take to get workers (not threatened by unemployment) to obey their instructions, managers to follow their rules, planners to defer to elected officials, and elected officials to neutrally adopt the interests of the electorate. At issue was not just the potentially differing preferences of the agents making up each link of this chain of political and economic transactions, but also the information and incentives available to the principals vis-à-vis each set of agents, that is, the effectiveness (and cost) of the mechanisms at hand for securing cooperation across those differences in preference.

As Daniel Bell notes in chapter 8, in 1920 Max Weber warned socialists against assuming that conflicts of narrowly conceived interest would disappear along with private property and market competition.[36] But the opposition in the subsequent calculation debates was, curiously, largely content to let stand the presumption that the agents in the Lange-Lerner system would be appropriately motivated, thereby deliberately abstracting from questions that would later be deemed central.[37] As Abram Bergson observed, "the critics apparently prefer to meet proponents on their own ground. Accordingly, they seek to demonstrate that *even if* the economy should be organized and administered as proponents suppose, efficiency will still be not as great as they contend."[38]

Ironically, the pathbreaking article on the nature of the firm, the pebble that set in motion the theoretical ripples that would ultimately change the way everyone (including socialists) comprehends principal-agent issues, was actually published at the height of the calculation debates (1937). Even more ironically, the article's author, R.H. Coase, had been a colleague of Durbin and Lerner and was still calling himself a socialist when he conceived his theory.[39] Coase accounted for the choice between markets and firms not in terms of production costs but in terms of *transaction costs* (the costs of ferreting out and consummating efficient exchange possibilities). The 1937 article was an invitation to explore the circumstances under which the comparative advantages of funneling transactions through a central directing authority could or could not be extended.

But almost a half-century would pass before socialists picked up Coase's invitation. By then, the dissection of planning and enterprise guidance failures (by Bergson, Kornai, Nove, and others) in both the unreformed command economy and in "central planning with regulated markets" had independently verified the centrality of questions about agency, politics, and organization in the socialist project. Nove appears to have been among the first (as he has been in many things) to have recognized Coase's relevance to the discussion of feasible socialism (see chapter 10).

Meanwhile, Coase's work had been combined with other seminal contributions (by Kenneth Arrow, Herbert Simon, Mancur Olson, Steven Cheung, Douglass North, Oliver Williamson, and many others[40]) to create a new "positive political economy" that subsumed the standard neoclassical explanation of why and how optimizing independent "factors" exchange within explanations of why and how optimizing interdependent agents contract. This was a change that radical economists could recognize as extending the analytic subject from the "administration of things" to the "governance of people" in markets and firms.[41]

## Markets and Hierarchies: From the Critique of Political Economy to Positive Political Economy

Granting its affinity to (and, keeping in mind Coase's intellectual background, even roots in) longstanding socialist concerns, the new contractual rights apple has fallen far from the old Marxian tree. The reasoning that separates positive political economy from the critique of political economy is worth dwelling on briefly, for it crisply charts the frontiers of the socialist arguments and dilemmas explored in this book.

Marx recognized "exploitation" in a modern economy primarily where a capitalist is able to capture the net difference between the price of labor power and the price of the commodities cooperatively produced with that labor power. In modern terms, we could say that Marx saw the capitalist as a "free rider" who is able (because his class, and not the working class, owns the means of production and commands the coercive powers of the state) to exhort cooperation from workers while he himself opportunistically "defects" from whatever it is that might urge reciprocal cooperation. But this sort of selfish behavior would, in Marx's view, be excluded by common ownership by "an association of free men," for "[t]he social relations of the individual producers . . . are here transparent in their simplicity, both in production and in distribution."[42]

However, modern positive political economy detects propensities for free-riding and other forms of noncooperation, in almost *any* exchange involving specialization and interdependence, not just in those occurring across the thresholds currently separating "capital" and "labor power."[43] This is because the division of labor precludes "transparency" of social relations *by definition*. Rather, specialization necessarily entails private knowledge and adjustment of effort ("hidden information" and "hidden action"), which means that contracts setting the terms of exchange between parties cannot stipulate *exactly* what will be rendered ("incomplete contracting"), which means that some of the benefits of cooperation are in effect public goods ("common property") that can be appropriated without compensating the party providing them. Efforts to limit the play of hidden information and hidden action in open markets incur *bargaining costs*, which can dissipate some or all of the benefits of exchange and reduce cooperation below otherwise optimal levels.[44]

When the bargaining costs associated with the use of decentralized, unsupervised markets are high, transactions may be embedded in organizations (such as firms) governed by a "discretionary centralized authority."[45] Governance entails a license to monitor, instruct, and sanction activities in ways that may modify not only the behavior but even the preferences of members or agents.[46] Nevertheless, as interdependent specialization is enveloped within a governed organization, hidden information and hidden action do not disappear, but are internalized also, accompanied by what are called *influence costs*.

Such costs arise because, in Paul Milgrom and John Roberts's words, "the very existence of [discretionary] authority makes possible its inappropriate use."[47] On the one hand, principals can themselves succumb to temptations to defect, using their authority to feather their own nests at the expense of others in the organization, or of the organization as a whole. Indeed, the literature on "incentive compatibility" shows that such temptations are ingrained in the procedures used to elicit information and cooperation from subordinates.[48] (When principals delegate discretionary authority to fiduciaries—as in the large corporation's much-debated separation of ownership and control—opportunities for noncooperation can be pursued in this direction as well.[49])

On the other hand, a principal's discretionary authority to allocate common-property type benefits within organizations creates internal "winners" and "losers" and elicits efforts by rationally self-interested agents to sway these decisions. Who gets the promotion? Which division's balance sheet will be favored by the firm's internal transfer pricing policies? The time and effort inevitably diverted into campaigning for different interventions—biasing information flowing to principals, or for that matter coping with routinized procedures contrived to insulate principals from campaigns and information bias—all this dissipates the benefits of mutual cooperation.

In sum, the idea that it is possible to create a discretionary centralized authority that will make *only* "benign, costless *selective interventions*" (Milgrom and Roberts) is a chimera.[50]

## "Networks"—a Critique of Positive Political Economy?

It is clear, even before proceeding to its analysis of the state, that positive political economy gainsays unlimited substitution of discretionary centralized authority for unsupervised exchange. But is there a cooperative "third way" between these two imperfect allocative mechanisms—in Michael Best's words, "an alternative to either extra-firm (market) or intra-firm (hierarchical) coordination"?[51] And does positive political economy betray its own deficiencies by failing to adequately comprehend this alternative?

According to Best and a number of other sophisticated critics (mostly on the left), the answers are yes and yes. As Michael Dietrich puts it, "resource allocation involves *three* principal governance structures: markets, hierarchies, and networks.... Networking involves mutual trust and cooperation with a long-term perspective and respected codes of behavior" and arises as a dominant strategy out of repeated interactions among mutually dependent parties.[52] Similarly, Best holds that "[t]he choice for a firm is not simply whether to make or buy," as transaction cost analysis argues, "but whether to make, buy, or collaborate." This third choice involves inter-firm cooperation (sometimes called relational contracting or quasi-integration) that "presumes an administrative governmental structure which does not base decision-making authority on ownership."[53] Here, Walter Powell argues, "transactions occur neither through discrete exchanges nor by administrative fiat, but through networks of individuals engaged in reciprocal, preferential, mutually supportive actions." The "open-ended, relational features of networks, with their relative absence of explicit quid pro quo behavior," gives them a particular advantage over both markets and hierarchies in fostering the sharing of "tacit knowledge" of technological or organizational potentials among producers.[54] (Elinor Ostrom and her associates have broadened the case for networks by documenting the viability—in many cases, superiority—of such collective governance structures in managing common-pool resources.[55])

In Northern Italy's industrial district, production networks are, according to Best, "led by internationally competitive independent small firms, strong unions, leftist political parties, and an active citizenry on the local level."[56] It is hardly necessary to spell out the attractiveness of "the Third Italy" as a prototype for a new incarnation of market socialism—or, if that label is rejected, for what Paul Hirst and others call "associative democracy."[57]

The fact that here "trust and cooperation can coexist with self-seeking behavior rather than being mutually exclusive characteristics" is said by Dietrich to make the transaction cost " 'opportunism' assumption . . . inappropriate as a central principle with networking."[58] For Best, "an analysis of comparative transaction costs misses the point" because networking firms specialize in complementary (rather than competitive) activities.[59] Networks do not, of course, drive transaction costs to zero; Powell recognizes that they take a lot of work to maintain, can involve conflict and dependency, and tend to exclude outsiders. But they do yield benefits—"network externalities"—that elude institutional theories (as well as institutional alternatives) that are overly preoccupied with rational egoism and reduce reciprocity to equivalent exchange.[60]

These assertions, however, are open to dispute. Michael Hechter musters evidence showing that "obligatory groups" such as producer networks or trade associations (or political parties or communes), no less than "compensatory groups" such as firms, require formal controls involving both monitoring and sanctions in order to sustain solidary behavior among members; mutual dependence and repeated interactions are not themselves sufficient.[61] Todd Sandler remarks the fragility of mutual cooperation strategies as the number and heterogeneity of unsupervised common-pool resource users increases.[62] Marc Schneiberg and J. Rogers Hollingsworth return only a qualified affirmative to the question, "can transaction cost economics explain trade associations?" but conclude that "the evidence largely confirms" the propositions that "bounded rationality and opportunism expose association members to problems of contracting" and that "the structural reforms of the associations are driven by an interest in transaction cost economizing."[63]

Meanwhile, some of the most telling evidence of the limits of networks as alternatives to markets and hierarchies comes from "the Third Italy" itself. Bennett Harrison relates how Prato's highly specialized textile producers, under increasing pressure to shorten contract cycles, spurned an innovative plan to boost collaboration by linking up all the workbenches and middlemen of the district in a telecommunications network. Terminals were actually installed but mostly lie idle. "Why? Because the actors, the participants, and the partners in the cooperatively competitive Prato regional production system have been too *distrustful* of one another to reveal the details of their operation." It seems that rational egoism and quid pro quos are not quite as exotic here as had been hoped or assumed, and that networks, like markets and hierarchies, have their own ways of "impacting" strategic "tacit knowledge."[64]

Harrison also argues that to a much larger degree than heretofore recognized, "network firms"—even in Northern Italy—are themselves dependent (or are becoming dependent) on large hierarchal corporations. While production itself is decentralized in networks, "the locus of ultimate power and control ... remains concentrated within the largest institutions." Harrison therefore believes that we should "characterize the emerging paradigm of networked production as one of *concentration without centralization.*"[65]

In truth, the breach between champions and doubters of networks is not as complete as this quick survey suggests. Powell, for example, recognizes that although network forms of organization may flourish within relatively homogeneous groups, "[w]hen the diversity of participants increases, trust recedes, and so does the willingness to enter into long-term collaborations."[66] We should not on that account dismiss the progressive possibilities in the devolution of (at least some) authority in the kinds of community-based producer networks found in Northern Italy. We should, however, resist jumping to the seductive conclusion that networks will fully *supersede* corporate capitalist hierarchy—a development that would be as providential for socialists wary of central planning as hierarchy's full supersession of market exchange *would have been* for socialists who eagerly awaited central planning. It seems more correct to view network firms as (very much market-oriented) complements to large corporations, and to recognize that market socialism (and any associationist alternative or variant) still must pick its way through the mine field of institutional costs and trade-offs illuminated by positive political economy.

## The State

Like Marxian economics, positive political economy emphasizes the fact that institutional choice does not take place in an institutional vacuum. Much work is devoted to showing, in Thráin Eggertsson's words, "how the structure of property rights affects individual behavior and output by influencing the range of internal rules of the game of the firm—or rather by affecting the costs of using alternative contractual arrangements."[67] This focuses attention on the state, which is, like the firm, an abode of centralized authority. But here the capacity to make discretionary interventions is sometimes limited and directed (as it rarely is in private firms) by subordinating such authority to democratic control.

Marxism provides a rich and varied menu of arguments concerning the liberal democratic state as a (more or less autonomous) arena and instrument of class conflict. However, positive political economy embeds class issues in a more general explanation of why democracy, while better than its alternatives, does not eliminate influence activity and abuse of discretionary authority by government.

This explanation starts with Kenneth Arrow's famous Impossibility Theorem—his proof that individual preferences cannot be aggregated into consistent, stable social choices without imposing an exogenous constraint on the choice process that favors some individuals and prejudices the outcome.[68] This may take the form of rules limiting the domain of choices and predetermining the order in which choices are considered—both of which are, in fact, prominent features of the stepwise voting procedures (involving parties, primaries, runoffs, and so on) that select candidates for government office, as well as of the stepwise voting procedures (involving "subgovernments" of committees linked to administrative agencies, "germaneness" rules for amendments, and the like) used by collective bodies to select issues for deliberation.[69] These procedures bring a needed measure of "structure-induced" order to social choice processes, but it is a necessarily biased, unavoidably arbitrary order—not a trivial concern for democratic socialists who, like Michel Rocard, "call socialism the collective wish for social justice [and] for less arbitrariness" (chapter 4). Nove puts his finger on the problem when he shows how unsuitable (that is, how arbitrary) voting is as a means of expressing consumer preferences because (unlike competitive market prices) votes can't measure *intensity* of preference (chapter 10).[70]

This problem is compounded by the fact that the discretionary interventions of public authorities, like those of private authorities within firms, distribute common property in ways that create winners and losers (inside as well as outside of government). As Peter Ordeshook has succinctly put it, "if markets fail whenever costs are private and certain goods are public, then the public sector can fail as well because, even in regulating the supply of public goods, *it must confer private benefits (e.g. benefits to interest groups) at public cost.*"[71]

Hence, as public policy choices are ordered and restricted by legislative and bureaucratic subgovernments, these become magnets for what Mancur Olson calls *distributional coalitions* (interest groups, lobbying organizations) that form to safeguard the private benefits that public allocations provide to members, and that members come to see as entitlements.[72] This of course is a prescription for incessant and far-reaching influence activity.

Here Olson's "logic of collective action" takes over.[73] It is easy to sustain distributional coalitions around political resource allocations that bring a substantial benefit to each member of a concentrated group, but much more difficult where allocations bring a modest benefit to each member of a widely dispersed group. (Here is where intensity of preference comes into play, but the problem of arbitrary—or procedure-dependant—aggregation of preferences remains.)

Thus, to cite an example with a certain salience for socialists, in 1993 the employees of France's money-losing state airline mounted an impassioned—and at least temporarily successful—campaign to maintain the government subsidies (soft budget constraints) needed to forestall retrenchments that threatened their wages and jobs. But there was no collective action by the French taxpayers whose incomes were (or will be) marginally reduced by that subsidy. This might have signaled a general consent to the idea that the public good provided by the Air France subsidy outweighed the private costs. (That subsidies may provide such a good is not in dispute.) Or it might have just indicated that while the private costs outweighed the public benefit, these costs were dispersed so broadly that it wasn't worth anyone's while to take a strong stand against the subsidy. The point is that if social justice wasn't served here—

or if it was simply *impossible to know* if it was served—it wasn't because "the economic" was not adequately politicized, or because "the political" was not reasonably democratic.[74]

When the state moves from setting the rules of the game for economic players to plotting its outcome, restricting the exercise of discretionary authority to "benign, costless *selective interventions*" becomes especially important—and especially difficult. As John Waterbury found in his study of development planning, "the plan itself was frequently more an elaborate bargain arrived at by various government claimants than a rational blueprint for coherent government action. Planners acted as brokers among sectoral lobbies. . . . One way to satisfy everyone was to give in to expansion in all domains." Comparisons of state enterprise performance in countries with and without democratic accountability (India being an example of the former) suggest "that the problems inherent in public ownership overwhelm mechanisms of legislative monitoring."[75]

Positive political economists do not conclude from all this that market allocation is genetically good and government allocation is genetically bad.[76] Rather, they conclude that the state's capacity to target corrections for market failure is genetically limited by its own intrinsic shortcomings as a cooperative exchange medium. As the Air France episode suggests (and countless other cases confirm), state-oriented influence activity is generally predisposed toward the status quo. If, as a rule of thumb (and not excluding many exceptions[77]), in market failure firms tend to shift the public costs of private investment mobility to others, then in government failure distributional coalitions tend to shift the private costs of public investment *im*mobility to others.

## Voices from *Dissent:* The Socialized Enterprise

Does what we have learned about agency issues, both from the painful failures of old socialist models and from the new political economy, leave open the possibility that alternative contractual arrangements can lower existing thresholds to cooperation? In short, can new arguments be marshalled to credibly affirm *why market socialism?* The essays in this book offer a gamut of answers to these questions, nearly all affirmative, some conflicting with others, and all showing how drastically the terms of the debate have shifted since the days, not along ago, when many socialists struggled to accept the mere *simulation* of competition in the "Competitive Solution."

One thing that almost all the authors here share is a discriminating appraisal—very much in the spirit of Mill—of where self-management will and will not succeed. Granting the advantages of workers' control in reducing conflicts of interest and free-riding in relatively small-scaled enterprises (for example, see Tom Weisskopf's argument in chapter 14), there is something close to a consensus among the essayists that this advantage can be dissipated in large firms. John Roemer (chapter 13) notes the paucity of examples of successful workers' control on a large scale (that is, larger than the oft-cited Mondragon cooperative). David Miller and Saul Estrin (chapter 11) hold that "[s]elf-management is not impossible in large, multi-plant diversified corporations ... but [here] the *costs of democracy* rise while the benefits for the workforce diminish" (emphasis added).[78] They warn of the welfare losses that could result if cooperatives "choose to sacrifice economies of scale for retaining relatively small size and effective workforce control over the firm." (This is an eerie obverse of the Soviet "gigantomania" that arose and persisted, despite its fabled wastefulness, because deliberately "concentrating and centralizing" production in a few large firms simplified the tasks of central planners![79])

Howe (chapter 2) urges the same point, invoking the prospect of a self-managed "socialist GM" and asking "how would it be possible to avoid the linked plagues of bureaucratism, demagogic manipulation, clique maneuverings, endless filibustering, ignorant narrowness, cronyism in elections, and a selfish resistance to the larger needs of society?" A pithier typology of influence costs under self-management one could not ask for. Howe took the prospect of selfish resistance to society's larger needs "as a warning against *exclusive* control of major enterprises by the workers within it."

This naturally raises the question of how and with whom control of major enterprises should be shared. Here our consensus evaporates, except insofar as most of our authors reject full capitalist ownership (and capital markets permitting large private accumulations of wealth) and recognize and wrestle with the constraints that agency and finance problems impose on the remaining choices. For Roemer, these problems rule out direct state control as well as full workers' control. He proposes to cut the Gordian Knot by attaching major firms to bank-led industrial groups—something like Japan's *keiretsu*—within which cross-shareholding would allow each firm's principal owner role to be played by a board representing the other firms and banks in the group. Both firms and banks would ultimately be socially owned: most profits would accrue to the state and be paid out as a "social dividend." Workers would have limited input into the choice of management but it would be enough to insure that "no politically powerful managerial class develops." The egalitarian distribution of wealth through "social dividends" would lower firms' incentives to boost profits by producing public "bads."

Fred Block (chapter 19) offers a mixed ownership and control scheme involving (outside) shareholders, workers, and other interested parties (creditors, suppliers, consumers, environmental advocates), which he believes will foster "broader debate and discussion [that] should measurably improve the quality of executive decision making." But what looks like enriching debate to Block comes across as enervating discord to Miller and Estrin. They consider, then (initially) reject the capital-labor partnership approach, warning that "it reintroduces the possibility of conflict between one party whose interests are solely in levels of profit and a second party whose interests are more diverse." (Note that the diversity of interests within the second party— that is, among the workers—itself suggests the possibility of conflict, even in the absence of outside owners.)

In Miller and Estrin's model, the capital supply constraints associated with pure worker ownership might be stretched by investment agencies (which could be owned by the enterprises they supply capital to) that would—unlike Roemer's *keiretsu* banks—maintain an arm's-length relationship with what would still be self-managed firms. Anything still too big (presumably because of the "costs of democracy") to be run on a fully cooperative basis—and this might include most of the large, capital-intensive corporations making up the "commanding heights" of the economy—would be owned by the state. Nove (chapter 10) and Weisskopf (chapter 14) loosely endorse similar distributions of ownership types.

A key question in all this is whether, as Miller and Estrin argue, investment agencies should and will provide capital to cooperatives without exercising control rights that might circumscribe self-management, or whether, as Roemer and Block hold, outside institutions should and will take on close monitoring responsibilities. The evidence and argument favor Roemer and Block. The Miller/Estrin proposal requires asset owners and managers to combine an arms-length "American" supervisory relation to asset users with a customized "European" financial and entrepreneurial commitment to these users. Investment agencies are being asked to bear substantial capital risk while recusing themselves from many of the decisions bearing on that risk. This is unlikely to be a stable setup. This may be why in his own essay (chapter 12), Miller softens his stance on labor-capital partnerships in capital-intensive industries, even though this means less pure workers' management and more investment income inequality in the market socialist system.[80]

It is important to mark the fact that outside monitoring (labor-capital partnerships) can be viewed not as a regrettable impurity but as a positive aid to participatory enterprise management. This important argument has been advanced by Masahiko Aoki, who notes that under pure workers' control, "room for local collusion within a subset of the [large-scale participatory] network may become greater, and there is no guarantee that such local collusion is consistent with the pursuit of the goal of the larger system." (This is, of course, the problem of hidden action discussed earlier.) However, "the existence of an agent external to the [participatory] network who shares the . . . (positive or negative) [rent from participation] with the internal members may have positive incentive impacts on the latter in curbing their free-riding."[81] Aoki's formal analysis assumes a homogeneous workforce; when an enterprise workforce is heterogeneous, the procedural stability provided by the external monitor may play an even greater role in defusing intrafirm conflicts raising the "costs of democracy" in large-scale enterprises.[82]

Aoki's external monitoring agent could be a "bank-like financial institution" of the type found in Germany and Japan, which is also the prototype for Roemer's socialist enterprise monitor. But some uncertainty remains as to Roemer's claim to have shown that "the equal distribution of profits does not entail highly diffuse, and therefore unsuccessful, monitoring of firms" (chapter 13, reply). On the one hand, it is not entirely clear that the monitoring services provided by Japan's capitalist *keiretsu* member banks and firms, which retain a substantial share of the residual benefits or rents of principal-agent cooperation, would be performed with equal dispatch by socialist *keiretsu* member banks and firms, which retain a substantially smaller share (since the rest goes into the "social dividend"); there may be a free-rider problem here.[83] On the other hand, if the institutional agents in a socialist *keiretsu* do perform the principal owner role as well as their capitalist counterparts, it is not immediately evident how dispersing *individual* profit income will (as Roemer also asserts) limit the pursuit of corporate strategies generating public "bads." (That is, if the diffusion of "ultimate ownership" does not weaken the commitment of the firms' *proximate* monitors to profit-maximization, then it would seem to follow that managers will *not* be influenced by the fact that the median "ultimate owner" is less enthusiastic about increases in profits accompanied by increases in "bads.")

### Voices from *Dissent:* The Socialized Economy

While all of these alternatives eschew direct state planning of enterprise activity and endorse real market competition with real market prices, they also envision a significant public *cum* state role in determining the economy's overall investment priorities. In doing so, they revert to formulas that—at least at first blush—recall the old Lange/Brus model of "central planning with regulated markets."

Thus Alec Nove subscribed to the idea that the state would be responsible for investments "of structural significance, usually involving either the creation of new productive units or the very substantial expansion of existing ones," while enterprise management would control investments "that represent an adjustment to changing demand (or to new techniques)." Roemer (chapter 13) rejects the idea of direct governmental price-setting, but not the goal of "social control of investment," which, he argues, can be realized through manipulation of interest rate discounts and surcharges; the necessary price adjustments in all markets will follow. "What is *not* planned in this vision of market socialism is the composition of output . . . just the composition of investment." All this is much in the Langean spirit of entrusting the present to individual enterprise management and the future to the wisdom of central planners.

Ernest Erber likewise is willing to let things like shoe styles be determined "by the blind outcomes of the Market," but warns that "if global market share is the goal, the nation's consumers had better not be permitted to decide on the allocation of resources." Subordination of the market to "strategically planned priorities designed to serve an overriding common purpose" is needed here (chapter 17).

Miller and Estrin (and later Miller alone) also speak of state regulation of investment. Similar sentiments are expressed, more or less forcefully, by Harrington (but see below) and Rocard and Roosevelt. Block argues for regulation of international capital flows.

But now we have a publicly owned commanding heights, resource allocation without capital markets (or with highly regulated and restricted capital markets), and a strong state investment guidance function. What about the danger of soft budget constraints in public enterprises—or for that matter in "socially" or cooperatively owned enterprises dependent on public financing? Weisskopf suggests that it will be possible to erect a firewall between the state and public- or worker-owned enterprise management by running the supply of capital through autonomous and competing investment agencies (as proposed by Roemer and by Miller and Estrin). Block also proposes having the government launch "semipublic" investment and commercial banks that "would be subject to government oversight to assure that they fulfill their mandate to lend money in the public interest," but that nevertheless "would be insulated from partisan interference." But is this sufficient? Will the firewall be thick enough? Weisskopf's response is that

> First, a democratic political environment—conspicuously absent in the [pre-1989] East—can be expected to restrain the ability of enterprise managers to collude at the expense of the public. Second, pressures by enterprise managers to get special favors from government agencies are hardly unknown in capitalist economies—especially in the case of large and politically powerful private corporations that represent the capitalist counterpart to socialist public enterprises.

We have seen, however, that positive political economy raises fundamental doubts about how well (or at what cost) democratic oversight per se can constrain public enterprise rent-seeking. Nove, too, insisted that *"[t]he assumption of democracy makes [the state's] task more difficult, not easier,* since a variety of inconsistent objectives will be reflected in political parties and the propaganda they will undertake" (chapter 10, emphasis added). This concern was echoed by Howe, who saw a need to share socialist enterprise control with "the larger public, the democratic polity," yet foresaw "conflicts among autonomous enterprises as they compete for the credits, subsidies, tax breaks, and contracts that are to be had from the state." This danger is also recognized by Miller (chapter 12) with respect to publicly owned investment banks.

Positive political economists also strongly dispute the notion that public ownership doesn't increase the government's susceptibility to corporate influence activity yielding soft budget constraints.[84] Brus and Laski concur, stressing that even the oligopolistic capitalist corporation must pay the piper for improvident management sometime; unlike its socialist state enterprise counterpart, it "cannot destroy the principal rules of the game." Their conclusion is (for socialists) drastic: the old ideal of "politicization of the economic" cannot be salvaged, and democratization should be supported only "because no other guarantee can meaningfully exist for the maintenance of the depoliticization of the economy" (see chapter 7).

However, most of the other authors haven't accepted this conclusion yet—or use arguments and terminology that disguise the fact that they (very nearly) have. For example, Nove's unvarnished evaluation of democratic oversight of the state's economic role appeared to fit better with the new Brus conclusion that "the economy has to become depoliticized" than with the old Brus argument (recycled by Nove) that the state should own the commanding heights and control structurally significant investments. Likewise, Nove's brilliant analysis of the *"ex ante* illusion" in central planning[85] coexisted uneasily with statements that "the problem of [fallible *ex ante* decisions] is more serious when autonomous units orientate themselves in a market environment"; and "the greater the freedom allowed to enterprises or to individual citizens, the greater the risk that some undesirable act might be committed" (chapter 10).

All this suggests that Nove was trying to hold positions—in particular, regarding the relative importance of influence costs and government failure vis-à-vis bargaining costs and market failure—that have been outflanked by his own evidence and reasoning. But the reader should not forget how radical *any* talk of the limits of democratic planning was (in socialist circles) when chapter 10 first appeared in *The Economics of Feasible Socialism* in 1983. When Nove revisited feasible socialism in 1990, he still argued (against Kornai) that governments could resist influence activities and enforce hard budget constraints on unsuccessful state enterprises "if determined to do so" (chapter 18). (But would they be determined to do so?) Nevertheless, Nove's rejection of capital markets was considerably attenuated and he had embraced more of Brus and Laski's auto-critique.

Michael Harrington's essay (chapter 4) also bears the marks of powerful currents moving under a relatively unbroken surface.[86] Harrington had always identified democratic socialism with decentralized planning. But in his earlier writings, this did not mean that there would be no central *plan*. It was the process of formulating and implementing the national plan that would be dispersed, but only insofar as the plan's ability to "assert a decisive influence over the huge corporations" (as Harrington put it in 1972) was not sacrificed. Harrington was the first to concede that this would mean "an ever-present danger of inefficiency, dullness, poor services, and all the rest." But he was clearly more preoccupied with the risk that "if the socialist state . . . grants the socialized industry the right to independent action, the latter will probably follow its own purposes rather than that of the national plan."[87] Thus, as he wrote in 1978, while a market "could operate within the broad limit of the democratic plan . . . [t]he existence of such a market would not determine the basic priorities of the economy."[88]

In "Markets and Plans," Harrington continued to speak in terms of markets *within* plans. But now his priorities had clearly shifted: "if there is to be genuine grass-roots autonomy, then there must be market space—modified by planning priorities, of course—in which the democratic enterprises are free to exercise their communal imagination and *interact without supervision from above*" (chapter 3, emphasis added). Now when Harrington spoke of "the use of markets within a planning framework," what he had in mind was the active labor market policies of the Swedish social democrats.[89]

In fact, what Harrington persisted in calling "the use of markets within a planning framework" was now really the reverse: *the use of planning within a market framework*. The difference is not trivial. Markets within a planning framework means the existence of a synoptic plan (or set of plans), covering, at least in general terms, the major resource allocation choices of the national economy; markets are then used "simply" to *implement* these choices. Planning within a market framework means that for the most part the pattern of resource allocation emerges directly from competitive interactions involving relatively autonomous producers and consumers; planning then consists of "selective measures" that "change the consequences of [a particular] market outcome."[90]

This metamorphosis of the meaning of traditional (market) socialist locutions is also exhibited through the comments and replies following the models presented in Part IV. Thus, Robert Blair responds to Miller and Estrin's preference for "either no market at all, or a well-regulated market in labor and capital" by suggesting that they are underestimating "the limitations of governmental efficiency, wisdom, and benevolence." Why not, he asks, deal with problems in labor and capital markets "by supplementing the market process with limited social legislation rather than by abolishing markets?"

Estrin and Miller reply that Blair got it all wrong: they really do *not* "favor nonmarket allocative procedures for labor and capital." Labor markets would operate freely except for wage floors and government interventions to prevent unemployment. In the case of capital allocation also, their "predisposition remains for free-market outcomes wherever possible"—except that (as noted above) individual private ownership would be curtailed and the "market-socialist capital market" would operate through public and/or cooperatively owned investment banks. Apart from that, instances of capital market failure would be addressed in an "indicative planning framework" and government intervention in the accumulation process would be selectively "triggered by predetermined criteria" (chapter 11).[91]

Similarly, when Barkan and Belkin argue that Roemer's scheme to socially plan the composition of investment through credit controls may be overly ambitious, Roemer protests that he has been taken too literally and has in mind only selective interventions—perhaps on the order of what goes on in South Korea, or Japan, or France; Barkan and Belkin had not thought to characterize these as examples of social(ist) control.

The content of the idea of social ownership appears to be changing as well. The cross-shareholding among member firms in Roemer's socialist *keiretsu* admits some income derived neither from one's direct labor nor from social citizenship. Roemer insists that no more than the capitalist camel's nose is being allowed into the socialist tent, as only "an extremely small fraction" of an individual's outside investor income will come from the profits of any one firm. Yet, as Barkan and Belkin point out, that fraction (or its aggregate among *keiretsu* shareholders) must be high enough to overcome the owner free-rider problem and elicit the close monitoring needed to minimize information asymmetries and effectively limit managerial rent-seeking.[92]

In his comment on Miller (chapter 12), Roosevelt also flags the fact that share ownership of investment banks by cooperatives allows individual members to receive what socialists once would have called "*unearned* income." Weisskopf notes that while proposals for increasing market socialist enterprise autonomy "do not amount to the restoration of full capitalist private property rights, they often do open up opportunities for individuals to receive some forms of capital income." Horvat's comment on Weisskopf sets aside any qualms on that score, declaring that a "social corporation . . . may issue external shares" and that a capital market and "[p]rivate dividends are compatible with socialism."

Needless to say, issues remain. Those that concern the role of the state in market socialism are more acute than those concerning enterprise ownership and control, discussed in the last section. (Of course, there is considerable overlap between these two sets of concerns.) When we are assured that a democratic socialist government with potent means of intervening in the investment process—credit controls, public ownership of investment banks and/or the "commanding heights," jurisdiction over the "social dividend"—is going to use these powers sparingly, we are entitled to ask how *this* formidable specimen of discretionary centralized authority will manage to shrug off subgovernmental hubris and influence activities by distributional coalitions, and restrict itself to only "benign, costless selective interventions."[93]

## Conclusion

In this real market socialism, then, the use of markets in a planning framework shades into planning in a market framework, and social ownership shades into mixed ownership. Does market socialism then simply shade into social democracy? Many of the contributors here remark on the convergence. Nove summed up his differences with Kornai by wondering if "[p]erhaps we would both settle for a kind of welfare-capitalism-with-a-human-face, not easy to distinguish from a 'socialism' with a big role for private capital and individual entrepreneurs?" (chapter 18). At the end of Barkan's exploration of the terrain beyond "slightly imaginary Sweden (SIS)," it turns out that "the socialist opts for a level of planning and an economy of mixed ownership that resembles more than anything else . . . well . . . SIS."

A similar end point is reached by Daniel Bell (chapter 8), who rejects the possibility of substituting the optimal planning methods of Kantorovich and Leontieff for the market mechanism, but accepts the idea that " 'planning' could remain as a *normative economic tool*, a shadow *'tableau economique'* to model different paths of growth and different assumptions of optimality and cost, against which the actual economy could be judged. . . . A modest role, perhaps. But we need to live in modest times."

Weisskopf also closes his essay by talking about how blurred the differences between market socialism and social democracy have become in recent years—and not because the model of social democracy has changed. Sober truths have particularly touched the socialist imagination with respect to what can be expected of enterprise management, and Weisskopf speaks of the need for government regulation "to prevent autonomous public enterprises or worker self-managed firms from acting in their own particular interest, as against the general social interest." The warning that Kautsky issued seventy years ago—prophetically in the case of "central planning with regulated markets"—has at last fallen on open ears.

It is Brus and Laski who perhaps state the case in the most unflinching terms, declaring that "[t]he recourse to [market socialism] means that *socialism should actually cease to be perceived at all as a bounded system*" (quoted in chapter 7, with emphasis added).

But none of the writers here regard the case as completely closed. Robert Dahl (chapter 16), doubts "whether . . . people in any . . . democratic country will ever manage to arrive at a point where market and nonmarket forces are all at a stable equilibrium, politically speaking." Weisskopf does not really disagree, but he believes that even if little else is different, market socialism can be distinguished from social democracy by changes in property rights that will more deeply root progressive social policy regimes. And Barkan reminds us that it is as hard to reconcile a system that goes slightly-beyond-social-democracy with classical images of capitalism as with classical images of socialism.

But this system does summon one classical image—that of the liberal socialism of John Stuart Mill and the other "forgotten precursors" who first made the connections between competitive means and socialist ends that we have only now rediscovered. Mill's enunciation of those ends still seems the most elemental, the most bare of extraneous elements: "the aim of improvement should be not solely to place human beings in a condition in which they will be able to do without one another, but to enable them to work for one another in relations not involving dependence."

As this collection of "Voices from *Dissent*" shows, the current debate over market socialism is marked—transformed—by an increasingly sophisticated awareness of the institutional problems that must be solved to realize Mill's goal. It is still not clear whether, in the end, these problems will be solved—or at any rate solved in a way that definitively answers the question "why market socialism?" But perhaps it is the question more than any particular answers that matter. In the end, the labels we attach to our endeavors should be, as they were for Irving Howe, less important than "the yearning for a better mode of life."

## Notes

1. Karl Kautsky, *The Labour Revolution* (London: Allen and Unwin, 1925 [German original, 1922]), pp. 102–3.

2. See Thomas Weisskopf, "The Drive Toward Capitalism in East Central Europe: Is There No Other Way" (mimeo, 1991), especially pp. 60–65 on "the weakness of the capitalist tradition," "the strength of the working class tradition," and "the strength of the commitment to economic security" as legacies of Communist rule.

3. Ludwig von Mises, "Economic Calculation in the Socialist Commonwealth" (1920), English translation in F.A. Hayek, ed., *Collectivist Economic Planning* (originally published 1935; reprint Clifton: Kelley, 1975). Mises expanded his argument in

*Socialism* (1922, English translation 1969, reprint Indianapolis: Liberty Classics, 1981).

4. This proof was inspired by Vilfredo Pareto's and Enrico Barone's earlier argument that (for a given distribution of individual endowments and wants) optimizing socialist planners would have to set the same exchange (or factor substitution) ratios as would obtain in a perfectly competitive market economy. (Barone's 1908 paper on "The Ministry of Production in the Socialist State" is translated in Hayek, ed., *Collectivist Economic Planning*.) At the time this was offered and taken as a reproof against the orthodox Marxian belief that interest rates and the "law of value" could be discarded in a planned economy. But Lange et al. turned the observation that it was possible *in principle* for the Central Planning Board to calculate optimal shadow price ratios from information about supply and demand schedules into an argument that it would be possible *in practice* for the CPB (acting as a kind of Walrasian auctioneer) to derive optimal ratios. This would be true particularly if the Board confined itself to adjusting "parametric" capital goods prices and interest rates and otherwise allowed markets for labor services and final products to function "freely."

5. For Dobb's views, see the "Three Articles on the Problem of Economic Planning in a Socialist Economy" (originally published in 1933, 1939, and 1953), reprinted in Maurice Dobb, *On Economic Theory and Socialism: Collected Papers* (London: Routledge & Kegan Paul, 1955). For Hayek, see the three articles on "Socialist Calculation" (originally published in 1935 and 1940), reprinted in Friedrich Hayek, *Individualism and the Economic Order* (Chicago: University of Chicago Press, 1948).

6. Kornai's influential critique of orthodox planning and of the attempted Hungarian reform (of which he was himself a leading architect) is contained in such works as *Contradictions and Dilemmas: Studies on the Socialist Economy and Society* (Cambridge: MIT Press, 1986); *Vision and Reality, Market and State* (New York: Routledge, 1990); and *The Socialist System: The Political Economy of Communism* (Princeton: Princeton University Press, 1992).

7. It was a less heralded aspect of NEM, de facto legalization of Hungary's nonstate "second economy," that contributed more to Hungary's economic prospects. Apart from Kornai's work, a very valuable study of the shortcomings of NEM and their implications for Western socialists is also provided by Nigel Swain, *Hungary: The Rise and Fall of Feasible Socialism* (London: Verso, 1992).

8. In Yugoslavia, some of the particulars were different from the Hungarian case: Budget constraints were softened by the capture of credit institutions by self-managed enterprises as well as by state maneuvers. However, the politically expedient but economically perverse end result was much the same—markets without bankruptcies (or even the threat of bankruptcies), and consequently without enough of the investment mobility ("creative destruction") that accompanies and pushes productivity growth. See Kornai, *The Socialist System*.

In chapter 6, Tadeusz Kowalik argues that "[e]ven if [Lange's] model contained a clearly utopian (unrealistic) element" (meaning its demand for "a strict division between the system of economic planning and management and the political system"), "the Yugoslav model went to the other extreme in its politicization of the economy." However, unlike Kornai, Kowalik does not consider the Yugoslav failure to be "conclusive" with respect to "the viability of market socialism."

9. In *Socialism* (New York: Saturday Review Press, 1972), Michael Harrington distinguished "socialist socialism," which he conceived in Langean market socialist terms (public ownership, partially decentralized democratic planning, partial decommodification, and so forth), from both "socialist capitalism"—the model evolved by social democratic reformers for running capitalism better than it could run itself—and from "capitalist socialism," the authoritarian state system imposed by Stalin's "revolution from above." Only the first variant was "socialism itself."

10. On the Swedes see Tim Tilton, *The Political Theory of Swedish Social Democracy: Through the Welfare State to Socialism* (Oxford: Clarendon Press, 1990), especially chapter 4, "Nils Karleby and Rickard Sandler: The Theory of a Socialized Market Economy." On the British experience see Elizabeth Durbin, *New Jerusalems: The Labour Party and the Economics of Democratic Socialism* (London: Routledge & Kegan Paul, 1985). Evan Durbin's story is of particular interest, for at the same time as he was involved in the socialist calculation debate, developing abstract market socialist models to facilitate "planning which results in the general supersession of individual enterprise as the source of economic decisions," he was *also* in the New Fabian Research Bureau, developing practical policies for "planning meaning simply the intervention of the government in a particular industry at a time when the greater part of the economy still remains in private hands" (ibid., p. 178).

11. See Kowalik, chapter 6, on the later Lange's fascination with "computopia." On the hopes and disappointments of "optimal planning" overall, see Pekka Sutela, *Economic Thought and Economic Reform in the Soviet Union* (New York: Cambridge University Press, 1991), and Martin Cave, *Computers and Economic Planning: The Soviet Experience* (New York: Cambridge University Press, 1980).

12. John Stuart Mill, *Principles of Political Economy* (Clifton: Kelley, 1987 [reprint of Ashley edition of 1909; first edition 1848]), p. 763 (quoted passage first appeared in the third edition, 1852), emphasis added.

13. Ibid., p. 211.

14. Ibid., pp. 113–15.

15. Ibid., pp. 111–12. Here Mill drew extensively on Charles Babbage, *On the Economy of Machinery and Manufactures* (Clifton, N.J.: Kelley, 1986 [1832, 1835]). But Babbage—of greater fame today as the pioneer of the computer—was himself preceded on the issue of trust in exchange by David Hume, who analyzed what is today known as the free-rider problem in *A Treatise of Human Nature* (Oxford: Clarendon Press, 1978 [1737]).

16. Mill, *Principles*, p. 790. The arguments for profit-sharing—but not worker ownership—were again drawn from Babbage. Marx flayed away at Mill for separating distribution from production in economic analysis (*Grundrisse*, New York: Viking, 1973 [1857–58], pp. 86 et seq.), but Mill's discussion of the advantages and disadvantages of capitalist, cooperative, and social ownership shows that Mill was fully alive to the potential impact of different property and distribution regimes on productive efficiency.

17. Mill, *Principles*, pp. 790–91. This passage was added in the sixth edition (1865).

18. Ibid., p. 793.

19. Morris Hillquit, *Socialism in Theory and in Practice* (New York: Macmillan, 1909), pp. 134, 112.

20. There were, of course, "left" critics of one-big-trust socialism like William Morris and G.D.H. Cole who were far removed from any temptation to consider markets as a tool of socialist decentralization.

21. Albert Schäffle, *The Quintessence of Socialism* (London: Swan Sonnenschien, 1889 [translation of eighth German edition; first German edition 1874]), pp. 95–96.

22. Here she was characterizing socialism's initial—and lasting—appeal to her husband. Dame Margaret Cole, *The Life of G.D.H. Cole* (New York: St. Martin's Press, 1971), p. 34.

23. In her polemic against Bernstein, Rosa Luxemburg argued that workers forming a production cooperative in a competitive milieu would be "faced with the contradictory necessity of governing themselves with the utmost absolutism," intensifying or reducing labor "according to the situation on the market" just like any capitalist enterprise ("Reform or Revolution" [2nd edition, 1908], reprinted in *Rosa Luxemburg Speaks* [New York: Pathfinder, 1970], p. 69). In later debates on self-management, critics doubted if cooperatives *could* adjust to market conditions like capitalist enterprises.

24. Quoted by R.H. Coase in "The Nature of the Firm" (1937), reprinted in Oliver Williamson and Sidney Winter, eds., *The Nature of the Firm: Origins, Evolution, and Development* (New York: Oxford University Press, 1993), p. 19.

25. Yoram Barzel, *Economic Analysis of Property Rights* (New York: Cambridge University Press, 1989), p. 47, emphasis added.

26. Harold Demsetz, "The Theory of the Firm Revisited," in Williamson and Winter, *The Nature of the Firm*, p. 160 (emphasis added).

27. Douglass North, *Structure and Change in Economic History* (New York: Norton, 1981), p. 61.

28. Karl Marx, *Capital*, Volume 1 (New York: Vintage, 1977 [1867]), pp. 475–76.

29. Thomas Hodgskin, *Labour Defended Against the Claims of Capital* (Clifton: Kelley, 1969 [1825]), p. 85.

30. Ibid.

31. Marx, *Capital*, Volume 1, p. 477.

32. Karl Marx and Frederick Engels, *The German Ideology* (Moscow: Progress Publishers, 1976 [originally written in 1846]), p. 54.

33. As Nove points out in chapter 10, an "analysis [that] can show us ... where the cost of centralization exceeds the benefits ... or where the cost of *not* decentralizing can be excessive" comes "with a built-in preference for small scale" that is "quite contrary to the Marxist tradition." I would amend this to say that it is the correlation of decentralization with market exchange that puts it contrary to the Marxist tradition.

Harrington makes a heroic effort in chapter 3 to show that Marx's methodology and values can argue for a socialism with markets, "even though Marx in one persona clearly rejected markets altogether." In chapter 5, however, Roosevelt argues persuasively that "Marx arrived at his rejection of the market as the logical outcome of his critique of capitalism," and that while a market socialism tempered by Marx's moral objections to markets is conceivable, a Marxist market socialism is not.

34. V.I. Lenin, *The State and Revolution* (New York: Penguin, 1992 [1917, 1919]), p. 91.

35. If it seems a little unfair to tar all classical socialism with the coarse brush of Lenin, the reader should note that the "simple bookkeeping" fable was fairly common coin in fin-de-siècle Marxist circles, its circulation extending from William Morris to Daniel de Leon. And it should be kept in mind that those Second International socialists who went furthest in acknowledging the complexity of the managerial tasks facing the working class "on the morrow of the revolution"—men like Bernstein and Vandervelde—were also regarded with the deepest suspicion by their comrades.

36. Weber mapped many of the dilemmas of administrative control—differences between formal and substantive economic rationality, conflicts between personal wealth maximization and enterprise profit-maximization, and the like—that would eventually enter the new theory of economic organization. This allowed Weber to thoroughly debunk the notion that socialism could appropriate industrial capitalism's "irresistible advance of bureaucratization" (*Economy and Society*, Berkeley: University of California Press, 1978 [1920], p. 1403) as a vehicle for empowering workers. There can be little doubt that the socialist calculation debate would have proceeded on different and more fruitful paths if Lange had paid as much heed to Weber's critique as to Mises's.

37. While pressing fundamental informational issues during the debates, Hayek explicitly assumed that socialist managers would be "as capable and as anxious to produce cheaply as the average capitalist entrepreneur" (Friedrich Hayek, "Socialist Calculation: The Competitive Solution," originally published in *Economica* [1940], reprinted in Hayek, *Individualism and the Economic Order*, p. 196). Pranab Bardhan and John Roemer hold that without bringing in agency issues, Hayek's case against Lange-type systems falls short ("Introduction," in Bardhan and Roemer, eds., *Market Socialism: The Current Debate*, New York: Oxford University Press, 1993, p. 5).

38. Abram Bergson, "The Politics of Socialist Efficiency" (1980), in Bergson, *Selected Essays in Economic Theory* (Cambridge: The MIT Press, 1982), p. 210, emphasis added.

39. See R.H. Coase, "The Nature of the Firm: Origins" in Williamson and Winter, *The Nature of the Firm.*

40. The first main works of synthesis were North, *Structure and Change*; Oliver Williamson, *Markets and Hierarchies: Analysis and Antitrust Implications* (New York: The Free Press, 1975); and Williamson, *The Economic Institutions of Capitalism* (New York: The Free Press, 1985).

41. See Samuel Bowles and Herbert Gintis, "Post-Walrasian Political Economy," in Bowles, Gintis, and Gustafsson, eds., *Markets and Democracy: Participation, Accountability, and Efficiency* (New York: Cambridge University Press, 1993). Also see Bardhan and Roemer's discussion of the five stages in the market socialist debate, with the agency-theoretic question of incentive compatability moving to center stage in the fifth (and current) stage ("Introduction" to Bardhan and Roemer, eds., *Market Socialism*).

42. Marx, *Capital*, Volume 1, pp. 171–72. "[T]he positive supersession of private property," wrote the young Marx, entailed no less than "the *genuine* resolution of the conflict between man and man . . . [and] between . . . individual and species." Karl Marx, "Economic and Philosophic Manuscripts of 1844," in Marx, *Early Writings* (New York: Vintage, 1975), pp. 350, 348.

43. The rest of this section (and the beginning of the next) is largely based on

Paul Milgrom and John Roberts, "Bargaining Costs, Influence Costs, and the Organization of Economic Activity," in James Alt and Kenneth Shepsle, eds., *Perspectives on Positive Political Economy* (New York: Cambridge University Press, 1990); Gary Miller, *Managerial Dilemmas: The Political Economy of Hierarchy* (New York: Cambridge University Press, 1992); and Thráin Eggertsson, *Economic Behavior and Institutions* (New York: Cambridge University Press, 1990).

44. Here we might briefly note that Marx's familiar formula, "from each according to their ability, to each according to their need," either implies indifference to the question of reciprocity in exchange, or assumes some costless mechanism—presumably, those "transparent" relations—for verifying that each *really is* giving as much as he or she is able and taking no more than he or she requires. Otherwise Marx's belief that the "positive supersession of private property" would *reduce*, not increase, agency costs lacks a logical foundation.

45. Milgrom and Roberts, "Bargaining Costs," p. 79.

46. The "nexus of treaties" that defines a centralized organization like a firm (cf. Masahiko Aoki, Bo Gustafsson, and Oliver Williamson, eds., *The Firm as a Nexus of Treaties*, Newbury Park: Sage Publications, 1990) involves not only enforceable obligations to fulfill the letter of contracts and rights to monitor fulfillment—much of which, as many have pointed out, is also found in open-market exchanges—but also binds agents to "an affirmative, open-ended duty" to act in the interests of principals, who in turn assume liability for the agents' actions (see Scott Masten, "A Legal Basis for the Firm," in Williamson and Winter, eds., *The Nature of the Firm*). Mieke Meurs has noted and Gary Miller has underscored the importance of preference-modifying *leadership*—a factor usually overlooked in the literature of organizational theory but accented in organizational psychology—in overcoming managerial dilemmas and lowering agency costs (see Mieke Meurs, "Agency Problems and the Future of Comparative Systems Theory," in Bowles, Gintis, and Gustafsson, eds., *Markets and Democracy*, p. 117, and Gary Miller, *Managerial Dilemmas*, chapter 11).

47. Milgrom and Roberts, "Bargaining Costs," p. 79.

48. This literature shows that to elicit optimal effort or accurate revelation of hidden information by subordinates, incentive schemes must be designed to include budget residuals—which the claimants can (in the short run) enlarge by opportunistically subverting those same incentive schemes! See Miller, *Managerial Dilemmas*, pp. 142–58. For a more technical survey of the results, see John Ledyard, "Incentive Compatibility," in John Eatwell, Murray Milgate, and Peter Newman, eds., *The New Palgrave: Allocation, Information, and Markets* (New York: Norton, 1987, 1989), pp. 141–51.

49. As in the case of managers aggrandizing themselves at the expense of stockholders by, for example, pushing mergers that lead to increases in management earnings and prestige but reduce organizational efficiency and share value. Michael Jacobs, *Short-Term America: The Causes and Cures of Our Business Myopia* (Boston: Harvard Business School Press, 1991), makes a compelling argument that regulatory barriers exacerbating the separation of ownership and control—in transaction cost terms, increasing the information asymmetries among managers, boards of directors, and stockholders—are responsible for increasing investment risk and shortening planning horizons in the United States, while also forcing investors to rely excessively on takeovers to deal with management failures.

50. Milgrom and Roberts, "Bargaining Costs," p. 79.

51. Michael Best, *The New Competition: Institutions of Industrial Restructuring* (Cambridge: Harvard University Press, 1990), p. 131.

52. Michael Dietrich, *Transaction Cost Economics and Beyond: Towards a New Economics of the Firm* (London and New York: Routledge, 1994), p. 101 (emphasis added). Dietrich is (for the moment) deliberately abstracting from the role of the state.

53. Best, *The New Competition,* pp. 131, 225.

54. Walter Powell, "Neither Market Nor Hierarchy: Network Forms of Organization," in Barry Straw and Larry Cummings, eds., *Research in Organizational Behavior,* Vol. 12 (Greenwich: JAI Press, 1990), pp. 303–4. Tacit knowledge is said to be "impacted" or "sticky" in markets and hierarchies.

55. Elinor Ostrom, *Governing the Commons: The Evolution of Institutions for Collective Action* (New York: Cambridge University Press, 1990); Elinor Ostrom, Roy Gardner, and James Walker, *Rules, Games, and Common-Pool Resources* (Ann Arbor: University of Michigan Press, 1994).

56. Best, *The New Competition,* p. 225.

57. See Paul Hirst, *Associative Democracy: New Forms of Economic and Social Governance* (Amherst: University of Massachusetts Press, 1994), and "Associative Democracy," *Dissent* (Spring 1994). Unfortunately, this important article appeared too late for inclusion in this volume. Also see Joshua Cohen and Joel Rogers, "Associative Democracy," in Bardhan and Roemer, eds., *Market Socialism.*

58. Dietrich, *Transaction Cost Economics and Beyond,* p. 101.

59. Best, *The New Competition,* p. 101.

60. Powell, "Neither Market Nor Hierarchy," pp. 304–5. Powell associates this reductionism with the view—which Powell rejects—that networks are simply an intermediary form ("some mongrel hybrid") along a continuum between markets and hierarchies. They should be seen, he insists, rather as "a distinctly different form" (p. 299).

61. Michael Hechter, *Principles of Group Solidary* (Berkeley: University of California Press, 1987), chapters 4–6, 8. According to Hechter, participants submit to the regimens of "compensatory groups" in exchange for the income derived from joint production of goods marketed mostly for consumption by nonmembers. The attraction of "obligatory groups" is the direct utility derived from joint consumption of *immanent goods*—anything from friendship and security to political clout and market power—that are relatively inaccessible to nonmembers. Hechter also makes the key point that large corporations themselves are really "quasi-obligatory groups" since their internal labor markets provide members access to immanent goods (career ladders, seniority protections, welfare services, etc.) as well as wage income (chapter 7).

62. See Todd Sandler, *Collective Action: Theory and Applications* (Ann Arbor: University of Michigan Press, 1992), pp. 122, 139. Ostrom herself is careful to document the failures as well as successes of voluntary organizations in overcoming "the tragedy of the commons."

63. Marc Scheiberg and J. Rogers Hollingsworth, "Can Transaction Cost Economics Explain Trade Associations?" in Aoki, Gustafsson, and Williamson, eds., *The Firm as a Nexus of Treaties,* p. 340. Also see Leon Lindberg, John Campbell, and J. Rogers Hollingsworth, "Economic Governance and the Analysis of Structural Change in the American Economy"; Hollingsworth, "The Logic of Coordinating American Manufacturing Sectors"; and Campbell and Lindberg, "The Evolution of Governance Regimes"; all in Campbell, Hollingsworth, and

Lindberg, eds., *Governance of the American Economy* (New York: Cambridge University Press, 1991).

64. The problem, Harrison notes, might not have been mutual distrustfulness per se, "but rather the bureaucratic attempt to substitute remote for face-to-face communication—a cornerstone of the district system." But even if this is so, "this only provides further evidence of how 'trust,' when it becomes a force for defending the old ways, can actually *suppress* innovation." Bennett Harrison, *Lean and Mean: The Changing Landscape of Corporate Power in the Age of Flexibility* (New York: Basic Books, 1994), pp. 100–1.

The Prato story should give pause to enthusiasts of Michael Albert and Robin Hahnel's scheme for restoring "socialism as it was always meant to be"—coordinated from the ground up, without markets and with a minimum of central control—through computer networks "directly" linking producer and consumer associations in a giant exercise of iterative mathematical programming. Even if the (still very formidable) technical problems of presenting—but not overwhelming—network participants with the relevant information on production and consumption possibilities could be solved, the question of agent motivation remains deeply troubling to Albert and Hahnel's many critics. The message of Prato is that incentive compatibility problems can confound networks as well as hierarchies. (This message is reinforced by the growing portents of a breakdown of solidary norms on the heretofore self-policed Internet—the increase in "spamming" and other opportunistic activities—raising the specter of a "tragedy of the virtual commons.") For their latest full-scale attempts to address these issues, see Albert and Hahnel, *The Political Economy of Participatory Economics* (Princeton: Princeton University Press, 1991), and *Looking Forward: Participatory Economics For The Twenty First Century* (Boston: South End Press, 1991). For recent critiques, see Nancy Folbre's contribution to "Looking Forward: A Roundtable on Participatory Economics," *Z Magazine,* July/August 1991, and see Thomas Weisskopf, "Towards a Socialism for the Future, in the Wake of the Demise of the Socialism of the Past," *Review of Radical Political Economics* 24, nos. 3 & 4 (Fall/Winter 1992).

65. Harrison, *Lean and Mean,* p. 9.

66. Powell, "Neither Market Nor Hierarchy," p. 326.

67. Eggertsson, *Economic Behavior*, p. 127. Eggertsson is specifically referring to reformulations of the neoclassical production function by Michael Jensen and William Meckling.

Transaction cost economics in general, and Oliver Williamson in particular, have been accused of neglecting the role of property rights (and hence of the state) in determining the "technical" conditions—relative degrees of capital and labor asset specificity, for example—that in turn determine the relative efficiency of various contractual alternatives. The suggestion here is that property rights regimes are self-perpetuating, so that, for example, "[d]emocratic rights at the work-place and the technological specification of resources associated with them may be blocked by the ability of capitalist property rights to reproduce themselves"—as opposed to more generic efficiency considerations (see Ugo Pagano, "Organizational equilibria and institutional stability," in Bowles, Gintis, and Gustafsson, eds., *Markets and Democracy,* p. 112).

Two brief comments: first, as we have seen above, property rights questions *are* in fact central to positive political economy (if this is not clear in Williamson, then it certainly is in Barzel or Eggertsson). Second, as we have also seen above, the malleability of technique has its limits: there was *no* "technological speci-fication of resources" associable with state ownership and central planning that could overcome the large efficiency deficits of that particular property rights regime. It sustained itself as long as it did not just by configuring human and physical capital in ways that made it difficult for alternative institutional forms (like open markets and capitalist firms) to compete and catch on, but by forcibly *prohibiting* alternative institutions.

In contrast, the relatively open competition between (and within) American, Ger-man, and Japanese capitalisms does limit the ability of these respective property rights regimes to constrain technological choices: manifestly inferior techniques will tend to yield (eventually) to more competitive ones, even if some mutation of prop-erty rights is necessary to accommodate the change. This is, after all, how the networks discussed in the previous section have themselves emerged as (partial) alternatives to traditional hierarchal corporations.

As we shall see, the question of whether a market socialist regime would be self-sustaining—would stay close to whatever is the comparable efficiency frontier—in the face of relatively open regime competition is very far from settled. What should be settled is that it would be fatal to depend on the suppression of such competition.

68. Kenneth Arrow, *Social Choice and Individual Values* (New Haven: Yale University Press, 1963, 1951).

69. See William Riker, *Liberalism Against Populism: A Confrontation Between the Theory of Democracy and the Theory of Social Choice* (Prospect Heights: Wave-land Press, 1988, 1982) and Matthew McCubbins and Terry Sullivan, eds., *Congress: Structure and Policy* (New York: Cambridge University Press, 1987). On "sub-governments" see Jack Knott and Gary Miller, *Reforming Bureaucracy: The Politics of Institutional Choice* (Englewood Cliffs: Prentice-Hall, 1987).

70. Actually, cumulative voting schemes can capture intensity of preference to some degree, but none without violating one or another of Arrow's "im-possibility" conditions. See Riker, *Liberalism Against Populism*, and Alfred MacKay, *Arrow's Theorem: The Paradox of Social Choice* (New Haven: Yale University Press, 1980).

71. Peter Ordeshook, "The Emerging Discipline of Political Economy," in Alt and Shepsle, eds., *Positive Political Economy*, p. 16 (emphasis added).

72. See Mancur Olson, *The Rise and Decline of Nations* (New Haven: Yale University Press, 1982).

73. Mancur Olson, *The Logic of Collective Action: Public Goods and the Theory of Groups* (Cambridge: Harvard University Press, 1965, 1971). See also Sandler, *Collective Action*.

74. Likewise it was not through any lack of democratic accountability that a distributional coalition of mental health worker unions and local politicians in New York State was able to delay reallocation of public mental health dollars to downstate community treatment programs *for thirty years* after deinstitutionalization emptied out upstate mental institutions and dumped their former patients into the SROs and streets of New York City.

75. John Waterbury, *Exposed to Innumerable Delusions: Public Enterprise and State Power in Egypt, India, Mexico, and Turkey* (New York: Cambridge University Press, 1993), p. 109.

76. In fact, positive political economy has reinvigorated Keynesian economics by showing how rational microeconomic responses to hidden information (paying agents above-market clearing "efficiency wages" to minimize influence costs) precipitates spells of macroeconomic disequilibrium (unemployment) that can be shortened by active monetary policy. See George Akerlof and Janet Yellen, eds., *Efficiency Wage Models of the Labor Market* (New York: Cambridge University Press, 1986), and N. Gregory Mankiw and David Romer, eds., *The New Keynesian Economics, Volume 1: Imperfect Competition and Sticky Prices, Volume 2: Coordination Failures and Real Rigidities* (Cambridge: The MIT Press, 1992). For a lucid, nontechnical exposition, see Paul Krugman, *Peddling Prosperity: Economic Sense and Nonsense in the Age of Diminished Expectations* (New York: Norton, 1994), chapter 8.

77. State action is also at times able to profoundly shift resource allocations. We don't have to look afar to Japan or South Korea for successful examples of this; here in the United States, the New Deal (and subsequent economic mobilization for World War II) engineered a huge reallocation of investment activity to the underdeveloped South and West. It is worth noting, though, that this reallocation was expedited by a one-time massive expansion of public spending that effectively masked the redistributive aspects of its regional focus (this is just what Waterbury's analysis would have led us to expect), and that it was not the subject of very much public deliberation. (See Jordan Schwarz, *The New Dealers: Power Politics in the Age of Roosevelt,* New York: Random House, 1993.) In more normal times, public investment patterns here are hemmed in, for good and ill, by innumerable subgovernmental quid pro quos. (As noted below, these are exacting their toll in Japan and South Korea as well.)

78. Presumably, then, when Miller later argued that compared to conventional capitalist firms, cooperatives would show "a greater willingness . . . to adapt to changes in the market and use the skills of their members in new ways" (chapter 12), he was referring to cooperatives small enough to have relatively homogenous workforces and relatively low "costs of democracy." Otherwise, as Mill pointed out, these kinds of entrepreneurial adjustments would be just where the "individual management" of the capitalist firm would shine to its greatest advantage.

79. In this the Russians were only pursuing a strategy prescribed by Kautsky, more than a decade before the Bolsheviks came to power, to overcome capitalism's vexing refusal to bring concentration and centralization to the logical conclusion predicted by Marx.

80. It's not clear to what extent the capital-labor partnerships would displace public ownership of the "commanding heights" or cooperative ownership with arm's-length finance.

81. Masahiko Aoki, "The Motivational Role of an External Agent in the Informationally Participatory Firm," in Bowles, Gintis, and Gustafsson, eds., *Markets and Democracy*, pp. 237, 244. (Aoki also recognizes and discusses the incentive compatibility problems in which the external agent might become ensnared.) See also Aoki's important analysis of the "coalitional firm" in *Information, Incentives, and Bargaining in the Japanese Economy* (New York: Cambridge University Press, 1987).

82. On the impact of workforce heterogeneity on worker ownership, see Henry Hannsman, "When Does Worker Ownership Work? ESOPs, Law Firms, Codetermination, and Economic Democracy," *Yale Law Journal* (99), 1990, and

Hannsman, "The Viability of Worker Ownership: An Economic Perspective on the Political Structure of the Firm," in Aoki, Gustafsson, and Williamson, eds., *The Firm as a Nexus of Treaties*.

83. A similar argument has been developed by Louis Putterman, "Incentive Problems Favoring Noncentralized Investment Fund Ownership," in Bardhan and Roemer, eds., *Market Socialism*. It would take us beyond the scope of the present discussion to consider how far these problems are overcome in the related "bank-centric" system in Bardhan, "On Tackling The Soft-Budget Constraint in Market Socialism," or in the "coupon economy" alternative presented in Roemer, "Can There Be Socialism After Communism" (both in Bardhan and Roemer, *Market Socialism*).

84. Here John Waterbury's comment is germane: "When one reads that in 1982 Exxon slashed 80,000 employees of a total of 182,000, including 1,000 of 1,360 bureaucrats in its New York headquarters, without sacrificing production, one must question the distinction between public and private" (that is, in terms of feebleness of monitoring efforts). "There is, however, a difference: had Exxon been an SOE [state owned enterprise], *it might not have made the personnel cuts*." Waterbury, *Exposed to Innumerable Delusions*, p. 14 (emphasis added).

85. That is, the illusion that central planners would be equipped with something like perfect foresight. Nove's devastating critique of this notion is contained in a section of *The Economics of Feasible Socialism* (London: Allen and Unwin, 1983) that is not excerpted in the 1985 *Dissent* article reprinted here.

86. The following discussion of Harrington is drawn from David Belkin, "From 'What Socialists Would Do' to What Socialists Wouldn't Do: Tradition and Change in the Vision of Michael Harrington" (unpublished paper, 1990).

87. Harrington, *Socialism*, pp. 370–71.

88. Michael Harrington, "What Socialists Would Do in America—If They Could," *Dissent*, Fall 1978, p. 450.

89. Similarly, when Erber characterizes "the corporate state strategy" as being about not "letting the market decide," it is the example of Sweden and Japan that he is extolling.

90. As Joseph Schumpeter once observed in a slightly different context, "[t]he decisive difference is whether, apart from any monopoly position which it might secure for itself, the state does or does not continue to work within the framework of a free economy whose data and methods it has to accept in its own enterprises" (Joseph Schumpeter, "The Tax State" [1918], reprinted in Richard Swedberg, ed., *Joseph A. Schumpeter: The Economics and Sociology of Capitalism* [Princeton: Princeton University Press, 1991], p. 116, emphasis added).

91. In chapter 12, Miller himself draws attention to the retrenchment of several traditional socialist goals. While describing the market socialist state's role in familiar terms as "set[ting] the parameters of the market" and the "regulation of investment," Miller makes it clear that this should not "preempt major policy decisions . . . about the nature and volume of production."

92. See the note above referring to Putterman, "Incentive Problems."

93. The recent well-publicized struggles of elected heads of state against entrenched planning bureaucracies in Japan and South Korea should give pause to those who cite these countries as success stories of benign self-limiting intervention.

# PART II

---

## The Democratic
## Socialist Perspective

# 2

# Thinking About Socialism: Achievements, Failures, and Possibilities

## (Fall 1985)

## *Irving Howe*

Christianity did not "die" in the nineteenth century. Millions held fast to the faith; churches survived; theological controversies flourished. Yet we can now see that in the decades after the Enlightenment, Christianity suffered deep wounds that could not be healed, sometimes were even made worse, by the sincere efforts of various thinkers to refine and revise the faith. Gradually Christianity lost its claim to speak for the whole of Western culture; gradually it lost the ability to seize and hold the imagination of serious young people. Some of them it could still attract, but not with the assurance of the past.

Has something like this been happening to socialism these past several decades? Powerful parties in Europe still employ the socialist vocabulary and millions of people still accept the socialist label; yet some deep inner crisis of belief, to say nothing of public failures and defeats, has beset socialism. The soaring passions of the early movement are gone, and those of us who strive for socialist renewal cannot help wondering whether we are caught in a drift of historical decline, perhaps beyond reversing, perhaps to yield at some future moment to a new radical humanism. And perhaps, too, it does not really matter: each generation must do what it can.

## I

> To the question of the elements of social restructure [that is, socialism] . . . Marx and Engels never gave a positive answer, because they had no inner relation to this idea. Marx might occasionally allude to "the elements of the new society" . . . but . . . the political act of revolution remained the one thing worth striving for.[1]

This observation by Martin Buber, while slightly overstated, embodies an essential truth. Marx and Engels praised the early nineteenth century "utopian socialists" for their boldness in projecting visions of a new Golden Age, but they were also contemptuous of the utopians' habit of indulging in detailed "future-painting." Where the utopians, wrote Marx, pictured a socialist society as "an ideal to which reality will have to adjust itself,"[2] he saw the movement toward socialism as a necessary outcome of concrete social conflicts. Marx wanted to place the socialist project within the course of historical development, and this he did by specifying two driving forces within history: first, the evolution of economic techniques and structures, leading to a concentration of ownership and wealth, a recurrence of social crisis, and a sharpening of class conflict; and second, the gathering strength and rising consciousness of the working class, derived from or enabled by its crucial position within the capitalist economy. By now it seems clear that Marx was keener in analyzing the "driving forces" of the economy than in allocating the "tasks" of the proletariat, a class that has shown itself capable of intermittent rebellion but not, at least thus far, of serving as the creator of a new society.

To read the passages in Marx's writings that deal with the socialist future—they are scattered, infrequent, and fragmentary—is to recognize how valid the charge is that on this matter he slips into a vague and static perfectionism. From his remarks we get a vision of a world marvelously free of social—and indeed nonsocial—conflict: no longer in thrall to alienation, exploitation, and social fetishism, humanity reaches, for the first time, a high plateau of the human. In the Marxist anticipation of the good society there is little recognition of the sheer recalcitrance of all social arrangements, the limitations that characterize the human species, the likely persistence into the future of error, stupidity, and bad will. Even convinced socialists must by now feel some skepticism about this version of utopia.

Marxists would reply, with some irritation, that their vision of ultimate social harmony depends on the unfolding of a lengthy historical sequence during which not only new values and habits, but a new humanity would emerge. Perhaps so. There is no way to disprove such expectations, any more than to dispel the skepticism they arouse. Far more troubling, at least for a socialist living toward the end of the twentieth century, is the fact that this vision of a society in which "the state withers away" and "the antithesis between physical and mental labor vanishes" does very little to help us achieve a qualitatively better, if still imperfect, society—the kind that some of us call socialism.

It's only fair to add that Marx's failure to engage critically with the problem of the envisaged socialist society did have some positive aspects. If the society of the future is to be entrusted to its living actors, then Marx was right, perhaps, in thinking it imprudent to detail its features in advance. History must be left to those who will make it.

But there is another, less attractive reason for Marx's failure to draw "the face" of a socialist society. Marxism offers a strong theory of social change but has little to say about political arrangements—structures of government, balances of power, agencies of representation. Marxism has usually failed to consider with sufficient attention what we might call the trans- or supra-class elements of politics—those elements likely to be present (and perplexing) in any society. Except for some brilliant remarks in his *18th Brumaire of Louis Bonaparte*, Marx gave little weight to politics as an autonomous activity, politics as more than epiphenomenon, politics as a realm with its own powers, procedures, and norms. As Paul Ricoeur has written

> Politics embodies a human relationship which is not reducible to class conflict or socioeconomic tensions. . . . Even the state most in subjection to a dominant class is also a state precisely to the extent that it expresses the fundamental will of the nation as a whole. . . . On the other hand, politics develops evils of its own—evils specific to the exercise of power.[3]

From such perceptions emerges a problematic view of the entire process of change that is supposed to lead to socialism. But if some sophisticated Marxists have recently begun to recognize the autonomy of politics, it must in honesty be added that this was by no means the prevalent view of the socialist movement during its formative, most powerful years. During the three or four decades after Marx's death, the movement as an institution grew stronger, but its vision of the goal for which it was striving declined into a slackness of perfection, only tenuously, through a papery chain of rhetoric, related to the issues and struggles of the moment. Socialism came gradually to be "defined" as a condition of classlessness, seen more as premise than problem; and since the inclination of Marxists was to think about conflicts and evils as the consequence of class domination, it followed—did it not?—that the eradication of classes must sooner or later mean the disappearance of these afflictions. I exaggerate a little, but not, I fear, very much.

Among social democrats this habit of thought encouraged an easy confidence in the benefits of historical evolution; among revolutionary Marxists, a faith in the self-elected vanguard party that would satisfy the ends of history.

Until about the First World War, this genial mythicizing of an assured future may not have done too much damage, for in those years the main work of the left was to rouse the previously mute lower classes to the need for historical action. Indeed, the visionary tone of early Marxism helped give the workers a quasi-religious confidence in their own powers. Had the movement achieved nothing else, this arousal of the plebes would still be to its credit. In fact, it also helped bring about valuable social changes, a sequence of reforms eventuating in the welfare state.

The problem of socialism would become acute when a socialist movement approached power or, in quite different circumstances, when it was weak and under sharp intellectual attack. In both of these extreme circumstances, the poverty of Marxist (not all socialist) thought regarding the "face of socialism" becomes very serious. Between immediate struggles for specific reforms and rosy invocations of the cooperative commonwealth still to come, *a whole space is missing*—the space of social reconstruction. In the writings of the English guild socialists we find some hints on these matters, but not enough. Only in the last fifteen or twenty years, under the impact of crisis and defeat, has some of that "missing space" been occupied through the writings of a number of serious thinkers—I shall discuss them later—who have tried to offer some guidelines (not blueprints) for a socialist society. The work is just beginning. Can it still be in time? I do not know.

## II

Why has the European social democracy been unable to advance further than the welfare state of Scandinavia? I list some of the possible answers: Social democratic parties often have come to office without parliamentary majorities, which meant they had to enter coalitions that imposed severe constraints. Social democratic parties were often voted into office at moments when capitalist economies were suffering breakdowns, which meant that precisely the condition prompting their victories also limited their capacity for taking radical measures. Social democratic parties in office frequently had to face flights of capital, a problem that, within the limits of the nation-state, proved very difficult to cope with. And social democratic parties, settling into the routines of institutional life, began to lose their radical edge.

For my present purposes, I want to stress another, important if not decisive, reason for the difficulties of social democratic parties. They often had no clear idea, no worked-out vision, of what a socialist transformation might entail. Given their commitment to democracy, their justified distaste for Bolshevik dictatorship, and their recognition that a good part of their electorate cared more about particular measures than a new society, they began to find the idea of socialism increasingly slippery, evanescent, insubstantial. No doubt, in some instances there were also the betrayals of principle that the far left charged against social democracy, but most of the time, I think, social democrats were victimized by their own intellectual slackness. They thought they knew what had to be done the next day, but when it came to their sacred "historic mission," they often grew uncertain and timid. And sometimes they were struck dumb.

Not so the Bolsheviks. *They knew.* Their aura of certainty, their persuasion that history lay snugly in the party's fist helped the Communists win the support of many European workers and intellectuals during the years between the world wars. Yet even a glance at the Bolshevik record after the November 1917 revolution will show that Lenin and his comrades had only the most sketchy and confused ideas about the socioeconomic policies that might enable a socialist transformation. The seizure of power—about *that* they could speak with authority.

Shortly before the Russian Revolution, Lenin had written that if the Bolsheviks came to power in backward, war-devastated Russia they would establish "workers' control" over industry; but he did not propose large-scale nationalizations. From November 1917 to the summer of 1918, the Bolsheviks favored what we'd now call a mixed economy, in which, for a time at least, large areas of private ownership of industry would continue, but production and investment decisions would be controlled by the leftist state together, presumably, with working-class institutions.

This view was in accord with Lenin's realistic understanding that socialism—seen traditionally by Marxists as a society presupposing economic abundance and a high level of culture—could not be achieved in a country such as Russia, certainly not without substantial aid from the industrial West.

Once in power, the Bolsheviks veered wildly in their economic policies. At the start of the civil war they abandoned their initial moderation and introduced the draconian measures of war communism: virtually complete nationalization of enterprises, the requisitioning of agricultural products, and a highly centralized political-economic command. Many Bolsheviks came to regard all this as the appropriate road to socialism, though in later years some of them would admit that grave errors had been made.

War communism intensified the economic disaster that was by then well advanced as a result of Russian defeats in the war. There now followed a sharp drop in production: further depletion of industrial plants; a radical cut in the size of the working class; a decline in labor productivity; and so on. Some of these conditions were a result of difficulties created by the civil war; some because of a mixture of Bolshevik arrogance and inexperience; but some were the fruit of a by then habitual refusal on the left to think concretely and problematically about the social transformation that might follow upon the assumption of political power.

Between 1917 and 1923 Bolshevik oscillations on economic policy found a vivid reflection in Trotsky's writings. At one point he proposed the creation of labor armies, a kind of militarized garrison economy; this ghastly idea, meeting with bitter resistance from Bolshevik and other trade unionists, was rejected. At another point, veering sharply, Trotsky proposed an economic course anticipating the New Economic Policy that would in fact be introduced in 1921: a considerable loosening of state controls, a return to a partially free market, something like a mixed economy. This proposal was at first rejected by the Bolsheviks, but under the pressures of reality they finally introduced the NEP. What we can see here is a deep incoherence, a floundering by gifted ideologues who had not anticipated, while still out of power and in a position to think theoretically, that the taking of power would by no means exempt them from the difficulties faced by their adversaries.

In his biography of the "right" Bolshevik leader Bukharin, Stephen F. Cohen remarks that Lenin took a "censorious attitude toward discussing future problems. He preferred Napoleon's advice, 'On s'engage et puis . . . on voit.' " (One engages, and then . . . one sees.)[4] Alas, we have seen.

## III

Were I writing here a comprehensive study of modern socialism, a central emphasis would have to be put on the enormous damage wrought by Stalinism once it became a powerful force in the 1930s. Insofar as right-wing and left-wing dogmatists found it convenient to identify the Russian dictatorship with socialism, they joined to discredit the entire socialist idea. And insofar as the identification was popularly accepted, so was the discrediting.

One result was that the already festering crisis of socialist thought grew much more severe. And now, for the past several decades, the socialist experience has involved a dislodgment of received persuasions, a melting-down of ideological structures, and a search for new—or for cleansed and reaffirmed old—values. For socialists, individually, this was often a clarifying and chastening experience; but for their movement it brought grave difficulties. Introspection rarely makes for public effectiveness.

Many socialists of my generation would customarily defend their belief through what I'd call a hygienic negative: "We entirely reject any sort of party-state dictatorship: the very thought of it is appalling. Nor do we want a complete nationalization of industry. . . . Less and less does that seem an avenue to the cooperative commonwealth."

After a time such responses came close to being instinctive. Serious socialists would now describe the desired society by invoking desired *qualities*, with a stress on sentiments of freedom, attitudes of fraternity, and, sometimes, priorities of social allocation. They proposed, first of all, to secure the socialist idea in the realm of values, whereas, to simplify a little, the tradition in which some of us had been raised was one that focused on institutional changes. In making this shift, these socialists were doing something morally and politically necessary but also tactically disabling. For unless plausible social structures and agencies could be located for realizing the values that were now being placed at the center of socialist thought, we were finally left with little more than our good will.*

---

*An illuminating parallel can be found in a passage from the British philosopher Stuart Hampshire:

> For me socialism is not so much a theory as a set of moral injunctions, which seem to me clearly right and rationally justifiable: first, that the elimination of poverty ought to be the first priority of government after defensé; secondly, that as great inequalities in wealth between different social groups lead to inequalities in power and in freedom of action, they are generally unjust and need to be redressed by governmental action; thirdly, that democratically elected governments ought to ensure that primary and basic human needs are given priority within the economic system, even if this involves some loss in the aggregate of goods and services which would otherwise be available. How these moral requirements are best realized, at particular times and places . . . are matters for the social sciences and also for a critical reading of history; after them also for personal experience and for worldly insight.[5]

Now I find this very sympathetic, but suspect it's open to the charge that it contains nothing distinctively socialist. Could not many liberals endorse Stuart Hampshire's "moral injunctions"? It's only when we come to specific proposals for putting these injunctions into practice that the socialist case can be said to stand or fall.

Nevertheless, the clarification of socialist values was the essential task during, say, the past half-century: little of importance could be accomplished on the left until that was done. And if these values are now accepted as truisms, it is because a bitter struggle had to be conducted in their behalf. It is useful to restate a few:

- There is no necessary historical sequence from capitalism to socialism, nor any irrefutable reason for supposing history moves along a steadily upward curve. Unforeseen societies—mixed, retrogressive, opaque—can persist for long periods of time.

- The abolition of capitalism is not necessarily a step toward human liberation; it can lead, and has led, to societies far more repressive than capitalism at its worst.

- Socialism is not to be "defined" as a society in which private property has been abolished; what is decisive is the political character of the regime exercising control over a postcapitalist or mixed economy.

- Socialism should be envisaged as a society in which the means of production, to an extent that need not be rigidly determined in advance, are collectively or socially owned—which means, democratically controlled. An absolute prerequisite is the preservation and growth of democracy.

- A "complete" transformation of humanity is a corrupt fantasy that can lead to a mixture of terror and apathy.

One painful yet predictable result of this reshaping, or cleansed reassertion, of the socialist idea was that in the very course of being given an increasingly humane and democratic character, it also came to suffer from greater uncertainty with regard to social arrangements and institutional mechanisms. The reassertion of values led to skepticism about major elements of traditional Marxist thought. Three instances:

1. *The assumption that the proletariat would serve as the leading agency of social transformation.*

    History has vetoed this idea. The working class has not been able to "transcend" its role within capitalist society, except perhaps during brief outbursts of rebellion; and now, as a result of technological innovations, its specific gravity as social class and political actor seems to be in decline.* As if in response to this development, there has appeared a tendency to regard socialism as a goal transcending the interests of one or another class. There is something attractive about this, but also something that betrays political uncertainty. For to say that a social vision is the province of all risks making it the passion of none.

2.  *The assumption that the nationalization of industry would, if accompanied by a socialist winning of office, smooth the way for the new society.*

Significant socialist texts can readily be cited making it clear that nationalization is not necessarily to be taken as an equivalent or even precondition of socialism.† Yet it would be misleading to lean too heavily on these texts, since I am certain that older socialists share the recollection that there was a strong habitual tendency to put great faith in the value of nationalization.

In the Communist dictatorships the mere takeover of industry has made for a frightful concentration (and fusion) of political and economic power. In some capitalist countries, portions of the economy have been nationalized, sometimes because socialist governments wished to make at least a dent in bourgeois owner-

---

*As a matter of historical justice I should add that once we free the working class from the "tasks" imposed on it by Marxism, we can recognize that, as the main unpropertied class in modern society, it has exerted a strong and positive pressure to bring about major improvements in the social order.

† As far back as 1892, Karl Kautsky, an accredited legatee of Marx, wrote: "It does not follow that every nationalization of an economic function or an industry is a step toward the cooperative commonwealth. . . . If the modern state nationalizes certain industries, it does not do so for the purpose of restricting capitalist exploitation, but for the purpose of protecting the capitalist system. . . . As an exploiter of labor, the state is superior to any private capitalist."[6]

And Morris Hillquit, the American Socialist leader: "Socialists entertain no illusions as to the benefits of governmentally owned industries under the present regime. . . . Its effect may be decidedly reactionary. . . . The demand for national or municipal ownership of industries is always qualified [by socialists] with a provision for the democratic administration of such industries."[7]

I cite these two influential figures to show that such ideas do go back to earlier generations of socialist thinkers.

ship, sometimes because governments, bourgeois or socialist, came to the rescue of enterprises on the brink of bankruptcy. The results have not been very inspiring, especially when no efforts were made to introduce democratic workers' participation in the management of newly nationalized industries.

Serious problems have arisen in the operation of such industries, some of them caused by the inherent difficulties of functioning through a calculus of profit while trying, within an economy still largely capitalist, to satisfy social goals. What should be the criteria for measuring efficiency in nationalized enterprises? If taken over because they have failed in private hands, what order of losses should society be prepared to accept? How are decisions to be made regarding capital investment? Such questions can be answered; and in part the answers are similar to those that might be provided with regard to private enterprise (since the criterion of profitability cannot simply be dismissed); but the answers should also be different from those prevailing under private enterprise (since such factors as "externalities" are now to be taken into systematic account).

Nationalization of industry has been part of a worldwide drift toward the interpenetration of state and society. It can be a device for trying to solve a crisis of capitalist economy; it can perhaps help to create a modern infrastructure in third-world economies; it can form part of the breakdown of "civil society" that enables the rise of totalitarianism; and it can be initiated by a socialist government intent upon deepening democratic practices in all areas of social life. Nationalization seems, in short, to be a somewhat neutral device, available to just about every kind of government; but, whatever else, it is surely not a sufficient condition for a socialist transformation.

3. *The assumption that economic planning is a unique aspect or virtue of socialist society, ensuring both justice and orderliness in economic affairs such as unplanned economies are not likely to match.*

By now we have learned otherwise. Planning does not necessarily offer an encompassing method for the solution of socioeconomic problems. As earlier Marxists such as Kautsky and Bukharin glimpsed, planning does not have to wait for the happy

arrival of socialism, but is at least partly to be found in "late"—
that is, monopoly or cartel—versions of capitalism. Like any other
human enterprise, planning is subject to error, manipulation, bureaucratic sluggishness, and sheer bad will, so that it must always
be tentative, proximate, and fallible. "Total" planning—that is, a
command economy—entails authoritarian political structures.

Democratic planning, in which many socialists place great
hope, is at once attractive, complex, and problematic. There are
ways in which planning must always be somewhat at odds with
democratic procedures, if only because it often depends, in modern societies, on skilled professionals who are likely to develop
their own caste or bureaucratic interests. On the other hand, "popular participation [can] inform the planner about the social terrain
he is trying to map; the planner [can] facilitate the democratic
process by presenting to the people intelligent alternatives for
their choice."[8] No assertion of general principles can remove the
constant need for a nuanced and vigilant mediation between
agencies of planning and a political democracy.

If, then, one turns to the revisions in socialist thinking that we have
had to make in recent decades, it becomes clear that we find ourselves
in an uncomfortable but, I would contend, worthwhile difficulty—re-
fining our values, growing somewhat uncertain about our means.
Leszek Kolakowski puts it well:

> Where are we now? What we lack in our thinking about society in socialist
> terms is not general values . . . but rather knowledge about how these values
> can be prevented from clashing with each other when put into practice. . . .
>
> Are we [then] fools to keep thinking in socialist terms? I do not think
> so. Whatever has been done in Western Europe to bring about more
> justice, more security, more educational opportunities, more welfare . . .
> could never have been achieved without the pressures of socialist ideolo-
> gies and movements, for all their naivetes and illusions. This does not
> mean that we are exculpated in advance and allowed to cherish these
> illusions endlessly, after so many defeats.[9]

During the last fifteen or twenty years, then, we have seen a significant shift in the nature and direction of socialist thought. The clarification of values to which some of us had to devote major energies has

now been achieved, at least in part, and as a result socialist thinkers have been able to turn to a study of those institutions and mechanisms through which these values might be realized.

## IV

A number of writers have tackled the problems that seem likely to appear during a "transition period" between capitalism and socialism. Such writers as Alec Nove, Michael Harrington, and Radoslav Selucky have offered proposals for the kind of immediate reforms (civil rights, women's rights, racial equality) that are not uniquely socialist in character but upon which liberals and socialists can happily agree. Next would come "structural reforms," such as tax proposals aiming at a gradual redistribution of income and wealth and efforts to achieve full employment, which would surely entail some overall economic planning. These latter "structural reforms" might be described as extending and deepening the welfare state. Beyond this second group of proposals lies a third—the kind that would begin to change the fundamental relationships of power and property, such as—

> [a] challenge to corporate control of the investment process by insisting that public policy concern itself with what is produced ... [to] include public controls over private investment decisions, such as specifying the conditions under which corporations can leave a locality or oligopolies can raise prices.[10]

Steps might also be taken toward creating "social property," pilot projects of enterprises democratically owned and controlled by employees, with the government encouraging, through generous credit and other provisions, the establishment of producer and consumer cooperatives, "small-scale, de-alienating, good for training workers in running their own affairs."[11]

Such a bundle of reforms, graduated in their social penetration, would signify a radical series of changes, even if not yet reaching a socialist society. One lesson to be learned from past efforts of socialist governments is that much depends on pacing. Too slow a rate of change disappoints enthusiastic followers; too rapid a rate can lead to the loss of middle-class support, excessive inflation (there is bound to be some), and serious disturbances. Choices would have to be made, so that fundamental socioeconomic measures would not be jeopardized by divisions over secondary or symbolic issues. And a socialist government, it should be remembered, would also have a stake in maintaining a good measure of national cohesion and civility, even if its legislation antagonized large property owners and small ideologues.

Such transitional measures, whatever their ultimate benefits, are certain to create immediate difficulties. Substantial benefits for the poorest segments of the population—absolutely; but if on too lavish a scale, these can result in an inflation threatening both the economic program and political stability of the government. Sweeping tax reforms—desirable; but if too sweeping, they can alienate segments of the middle class, whose support a socialist government needs. A wealth tax—attractive; but it can lead to capital flight. Economic controls—probably unavoidable; but they entail the likelihood of shortages, black markets, misallocation of resources, economic imbalances.

One suggested way of alleviating these difficulties would be to stress the need for higher productivity, "a larger cake" so that most segments of the population would be satisfied with immediate benefits. But it's by no means certain that in a transitional period this could be achieved. And such proposals for economic growth would encounter a bumpy course: they would be opposed by people who fear the ecological consequences and think "consumerism" at variance with the socialist ethos, as well as by entrepreneurs and managers reluctant to help raise productivity at the very moment their "prerogatives" are being curbed. At least with regard to the managers, however, an imaginative government would work very hard to gain their cooperation, arguing that many of them, especially at middle levels, have no unalterable stake in perpetuating corporate control of economic life or in vast social inequities.

A democratic commitment—unconditional as it must be—may well delay and even thwart socialist programs. Socialist governments do not rest on undifferentiated popular support, and many of their voters might not wish them to go beyond limited reforms. Socialist governments must put into office people who lack experience and often, in consequence, make mistakes or slip into confusion. Socialist governments need to find channels to capital growth, but the tensions created by the changes they initiate can lead to panic and "sabotage" in capital markets. And even the best-conceived program of transition is likely to be hostage to the business cycle, as well as to imbalances of wealth and power among the nations.

A painful irony must here be acknowledged: many of the criticisms Leninists have made of social democratic reformism have a point, for instance, that timidity would inhibit radical initiatives, while radical excess could drive people of the political and social middle to become outright opponents. The Leninist conclusion is that the "transition period" requires a "temporary" abrogation of democracy, in the name, to be sure, of a "higher democracy." This cure, however, is far worse than any malady one can imagine, since "temporary" dictatorships have a way of slipping into permanence, especially those established by Communist parties. What's more, they usually fail to cope with the economic problems they alone are supposedly able to solve.

There is no undemocratic road to socialism; there are only undemocratic roads that can bring, and have brought, nations to barbaric mockeries of the socialist idea. If we were forced to conclude that there cannot be a democratic road to socialism, then we would also have to conclude that the entire socialist enterprise is illusory.

We understand now—experience must teach us *something*—that the transition from capitalism to socialism is likely to be a lengthy process, interrupted by setbacks, and fraught with tensions, conflicts, difficulties, and errors. But if it is to be a socialism of free men and women, there can be no other way.

## V

Between the period of "transition" and a "full" or achieved socialism there is no thick or impenetrable wall. The distinction is mostly an analytical convenience. A healthy society must always be in transition; a dynamic socialism can never be "full."

What, then, would the social structure of a democratic socialist society look like? Mulling over this question, I find myself in some sympathy with the traditional leftist reluctance to indulge in "future painting." Certainly, there can be no call, at this point in history, for either prediction or prescription. But it is also too late to trust simply to the workings of history; tokens must be offered of the *direction* in which we hope to move.

But must not any discussion of a socialist society now seem remote, unrelated to current needs and concerns? It all depends on the spirit and terms in which we approach the matter. Everyone knows that today in the United States socialism is not on the political agenda; but can anyone be certain that there will not be new or recurrent social crises that will give an unexpected relevance to at least some of the basic socialist proposals? Within or close to a number of European socialist parties there are significant groups of political people seriously trying to sketch out "the face of socialism." They understand that, in view of the volatility of modern history, it is necessary to think now with regard to what may be done the day after tomorrow. (And perhaps the day after tomorrow will come tomorrow.) There is, furthermore, one great advantage in being powerless, and that is that it enables, sometimes stimulates, serious thought. So with all the necessary qualifications as to tentativeness and speculativeness, I proceed to offer a sketch of a sketch, cheerfully pilfered from the work of several recent writers (including, among others, Oskar Lange, Abram Bergson, George Lichtheim, Radoslav Selucky, Henry Pachter, Wlodzimierz Brus, Michael Harrington, and Alec Nove).

Let us focus on two models for a democratic socialism offered by Radoslav Selucky, a Czech exile now living in the West, and Alec Nove, an economist living in Scotland.\* As a matter of strict principle, both agree on the need for multiparty democracy. Anything remotely like the centralized "command economies" of Eastern Europe must be entirely avoided, since these are economically inept, politically repressive, and intellectually intolerable.† Both writers agree also on the need for a

---

\*Alec Nove's deeply interesting discussion appeared in the Summer 1985 issue of *Dissent.* [Editors' note: Nove's essay is reprinted as chapter 10 of this volume.]

†As Selucky points out, the centralized, authoritarian structure of the East European societies

> requires that all basic economic decisions be made at the top of the social hierarchy. Because the producers are dispersed, of technological necessity, the basic division of labor between those who rule, control, plan and manage, and those who are ruled, controlled, planned and managed, cannot but remain in existence despite the nationalization of the means of production. From the functional point of view, it is irrelevant who has a formal title to property; *what is relevant is who disposes of it, who decides on it, who manipulates it, in whose interest one makes decisions and in whose interest controlling functions are exercised."* [Emphasis in original.][12]

market economy, subject to controls by a democratic polity: laissez-faire would be quite as inoperative under advanced socialism as it has turned out to be under advanced capitalism. Where they differ significantly is with regard to structures of property and productive relations in a "market socialism." Selucky strongly favors social controls from below, while Nove would encourage a greater variety in the modes of ownership. Selucky's views on this matter seem more attractive, Nove's more realistic.

Selucky lists a number of concise premises for his model, and I quote the essential ones:

> The means of production are owned socially and managed by those who make use of them.
>
> Social ownership of the means of production is separated from the state.
>
> Producing and trading enterprises are autonomous from the state and independent of each other. They operate within the framework of the market, which is regulated by a central indicative plan.
>
> The institutions which provide health, education, and welfare services are wholly exempt from the market.
>
> The right to participate in direct management of the work units *operating in the market* is derived from labor.
>
> The right to participate in direct management of the work units *exempt wholly or partly from the market* is derived proportionally from labor, ownership, and consumption of the provided services and utilities.
>
> The right to participate in indirect political control over, and regulation of, the socially owned means of production is derived from one's position as a citizen.
>
> Health and education services and social benefits for the disabled are distributed according to one's needs.
>
> The principle of self-management is limited to microeconomic units only.[13]

This model, attractive in several respects, stresses—as, after the experiences of our century, socialists must stress—the separation of political and economic power. It proposes a dispersal of economic power in horizontal enterprises, each largely self-sustaining and freely administered, though subject both to market signals and social regulation. It provides consumers with freedom of choice, and citizens with free occupational and educational choices. It favors a market mechanism that would be interdependent with "indicative" planning—that is, planning not merely imposed from above but with institutional mechanisms for democratic decision-making and checks from below. And it rests on direct democracy within the workplace insofar as that is possible, and on representative democracy in the society as a whole.

This model presupposes the flourishing of "civil society" and its autonomous "secondary institutions" (such as trade unions, political groups, fraternal societies) apart from and, when necessary, in opposition to the state. The intent is clearly to enable a pluralist flexibility that is present in, though often only claimed for, capitalist democracy, while at the same time eliminating many of its socially retrogressive features.

In such a socialist society, wage levels would be subject to the law of supply and demand, shaped in part through collective bargaining undertaken by free trade unions, though also (as is sometimes now true in industrial nations) bounded by social regulations such as "incomes policies." Wage differentials would remain, in accordance with pressures of scarcity and skill, though again subject to social boundaries. The market would provide goods and services, regulating those prices not controlled for purposes of public policy (or those products the society might decide to provide without cost). And while, in its initial phases, a democratic socialist society would have to strive for increases in production and higher productivity, it might, after a time, through modest increments, supersede the efficiency principle in behalf of more attractive social ends.*

---

*In such a society, observes Abram Bergson,

> managers of socialist plants and industries—the former responsible primarily for current operations, the latter for larger investments, especially introcution of new plants—are allowed similarly to determine autonomously inputs of factors and corresponding outputs. In the process, however, each is supposed to observe two rules: (1) to combine factors in such a way as to assure that at the prices established for such inputs any given output is produced at a minimum cost and (2) to fix the scale of output of any commodity produced at a point where its marginal cost equals the corresponding price.[14]

[Editors' note: In this passage Bergson is actually discussing Oskar Lange's model of market socialism (see chapter 6, this volume), which differs in important respects from the Selucky model that Howe is summarizing here.]

Alec Nove's model for democratic socialism differs from Selucky's in one crucial respect. Selucky, writes Nove,

> appears to envisage an evolution toward one type of producing unit. In my view it is possible and desirable to have several. . . . It is essential to recall the assumptions of political democracy. The citizens can choose, for example, what sorts of private initiative to encourage or to tolerate, the desirable forms of cooperatives, the extent of workers' participation in management, and much else besides. They can experiment, learn from experience, commit and correct errors. . . .
>
> Suppose that we have a legal structure which permits the following species:
> 1. State enterprises, centrally controlled and administered, hereinafter [called] *centralized state corporations.*
> 2. State-owned (or socially owned) enterprises with full autonomy and a management responsible to the workforce, hereinafter [called] *socialized enterprises.*
> 3. *Cooperative enterprises.*
> 4. *Small-scale private enterprises,* subject to clearly defined limits.
> 5. *Individuals* (for instance, freelance journalists, plumbers, artists).[15]

The idea of a greater diversity of production units is in principle appealing, since the aim of a socialist society ought to be the maximizing of opportunity, choice, and freedom within democratically agreed-upon bounds. The "centralized state corporations" would include banks and enterprises necessarily very large or occupying a monopoly position, or both—and with regard to all this there would be significant, large-scale economies.

Among examples of such "state corporations" are power stations, oil and petrochemical complexes. But the criterion here ought to be technological, not the corporate structure that prevails today, since some present-day corporations are large because of the power it gives them over the market rather than because of any criteria of efficiency. There might be the danger that some of these giant enterprises would assume a monopoly posture under socialism as disadvantageous to consumers and workers as it can be under capitalism. In order to rein in such enterprises, both of our models envisage "tripartite management" (government, consumers, workers).

In the socialized and cooperative enterprises, according to the Nove model, managers would be appointed by an elected committee representing the employees and would be responsible to that committee for basic policy. One main difference between socialized and cooperative enterprises is that in the former the state would have "a residual responsibility for their use or misuse, or for debts incurred," while a cooperative could freely dispose of its property or decide to go out of business (again, no doubt, within the bounds of social regulations). As for small-scale private enterprise,

> Presumably even the fanatical dogmatist would accept the existence of freelance writers, painters and dressmakers. My own list would be longer. Indeed, there should be no list. If any activity (not actually a "social bad" in itself) can be fruitfully and profitably undertaken by any individual, this sets up the presumption of its legitimacy. . . . So long as it is one individual, there would probably be no objection. . . . But there would be also the possibility of a private entrepreneur actually employing a few people, which makes him an "exploiter" insofar as he makes a profit out of their work. . . . Subject to limits, this should be allowed. . . .
>
> Subject to what limits? This could be decided democratically in the light of circumstances and experience. The limit could be on numbers employed, or on the value of capital assets, and could be varied by sector. One possible rule might be that above this limit there be a choice either to convert into a cooperative or to become a socialized enterprise, with proper compensation for the original entrepreneur. . . . Be it noted that there is no provision for any class of capitalists; our small private entrepreneur *works*, even when employing a few others. There is then no *unearned* income, arising simply from *ownership* of capital or land.[16]

Scale as well as structure is important. The larger the enterprise, the more difficult self-management becomes and the more likely its bureaucratic deformation. But I do not see why even in subdivisions of Nove's "centralized state enterprises" there could not be nurtured at least a measure of workers' control regarding such matters as relations and pace of work even if it is granted that on large overall decisions (how much oil should Britain extract from the North Sea?) there would have to be vertical decision-making subject to the check of the democratic polity.

In Nove's model the extent of central planning is, then, greater than in Selucky's. Major investment decisions; monitoring decentralized investments; administering such "naturally" central productive activities as electricity, oil, railways (today "public," actually private, utilities); setting ground rules for the autonomous economic sectors, "with reserve powers of intervention when things got out of balance" (today bailing out Chrysler, Penn Central); drafting long-term plans—all these, subject to decision and check by Parliament or Congress, would be the responsibility of central planning, thus entailing a greater concentration of economic power than many socialists, myself included, would prefer. But who can say with assurance? One encounters here a deep and inescapable tension between the technological economic realm and the democratic-social arrangements of a socialist (and perhaps any modern) society.

In all such projected arrangements a crucial factor must surely be the morale and consciousness of the people. It isn't necessary, or desirable, to envisage a constant state of intense participation in public affairs, a noisy turmoil of activists, in order to recognize that the felt quality—as distinct from the mere economic workability—of such a society would depend on the fundamental concern of a sizable portion of the population. "No social system," Joseph Schumpeter has remarked, "can work that is based exclusively upon a network of free contracts . . . and in which everyone is supposed to be guided by nothing except his own (short-run) utilitarian ends."[17]

If put to the test of reality, such projections would surely require many changes. But the purpose of a model is not to "appropriate" the future, it is to indicate the nature of thought in the present. Nor need it be denied that such models contain within themselves a good many unresolved problems, tensions, perhaps even contradictions. They *should* contain them, for that is what lends a savor of reality. Let me now, in no particular order, consider a few of these problems:

- The Selucky and Nove models of ownership suffer from opposite difficulties. Selucky's lacks variety and flexibility in its proposals: why should there not be a range of democratic structures in economic life just as in political life? Nove's model, by contrast, gives an uncomfortably strong place to "centralized state corporations." The ogre of bureaucratism rises with regard to both—in opposite ways, the one through rigidity and the other through concentration. In principle one would like to combine Selucky's stress upon worker self-management with Nove's stress upon varieties of property, but that may be asking for the best of all possible worlds, something actuality is chary of providing.

- Neither of our model-makers discusses sufficiently a major problem: the place of unions in a democratic socialist society. If the workers own an enterprise cooperatively or if they manage one democratically, is there still a need for unions? I would say yes, unambiguously. Insofar as we think of a socialist society as one with autonomous institutions and enterprises, this entails the likelihood and even desirability of democratically contained conflict. The weaker segments of the population should be able to protect themselves through organization. It's possible to foresee a situation in which a minority of workers in a self-managed enterprise believes it is being mistreated by the majority; that minority thereupon organizes itself into something very much like a union. In the "centralized state corporations" that Nove proposes as one mode of socialist ownership, there would surely be a need for strong unions to resist bureaucratic dictate. As for cooperatives, take the example of the Israeli kibbutzim. They function pretty much like cooperatives but also hire outside labor at wage rates; the people so hired may well feel they need a union to protect themselves against the benign or not-so-benign edicts of the cooperatives. So it could be in many areas of a socialist society. A pluralism of institutions signifies a plurality of interests, and these must express themselves openly through modulated conflict-and-cooperation.

- It would be hard, according to the economist Abram Bergson, to work out satisfactory criteria of success and reward in a socialist society for managers of the autonomous productive units. Pressed by the often clashing interests of the worker-employers and the central planning agencies of the state, managers might hesitate to take risks or use their initiative. They would need, also, to adjudicate between local interests and larger, more distant social goals, which might put them in a crossfire and cause them to yield to whichever side was the strongest. Incentives would have to be attached to their jobs, allowing them sufficient authority to display leadership while still being subject to the democratic check of worker-employers.

• Nor is it difficult to foresee conflicts among autonomous enterprises as they compete for the credits, subsidies, tax breaks, and contracts that are to be had from the state. Just as under capitalism competition tends to destroy competition, so it is by no means excluded that self-managed enterprises can form rings or cartels. This would have to be resisted, except perhaps in circumstances where economies of scale are very substantial. It might even be necessary to introduce a species of "socialist antitrust" legislation. For until the society reached an unforeseeable state of material abundance, a major source of conflict could well be that between general and partial interests, society as a whole and its regions, social groups and industrial units.

As Selucky says very sensibly, "Since no [complete] harmony of interests is possible at every level of society," there would have to be mediators to control the conflicting interests. "To regulate the conflicts, two mediators are necessary: the market mechanism for economics and the multiparty system for politics."[18]

• Employment and income policies could also bring serious difficulties—for instance, coping with tendencies toward local monopolizing of jobs where enterprise profits are high; working out income policies that might arouse opposition from unions but could be seen as justifiable for the common good; finding ways to help workers whom technological changes in a given industry or enterprise have rendered superfluous; deciding upon or how to decide upon appropriate surpluses for capital investments and new technologies as against the "natural" inclination of self-managed communities to reap immediate rewards, and so on. For that matter, it is foolhardy to suppose that unemployment might not be a problem in a democratic socialist society: all one can reasonably expect is a readiness to deal with it quickly.

• Another complex of problems worth at least pointing to concerns how, when, and whether the state should intervene if a self-managed enterprise is failing. For some would fail, the operation of even a regulated market under socialism having certain parallels to its operation under capitalism.

• Many such problems constitute disadvantages probably inseparable from the advantages of a regulated market, and they seem to reinforce the traditional critiques, both Marxist and romantic, of the market. That the market subjects the human encounter to the fetishism of commodities, signifying that men are not free from the rule of impersonal exchange and wage labor, is true. But unless we can suppose an implausible cornucopia of goods and services, we had better accept the idea of a regulated market as necessary under a feasible democratic socialism.

A socially controlled market would also have some attractive features. The argument against capitalism first made by R. H. Tawney still holds—not that it's bad if people take some risks but that in a society where a few have much and most have little or nothing, the majority doesn't enjoy the privilege of taking risks. Risk, thought Tawney, is "bracing if it is voluntarily undertaken," and in a cooperative commonwealth self-managed enterprises and producers' cooperatives could take socially useful risks that would bring into play their energies and minds.

Still, the market has drawbacks traditionally noted by the left, and one possible way of getting past some of these, and also perhaps moving a bit closer to Marx's vision of "free associated producers," is a modest increase in society's provision of free goods. Some commodities could be produced in such abundance and at so small a cost, it would be economical to dispose of them at zero price rather than incur the overhead costs of charging for them. Even today water, some health, and many educational services are free, which in actuality means carrying them as a shared or social cost. In a cooperative commonwealth, such provision might be extended to milk and perhaps even to bread. Would people take more than they need, would there be waste at first? Probably; yet that might not be as wasteful as many of the practices we simply take for granted in a capitalist society. And as free access to a modest number of basic goods would become customary, misuse of the privilege would probably decrease. Nevertheless, in a market socialism such free provision could only be marginal.

• All these problems are instances of a larger problem often cited by conservatives for whom socialism is anathema, as the market is for doctrinal Marxists. It is possible that the autonomous enterprises might repeat some of the socially undesirable behavior with which we are familiar in corporate capitalism, functioning as "socialist corporate" units in quite as selfish a spirit as present-day corporations are known to do. When doctrinaire leftists (or rightists, for that matter) point to possible abuses in a market socialism, they are almost always pointing to risks present in *any* democratic society. Mistakes and abuses are always with us; this is a condition of freedom and can be eliminated only by eliminating freedom itself.

What would be needed in a democratic socialist society (as today in a democratic capitalist society) is some version of the welfare state. Through electoral decisions, compromises and bargaining, it could adjudicate among conflicting parts of the population, setting rules for the operation of the market while protecting both the norms of the society and the rights of its citizens.

## VI

Finally, the socialist aspiration has less to do with modes of property ownership than with qualities of social life. That is why the case for socialism rests not just on its proposed reduction of inequities in wealth and power, but on its wish to democratize economic practice. The two values—equality and freedom—are sometimes, of course, in tension, but when regarded in a spirit of generosity and humaneness, they flourish together, as they seem to have flourished, partly, during the early days of the American republic.

The egalitarian ideal has been very strong in socialist thought and tradition. It should be. There is something morally repulsive in the maldistribution of wealth and income in a country like the United States. And not only is this state of affairs morally repulsive, it is socially unjust, a major barrier to the genuine realization of the democratic idea. Now, any proposal can be pushed too far, turning into a vicious parody of itself. An egalitarianism enforced by authoritarian decree—what's called in Eastern Europe "barracks egalitarianism"—is utterly alien to the socialist idea. Our vision of egalitarianism implies a steady, perhaps slow and surely gradual rectification of inequities through education, legislation, and popular assent. It aims not for some absurd version of total equality (whatever that might mean) but rather for a progress toward the fair sharing of socioeconomic goods and political power that would allow each person to fulfill his or her potentialities.

One precondition is both political and economic democracy, with the latter signifying the replacement, insofar as possible, of "vertical" hierarchical structures by "horizontal" egalitarian ones. Workers' control, self-management by those who work in an enterprise—some such concept is crucial to the socialist hope. One needn't be a fanatic and set up standards so impossibly high that they will fall of their own weight. In the end socialists have no choice but to accept the wager— either a genuine, if imperfect, economic democracy is realizable or the entire socialist enterprise must be relegated to historical fantasy.

A classic case for workers' control appears in John Stuart Mill's *The Principles of Political Economy*:

> The form of association . . . which, if mankind continues to improve, must be expected in the end to predominate, is not that which can exist between a capitalist as chief, and workpeople without a voice in the management, but the association of the laborers themselves on terms of equality, collectively owning the capital with which they carry on their operations, and working under managers elected and removable by themselves.[19]

No longer tolerating their reduction to mere factors of production, workers would learn through experience to demand their rights as free, autonomous men and women. They would form cooperatives. They would acquire some of the skills of management (those arcane mysteries, it's sometimes said, which must forever remain beyond the reach of the lowly). And in time there could be a trade-off between some of the efficiencies allegedly brought about by authoritarian forms of organization and the growing creativity of cooperative production.

Too often in recent socialist literature the idea, sometimes merely the slogan, of workers' control has remained gloriously vague. What does it mean precisely? That decisions regarding production, prices, wages, and investment in a giant enterprise like a "socialist GM" would be made by the assembled workers or even their representatives? And if so, how would it be possible to avoid the linked plagues of bureaucratism, demagogic manipulation, clique maneuverings, endless filibustering, ignorant narrowness, cronyism in elections, and a selfish resistance to the larger needs of society?

One frequent argument against self-management proposals is that their advocates tend to minimize the sheer complexity of modern enterprise. Lay people (workers) would have difficulty in securing relevant information from managers; they would often be unable to grasp the technical aspects of the information they got; and they would lack the time needed to reflect upon what they did grasp in order to arrive at coherent plans. There is of course some truth to this argument, though it largely proceeds on the assumption that workers in a better society will remain quite as workers are today. But there is reason to expect that with higher levels of education and a greater provision for time, leisure, and training within the organized work community, some of these problems could be overcome. Lethargy isn't a universal constant; it is a socially conditioned phenomenon open to change. "Full" participation in managerial activities might, in some situations, be a chimera; but there surely could be a large measure of selective control by workers even in giant enterprises, with technicalities left to managers and large policy issues decided through democratic mechanisms.

A somewhat different problem is raised in a recent study by Allen Graubard, who sees workers' control, narrowly conceived, as clashing with public rights. A large corporation

> is a national resource. . . . The same argument against private control of the founder-owner or by the current corporate owner works . . . against private control by the community of employees. The authority for major decisions of the enterprise should rest in the larger public, the democratic polity.[20]

This criticism can best be regarded as a warning against *exclusive* control of major enterprises by the workers within it—though even that should not preclude a good measure of self-management with regard to intraplant arrangements. About such matters it would be foolish to be dogmatic; far better to recognize a multiplicity of interests and outlooks, with the certainty that, if ventures in self-management are undertaken, they will be subject to many difficulties.

The practical impediments to workers' self-management that both sophisticated organization theorists and "the man in the street" detect are often real enough—but are the consequent objections very much more cogent than similar arguments once used against the feasibility of political democracy? An excrescence of bureaucratism might indeed flourish on the structure of self-management. Who in the twentieth century can deny that possibility (or *any* possibility)? Here

everything depends on conscious effort, the vigilance that had better
be eternal—quite as with regard to political democracy. And there is
much cogency in an argument advanced by George Lichtheim that

> A future advance will probably have to start from a concept of technical
> education which envisages it not simply as a means of improving effi-
> ciency, but as a link between the worker and the planner. . . . For the
> worker technology holds the most direct access to science and everything
> that lies beyond it. But technical education without responsible participa-
> tion soon loses its spur. . . . For [socialists], its significance . . . lies in the
> fact that it arises spontaneously out of the modern process of work, while
> at the same time it enables the worker to develop his individuality.[21]

In practice self-management would sometimes thrive, sometimes
stumble, but always be marked, like all human enterprises, by imperfections. There is one argument, however, against self-management
that seems to me peculiarly insidious: it is offered, as you might expect, by ex-radicals, and its main thrust is that workers "show little
interest" in the idea.

In certain empirical respects, this is not even true. Through their
unions, workers have often fought very hard for such noneconomic
rights as grievance mechanisms and a proper work atmosphere. These
inroads on traditional "management prerogatives" often constitute
modest beginnings of economic democracy, whether or not those who
make the inroads so conceptualize them. Still, for the sake of the
argument, let us grant the conservative claim that workers today
"show little interest" in self-management proposals. To stop there
would be to acquiesce supinely in "the given." For this argument
against self-management is essentially an extension of a larger skepticism about democratic politics. How often have we not heard that
most people care more about their bellies than their freedoms? Or that
in the United States millions of citizens don't even bother to vote?
Notions of self-management, our conservatives tell us, are mere futile
efforts by small groups of intellectuals to "impose their fantasies"
upon ordinary people who seem quite content to allow the corporations to determine their work lives.

Few of us are born passionate democrats. The values of freedom
have to be learned. Centuries passed before masses of men came to

feel that democracy is a necessity of life. All the while it was a not-very-large company of intellectuals who sought to "impose their fantasies" about democracy upon ordinary people. Even today, who can say that this persuasion has taken deep enough root?

It may be a long time before the value of democratic norms is secured in socioeconomic life. An independent Yugoslav writer, Branko Horvat, reports that in his country "inherited authoritarian attitudes are so deeply ingrained that they are unconsciously carried into self-management."[22] Could it be otherwise—especially in a country with little experience in political democracy, before or after Tito?

Nothing is ordained. Socialism, self-management, economic democracy are options, sometimes brighter, sometimes dimmer. The realization of the socialist hope depends on the growth of consciousness, a finer grasp of the possibilities of citizenship and comradeship than now prevails. Times change. We will emerge from our present slough of small-spirited conservative acquiescence and live again by more generous aspirations. The idea of self-management could then take a somewhat more prominent place on the agenda of public discourse— kept alive by "unrealistic intellectuals," "visionary socialists."

## VII

Amid such turnings of political thought, a harsh question intrudes itself: Does the socialist idea, even if rendered more sophisticated than in the past, still survive as a significant option?

Historical energy and idealism cannot be supplied on demand. Once an idea becomes contaminated or a generation exhausted, it takes a long time before new energies can be summoned, if summoned at all. Whether socialism can be revived as a living idea—which is something different from the mere survival of European social democratic parties—is by now very much a question. So too is the possibility, or hope, that it may serve as a bridge toward a radical new humanism.

In any case, socialists remain. They engage themselves with the needs of the moment, struggling for betterment in matters large and small, reforms major and modest: they do not sit and wait for the millennium. And they continue also to grapple with fragments of a tradition. This intellectual effort, it must be admitted, can handicap them politically. Not many people became socialists because they were persuaded of the correctness of Marxist economics or supposed the movement served their "class interests." They became socialists because they were moved by the call to brotherhood and sisterhood; because the world seemed aglow with the vision of a time in which humanity might live in justice and peace. Whatever we may now claim for a refurbished socialism, we can hardly claim that it satisfies the emotions as once the early movement did.

If it is true that utopian-apocalyptic expectations are indispensable to a movement advocating major social change, then democratic socialists are in deeper trouble than even they recognize. For in politics, as elsewhere, choices must be made. You cannot opt for the rhythms of a democratic politics and still expect it to yield the pathos and excitement of revolutionary movements. Our hope must be that there are other kinds of fervor—quieter, less melodramatic, morally stronger—which a democratic reformist politics can evoke.

I have been speaking about the problem of socialism as if it were self-sufficient and self-referential; but that is no more than a useful analytic device, an abstraction from the real world in which the fate of socialism must be bound up with the fate of capitalism. We cannot be certain. The recovery of Western capitalism during the several decades after the Second World War has come to a halt; there is clearly in the West a serious crisis regarding such problems as unemployment, technological change, relations with the underdeveloped world. And how well democratic capitalism will be able to deal with these problems is very much a question.

Our problem may be restated as that of utopianism—does the utopian vision still have value for us?

The "utopia" imposed through force and terror by a self-chosen vanguard is hell. The utopia of a "withering away of the state" is a fantasy gone stale. But there remains a utopian outlook that relates immediate objectives to ultimate goals, and it is to this that socialists cling. As Leszek Kolakowski has written:

> [G]oals now unattainable will never be reached unless they are articulated when they are still unattainable. . . . The existence of a utopia as a utopia is the necessary prerequisite for its eventually ceasing to be a utopia.[23]

"Very nice," a friendly voice interjects, "but socialism—has not that name been soiled in the pillagings of our century? Might it not be better for a movement to shake itself clear of all the old confusions, defeats, betrayals?"

I can well imagine that a movement in America might choose to drop the socialist label: who needs, once again, to explain that we do *not* want the kinds of society that exist in Russia and China, Poland and Cuba? But at least with regard to America we continue to speak of small groups trying to keep alive a tradition. Suppose, indeed, we were to conclude that the socialist label creates more trouble than it's worth: we would then have to cast about for a new vocabulary, something not to be won through fiat. How much would actually change if our words were to change? If, say, we ceased calling ourselves socialists and instead announced that henceforth we are to be known as—what? "Economic democrats" or "democratic radicals"? The substance of our problems would remain, the weight of this century's burdens still press upon us. We would still regard capitalism as an unjust society, still find its inequities intolerable, still be repelled by its ethic of greed, and still be trying to sketch the outlines of a better society.

Isaiah Berlin has written that liberalism is "a notoriously exposed, dangerous, and ungrateful position." I would borrow his words for democratic socialism, which is not quite the same as but, in my sense of things, has a kinship with his liberalism.

For those socialists who have experienced in their bones the meaning of our century, the time has not yet come, I believe, to cast off its burdens. It may come. Meanwhile, we hope to serve as a link to those friends of tomorrow who will have so completely absorbed the lessons of our age that they will not need to rehearse them. Whatever the fate of socialism, the yearning for a better mode of life, which found expression in its thought and its struggle, will reappear. Of that I am certain.

## Notes

1. Martin Buber, *Paths in Utopia* (Boston: Beacon Press, 1949, paperback), p. 96.
2. Karl Marx and Friedrich Engels, *The German Ideology* (London, 1942), p. 26.
3. Paul Ricoeur, "Power and the State," in Irving Howe, ed., *Essential Works of Socialism* (New Haven: Yale University Press, 1976), p. 736.
4. Stephen F. Cohen, *Bukharin and the Bolshevik Revolution* (New York: Vin-

tage Books, 1975, paperback), p. 54.

5. Stuart Hampshire, "Epilogue," in Leszek Kolakowski and Stuart Hampshire, eds., *The Socialist Idea* (New York: Basic Books, 1974), p. 249.

6. Karl Kautsky, "The Commonwealth of the Future," in *Essential Works of Socialism*, p. 169.

7. Morris Hillquit, quoted in William English Walling, *Progressivism and After* (New York: Macmillan, 1914), pp. 169–70.

8. Harold Orlans, "Democracy and Social Planning," *Dissent* (Spring 1954), p. 194.

9. Leszek Kolakowski, "Introduction," in *The Socialist Idea*, p. 15.

10. Michael Harrington, "What Socialists Would Do in America—If They Could," in Irving Howe, ed., *Twenty-Five Years of Dissent: An American Tradition* (New York: Methuen, 1979), p. 23.

11. Alec Nove, *The Economics of Feasible Socialism* (London: Allen & Unwin, 1983), p. 174.

12. Radoslav Selucky, *Marxism, Socialism, Freedom* (New York: St. Martin's Press, 1979), p. 36.

13. Ibid., pp. 179–80.

14. Abram Bergson, "Market Socialism Revisited," *Journal of Political Economy* 75, no. 5 (October 1967), p. 656.

15. Nove, *Feasible Socialism*, p. 200.

16. Ibid., pp. 206–7.

17. Quoted in *ibid.*, p. 204.

18. Selucky, *Marxism, Socialism, Freedom*, p. 185.

19. John Stuart Mill, *The Principles of Political Economy* (Toronto: University of Toronto Press, 1965).

20. Allen Graubard, "Ideas of Economic Democracy," *Dissent* (Fall 1984), p. 421.

21. George Lichtheim, "Collectivism Reconsidered," in *Essential Works of Socialism*, p. 757.

22. Branko Horvat, *The Political Economy of Socialism* (Armonk, N.Y.: M. E. Sharpe, 1983), p. 255.

23. Leszek Kolakowski, "The Concept of the Left," in *Essential Works of Socialism*, p. 686.

# 3

# Markets and Plans: Is the Market Necessarily Capitalist?

## (Winter 1989)

### Michael Harrington

China, one has been told since Deng Xiaoping's market-oriented reforms began in the late 1970s, is becoming capitalist. So is the Soviet Union under Gorbachev, similarly with Hungary, Angola, Vietnam, and all the other economies that were once centrally planned and have now introduced markets to achieve efficient production.[1]

If this were simply one more example of a superficial journalistic dichotomy—either a society is planned and socialist or relies on markets and is capitalist—it would not be too bothersome. But it goes beyond that. Serious scholars employ this facile distinction. And there are not a few socialists who believe that tolerating markets may be a political necessity but still somehow represents a surrender of rectitude, compromising the basic vision.

The fact is that we cannot evaluate, or even describe, the workings of markets independently of the social structure in which they operate. The "free choice" of goods, jobs, or investments is one thing in a laissez-faire economy of extreme inequality; another in a monopoly or oligopoly system; still another in a democratic welfare state; and quite different in a communist dictatorship. And, under conditions that must be carefully specified, free choice—without quotation marks—would have a completely new, and potentially positive, significance in any fore-seeable transition to a socialist society. Generalizations about the mean-ings of markets in the abstract are, then, all suspect.

In a sense, the superficial dichotomy of plan and market, an abstrac-tion par excellence, is the heir—usually unwitting—of a central tradi-tion in capitalist thought. In that perspective, there is an economic "human nature" that exists throughout history even if it is imperfectly developed in precapitalist societies. The stone tool of paleolithic hu-manity is an embryonic form of capital, the precursor of an automated factory. And a market is a market is a market. Thus the announcement of "the emergence of capitalism" in China or the Soviet Union is made triumphantly as a proof that the eternal verities have again prevailed.

The point is not just to make a critique of a bad theory. It is to understand the very different relations between planning and markets in various societies and to free the socialism of tomorrow from the assumption that a market in a social order of increasing equality and popular democratic control is somehow as reprehensible as a market that functions to provide shacks for the poor and mansions for the rich.

Let me put my point paradoxically: only under socialism and demo-cratic planning will it be possible for markets to serve the common good as Adam Smith thought they did under capitalism.

I am not proposing that the new socialism project a market utopia. Far from it. In the advanced welfare states socialists have already removed critical areas of life from the market economy. In every one of them, save the United States, basic health care is collectively financed and provided without reference to income—and that process will, and should, con-tinue. And the actual functioning of some of the most important contem-porary markets—the capitalist world market that integrates North and South, for instance—are viciously and completely at odds with the vir-tues still imputed to them. Nevertheless, I insist that, in the dimly foresee-able and utterly international future of, say, the next fifty years, markets can be an important instrument of free choice rather than of perverse maldistribution if they are reorganized within a socialist context.

## Ambivalence in the Marxist Tradition

It may seem strange that I begin an analysis of current and future markets by going back to Marx. But, as Keynes said, the pragmatic, no-nonsense proponents of the simplistic plan/market dichotomy often repeat abstractions that are more than a century old. Marx, I am afraid, is a major source of the contemporary confusion, not the least because he provides solid authority for contradictory positions. Even more to the point, a careful reading of *Das Kapital* yields, of all things, a Marxist methodology capable of grasping the positive potential of markets even as that book brilliantly denounces their functioning under laissez-faire.

At first glance there seems to be no ambiguity. It is, one would think, painfully obvious that Marx equated markets with capitalism and socialism with their abolition. The opening chapter of *Das Kapital* defines the "commodity" as the very basis of the capitalist system. And the commodity is, of course, not simply a useful good or service but a useful good or service that is produced to be sold on a market at a profit. Commodities, Marx argued, have existed ever since human beings, in the mists of time, went beyond subsistence production and began to make things to exchange with one another. But it is only with the rise of capitalism that commodity production—market production—becomes the dominant activity of an entire society. Isn't it inescapably clear, then, that the system is defined by markets?

Those markets, Marx continues, are pernicious. Where people produced for their own needs—in families, tribes or self-contained communities—there was misery as a result of the low level of economic development and periodic hunger and famine when the harvest failed or the fishing gave out. But there were not such things as overproduction and underproduction, no economic breakdowns that occurred because there was "too much" to be sold at a profit. It was only with the dominance of commodity production that poverty resulted from glut. At the same time that this market process regularly plunged masses into a social abyss, it enormously increased the wealth of the successful rich. Markets were, Marx held, engines of social inequality, reproducing elite domination as well as physical products.

So far, the attack on the market is straightforward and principled. But then, when he turns to his central theory of exploitation, Marx becomes more complex. In the calculated oversimplification of his basic analysis, which generations have mistaken for a flawed description of the real world, it was assumed that raw materials, machines, and finance were all exchanged according to their value and that sellers charged buyers a fair price. Where, then, was the source of profit? In the labor market. The workers sold their labor power like any other commodity. In theory, the resulting wage was the outcome of a bargain between equals, each of whom was "free" to deal with the other. In reality, this was a deal between unequals: between a wealthy buyer and a precarious seller trying to keep body and soul together. The content of the market agreement was, then, determined, not by markets *per se* but by the social conditions under which the markets operated.

So labor markets under capitalism, based on economic rather than political coercion, forced workers to "freely" sell their labor power at a fair value that produced more for the capitalist than it cost. But that opened up the possibility that, if one changed the circumstances under which the wage bargain was made, the market outcomes would be different. And in an analysis of a historic event of enormous importance for his theory, Marx went on to show that that eventuality had taken place.

The discussion of the Ten-Hours Law, which legally limited the working day in Britain, occupies a central place in Volume I of *Kapital* because it was the basis of a crucial distinction between "absolute" and "relative" surplus value. If one assumes that the worker produces enough to "pay back" his or her wage during only a portion of the working day, then an obvious way to increase profits is to extend that working day. That was the first capitalist strategy. As a result of this savage process, "every limit of morality and nature, of age and gender, of day and night, was destroyed." This was the drive for "absolute" surplus value.

But then, continues Marx, a number of things happened. The physical brutalization of the working class literally threatened its biological existence and thereby the future of the system itself. The landlords, still furious with the industrial capitalists for having abolished agricultural protectionism in order to cheapen the price of bread and thereby the subsistence wage, were willing to make common cause with the reformers and the workers and to join in a campaign to put a limit on the working day. The official economists predicted, of course, that such a move would destroy capitalism. In fact, Marx argued, it forced capital to seek more profits by increasing productivity, by working labor intelligently rather than working it to death. And one of the consequences of this political struggle was that capitalism now oriented itself toward "relative" surplus value, toward getting more out of each hour of work rather than simply extending the hours. This was one of the many reasons why it was superior—economically and even morally—to the brutal exploitation of the past.

What is relevant here is that Marx regarded the Ten-Hours Law— only a minimal humanization of the laissez-faire labor market—as nothing less than a "modest Magna Carta," as "the triumph of the political economy of the working class over the political economy of the middle class." A merely reformist change in the structure of the labor market could profoundly affect the very meaning of the market economy and even give rise to a new epoch in the history of capitalism. These texts provide clear warrant for the notion that, under the radically changed circumstances of a socialist-tending society, markets would have an utterly different meaning than under capitalist laissez-faire. Unfortunately, *Das Kapital* also provides solid reasons for arguing a contrary proposition: that socialism must totally dispense with markets. Small wonder that matters get confused.

Ironically, Marx gets into this contradiction in the process of once again making the point that markets do not have a fixed, immutable content. Indeed, under capitalism they inexorably tend to turn into their opposite: It is the "historic tendency" of competition to culminate in monopoly. At that point, Marx argued, the pursuit of private profit no longer motivates the capitalist to act as the greedy agent of progress by constantly revolutionizing the productivity of the entire society. Now, monopolists "fetter" production precisely because they can dictate to markets and are therefore no longer subjected to the discipline of efficiency. As the system falters, the working class, which needs more productivity in order to raise its own living standard, becomes the economically dynamic class.

This means many things. What is particularly relevant here is that socialism is defined as a monopoly—a democratic, socially conscious monopoly, but a monopoly nevertheless, a system without effective markets. As Radoslov Selucky, who brilliantly understands this contradiction, has put it, in this context "Marx's economic concept of socialism consists of a single social-wide factory based on vertical [hierarchical] relations of superiority and subordination." This is the planned, marketless society with a vengeance. But at the very same time, Marx's "political concept of socialism consists of a free association of self-managed work and social communities based on horizontal relations of equality. Whoever accepts in full Marx's first concept has to give up the latter, and vice versa: they are mutually exclusive."

In short, even though Marx in one persona clearly rejected markets altogether, his methodology allows room for the assumption that the markets of a socialist future need not be anything like the markets of the capitalist past. And, much more important, his basic political values, his commitment to freedom and human emancipation, are simply at odds with the consequences that follow from his own analysis of socialism as a centrally planned society or a progressive monopoly. When Karl Kautsky concluded that in the good society workers would not have the right to change their jobs at will—because there would be no labor markets—he had solid grounding in Marx at the same time as he was contradicting the latter's vision of a truly free and communitarian association of the direct producers.

Piety about an ambiguous tradition should not, then, keep socialists from seeing that markets can, and must, play a role in the transition to a humane future. All one needs to do is to choose the libertarian Marx over the centralist Marx and then confront reality instead of texts.

## How the Bolsheviks Coped, or Didn't

The first socialists to confront reality, in the sense of actually taking responsibility for the organization of an entire economy, were the Bolsheviks. And their experience, as the Soviet rehabilitation of Nikolai Bukharin in the 1980s testifies, is relevant to the present and future.*

---

*I regard Stalinism as an "anti-socialist 'socialism,'" as a system of bureaucratic collectivism and do not see its history as part of the socialist tradition. But even though the Bolsheviks before Stalin, including Lenin, approved measures that laid the basis for the later tyranny, they were in the 1920s sincere and committed Marxists, however wrong, and their experiences do belong to that tradition.

Indeed, the thesis that any reliance on markets is a sure sign of capitalism, so popular in the eighties with regard to China and the Soviet Union, first surfaced in the 1920s under Lenin's New Economic Policy (NEP). The anti-socialist press gleefully reported that the Soviets were making the transition from communism to capitalism because they had turned to market forces, a judgment that proved to be spectacularly wrong and about as substantial then as it is now.

Bukharin was a champion of "socialism at a snail's pace," which would make use of market incentives. But Trotsky, who was then Bukharin's principal antagonist and the chief defender of "planning" as against "markets," also recognized that the latter had a critical role to play throughout the entire period of transition. Trotsky was ultimately committed to the vision of a planned society that would dispense with markets; but he was equally emphatic that, on the road to that final goal, it was necessary to have a sound currency to measure the market value of investment costs and consumer goods. Stalinist planning—a command economy operated bureaucratically from a single center—was, he rightly thought, a political and economic disaster.

But before turning to Trotsky's advocacy of markets, two of Bukharin's particularly illuminating insights in this area are worth remembering.

In a 1924 polemic, Bukharin raised the problem of the "tendency toward monopoly" in Soviet society. That, he said, could indeed allow the state to get an extra profit without any effort at all. "But isn't the result of that the danger of parasitism and stagnation? . . . Our economic administrators," he went on, "work for the proletariat, but they are not exempt from human weakness. They can doze off in a beatific quietude instead of being constantly concerned for progress toward communism." In order to keep up the pressure on the bureaucrats, Bukharin said, they must be driven to meet the needs of the people. That means the cheapest prices for the mass of consumers, which can only be delivered if the costs of production are kept to an absolute minimum. Efficiency was thus an imperative of the commitment to a higher living standard for all.

This theme—that the replacement for the capitalist profit motive was the drive to satisfy consumers—was shared by Preobrazhensky,

Trotsky's economic theoretician, who differed with Bukharin only in being much more confident that it would be effective. Stalin, of course, did exactly the opposite of what Bukharin and Trotsky proposed. He cut consumption and turned the state into an absolute monopolist that financed the industrialization of the society precisely by the super profits that could be derived thereby. The result was a system that by totalitarian pressure could effectively squeeze resources out of the masses of workers and peasants and an economy that, as Mikhail Gorbachev realized in the eighties, had all of the drawbacks that Marx—and Bukharin—had ascribed to capitalist monopoly. The Soviet state, rather than the international bourgeoisie, became a "fetter" on production and productivity. In the West there were computers; in the East, the abacus.

In another essay, published in 1925, Bukharin speculated that in his final writings Lenin had broken with his theory that the road to socialism was along the path of state capitalism, i.e., the monopoly stage of capitalism. Lenin's remarks on the importance of cooperatives, Bukharin said, "puts us in the presence of a program that is totally different [from the perspective of state capitalism]." He quotes Lenin: "Now we have the right to say that the *simple development of cooperatives . . .* becomes identified for us *with the development of socialism itself.*" Did Lenin actually go that far? We will never know. But it is at least possible, and even plausible, that before he died the Bolshevik leader sensed the dangers of centralization in a command economy, what he called "a bureaucratic utopia."

About Trotsky we need not speculate. In a 1932 essay, "The Soviet Economy in Danger," he wrote:

> The innumerable living participants in the economy, state and private, collective and individual, must serve notice of their needs and of their relative strength not only through the statistical determinations of plan commissions but by the direct pressure of supply and demand. *The plan is checked and, to a considerable degree, realized through the market* [emphasis added]. . . . The blueprints produced by the departments must demonstrate their economic efficacy through commercial calculation.

And in his critique of the Stalinist planners in *The Revolution Betrayed*, Trotsky commented that the obedient professors managed to create an entire theory according to which the Soviet price, in contrast to the market price, has an exclusively planning or directive character. . . . The professors forgot to explain how you can "guide" a price without knowing real costs, and how you can estimate real costs if all prices express the will of the bureaucracy and not the amount of social labor expended. . . . [Socialist construction is unthinkable] without including in the planned system the direct personal interests of the producer and consumer, their egoism—which in its turn may reveal itself fruitfully only if it has in its service the customary reliable and flexible instrument, money.

There are two aspects to these statements by Trotsky and Bukharin. First, both the "left" and "right" Bolshevik critics of Stalin agreed that markets were an indispensable element in the transition to socialism (if not, to repeat, in the blessed "final state" of socialism itself). Without them, they argued, the system would become bureaucratic, wasteful, inefficient, and incapable of satisfying those basic human needs that were supposed to be the driving force, and the proof of the moral superiority, of the new economy. Second, Trotsky and Bukharin were right, as at least a portion of the present Soviet leadership has tacitly acknowledged (in Bukharin's case, the admission is even spoken aloud).

Stalin, however, settled the political argument by force and in the process liquidated both Trotsky and Bukharin. He proceeded to a version of total planning in which the omnipotent state swallowed up not just the economy but the whole of society.

This does not mean that there were no markets under Stalin. Even in the most extreme days of his rule, people bought consumer goods with money. But the basic decisions with regard to work, production, and consumption were taken by a centralized bureaucracy from on high and almost all the institutions that might mediate between government and citizens were turned into "transmission belts" for official policy. In 1938 and 1940, for instance, it was decreed that everyone would have a work book, that no one could leave a job on pain of criminal punishment for "flitting" from post to post, that the first offense of absenteeism would be punished by "forced labor at the place of employment" (which involved a 25 percent cut in wages), and the second offense by a mandatory jail sentence, and so on. This draconian attack on the rights of workers was introduced at the initiative of "trade unions" reduced to organs of state discipline. And the most severe rules were put in place, not under the siege conditions of World War II, but during a period when Stalin was trusting in his deal with Adolf Hitler.

The investment and production decisions were fixed according to planned, quantitative targets, which facilitated both waste and shoddy goods. If, a believable joke reported, a Soviet pin factory were assigned a quota of so many tons of pins, it would turn out one, monstrously large and unusable pin; and if it were told to produce a certain number of pins, it would achieve the numerical goal with a myriad of pins so thin that they were also useless. The collective farms were required to deliver their crops to the state at less than their cost of production. And consumption goods were manufactured, not in response to demand, but according to a preset planners' decision, which meant that waiting in line to buy items in short supply became a major cause of squandered energy in the Soviet Union.

Yet this system, for all of its intolerable human and social costs, "worked," i.e., it allowed the Soviets to create an industrial infrastructure in the space of a decade. Marx gave capitalism enormous credit for having similarly raised the level of economic development by the savagery of "primitive accumulation" *and* denounced the process as morally vicious. But even leaving morality aside, this kind of "planning" was laying the groundwork for the economic crisis of the seventies and eighties.

It is possible to make the initial physical investments in modernization in a brutal way. The slave laborers of the Gulag could be, and were, driven to dig canals because the productivity of a person with a pick or a shovel is not of great moment. That is what the Soviets now refer to as "extensive" growth, and it corresponds to the period of "absolute surplus value" when capitalism thrived by working people to the edge of death. But the basis of a truly modern system, particularly in the age of automation and the computer, is "intensive" growth, an exponential increase in productivity that rests upon the facility of both human beings and machines. That requires a concern for the quality of work that slaves, or driven workers, will never exhibit. And even though the Soviet economy was significantly modified between Stalin's death in 1953 and Gorbachev's rise to power in the eighties, the institutional bias remained centralist, quantitative, "extensive," which all but guaranteed the declining growth rates of the last decade and a half.

In Stalin's day, however, there was little or no relief from bureaucratic commands backed up by a repressive state. It was this reality that gave rise to the theory of "totalitarianism," the idea that a totally controlled society without any real sources of internal opposition had actually come into existence. There was an attempt to mobilize the economy by a state that absorbed all of society into its dictatorial political system. In theorizing about this phenomenon, Hannah Arendt wrote in her influential *Origins of Totalitarianism* that "total domination succeeds to the extent that it succeeds in interrupting all channels of communication, those from person to person inside the four walls of privacy no less than the public ones which are safeguarded in democracies by freedom of speech and opinion." The aim, she said, was to make "every person incommunicado."

There were political consequences. If there was no possibility of internal change within the Stalinist empire, that made a hawkish cold war policy of "liberation" all the more logical, since there was no hope that, as the original American "containment" theory of 1947–48 held, time and history would eventually soften Soviet policy. Arendt's book came out when Stalin was still alive, in 1951; a second edition, with an epilogue to deal with the anti-Stalinist rebellions in both Poland and Hungary in 1956, came out in 1958. Even then, Arendt was convinced that the Khrushchev reforms in the Soviet Union had already run their course, that the system was returning to type.

On a more superficial—even frivolous—level, Friedrich Hayek, normally a serious thinker, declared in *The Road to Serfdom* that the British Labour government of 1945 was a precursor of a totalitarian system. This was an attempt to make the case that Stalinism was an inherent tendency of any socialism, even a democratic socialism, a proposition refuted by every event that has occurred since it was first stated.

Stalinism terrified its external enemies as well as its own people. Yet it turned out that opposition and criticism had not been abolished as Arendt thought. Hardly was the tyrant dead than some of the most repressive features of the regime were modified. In 1956, Khrushchev gave his famous speech in which he began to acknowledge the bloody historical record. Contrary to Arendt's 1958 speculation that the event was a momentary aberration, the anti-Stalin campaign was most marked between the Twenty-Second Party Congress of 1961 and Khrushchev's downfall in 1964.

The most dramatic break with Stalinist orthodoxy took place in China, not the Soviet Union, under the leadership of Deng Xiaoping.

Mao had turned on the Soviets as early as the late fifties. The "Great Leap" was a repudiation of the model of centralized command planning, of giant factories, and a celebration of the utopian potential of the people. But despite the utopian content of both the Great Leap and the Cultural Revolution (the latter directed against the evils of bureaucracy that Mao saw writ large in Soviet society), the mode of leadership was still quite Stalinist. That is, Mao believed that he could "write" on the Chinese people, whom he compared to a blank page. And from on high he engineered a revolution-from-below, a reality that became quite apparent in mid-1968 when Mao turned off the enthusiasm of the Red Guards, which he himself had originally decreed and relied on to enforce his will. Decisions were, in short, still taken on a political basis by small cliques—or by one man—and behind closed doors.

Mao died in 1976 and there was an interregnum that lasted until Deng took control in 1979. When that happened, the government decreed that individual peasant families, under the "household responsibility system," could—after paying their taxes, selling a quota of their output to the state, and meeting fees to the collective, which still owned the land—dispose of their surplus in any way they wanted. Industrial enterprises were made more autonomous and they, too, could decide how they used their surplus. Some radicals wanted to go further. They proposed to make the market, rather than the plan, the basis of the economy, to have "regulation" rather than control, and to significantly increase political pluralism.

In the wake of the 1979 changes there were problems and the moderates counterattacked the radicals. But in 1983 there was another period of reform with enterprises given much more latitude to take initiatives on their own, a strengthening of the "household responsibility system," and a new emphasis on foreign trade. In the retail sector, markets became more and more important, capital markets were created, and some enterprises actually sold stock. At the end of 1984, the conservative columnist William Safire wrote in the *New York Times* that the biggest event of the year had been "the embrace of capitalism" by the Chinese Communist party.

That assumed that markets per se, without any regard for their context and content, are always capitalist, an over-simplification that is not at all helpful in explaining what is going on in China. In the midst of the reforms, for instance, Deng at all times insisted on "four cardinal principles": Marxism-Leninism, Mao's thought, party leadership, and continuation of the existing state structure. In 1986, two years after Safire's discovery of "capitalism" in China, 68.7 percent of the industrial output came from the state sector, 29.2 percent from collectives, and 0.3 percent from private enterprises. In retail, the respective figures were 39.4 percent, 36.4 percent, and 23.9 percent, which did indeed mark a significant shift. But exactly how a stratified economy, run by a single party, which uses markets to forward its own planned policies, qualifies as "capitalist" is a mystery.

As John King Fairbank put it, "Anyone who concludes that Chinese agriculture, having seen the light and wanting to be more like us, has gone 'capitalist' is making a grievous error. The contract system [Fairbank's translation of the "household responsibility system"] must be seen as the latest phase of statecraft, how to organize the farmers in order to improve their welfare and strengthen the state." And a little later Fairbank writes, "the Deng reforms are not bringing Western-style capitalism to China, except for the state capitalism of corporations that make deals with foreigners, but rather they are bringing an expanded form of what might be called 'bureaucratic socialism'.... In other words, a modernization that elsewhere has generally produced a new middle class, in China seems likely to produce a local and mid-level leadership that remains essentially bureaucratic."

It is, at this writing, impossible to say how the economic reforms put into practice in the Soviet Union at the beginning of 1988 will change that society. Clearly, Gorbachev has decided to take seriously the need for "intensive growth," productivity, qualitative rather than quantitative measures of output, and the use of market criteria in investment policy. In a major report to the Party Central Committee in February 1986, for instance, the Soviet leader told his colleagues that "we must radically change the substance, organization, and methods of the work of the financial and credit bodies. Their chief aim is not to exercise petty control over the work of enterprises but to *provide economic incentives and to consolidate money circulation and cost accounting, which is the best possible controller.*" (Emphasis added.)

That means a fundamental reorganization of the State Planning Committee, one of the most powerful bureaucracies in the society. It would also put the state in conflict with the least efficient enterprises, which would not be able to meet the requirements of profitability. And it opens up the possibility, in a society that, for all of its manifold faults, has prided itself on guaranteeing a job to every citizen (even if inefficiently), that unemployment, or at least firings, would become a necessary concomitant of market policies.

Dealing with that problem—putting market mechanisms at the service of social priorities rather than in command of the economy—is an area in which democratic socialists have contributions to make. But before turning to those specifics, it is important to locate the very possibility of a democratic socialist dialogue with communist reformers in a much larger context.

It may well be that the changes now taking place within the communist world define the beginnings of a new era in the relationship between democratic socialism and communism. The definitive split between those two ideologies occurred in the 1930s, when Stalin appropriated a socialist rationale to create a new, antisocialist system. The resulting hostility was not based on misunderstanding. It was the consequence of a real-world conflict between fundamentally different conceptions—and the actual practice—of how to organize, not simply society, but the world. And it was, of course, made all the more acute by the fact that most of the effective democratic socialist parties in the world were European and supported the Atlantic Alliance in the cold war.

Indeed, that geographic dimension of the ideological quarrel was one of its most disturbing aspects, as Willy Brandt openly admitted when he became president of the Socialist International in 1976. Democratic socialism was "Western," largely confined to a European ghetto; communism was "Eastern" and a road of forced modernization for backward economies; and there was a nonaligned Third World, in which, in most cases, "socialism" had strong authoritarian tendencies.

The economic and structural sources of that ideological geography have not been abolished simply because communist reformers have changed their attitudes toward markets. China remains, for all of its material progress, a very poor country, subject to the vicious anti-socialist constraints that Marx outlined well over a century ago. The Soviet Union is obviously at a higher economic stage but the institutional weight of its Stalinist history puts an enormous limit upon change. And it is, of course, true that in both the Soviet Union and China reform has come from concerned bureaucrats, none of whom propose mass democratic participation.

At the same time, the old-line Soviet conservatives, committed to defending the very structure of the state, are right: it is extremely difficult to segregate economic and political change, to embark on a course of liberalization in the one sphere without opening up the other. It is not an accident that *glasnost*, with all of its evident limitations, and *perestroika* were introduced together. For it is simply impossible to demand initiative and creativity from a labor force that, the moment it leaves the job, is not allowed to think aloud and to discuss freely. Does this mean that democratization will follow quickly and inevitably upon markets? Of course not.

Yet *possibilities* are opened up, not the least because no one knows where reform will lead. And that offers openings for democratic socialism that have not existed for more than half a century.

A particular example is relevant here. The adoption of market criteria of efficiency by communist reformers could, we have just seen, mean that workers will lose their jobs in inefficient plants. But doesn't that show that the communists are, willy nilly, driven to accept the classic capitalist discipline, with its special cruelty toward those at the bottom? Not necessarily. For one of the most imaginative socialist attempts to deal with that problem—and one of the most creative illustrations of the use of markets within a planning framework—might become germane to the communist reformers. I refer to the Swedish active labor market policies.

## In the Light of European Socialism

At the very outset, it is necessary once again to acknowledge "Swedish exceptionalism," which, in the case of the active labor market policy, is particularly strong. The point is not so much to propose a model for imitation as to examine a rich example of how socialists can combine elements of democratic planning and market efficiency. It is that mix which is relevant to a new international socialism which could make a contribution to democratization in the East.

As far back as the 1920s, the industrial unions of Sweden, the Swedish Labor Federation (LO), had declared their concern with the low-paid workers of the land and the forests. But it was not until 1936, with the metal workers taking an important role, that the notion of a "solidaristic wage policy" came to the fore and only in 1951 was it decisively formulated. According to that concept, the unions would use their bargaining power to reduce the wage differentials within the working class by maximizing the gains for the lowest paid in negotiations with the employers.

There were a number of reasons for adopting this attitude and one of them had to do with a refusal to accept the verdict of the existing labor markets. Under "normal" capitalist circumstances, the employees of the most backward sectors would receive lower wages than those who worked for advanced, highly competitive companies. But the labor movement, the LO concluded, should favor the universalistic principle that there should be the same pay for the same expenditure of effort throughout the entire economy. And that meant that the unions should have a conscious policy of reshaping the outcomes of the labor market. This tactic was adopted on "trade union," not feminist, grounds but it was one of the reasons why women in Sweden were to reach near parity with men. They benefited from a policy directed not to their gender but to the inferior position to which the "normal" workings of markets would have assigned them.

That policy was definitively adopted in 1951. Now, however, the economic environment was completely different from that of the thirties. Instead of mass unemployment and depression, there was full employment and the danger of inflation. How could the solidaristic wage policy, and all the other social goals of the unions, be made compatible with price stability? The answer was formulated by two union economists, Gosta Rehn and Rudolf Meidner, and it was taken up by the LO.

Ten years before the economist A. W. Phillips published his famous article on the relationship between joblessness and wages, the Swedish unions had identified what came to be known as the "Phillips Curve."* That was the theoretical basis in almost all of the Keynesian countries of the 1960s for the notion that there was an inevitable "trade off" between full employment and price stability, something that Keynes himself believed and that Phillips had documented as a historical fact during a century of British experience. But the Swedish unions and socialists were not willing to accept periods of unemployment, even at relatively low levels, in order to deal with inflation and to make other social priorities possible.

As Meidner and his associate, Anna Hedborg, put the LO attitude in a retrospective of the early eighties, "The Phillips curve states propositions about certain economic relations under given institutional and economic policy assumptions. It is these assumptions that must be changed."

Prior to the adoption of the active labor market policy, particularly in 1949–50, the Swedish unions had effectively experimented, like their counterparts throughout the West, with an "incomes policy" as a way of dealing with the problem. That is, the unions voluntarily accepted a two-year moratorium on wage increases and took much of the responsibility for dealing with inflation upon themselves. Relying on the "general" mechanisms of economic policy, it turned out to be a most fallible instrument of fighting even wage increases. For despite the moratorium there was an upward "wage drift." It was the result of local conditions, of piece workers making more money, of entire new categories of labor coming into the market, and other factors that escaped the macroeconomic net.

Wage restraint also posed the incongruous issue of unions policing workers' demands rather than fighting for them. It also affected both the solidaristic wage policy and the efficiency of a national economy that was very much oriented toward competition on the world market. Ironically, the refusal to countenance low wages meant that marginal

---

*In "The Relation Between Unemployment and the Rate of Change of Money Wages in the United Kingdom, 1861–1957," *Economica* 25 (November 1958), Phillips argued that low unemployment led to higher wages (and inflation) and joblessness to a downward pressure on wages.

enterprises, which could survive in other economies, were subjected to particular pressure because they had the highest number of the under-paid. They could solve this problem either by becoming more productive—which would raise the efficiency level of the entire economy—or by going out of business. The Swedish socialists did not retreat in the presence of that last possibility of a plant shutdown (and the relevance to the Soviet problems of restructuring is, I assume, obvious). They proceeded to change the consequences of that market outcome by selective measures that saw to it that the workers would not suffer as a result of shutdowns or rationalization.

Local labor exchanges were created under the direction of a national Labor Market Board. A whole range of options was made available for dealing with the specific conditions of an enterprise or industry in a given area. There were job retraining, public works employment, a sophisticated system of identifying new openings, aid to employers in creating new jobs, subsidies to cover the moving costs of those who had to go to a new region, and, in many ways last and least, unemployment compensation. In 1979, for instance, the Swedes devoted only 10 percent of the labor-market funds to jobless benefits, compared to 31 percent for retraining, 13 percent for support to cooperating employers, and 45 percent for other measures to help the individual find new work. The goal was not to tolerate even subsidized joblessness, but to find useful work for every single citizen.

There is no reason to depict these policies as Utopia in action. There were grave difficulties in the seventies and eighties because of the slowdown in Western growth, and a good part of the success of the Socialists after their return to power in 1983 was the result of an old-fashioned competitive devaluation of the currency. But there were also new measures of public employment to deal with the specific problems of youth joblessness. However, I don't want to go into the actual workings of the system in any detail. I want instead to generalize from this rich experience to an overall socialist attitude toward the relationship between plan and markets.

How, it might be asked, can policies designed to defend workers against the impact of capitalist markets be used as a model for the socialist future? And isn't this objection reinforced by the fact that those policies were adopted as pragmatic, trade-union responses to a specific economic problem? In fact, a conception of the relationship between markets and plan is implicit in this Swedish history that could be quite relevant to the new socialism of the twenty-first century.

The positive aspect of Swedish policy was well stated by Jacques Attali in 1978, a time when he, and the entire French socialist movement, was quite critical of "mere" social democratic solutions. Attali wrote that "plan and market are two inseparable sites of the encounter between the production of demand and supply: the plan participates in the creation of a market liberated from the logic of capital; the market transmits the collective demand elaborated under the plan to the enterprises." Translated into Swedish: the plan decommodifies the labor market and treats workers as human beings but it does so in response to signals from that labor market.

In putting these considerations in their larger context I will assume that the reality of the next half century or so will be nonutopian. Marx thought that ultimately there would be so much abundance that "economizing" would no longer be necessary; that, as Alec Nove put it, resources would be available at a zero price. As formulated in the anticipation of automation in Marx's *Grundrisse*, science applied to economic ends would so exponentially increase productivity that there would no longer be the possibility, much less the necessity, of measuring and compensating contributions to output in terms of hours of labor expended. At that point, "*the surplus labor* of the masses has ceased to be the precondition for the development of universal wealth and the *non-labor* of the few is no longer the precondition of the development of the universal power of the human brain."

Nove is quite right to reject this automated utopia as a guide to the formulation of socialist policy in the contemporary world. Whatever unimaginable potential there may be in technology, total abundance will not happen in the next fifty or even a hundred years, which means that it is irrelevant to even the most "long-run" planning. Yet I think Nove misses the possibilities of real-world approximations of that utopia. Hunger could be abolished in the next period even if scarcity cannot be, not least because the world already has the capacity to feed itself. And we must be sensitive, not simply to the material meaning of such a development, but to its moral capacity to transform "human nature" as well.

But for the world as a whole, economizing is clearly on the agenda for any time frame suitable to serious analysis. The question then is, how does one economize in socialist fashion? To answer that question we go back to some ABCs.

In any dynamic society this side of total abundance, there must be, over the not-so-long run, a surplus from the productive system. Society cannot consume all that it creates in a year or a decade; it cannot eat its seed corn. At a minimum, there must be provision for depreciation and new investment. This necessary surplus product takes the form of profit in, and only in, capitalism. It is only in that system that the surplus is the property of private individuals or corporations, which carry out the social function of depreciation and investment in order to maximize their own interest. In the Soviet Union under the Stalin model, for instance, there was a surplus product that was not assigned to a class of private capitalists, but rather was allocated by a class of bureaucrats who made sure, as Trotsky well put it, that the one thing the plan did not ignore was their own well-being.

In a democratic socialist society constrained by scarcity and committed to the global abolition of poverty, the surplus product would be socially and democratically allocated. And so long as the producers and/or the ecosphere are not violated in the process, such a society will, on grounds of solidarity and social justice, be as concerned with efficiency as is capitalism. That "efficiency" will be defined in a different way than under capitalism—to express social goals and not just private interest—is obvious. But there is still a moral, as well as an economic necessity, to minimize the human and material inputs in production—in the public sector as well as the private—in order to have a maximum surplus product for the work of justice.

Let me be specific on how this implies the use of both planning and market principles. It was, and is, one of the great accomplishments of European social democracy to have removed the minimum necessities of health care from market allocation. But in both Britain and Holland that accomplishment was under severe attack in the eighties. In part, that is because the socialization of health care does indeed increase demand as "ordinary" people want the kind of care once available only to the elite.

It is also true that the nonmarket sector can develop inefficiencies of its own. And that then opens it up to the attack of "privatizing" conservatives. In Margaret Thatcher's Britain, for instance, 10 percent of health care came under private health insurance policies, and in the discussion of National Health in the eighties there were more than a few who wanted to extend the scope of for-profit care. Indeed, Thatcher tried to quintuple its role and in many cases the assault on public health is being led by corporations from the socially backward United States. This threatens one of the greatest socialist triumphs over the "logic of capital."

When the National Health system was created by the 1945 Labour government, it was established as a *universal* entitlement. In part, this was an appropriately negative response to the means-testing of social programs in the depression; in part, it was the assertion of a basic socialist principle that medical care should be a right of the citizen, not of the poor citizen alone. With privatization, however, there is a tendency toward the "Americanization" of the entire system, i.e., toward the creation of two separate systems of medicine: a publicly financed one for those at the bottom and the middle of the income distribution; private financing—and superior care—for those at the top.

The private enterprise attack on socialist universality is, it should be noted, an inherent tendency of a society that is no longer entirely capitalist but certainly not yet socialist. Under such circumstances, private profit makers will try to "cream" off the affluent functions in a given sector and graciously allow the state to socialize the remaining losses. That trend cannot be successfully combated simply by appealing to egalitarian value systems (although in Britain in the eighties, it is clear that there is enormous political support for *National* Health). The public sector has to respond to the private market attack—to markets—by controlling costs without sacrificing quality or the principle of universalism. In the mid-1980s, the Swedish socialists also addressed this issue. They have introduced reforms that seek to achieve private, market levels of efficiency in the public sector without compromising the basic commitment to services based on need.

Sometimes critically important ethical problems, which deserve to be dealt with in a calculus more humane than that of profit and loss, are involved. Medical technology now makes it possible to prolong a life of sorts for the very old if major, and rather expensive, investments are made in sophisticated technology. Is that a morally and socially sound use of resources? In *Setting Limits*, the bioethicist Daniel Callahan argues that, in the name of other health and social priorities, one cannot make such an open-ended commitment to maintain life without regard to cost. In Britain, he notes with approval, National Health has emphasized "improving quality of life through primary-care medicine and well-subsidized home care and institutional programs for the elderly rather than through life-extending acute-care medicine." In the United States, with its two-tier health structure, there has been a tendency to invest in the high-tech care of those who can pay for it.

So questions of efficiency—sometimes posed as profound choices relating to life and death—are important even in the nonmarket sector. They are also critical if the new socialism is to commit itself to *decentralized* forms of social ownership that open up new spaces for personal freedom and creativity as well as providing for the possibility of bottom-up control of the economy on a human scale.

Either, Alec Nove argues, there is a centralized and authoritarian plan for the allocation of resources, or there must be markets. There is, he asserted in a debate with a sophisticated "orthodox" Marxist, Ernest Mandel, no third possibility. Nove, I think, overstates this counterposition and Mandel projects a vision of democratic planning that is at least possible. The problem is, Mandel's model requires heroic consumers who would be willing to attend endless meetings in order to assure that they get exactly what they want. I am not sure that is feasible; I am quite sure it is not desirable. For one of the most effective arguments against socialism, as Oscar Wilde realized long ago, is that it would create a society with interminable meetings.

More broadly, Nove is right if one is serious about decentralized social ownership. What is the point of having a variety of forms of participatory control at the base—in nationalized industries, cooperatives, small private enterprises—if all of the critical decisions are to be made centrally? That would obviate one of the greatest gains that could come from that structure of ownership—namely, the encouragement of independence on the part of workers. For one of the sources of socialist productivity should be precisely that liberation of creativity, which is, under capitalism, smothered by the antagonistic relations on the shop floor.

The French notion of "worker self-managed socialism" *(socialisme autogestionaire)* was subverted by the events that caused the Socialists to make a radical change of course while in government. But it has a relevance to the socialism of the future. And it is of some moment that all of the proponents of this approach understood that, if there is to be genuine grass-roots autonomy, then there must be a market space—modified by planning priorities, of course—in which the democratic enterprises are free to exercise their communal imagination and interact without supervision from above.

If, however, all decisions were taken by central planners, even if they were working under the instructions of the people, one would lose that new source of productivity. For the latter requires that the enterprise—private or public, large or small—have the possibility of coming up with new ideas and products. And that leads to what must seem to be a very heretical thought for a socialist: that there must be sources of individual and collective gain in this process.

Of course socialism will be marked by the expansion of nonmaterial incentives, by the degree to which people will strive for excellence on social grounds or simply because it is its own reward. But so long as there is scarcity and discretionary income, so long as there must be a *social* concern with economizing inputs and therefore linking performance and success, just so long is there a necessity for material incentives. And that situation will most certainly obtain for the foreseeable future. Obviously socialists will at the same time seek to radically narrow the inequality characteristic of capitalist society, which is not, as the system's defenders claim, a functional necessity but a matter of ethos and legitimated greed.

But isn't it true that markets, even under optimum socialist conditions, inherently encourage self-seeking and even greed? That they are antithetical to a society based on solidarity and cooperation?

The evidence is ambiguous. There is no doubt that, with the rise of the mass standard of living in advanced capitalism in the West, millions have been liberated from the primordial struggle for necessities and have freely chosen paths of culture, learning, and service. So we might optimistically hope that rising levels of material satisfaction, even if far short of abundance, will change human motivation and make people impervious to the corruptions that have historically accompanied competition. But at the same time, we know that the youth of the West in the sixties, sometimes proclaimed as a "post-materialist generation," were often as acquisitive as their elders, different only in what they coveted, not in coveting, disdaining suburban comforts and exalting consumer electronics. Even more dispiriting, not a few of these rebels became well-adjusted members of societies with chronic poverty and unemployment.

Socialists should not passively wait to see how these ambiguities turn out. The labor market can be consciously shaped so that there are more opportunities for socially meaningful work that do not require heroic sacrifice. The prejudice for the private over the public is, after all, an artifact of a system that carefully favors the former over the latter. In other words, the psychological reaction to a socialist use of markets is not a given, but a policy issue. At the same time, to repeat an earlier warning, there is no socialist market utopia. Making self-interest—including collective self-interest—the instrument of community purpose will be a contradictory, and even dangerous, idea for the foreseeable future. It is also necessary.

The insightful—and heterodox—Yugoslavian Marxist, Svetozar Stojanovic, has made a most important point in this regard. On the one hand, he writes, worker self-management can lead to a "decentralized oligarchy," to an egoism, a sort of collective capitalism, of the democratic enterprise. In that case, the logic of capital takes on a communal form within the framework of the market. On the other hand, "self-management is not only threatened by statism, but also by a utopian image of human nature that leads to the naive expectation that self-managed groups produce rationally, without being challenged by competition. In a system without competition, solidarity turns into its opposite, into parasitism." The market is not a sufficient condition for the socialist functioning of self-management, but it is a necessary condition.

Integrate Stojanovic's point with the Swedish labor market experience. One of the aims of the Swedish unions was, precisely, to counteract the market outcome according to which workers in advanced companies get higher wages than those in less successful industries. But at the same time, the Swedes did not abolish the labor-market mechanism itself; they restructured it to meet their priorities. In the case posed by Stojanovic, a similar solution would be appropriate: Planned policies to see to it that the productivity of worker-managed enterprises would be, in some measure, shared by the society without abolishing the local incentives for that productivity.

So there must be room in the new socialism for initiative from the base and one of the ways of encouraging that is precisely through markets that will reward—in the sense I have just defined—the most innovative producers. A cooperative should be motivated, say, to produce medical technologies that would make the nonprofit health sector more effective and free resources for other purposes; a hospital should be able to use its expertise to choose between medical technologies and to pick the one which most meets its needs. And this is particularly important, as Nove insists, in the area of capital goods where the "consumers" consist of other enterprises that must make a self-interested assessment of what they buy.

This means, as Jacques Attali suggests, that there must be room for failure in a socialist society. An incompetent cooperative or an ineffective management in a socialized industry wastes human skills and materials that could be put to a better social use and, as the Swedish socialists have understood within the context of capitalism, there must be socially acceptable ways of putting an end to such activities. The resulting "discipline" of markets must not be vicious, as it is now, where entire communities were sacrificed in Britain under Thatcher in order to make industry "lean" and competitive. But, particularly if one is serious about the commitment to abolish world poverty, there must be *a* discipline. Here the issue is not whether there are to be markets, but what kind of markets, with what kind of consequences.

That generalization applies to the area in which there is the most obvious case for socialist markets: consumer choice.

In the capitalist theory of "consumer sovereignty," it is the individual in the marketplace who dictates the patterns of production. In reality, monopoly capital produces that which will yield the largest profit, uses all the wiles of psychology and science to make sure that the consumer chooses what is good for the corporate bottom line, and will generate and satisfy pseudo-needs while desperate human needs—say for affordable housing in the decaying central cities of Britain in the eighties—are not met. Above all, under the consumer "democracy" of contemporary capitalism, the votes are determined by income and wealth and the market is thus a mechanism for transmitting the desires of the privileged.

But, as Anthony Crosland suggested in *The Future of Socialism*, if there were a much more egalitarian society, then, *and only then*, would the essential virtue of markets really come into play. They would function as a decentralized and instantaneous device for registering the needs of people as determined by the people themselves. This they cannot do under contemporary capitalism, so that one of the basic socialist critiques of the prevailing system is that it systematically rigs and frustrates the free choice it claims as its greatest virtue. The new socialists can, and should, argue that their policies would lead to the liberation of markets from the manipulation to which they are subjected under capitalism.

In at least three areas, then—the efficiency of the nonmarket sector, the relations between decentralized democratic enterprises, and consumer choice—markets have an important role to play in the new socialism.

Markets are obviously not acceptable to socialists if they are seen as automatic and infallible mechanisms for making decisions behind the backs of those who are affected by them. That is indeed a profoundly capitalist notion and the new socialism should reject it out of hand. But within the context of a plan, markets could be, *for the first time,* an instrument for truly maximizing the freedom of choice of individuals and communities.

The aim, then, is a socialism that makes markets a tool of its nonmarket purposes. Socialists can argue that, in liberating markets from the capitalist context which frustrates their virtues, the visible hand can use the invisible hand for its own purposes.

## Note

1. Editors' note: Citations to the sources of material quoted or referred to in this chapter may be found on pp. 295–98 of Michael Harrington, *Socialism: Past and Future,* (New York: Arcade [Little, Brown and Company], 1989), which reprints Harrington's essay in slightly different form as chapter 8.

# 4

# Justice and the Market

## (Fall 1991)

### Michel Rocard and
### Paul Ricoeur

The following discussion first appeared in the French journal *Esprit* and is reprinted here with the permission of the editors. For reasons of space and to omit references purely local to French life, we have edited and abridged the text, indicating cuts by ellipses. Paul Ricoeur is a leading French philosopher, and Michel Rocard was prime minister of France when this conversation took place.

Eds.

**PAUL RICOEUR:** If we are to discuss the kind of society we live in and what kind of society we wish to promote, then we must agree on a common description. That is why it seems necessary to clarify the vocabulary that you yourself have used repeatedly in your speeches. All the more so because the "springtime of peoples" in the East has convinced even the most recalcitrant that it is within our democracies—and democracy constitutes our definitive horizon—that we must build the most just future possible.

The failure of the administered economics in the East actually leaves a whole series of questions for the West. New light is being thrown on notions like "moderated capitalism," "social democracy," and "market economy." These are terms to which you have resorted on occasion; but are they really equivalents? And if not, how can they be distinguished? Plainly, references to the market are obligatory. Some say that economic modernization, of which you are a leading proponent, has unleashed the market in the most brutal form. Too much talk of the market quickly becomes advocacy of the naked logic of the marketplace and of the capitalist as chief economic actor; one becomes enslaved to a conception of society solely as a function of the capitalist organization of market goods.

There are many possibilities of misunderstanding here. I would suggest that we not take the capitalism-socialism antithesis as our starting point but rather start from the idea that society, as a network of institutions, consists in the first place of a vast system of distribution—distribution not in the narrow economic sense but in the sense of a system that provides all sorts of goods and benefits: economic goods, certainly, but also goods like health, education, security, national identity, and citizenship. Consequently, the problem is to determine which of these goods are best distributed according to the rules of the market and which require a different mode of distribution—and if so, what kind?

Only thus, it seems to me, will we be able to clarify notions like moderated capitalism, social democracy, or even socialism; this can be done by relating them to a vision of society conceived as a system of distributive institutions. . . . This view of things was suggested to me by Michael Walzer, of the American political journal *Dissent,* who in his book *Spheres of Justice* argues that a purely procedural view of justice is inadequate, and that we should take into account the nature of the goods to be distributed. . . . To do this, we cannot limit ourselves to simple procedures, to formal rules of allotment, . . . as is the tendency with other American theorists—notably John Rawls, the author of *The Theory of Justice,* which has had an important resonance in France, and which Walzer specifically criticizes. In other words, we should not distribute in the same manner goods like education, health, and commodities, and, even more so, such benefits of citizenship as the right of association, freedom of expression, the right to security, and so on. We thus avoid the quandary that lies in wait when we either want all goods to be market goods or want certain goods to stand totally outside the market. . . .

MICHEL ROCARD: I am very sympathetic to this approach. It takes into account the central question of what our conception of society should be. This conception cannot be based on an extension of market logic into all spheres of social and political life. I would augment this question with another one that you might say is more practical, or in any case less directly conceptual, and one that increasingly confronts me as a politician: how will we and how can we decide in favor of this or that system of distribution when several systems confront and compete with one another, despite what you said about the definitive horizon of democracy? How are we going to secure the adoption of whatever system emerges as the best? How can we ensure that the system that wins approval is not a pure and simple market society, given over entirely to competition?

Humanity has actually known several ways of responding to this question, but for the longest time the preferred response has been war or coercion. One system of social organization prevailed over another because it was imposed by force. That this is no longer the case represents an advance of civilization. We no longer kill or reduce to silence those who are not in agreement with us; now we have to convince them. How then can we convince those who adopt other systems of distribution?

My question can be raised with more urgency: according to what criteria do we distinguish between goods that depend on the market and those that do not? The rejection of violence and brute force does not imply the disappearance of antagonisms, of relations of force and conflict. We should try, then, to make explicit the values that underlie this or that choice, and transmit this explanation to public opinion. I detest the word *consensus,* which, finally, can be made to mean everything and anything, but something very much like it is at stake here: the enlarging of consent through the medium of democracy or some form of compromise. Without such compromise, it is illusory to distinguish "spheres of justice" and the plurality of goods (market or nonmarket), to which you alluded.

But what have we established? That there are no longer any values that are capable of eliciting consensus and imposing limits on the market or the reign of commodities and of money? In the West, medieval society was the last to have an ethical and religious regulation of the economy, through a legitimacy that was extraordinarily powerful because not subject to secular debate. The idea imposed by the church of a "moral economy" crumbled under the assaults of those who enriched themselves, especially the bourgeoisie of the towns. . . .

The drive for accumulation, then, produced a social rapaciousness—all the stronger because the market was a form of freedom and to the extent that there were no more impediments to the ability of the rich and powerful to enrich themselves further—by exploiting the work of others. Socialism was first of all an ethical utopia, the utopia of a radically nonmarket society, corresponding on the level of ideas to, say, Fourierism and on a practical level to all those mutual aid societies, cooperatives, and labor exchanges *(bourses du travail),* which provided hiring structures that avoided the marketing of human beings. In those early years the socialist movement did not envisage bringing into being a society different from the existing system of production but rather constructing something else, alongside it, in the name of a mainly ethical legitimacy, and therefore not in the name of the alleged "direction" of history. Marxist deviations subsequent to this movement resulted in a gigantic defeat, the defeat of the command economy in the communist world, which, in its ruin, has dragged down, for many, the very idea of socialism. This is not the case with me, though not because of any nostalgia or an inability to imagine another model. Along with the early founders of socialism, I call socialism the collective wish for social justice, for less arbitrariness, for a reduction of inequality to a level that corresponds to the distribution of talents, risks, and responsibilities.

Since we are clarifying our respective vocabularies, I would say that in my mind market society, which you have defined in a precise and original manner, is not in contradiction to a wish to create a workable version of what I still call socialism, even with its original aura of utopianism. . . .

**P.R.:** But doesn't the critique of the administered economy, of bureaucratic "socialism," and even of totalitarianism too often end up extinguishing all social imagination, all visions of social transformation? Doesn't it lead to renouncing the idea of utopia, or even any possible conception of the common good?

I think we have to admit that the critique of the administered economy is over—more precisely, that while the critiques of both totalitarian societies and even the welfare state must be pursued for as long as necessary, it is in a certain sense behind us. Instead, what we need to begin today is a critique of capitalism as a system of distribution that identifies all goods as commodities. If it is true that there is no alternative to democracy, we must not be content with simply opposing a moral discourse to a self-contained economic logic. . . .

## An Ethic of Responsibility

**M.R.:** I am in complete agreement. We must quickly undertake a critique of capitalism in the form you have mentioned. But let us not forget that we have just had a narrow escape. The French Socialist party still partly supported a project of an administered economy in the 1970s. Its failure has aggravated the problem; all legitimacy other than that of the market has been dangerously weakened.

Today, we hear in the East European countries demands for the freeing of the market, for the absolute reign of the economy of money. And when we say that they should not renounce politics, that they should preserve at least a few of the prerogatives of the state, they have the impression that we are dangerous accomplices of the Gulag. Thus it is not only the critique of the administered economy but the reality of it, too, that has blocked the social imagination. What we called the critique of totalitarianism has given rise to a vehement denunciation of political action itself. We saw this in France with people like Andre Glucksmann,* for whom the individual must henceforth struggle above all against the evils of power and institutions—in short, guard against evil rather than concern oneself with establishing the common good, since in his view the destiny of all utopian projects is to end up with concentration camps. The very idea of political action, then, is vigorously rejected. And I believe that this is not without its effects on the imagination and thinking of young people. Moreover, those like

---

*Editors' note: A "New Philosopher" of the 1970s who had been a radical in the 1960s.

Vaclav Havel, who devised the idea of "antipolitics," are obliged today to accept political action because they are responsible for the fate of their communities.

That said, I am of course searching for new sources of legitimacy other than that of the market. I therefore agree with you that certain types of goods must not be dependent on the market, and others must enter into graduated relations with market forces.

Take one of the greatest problems on the planet today: the environment. We cannot produce without polluting; this an undeniable fact. But when we see the accumulated results of past pollution, we discover damage that is frightful. By what authority can we impose costly measures to preserve the environment? Clearly it cannot be done according to the laws of the market; we have to refer to different values, such as respect for life, for all life, and even more to a projection of this respect into the future. Humanity must make itself capable of protecting and preserving its environment—not only acting for itself but also for the humanity to come. We have here a new human right, or rather a new understanding of human rights: their projection into the future. This responsibility for the future enables us to answer your question about the distribution of goods. There are goods (environment, health, education) that involve the future, and we cannot dispose of them as we please. These goods are precisely the ones that require strict regulation and prohibitions, and also expenditures that the laws of the market alone are not able to justify.

This ethic of responsibility for the future does not stop at the threshold of the market; it is equally valid at the heart of the economic sphere, where too often concern for the long-term is sacrificed to the short-term. One great weakness of the laws of the market resides in the fact that they suppose, so to speak, a quasi-absolute contemporaneity of actors and moments of exchange; in other words, they are based on the hypothesis that heterogeneous actions must occur all at once, with no regard for time. This denial of time is accompanied by a rejection of concert among actors, of coordinating actions with a view to future consequences. . . . This absence of planning for the future is not unconnected with the decline of conceptions of history in terms of ends or design. Ends, finalities should not always be associated with bad utopias. . . .

## From Procedures to Values

**P.R.:** From this agreement on the idea of a plurality of categories and goods, let us move on to the question of what conception our society can have of itself when we cease to perceive it in terms of the capitalism/socialism cleavage. Now, between liberal individualism, which refuses to accept any idea of a common good, and the desire to renew the *telos* of the ancients, there appears in outline a type of society where the question of goods is posed without necessarily referring to the simplistic antithesis between market and nonmarket. We now conceive of "goods" not as an antithesis between a single Good, in which all individuals partake in indistinct fashion, and a moral individualism that endlessly fragments the conception of the Good. We speak instead of kinds of goods, whose distribution must be organized in the fairest way.

We come to the second part of our inquiry: how to organize a hierarchy of these goods. We cannot accomplish this all at once, but it *ought* to be possible to establish for each epoch and each society an order of priority, as a result of democratic discussion. The question, then, is the following: what values are capable of emerging, beyond simple procedural rules of exchange, that would shape the choice of priorities?

**M.R.:** The question must be reformulated thus: according to what values do we rank the good to which we want to give preference? However, today the inquiry is even more ticklish for a politician to the extent that the state has lost a great deal of its legitimacy, and consequently, political action has lost a great deal of credibility for the citizen. Yet this phenomenon is ambiguous insofar as it testifies, at the same time, to an advance in democratic consciousness. The political actor has no choice: to act politically, he must legitimize his action. He not only acts in the name of the sovereign people, he acts in linkage with them, you might say. Hence the necessity of understanding public opinion, of listening to it without embracing it demagogically.

And this is no accident. Democracy is a system in which legitimacy is always in question, always being debated. No one form of legitimacy can definitively win the upper hand because it is always susceptible to challenge. . . . But then the risk is that democracy has no criteria to put forward other than its own procedures. This is what you call the procedural vision of the state, a vision implied by the idea of a society of law. Here I come back to your inquiry into the links between procedures and values. What in fact is the result of such a procedural vision of democracy?

In the first place, values are, so to speak, suspended, put in parentheses. That which is good, that which is bad—how are they to be distinguished in order to evaluate the systems for distributing goods? Can we simply rely on rules of procedure? To these questions we have to bring answers that engage our convictions: Procedural rules are not values in themselves. But right now it is difficult to carry on this debate. Either values are seen as things that politics muddles or destroys or else one contents oneself with more or less restrained panegyrics to "communication." It seems to me, first of all, that a certain kind of intellectual, the kind who sanctified Sartre, has veered sharply from ultraleftism and Maoism toward a valueless void, which is part of this concern for procedure. . . .

If you keep referring to values, people regard you as an archaic vestige. For once, it is I who feel archaic here! Because I am not prepared to renounce the values that underlie my political activity. There is a paradox here, for at the same time many reproach me for carrying out a politics that is overly cautious, and you have suggested that any reference to socialism is not without ambiguity.

**P.R.:** It seems, in fact, that one expects the process of discussion itself to make values manifest. Hence the strange situation we are in: on the one hand, politics is blamed for creating an excessive passion for conflict, for being still too bound up with nostalgia and utopianism; and on the other hand, politicians are accused of yielding too much to consensus, of no longer having a specific body of independent ideas, of no longer articulating the values that must weld together a historic community.

In these conditions, the critique of politics is not easy; it quickly becomes a radical indictment of political action itself. Either one is not sufficiently political, or else one is excessively political, which is identical with graft and Machiavellianism. . . .

I fear that speaking in terms of abstract values like liberty, equality, and solidarity merely reinforces an ambivalence with regard to politics. Either it is said that there are no values or else values are affirmed in a purely voluntarist and arbitrary manner. That is why I suggest that we start with the concrete situation, one that's characteristic of modern democracy: namely, the dialectic between conflict and concert. As Edgar Morin has noted, the more complex the society, the more it creates conflicts that are not necessarily conflicts to the death, or civil wars. There are confrontations between divergent interests and between divergent convictions. I would say that democracy is the regime in which all conflicts are open. That is the reason why it requires known and accepted procedures. But accepted on what basis? Procedure is the form of the discussion, but it needs to have a content. Content can only come from conviction, which is another term for enunciating the values that inform our actions. Democracy, one could say, at once demands rules and procedures for arbitrating conflicts and also convictions and values to sustain the procedures of arbitration and to decide among competing values. . . .

**M.R.:** I am always struck by the curious tropism of the French intelligentsia, which consists of favoring, in a romantic manner, both violence and perspectives a little too apocalyptic for my taste. There is a radical posturing that often borders on the "betrayal of the intellectuals" *(trahison des clercs)*. One example: The extraordinary legitimacy among intellectuals that Castro has enjoyed for so long—and which he still seems to enjoy a little—compared to the absolute indifference that this same intelligentsia later showed toward the prodigious reconstruction of democracy in post-Franco Spain. In the latter case, there was an unfolding of political intelligence, competence, and mutual respect that made Spain, in a few years, one of the most flourishing and best administered democracies in the contemporary world—and all this, I repeat, in the face of total indifference.

It is convenient to reduce all conflicts to a single conflict and seductive to envisage this conflict as total conflict, like a war. There is an allure to violence that is always dangerously tempting for intellectuals. What is responsible for this? In the French context I think it is useful to recall the old Catholic mistrust of money; money is dirty, and it is not romantic. Rather than engage in conflicts over the distribution of money, one turns to other enthusiasms: nationalism, the class struggle, anti-imperialism. Nevertheless, there are conflicts that urgently need to be brought into the open: the regulation of social welfare and health expenditures, the relationship between television and the market, the treatment of Third World debt, and so on. But then it is necessary to confront the question of money, of the distribution of wealth, which is less exalting than enthusiastic invocations to violence, or the contemporary withdrawal into an irritable skepticism.

From the moment one makes the choice, which we mentioned at the beginning, to renounce violence—that is, to coexist with the adversary—one necessarily enters into the logic of compromise. Those who are scandalized by this situation talk about a "feeble consensus" or else are nostalgic for armed conflicts. There is something unseemly about all this, especially when one refuses to discern the real conflicts of today, which revolve around the regulation of money and the redivision of wealth. We must put an end to intellectual oscillation between unanimity and civil war. It's necessary to live with a democratic culture that at once entails compromise, concert, and the reality of conflict.

**P.R.:** In short, you're saying that we can discern, even in radical critics of Bolshevism, the musty odor of Bolshevism itself, of revolutionary nostalgia. It seems to me that there is a strong tendency in French society for conflict to present itself always in a somewhat archaic form, which makes it unamenable to negotiation and arbitration. . . . We have a lot of trouble acknowledging the proliferation of conflicts and the corresponding necessity of their orderly regularities.

**M.R.:** From this point of view, I would plead for the reintroduction of a regulative function in the life of our societies. This regulative function has two aspects: one is related to the public authority, to the state, and the other to the contractual regulations of civil society. This latter dimension is very new in French society, because it has always relied on the state. Now, many social processes do not depend on state intervention but on collective negotiation regulated by contracts or agreements. Of course this is the case with social partnerships, but also with institutions, like the medical ethics committee or the *conseil* *superieur de l'audiovisuel,* even if they do not yet play the role they ought to.

Here I come back to the central line of inquiry. We have at our disposal some procedures, which certainly need to be improved, for arriving at a negotiated treatment of conflicts. But these procedures are not distinct from the values that must underlie them. Now, which values are we likely to favor today? Since we no longer make use of transcendent values, plainly there is no value available to us other than respect for human life. . . .

This idea of respect for human life enables us to link environmental protection, questions of bioethics, and also urgent requirements like economic regulation at the global level. It can also be made the basis for a certain respect for the market, insofar as the market is one of the constitutive elements of freedom. But respect for life also requires respect for the freedom of the other. Questions of values thus are not distinct from questions of procedure, for while there are domains proper to state intervention and those proper to contractual negotiation like the economy, others must be invented from this point of view: bioethics for example, and of course health, education, culture, and so on. . . .

**P.R.**: The absence of transcendent values has been given a name in the French tradition, that of secularism *(laïciser)*. And we have tried to make it a value in itself, to make it something positive and substantial. The secularization of the state was thus conceived as a process of putting convictions in parentheses. . . .

In this sense, the legitimacy of the secular state requires no strong conviction. The great struggle for secularization was a struggle to break from a legitimacy founded on tradition and to substitute for it a legitimacy founded on argumentation. . . . We need, once again, to give substance to the idea of a living secularism, one that provides for confrontation between diverse convictions, nourished by the diversity of our cultural heritage, which is for me the Judeo-Christian heritage, that of the Greeks and the Romans, the heritage of the Enlightenment and that of nineteenth-century socialism, to which we must of course add today the Islamic traditions, and perhaps others still. . . .

We have renounced, with good reason, a certain social utopianism, which inspired dreams of a transparent, limpid future, and which ended up legitimizing a totalitarian ideology. But utopianism makes another demand, that of the Harmonious Man *(l'homme réconcilié)* of people no longer prey to fragmentation and division, or alienation. Can we still act without a utopia of this kind, a positive utopia? You have sometimes given the impression of resigning yourself too quickly to the end of ideology and thus renouncing any project for society. But shouldn't some of the ideas that were part of this utopia of a better future be saved?

Translated from the French by Thomas B. Harrison.

# PART III

---

# Markets and the Socialist Tradition

# 5

# Marx and Market Socialism

## (Fall 1992)

## *Frank Roosevelt*

Karl Marx ruled out any role for the market in a post-capitalist economy. "Within the cooperative society based on common ownership of the means of production," he wrote in the *Critique of the Gotha Program,* "the producers do not exchange their products." Marx's collaborator, Friedrich Engels, stated their position (in *Anti-Düring*) even more bluntly: "The seizure of the means of production by society puts an end to commodity production . . . [and at that point the market is to be] replaced by conscious organization on a planned basis."[1]

Today, however, many democratic socialists are moving, both in theory and in practice, toward allowing markets a significant role. "Market socialism" is coming to be seen as a feasible way of implementing socialist values within an efficient economic system and, hence, as a chance to revive the socialist project in the face of nearly universal disenchantment with the orthodox model of central planning and state ownership.

The movement toward the market is not without some real problems for socialists. There is a strong possibility that markets will make it difficult or impossible to achieve some of the defining goals of socialism.[2] Although the market socialist critique of Marx must be taken seriously—I, for one, have come to reject his abolitionist position—it is still necessary to pay careful attention to Marx's argument. He exposed many of the defects of capitalist markets that will not just disappear with the establishment of market socialism.

## The Critique of Marx

The first task is to review the main criticisms lodged by market socialists against Marx. Why is the goal of abolishing markets simply not feasible? To begin with, there is the inescapable fact that there are only two known ways, broadly speaking, in which the economic activities of a modern society can be organized and coordinated—one being the market, and the other, some form of political process (that is, planning). Before advocating the elimination of either option, one should be reasonably certain that the other will work. Yet Marx does not seem to have thought this through. Take, for example, the well-known passage in *The German Ideology* in which he and Engels criticize the capitalist division of labor and project a future communist society in which a person could "hunt in the morning, fish in the afternoon, rear cattle in the evening, [and] criticize after dinner. . . ." For Marx, the freedom to change occupations was linked to the organization of the economy. Under communism, "society regulates the general production and thus makes it possible for me to do one thing today and another tomorrow. . . ." The problem is that Marx and Engels neglect to explain *who* is to represent "society" and *how* the "regulation of production" is to be accomplished in a way that allocates resources efficiently.

A great many writers over the years have pointed to the difficulty— or even impossibility—of effectively structuring a modern economy without relying on markets. In an unpublished paper, market socialist theorist David Belkin has recently offered a list of the more common problems that became pervasive in many of the former communist countries that tried to eliminate the market: bureaucratic domination of production and social life; resources tied up in obsolete investments; prices unrelated to costs, hence distorted allocation of resources; goods and services in chronic short supply; slow growth in real incomes; disguised unemployment, for example, people in unproductive jobs; poor motivation and work discipline; little reward for attending to environmental considerations. Although many of these problems are also prominent in capitalist countries, the point is that they remained in societies that claimed to have found an economic system superior to capitalism. At least one reason why the "socialism" instituted in Eastern Europe did not outperform capitalism was the mistaken idea, inspired by Marx, that the market could simply be abolished.

Furthermore, even if the vision of a marketless communist economy were applicable, it would be so only in a small and relatively simple society. It is just not an effective way to organize and coordinate the economic activities of a large and complex nation—much less the whole world. Once the market is eliminated, the allocation of economic resources has to be accomplished through some form of political process. In a relatively small and simple society (for example, an Israeli kibbutz), the political process can also be simple. Decisions about what to produce, how to produce it, and so on, can be arrived at without reference to market-determined prices because everyone involved in decision making can have direct knowledge of the relative costs of producing different things, and the preferences of the members of the community for various possible outputs will also be known. Assigning different tasks to specific people—achieving an acceptable "division of labor"—and motivating everyone to do their work well can also be accomplished.

It is otherwise in large and complex societies. Collection of essential information becomes more difficult, motivation becomes a problem, and the political process is altered as direct democracy ceases to be an option. Inevitably, a subset of the population is selected by some method to gather information and to make production and resource-allocation decisions. Impersonal mechanisms must be put in place to motivate people to perform the necessary tasks and to distribute the output of the economy. Information may be closely held or widely shared, and the procedures for making decisions at various levels may be more or less democratic. Still the fact remains that, in a large and complex economy, not everything can be done by everybody. The selection of those who perform the more important tasks and the methods by which this selection is accomplished necessarily become vital issues. A question arises as to what social interests those selected—the planners, politicians, bureaucrats—will actually represent. Is it likely that these "agents" will be able to, or even wish to, represent the interests of the "principals"—that is, the population as a whole? If not, how can the goals of socialism be achieved in a marketless society?

It is noteworthy that in the same sentence in the *Critique of the Gotha Program* in which Marx banished commodity exchange from communist society, he asserted that "now, in contrast to capitalist society, individual labor no longer exists in an indirect fashion but [exists] directly as a component part of the total labor." This rather mysterious statement builds on the first chapter of *Capital,* where there is a rough sketch of the economic organization of "a community of free individuals carrying on their work with the means of production in common. . . ." Marx argues that we can analyze the economic tasks of a socialist society in essentially the same way that we think about those of a single, isolated individual—Robinson Crusoe—only "with this difference, that they are social, instead of individual." But can we really think of a complex economy in this way? Marx's yearning for a marketless society (exemplified in the purest form by the Robinson Crusoe story) seems to have blinded him to the many difficulties involved in moving from the analysis of a one-person economy to the modeling of a multifaceted socialist economy.

Marx does allude (in the same passage) to one of the central problems of a socialist economy when he asserts that the "apportionment [of labor-time] in accordance with a definite social plan, maintains the proper proportion between the different kinds of work to be done [on the one hand] and the various wants of the community [on the other]." Indeed, one can judge the effectiveness of any economic system by asking how well it achieves this "proper proportion." In none of his discussions of a post-capitalist economy, however, does Marx ever take up the question of whether or not a centrally planned socialist economy—one that bans markets—actually can allocate the "different kinds of work to be done" in such a way as to provide effectively for the "various wants of the community." He simply assumes that this will be possible. Considering the widespread dissatisfaction today with centrally planned economies, this appears to have been an unwarranted assumption.

So what is the problem? Why is it not possible for a socialist economy to replace the market with planning? Another perspective on this question is supplied by Alec Nove's discussion of "the *ex ante* illusion" in *The Economics of Feasible Socialism*. This is the idea that the needs and wants of a community can somehow be determined before production takes place, thereby allowing production itself to be undertaken in a precise way to provide exactly the goods and services that the community wants. If things could actually be done this way, and done effectively, it would certainly eliminate a good deal of the waste that occurs in a market economy—where some resources are employed to produce things that nobody buys, and others are used just to persuade people to buy things that they may not need.

However, as Nove points out, there are several fundamental problems with this conception of a planned economy. One has to do (again!) with collecting the necessary information from the population regarding, say, the preferred design and size of shoes, in advance of production. Some people (myself included) do not know exactly what style and size shoe they want until they actually enter a shoe store, look around, and try on a number of different pairs. This way of allowing consumers to express (and form) their preferences is available only in a market economy, and the validation of the allocation of social labor occurs only *ex post*. In other words, one can only know whether or not society's labor-time was allocated "properly" *after* consumers have made their purchasing decisions. Inevitably, the shoes (or other items) that do not get purchased will represent wasted resources.

Even if all of the necessary information about consumers' preferences could somehow be obtained in advance of production, it is far from sure that precisely the desired quantities and qualities of products will be produced. If, for some reason, producers do not turn out precisely the quantity and quality of goods and services that the community wants, what recourse does the community have—either individually or collectively—to correct the production process?

Whatever its many deficiencies, a market economy provides consumers with choices and it can also give producers incentives to produce what consumers (or other producers) want.[3] A market economy makes possible the decentralization of production decisions and it allows prices to be established that, however roughly and imperfectly, reflect the relative scarcities of the available resources both in relation to each other (for example, wood, coal, water power, land, labor, machinery) and in relation to consumer preferences. If there is a workable degree of competition in the economy (that is, relatively little monopoly or monopsony power), these prices can serve as signals that not only transmit information about relative scarcities, production possibilities, and consumer preferences but also provide incentives for efficient production.

When Marx looked at the market and its corresponding money relations, he primarily saw their negative and mystifying effects on people. He failed to see that markets can also organize production in a way that allows resources to be used effectively to satisfy people's needs. Moreover, as Barnard College economist Deborah Milenkovitch has argued, market-determined prices are a necessary condition for popular sovereignty. It is only with the information provided by such prices that the citizens of highly complex modern societies can evaluate alternative public policies.

There is, however, one assumption that, if accurate, would permit us to ignore all of the problems entailed in Marx's proposal to abolish the market. That is the assumption of abundance. If everything were plentiful (including natural resources and capital goods) and if—as a result of advances in technology—human labor were many times more productive than it is today, then we would not have to worry about social priorities or concern ourselves with allocating scarce resources effectively. Rather, we could enjoy a state of affairs in which efficiency would be relatively unimportant and virtually all social needs could be easily satisfied.[4]

This appears to have been assumed in *The Communist Manifesto,* in which Marx and Engels observed that "the bourgeoisie cannot exist without constantly revolutionizing the instruments of production." With admiration they noted that "during its rule of scarce one hundred years, the bourgeoisie has created more massive and more colossal productive forces than have all preceding generations together." In Marx's view of history, it was the specific mission of the bourgeoisie to raise productivity to such a high level that an age of abundance could be inaugurated—an age in which scarcity and its attendant conflicts over goods and resources would be left behind. Indeed, in *The*

*German Ideology,* which Marx wrote with Engels shortly before they wrote the *Manifesto,* there was an explicit reference to "a great increase of productive power, a high degree of its development" as a precondition for communist society: "[T]his development of [the] productive forces . . . is an absolutely necessary practical premise [for the communist revolution] because without it *want* is merely made general, and with destitution the struggle for necessities and all the old filthy business would necessarily be reproduced."

Thus, in Marx's view, communist society would not have to wrestle with "the economic problem" but could pursue its goals in an environment of plenty. Yet how realistic is this assumption in today's world—one in which most of the population is still poor, and in which the effort to bring everyone's standard of living up to that of the average person in the industrialized countries is probably not ecologically feasible? Given present realities, embracing Marx's assumption of abundance seems naive at best and, if one takes into account the ecological constraints on further industrialization, irresponsible. An alternative approach would accept the continued presence of scarcity and would explore ways in which socialist societies might share its burdens while pursuing growth in ways that would be both equitable and ecologically sustainable.

## Marx's Critique of Markets

Was Marx simply naive? He spent a lifetime trying to analyze the market—did he really misunderstand it? That would be simplistic and misleading. Marx arrived at his rejection of the market as the logical outcome of his critique of capitalism. If market socialists are right, the major defects of our existing market economy can be remedied by altering its capitalist framework. But if Marx's critique of capitalist markets applies to markets per se, whatever their institutional setting, market socialists will have to find ways of counteracting those undesirable tendencies of markets that will persist even in a socialist framework. This is why we need to pay attention to Marx's critique.

One of Marx's most forceful criticisms is that capitalism exacerbates economic inequalities and necessarily pits people organized in social classes against each other. Anyone familiar with his analysis of the origins of capitalism will recall his account of how, in Britain, the division of society into capitalists and workers occurred as a result of the historical process of "primitive accumulation." There is, however, another argument in *Capital* that holds that "commodity production, *in accordance with its own inherent laws,* develops further [as soon as some people begin selling their productive capacities to others] into capitalist production." (Emphasis added.) It seems obvious to me that Marx was right about the inherent tendency of markets to generate inequality. Even if we could (somehow) start with an equal distribution of economic resources, the normal operation of markets themselves would lead, sooner or later, to increasing inequality, to class divisions, and to the well-known capitalist forms of domination and exploitation. If we are to retain the socialist goal of a classless society, market socialists will have to devise institutional mechanisms to counteract these tendencies.

A second defect of market economies that Marx brings to our attention is that they are inherently unstable. He argues that *any* market economy will be unstable as long as production decisions are made by individuals or firms without any social coordination. This leaves the economy vulnerable to swings in expectations about the future. When there is an optimistic mood in the air, firms will tend to expand production, hire more workers, and use more inputs until, for one reason or another, the optimism is replaced by pessimism and output rates are cut, workers laid off, and so on. Macroeconomic variables—total output, investment, employment, and the like—will tend to fluctuate because of the way in which the microeconomic decisions are made. As a result, a market economy will fail to utilize its human and material resources consistently over time and will not produce the amount of output that might otherwise be created and consumed. With resources often idle at the same time as there are unfulfilled human needs, a market economy can be said to be both irrational and wasteful.

Marx's criticisms of the inequality and instability of a market economy are primarily *economic*. However, his most powerful objections to the market were essentially *moral* arguments. Despite his commitment to "scientific" socialism, he engaged in a profoundly utopian exercise, linking his critique of markets to his vision of how things ought to be in a future society. At the most basic level, Marx's antipa-

thy toward the market was rooted in a profound communitarian im-
pulse. It represented a desire to achieve on a higher level the social
solidarity, based on a commonly accepted social ethic, that had prevailed in simpler societies before the appearance of class divisions, the
state, and the market (with its impersonal relations of commodity
exchange). Running through all of his critiques of capitalism is the
idea that markets gradually turn everything into a commodity and, in
the process, corrode social values and undermine community. Here the
young Marx presents his ethical critique of the market in *The Poverty
of Philosophy:*

> [With the spread of markets] there came a time when everything that
> people had considered as inalienable became an object of exchange, of
> traffic, and could be alienated. This is the time when the very things
> which till then had been communicated, but never exchanged; given,
> but never sold; acquired, but never bought—virtue, love, conviction,
> knowledge, conscience, etc.—when everything, in short, passed into
> commerce. It is the time of general corruption, of universal venality, or,
> to speak in terms of political economy, the time when everything, moral
> or physical, having become a marketable value, is brought to market to
> be assessed at its truest value.

The same point was made in a famous passage in *The Communist
Manifesto* in which Marx and Engels assert that capitalism "has left
remaining no other nexus between people than naked self-interest,
than callous 'cash payment.' " This posture is quite similar to that
adopted by moral philosophers ranging from Immanuel Kant to
Martin Buber, when they condemn any behavior which uses others
in an instrumental fashion or treats human beings as means rather
than as ends.

Much of Marx's well-known critique of alienation under capitalism
is even more utopian than his analysis of commodification. As Stanley
Moore has argued in his important book, *Marx on the Choice between
Socialism and Communism,* the project of overcoming social alienation requires a more radical change than the elimination of capitalist
exploitation and is inseparable from Marx's commitment to the goal
of a marketless communist society. An unalienated society could only
be achieved if "production for exchange" were to be replaced entirely

by "production for use." Not only is such a goal inappropriate to any society other than a very small and self-sufficient one, as Moore points out, it is not consistent with—or justified by—Marx's materialist conception of history since it does not grow out of any historical interaction between the forces and relations of production.

There is, however, one aspect of Marx's analysis of alienation that has important implications for market socialism, namely, the one pertaining to the capitalist way of organizing the work process. In the *Economic and Philosophical Manuscripts of 1844,* Marx asks, "What constitutes the alienation of labor?" and goes on to give the following response:

> First, that the work is *external* to the worker, . . . and that, consequently, he does not fulfill himself in his work but denies himself, has a feeling of misery rather than well-being, does not develop freely his mental and physical energies but is physically exhausted and mentally debased. The worker, therefore, feels himself at home only during his leisure time, whereas at work he feels homeless. His work . . . is not the satisfaction of a need, but only a *means* for satisfying other needs.

Clearly, human labor does not need to be organized as it is under capitalism. Any socialism worthy of the name must humanize the work process. Consequently, one of the most important questions for market socialists is whether—or to what degree—work can be humanized in enterprises that are competing with each other within a market framework.

Perhaps the most profound of Marx's objections to the market is an argument about the meaning of human freedom. He believed that reliance upon the market to coordinate economic activities prevents a society—and the individuals in it—from achieving freedom in the fullest sense of the word. In order to grasp the complexity of his argument on this point, it is necessary to recall his theory of "commodity fetishism" in *Capital.*[5]

Not long after people begin to exchange their products (commodities) in markets, this process takes on a life of its own. The people who do the exchanging come to see it as something that is independent of and superior to themselves. Using an analogy to the process in which "primitive" people carve a tree into a totem pole and then turn it into an object of worship, Marx called the modern tendency to reify the market "commodity fetishism." Once people attribute "objective" reality to "the forces of supply and demand" (forgetting that they themselves set the process of exchange in motion, that it did not fall from the sky), the "market mechanism" becomes an autonomous power and people lose control over certain very important social decisions (for example, what is to be produced, by what methods, where, and for whom). Indeed, people lose control over the direction of their society and allow crucial social choices to be made without deliberation (through representative bodies, for example) on them. Examples of such choices might include the process and pace of urbanization, choices among alternative technologies, priorities for developing energy sources, and the degree of inequality in the distribution of income and wealth.

Marx's analysis of commodity fetishism was first elaborated at length in *Capital,* but it was anticipated more than twenty years earlier in one striking sentence in *The German Ideology:*

> [As the market develops] . . . trade, which after all is nothing more than the exchange of products of various individuals and countries, rules the whole world through the relation of supply and demand—a relation which, as an English economist says, hovers over the earth (like the Fate of the ancients), and with *invisible hand* allots fortune and misfortune to people, sets up empires and wrecks empires, [and] causes nations to rise and to disappear—whereas with the abolition of the basis [of trade], private property, with the communist regulation of production (and, implicit in this, the abolition of the alien attitude of people to their own product), *the power of the relation of supply and demand is dissolved into nothing,* and people once more gain control of exchange, production and the way they behave to one another. (Emphasis added.)

Clearly, Marx's conception of freedom went beyond the classical liberal definition that focused on the rights of individuals to express themselves and to make choices without interference by the state. For Marx, individual choice and expression do not give a person freedom if he or she has an "alien attitude" toward the market mechanism and is without any power to influence the important social decisions affecting his or her life.

**Promoting Socialist Objectives**

If market socialists such as myself reject the abolition of markets but find valid insights in Marx's critique of them, what practical conclusions can be drawn concerning the implementation of market socialism? While it is beyond the scope of this essay to lay out a detailed model of a market socialist economy, a few suggestions are in order to indicate how to counteract the undesirable tendencies of markets and promote socialist objectives.

If markets, left to themselves, tend to generate inequality, what institutional mechanisms might counteract this tendency? Policies that rely entirely on income taxes and transfer programs often conflict with people's sense that they have a right to their income whether it derives from their property or from their labor. For this reason, it is necessary to promote a form of social ownership of the means of production that can distribute pretax income more equitably while avoiding the negative consequences of state ownership of property. Models that provide for worker- or community-owned enterprises might accomplish this objective. The greatest challenge is to devise a capital-providing mechanism that can foster the development of such enterprises, and it is especially important that this mechanism itself be socially owned, since private banks and capital markets are major generators of inequality and tend to exacerbate uneven development.

If market economies are inherently unstable, fluctuations in the rate of growth can at least be attenuated by using the kind of "indicative planning" that allows a multitude of economic actors to coordinate their decisions and set target rates of growth while avoiding the undesirable effects of central planning.

To counteract the tendency of a market economy to turn everything into a commodity, conscious efforts would be required to slow down—and eventually reverse—the process of commodification. Explicit boundaries would be drawn around the sphere of the market in order to defend other realms and relationships against its encroachments. Certain goods and services should be provided "free" through the public sector either because citizens have a right to them (for example, police and fire protection, legal services, education, health care) or because they are socially desirable but not likely to be provided by the private sector (for example, infrastructure, job training, public amenities). The expansion of a sector of worker-owned enterprises would in fact restrict the sense in which labor-power itself is a commodity (even while labor markets are retained in order to ensure freedom of occupational choice and to promote efficient use of human resources). The purpose of all these efforts to contain the market is ultimately to enable us to fashion and to preserve a social ethic, strengthen community life, and achieve a better balance between competition and cooperation.

Although we cannot expect to eliminate social alienation—because it is just not possible to organize most economic activities on the basis of "production for use"—we certainly can improve the quality of work experience for large numbers of people. This can best be done by promoting worker self-management and strengthening those regulations and workers' rights that ensure healthy and humane working conditions.

For Marx, freedom could not be fully achieved as long as markets dominated economic organization. In his view, wherever there are markets there will also be "commodity fetishism." Even if market socialists do not accept this doctrine, we can learn from Marx not to be intimidated by markets. While we do not seek to eliminate the play of supply and demand, we do refuse to hand over all power to "the market mechanism." Seeking the middle ground, we believe that, under the right conditions, markets can be used to achieve social objectives such as efficient allocation of resources, decentralization of decision making, and satisfaction of consumer needs. Demonstrating our liberation from "commodity fetishism," we would institute an "industrial policy" that would reflect democratically determined priorities and give us a degree of control over the direction in which our society is moving. In this way we would hope to achieve, among other things, a kind of economic progress that would be ecologically sustainable and supportive of less developed nations.

Of course, none of this will be easy. Simultaneous and commensurate progress toward all of these goals is impossible because some of the goals conflict with each other.[6] For example, democratic decision making at the grassroots level—say, within enterprises or local communities—may conflict with asserting control over the general direction of society, since achieving the latter objective would require either a society-wide consensus or centralized power. Similarly, one can imagine situations in which efficiency considerations (requiring competition and mobility of labor and capital) might conflict with worker-owned enterprises or stable community life. Nevertheless, we would have a much better chance of achieving most of our objectives if we faced these problems under market socialism rather than in capitalist society.

The most important lesson we might learn from Marx would be to take seriously his "materialist conception of history." As he wrote in a celebrated passage, "Men make their own history, but they do not make it just as they please; . . . [rather, they make it] under circumstances directly encountered, given, and transmitted from the past." Abolishing the market would seem to qualify as an effort by people to make history "just as they please." Accepting at least a few of the lessons of the past, we should try to find a way to incorporate the market within a framework that will allow us both to promote economic efficiency and to advance socialist values.

## Notes

1. For a more scholarly version of this essay with citations to the sources of all quotations, see chapter 14 in Ron Blackwell, Jaspal Chatha and Edward J. Nell, eds., *Economics as Worldly Philosophy: Essays on Political and Historical Economics in Honor of Robert Heilbroner* (London: Macmillan, 1993; New York: St. Martin's Press, 1993).

2. For my earlier views on this point, see F. Roosevelt, "Market Socialism: A Humane Economy?" *Journal of Economic Issues* 3, no. 4 (December 1969), pp. 3–20.

3. As Herbert Gintis has pointed out, the "power to switch" is the basis of whatever "sovereignty" consumers have in any economic system. See H. Gintis, "The Power to Switch: On the Political Economy of Consumer Sovereignty," in Samuel Bowles, Richard C. Edwards, and William G. Shepherd, eds., *Unconventional Wisdom: Essays in Honor of John Kenneth Galbraith* (Boston: Houghton Mifflin, 1989), pp. 65–79.

4. For an appealing projection of such a state of affairs, see John Maynard Keynes, "Economic Possibilities for Our Grandchildren," *Essays in Persuasion* (New York: Norton and Company, 1963), pp. 358–73.

5. For a more extended discussion of this topic, see F. Roosevelt, "Cambridge Economics as Commodity Fetishism," *Review of Radical Political Economics* 7, no. 4 (Winter 1975), pp. 1–32.

6. See David Miller, "A Vision of Market Socialism," *Dissent* (Summer 1991) and F. Roosevelt's comment on Miller, "Questions About Market Socialism," *Dissent* (Fall 1991), reprinted in chapter 12, this volume.

# 6

# Oskar Lange's Market Socialism: The Story of an Intellectual-Political Career

## (Winter 1991)

### Tadeusz Kowalik

Oskar Lange is known in the West, above all, as the author of the classical and widely criticized model of market socialism. An enormous amount has been written about this model, some of it developing Lange's idea and much of it criticizing its weaknesses. This article is concerned not so much with the systematic exposition and criticism of Lange's model as with discussing the place it occupied in the development of his views on socialism.

During his lifetime, Lange was able to observe firsthand all three of the worlds that currently coexist on this planet, and he encountered these worlds in the same order in which they follow each other in his scheme of the development of the modern world. Lange learned about economic backwardness and peripheral capitalism in prewar Poland. Later he spent more than twenty years in the bastion of modern capitalism, the United States. After returning to Poland in 1948, he linked his fate to the creation and then reform of the communist system.

## The Polish Background

Lange grew up in the western part of the region that had been partitioned by Russia. His father came from a family of assimilated German industrialists who had settled in Poland at the beginning of the nineteenth century and personified the "enclave" capitalism of a backward country. He produced largely for distant eastern markets, and when access to these was cut off, the Lange family became impoverished.

When Poland regained its independence in 1918, the fourteen-year-old Oskar underwent his own baptism of fire. He joined a band of youths who seized weapons from soldiers of the retreating German army. Two years later, during the Polish-Russian war, he signed up for an alternative to military service. It is worth recalling these symbolic events, because they typify the early road taken by many Poles who invested so much hope in the newly independent Poland and then were so sorely disappointed. Lange's preoccupation with unresolved social issues, his turn to socialism—first in its reformist and pacifist form and then its revolutionary version—reflected broader processes of radicalization in a country condemned to stagnation.

Prewar Poland was not simply a backward or, in the terminology of the United Nations, a developing country. Ludwik Landau, in his book *Gospodarka Swiatowa (The World Economy),* published in 1939, counted Poland among the "partly capitalist" countries. He thus situated Poland between such countries as Spain, Hungary, and Argentina, whose per capita national income was greater, and countries that were less developed, such as Romania, Yugoslavia, Bulgaria, and Greece. As a result of the Great Depression, Poland's many problems came to form a "trap" or "vicious circle" of backwardness. The main problems were the semifeudal structure of agriculture, with its latifundia on the one hand and the hidden unemployment of many millions on the other; the prominent role of foreign capital, which had little interest in developing domestic manufacturing industry; the preponderance of raw-material exports; and the absence of an entrepreneurial middle class.

Lange saw the main causes of Poland's economic stagnation in the growing role of monopolies in the world economy. It was this that had brought about the Great Depression, exacerbating negative tendencies and conserving backwardness. To Lange, it seemed that the only effective solution lay in the revolutionary overthrow of capitalism and the construction of a socialist system. Only such a radical change appeared to offer an effective means of eliminating poverty and backwardness.

This revolutionary message was set out in a collective book, *Gospodarka—Polityka—Taktyka—Organizacja Socjalizmu (The Economics, Politics, Tactics, and Organization of Socialism)*, published in 1934 and edited by Lange. This work sets out Lange's first vision of a socialist economy that would constitute an alternative to both capitalism and "state socialism" of the Soviet kind. A section of the book subtitled "The Road to a Planned Socialist Economy" was written by Lange together with Marek Breit, a brilliant young economist murdered by the Nazis. The proposals for a transition period, as well as the organization and functioning of a socialist economy, set out in this section foreshadowed Lange's classic work on socialism.

This early work clearly reveals Lange's basic characteristics as a socialist thinker. To Lange, socialism was not simply the negation of capitalism but also its continuation—something that is often distorted by the revolutionary language of much propagandistic writing. At the heart of Lange's views is the conviction that, by introducing fascism (which Lange considered genetically linked to monopolies and imperialism), the bourgeoisie was renouncing political democracy. Similarly, the growth of economic monopolies had destroyed the market and free competition. Thus, the task of socialism as a social movement was to salvage and broaden the scope of democracy and competition. Despite, then, the reference to a "planned economy" in the title and the terminology used in the text, it was not central planning but market competition that was to be the basis of the future economy.

If we compare the early Lange-Breit model with the Hungarian reform model of 1968, the radicalism of the former's approach to the market and the caution of the latter's approach to planning is immediately evident. At first glance, the Lange-Breit model seems similar to the Hungarian model of planning with the aid of financial parameters. In the Lange-Breit model, the central planning institution was to be the public bank. The bank was to determine the rate of accumulation and was to appropriate and allocate investment resources between individual enterprises and their associations (trusts). It was also to have the power to close inefficient enterprises and to transfer their assets to more efficient competitors and to check whether enterprises and trusts were employing "strict cost accounting."

The similarity with the Hungarian model is, though, of a purely formal nature, because the criteria governing the behavior of the central planners in the two systems were quite different, if not antithetical. In the Hungarian model, the center had the power to decide the scale of investment and to determine most prices on the basis of its own preferences. On the other hand, the public bank in the Lange-Breit model had no price-setting powers whatsoever, not even in relation to capital goods. All prices were to be determined by the market. Similarly, investment resources were to be allocated not according to the preferences of the center but according to market forces generated by the needs of consumers. The bank was simply supposed to "serve" the market.

Realizing that a monopolistic economy, and with it the artificial escalation of prices and wages, might reemerge, Lange and Breit proposed that the state oblige enterprises to employ all those who applied for work. The ensuing growth in output would bring down prices and, as a result, wages. The public bank would be obliged to provide investment loans to enterprises if warranted by the growth in employment:

> In this way [the authors declared] there will be no room for the arbitrariness in investment policy. It will be based on a specific and automatic indicator of intensity of demand for individual commodities. The Public Bank will not be able to depart from these principles. This will ensure that the socialist economy will produce goods according to intensity of demand.

The impracticality of this "practical" proposal is so obvious that any detailed criticism is superfluous. It is worth, however, noting the authors' intention, their effort to retain a commodity and labor market in the strict institutional sense such that the entire economy, including the investment process, would operate according to automatic, and thus objective, market mechanisms reflecting the intensity of consumer needs.

The Lange-Breit model differs from the Hungarian also in the demand that the entire organizational structure of the economy be based on a "system of workers' councils" from top to bottom (in other words, it would include a Chamber of Self-Management Representatives in the parliament). This was to constitute an effective antidote to the dangers of bureaucratization.

In Hungary the absence of such a countervailing force to the bureaucracy led to the transformation of the "new economic mechanism" into a system of indirect centralization, in which spontaneous market mechanisms were crushed by intervention in enterprise activity on the part of bureaucrats at all levels. Comparing the functioning of the Hungarian economy with the assumptions underlying the reform and with the vision of market socialism, János Kornai recently wrote:

> Power creates the irresistible temptation to make use of it. A bureaucrat must be interventionist because that is his role in society; it is dictated by his situation. What is now happening in Hungary with respect to detailed microregulation is not an accident. It is rather the predictable, self-evident result of the mere existence of a huge and powerful bureaucracy. An inherent tendency to recentralization prevails.[1]

In Lange's model, the workers' councils were intended to limit the power of the bureaucracy, to counteract what another Hungarian economist, Laszlo Antal, has called the "illusion of regulation."

The Lange-Breit approach bears some similarity to the Yugoslav model of a labor-managed market economy, a model that has its strong and weak points. Without engaging in discussion of whether workers' self-management is compatible with a high level of economic efficiency, we should take note of one danger, which has made itself felt with full force in Yugoslavia. Lange and his colleagues advocated, as did the Yugoslavs much later, a uniform system of self-management. Inherent in this model is the very real possibility that workers' councils will become bureaucratized as the result of a low level of social participation and lack of competence.

To sum up, Lange and his colleagues believed that this model of a socialist economy would be superior to the capitalist economy of the Great Depression (which would not have been difficult) and would avoid all the obvious defects of the Soviet economy. They considered that the latter was based largely on popular enthusiasm and on appeals from the leadership, which did not hold out the prospect of efficient functioning in the long run. This is what they wrote about the Soviet Union:

> We view the cultural and moral might of the Russian peasant and worker revolution with enormous admiration. . . . But we should remember that, in the long run, socialism will take root only if it manages to transcend its moral achievements to show that its economy functions better than capitalism.

Elsewhere they wrote in a similar vein: "If the socialist economy does not fulfill the hopes invested in it, then indeed it will not be worth the toil and sacrifice that the working masses have endured in the struggle to achieve it."

## Lange's Model

Lange published *On the Economic Theory of Socialism* in 1936, only two years after arriving in the United States. Thus, although his studies in the States had a substantial influence on his conceptual framework, his views on social issues were those that had been formed earlier, in Eastern Europe. In all its major points, including the call for revolution, this famous work continues themes developed earlier. It can thus be taken as the starting point of Lange's "American evolution."

Here it is worth recalling the main features of Lange's model. In its organization, the socialist economy was to be extremely simple. For simplicity, Lange assumed the existence of a public sector alone and ignored the private sector. The public sector itself was conceived as a system of three levels: industrial enterprises, branch associations in the form of industry trusts, and a central planning board. Economic management was to be separated from the political apparatus of the state. Enterprises and trusts were to be directed by "public officials" subject to "democratically organized control." A Supreme Economic Court was to supervise the entire economy to ensure that it functioned in accordance with the public interest.

The actual functioning of the future economy was to be equally simple and intelligible. It was based on the coexistence of two markets—a real market in the institutional sense and a market simulated by the central planning board. This combination was intended to provide free choice in consumption and occupation and also to make enterprises largely autonomous. Prices of consumer goods and wages were to be freely determined by the market, while prices of capital goods were to be set by the central planning board. The central planners were also to ensure that enterprises and trusts followed two rules: they were to choose factors of production in such a way that average costs were at the lowest possible level, and they were to set the volume of output in the industry as a whole at a level where marginal cost was equal to price. The first of these two rules was designed to help eliminate less effective alternatives; the latter was envisaged as a substitute for the free-entry rule in a private, competitive economy. Both were to function as substitutes for profit maximization. The central planning board was to use interest rates to determine the amount of national income to be allocated to accumulation.

Leaving aside the numerous interpretations of this model, many of them highly critical, it should be noted that Lange's classical model has most often been challenged on account of its lack of realism. Critics have doubted that production managers would keep to the two chief rules unless the central planning board had some means of forcing them to do so. On this issue, liberals and socialists have been in agreement. Referring to the trial-and-error method of simulating a capital-goods market, socialists have usually attacked Lange's model on the grounds that it abandons planning. Liberals, on the other hand, have argued that the central planning board would get bogged down in red tape and would be unable to react quickly enough to market signals, and that the economy would thus become too rigid.

In the second half of the book, Lange anticipated some of the criticisms that would later be directed at his work. For example, he wrote: "The real danger of socialism is that of the bureaucratization of economic life and not the impossibility of coping with the problem of resources."[2] He considered his own model of socialism also open to such danger, although less so than the centralized models. Comparing this aspect of his socialist model with the capitalism of large corporations, he added that the latter was open to the same or even greater danger and that "officials subject to democratic control seem preferable to private corporation executives who practically are responsible to nobody." Kornai is unjust, then, when he writes that the Lange of the thirties "lived in a sterile world of Walrasian pure theory and did not consider the socio-political underpinning of his basic assumptions."[3]

It is, however, a fact that Lange underestimated at that time the scale of the perceived danger and that it was precisely this danger that made the issue of the allocation of resources such a horrendously difficult problem. These are not two separate issues but two aspects of the same problem.

The basic weakness of both the Lange-Breit model and Lange's model is their static character. The person who summed this up most concisely was Lange's teacher at Harvard, Joseph Schumpeter: "A system . . . that at every given point of time fully utilizes its possibilities to the best advantage may yet in the long run be inferior to a system that does so at no given point in time, because the latter's failure to do so may be a condition for the level or speed of long-run performance."[4] Further: "The problem that is usually being visualized is how capitalism administers existing structures, whereas the relevant problem is how it creates and destroys them. As long as this is not recognized, the investigator does a meaningless job."[5]

Lange touched on this problem. He was on the right track when he wrote:

> The really important point in discussing the economic merits of socialism is not that of comparing the equilibrium position of a socialist and capitalist economy with respect to social welfare. Interesting as such a comparison is for the economic theorist, it is not the real issue in the discussion of socialism. The real issue is whether the further maintenance of the capitalist system is compatible with economic progress.[6]

Not only was Lange too pessimistic regarding the future of capitalism (in this he followed the example of his teacher), but, even worse, he did not raise the same question regarding the possibility of technical and economic progress in a socialist economy. It should be remembered, however, that Lange was dissatisfied with this work, and the subsequent evolution of his views led to his dramatic disavowal of the study that earned him world fame. Papers published after his death reveal the following story.

In early 1945 the University of Minnesota Press suggested publishing *On the Economic Theory of Socialism* in an updated version, together with several other essays. The first edition was no longer available; demand for the work remained high, as it was required reading for many college courses; and, the publishers argued, a new edition would afford Lange an opportunity to discuss Hayek's controversial work, *The Road to Serfdom*.

At first, Lange accepted the offer, promising to rewrite two chapters and add one on full employment. However, a couple of weeks later he sent the publishers the following letter:

> The essay is so far removed from what I would write on the subject today that I am afraid any revision would produce a very poor compromise, unrepresentative of my thoughts. Thus, I am inclined to let the essay go out of print and to express my views in a completely new form. I am writing a book on economic theory in which a chapter will be devoted to this subject. This may be better than trying to rehash old stuff.[7]

It is baffling, then, that the surviving list of fifteen chapters of the book that he then began to write contains not a single chapter entitled "socialism" or "the socialist economy." What was it that caused Lange to consider his classical work "old stuff"?

**Toward the Model of a Mixed Economy**

Probably the most important factor that caused him to change his views was his encounter with America. Lange's time in the United States coincided with the four-term presidency of Franklin D. Roosevelt. While fascism and war raged across Europe, the United States underwent an unusual spiritual and economic renaissance. This spiritual revival was partly due to the fact that during the period of the New Deal the United States provided a haven for political refugees from Europe. These refugees, including many Poles, found not only material financial support but also a place for social and political activity. The new immigrants contributed not only to American industry, particularly the military sector, not only to science and technology, but also to intellectual life, to which they brought many new ideas and proposals for reforms. Lange agreed with the description of the United States at that time as "the arsenal of democracy."

Lange's entire life was an exceptionally productive one, but his years in the United States were particularly rich in scholarly and sociopolitical activities. Not only did he make a rapid academic career for himself, but he immediately joined the struggle to restrict the economic and social might of large corporations, to make the New Deal program more coherent and long-lasting, and to broaden and secure the economic basis of democracy. Lange saw the New Deal as the beginning of a permanent policy of full employment. It was from this perspective that he viewed also the problem of mobilizing the American economy for the needs of war and its subsequent transformation to meet the needs of peacetime.

At the same time, Lange implicitly abandoned—at least in relation to the United States—his views of the 1930s regarding the unreformability of capitalism. His former argument for the overthrow of this system thus lost its validity, and socialism began to appear as a distant result of an evolutionary process. In a book that Lange wrote with Abba Lerner, *The American Way of Doing Business* (1944), all references to socialism were reduced to demands for the socialization of the largest corporations and for policies that would increase social welfare.

In an article entitled *"Ekonomiczne podstawy demokracji w Polsce"* ("The Economic Foundations of Democracy in Poland"), written in 1943, Lange's previous vision of a socialism that accorded a dominant, and eventually exclusive, role to public ownership was replaced by one that envisaged the socialization of large-scale industry only. Both medium- and small-scale industry were to remain in private hands, and the maintenance of such a structure of ownership was to be one of the goals of the state's credit policy. Lange argued for such a combination of ownership forms on the grounds that it would contribute both to democracy (the diffusion of ownership and thus of economic power) and to economic efficiency. The private sector, he wrote, gives the entire economy "a pliability and flexibility as well as an adaptive capability that private initiative alone can give."[8]

In many of his writings, Lange expressed his concern to reduce further the scope of central administrative intervention in the economy. He abandoned the demand contained in his model that the center be free to set the rate of accumulation. In a letter responding to criticism voiced by Hayek (1940), Lange wrote that his suggestion to empower the central planning board to fix capital-goods prices had been a methodological trick rather than a practical demand. In actual practice, said Lange, he would recommend free price-setting by the market wherever possible (where non-oligopolistic markets existed). He promised to explain this in an article that he planned to write but never did. In a series of public lectures entitled "On the Economic Operation of a Socialist Society," given in 1942,[9] Lange abandoned the idea of the state setting capital-goods prices, an idea that many of his critics considered to be the essence of his model.

In general, then, it can be said that Lange's initial sharp distinction between socialist and capitalist economies was subsequently eroded. Lange prepared the theoretical ground for the concept of the convergence of the two systems long before this concept became commonplace.

## The Central Planner and the Reformer

In the West, and more recently in Poland, the following question is frequently asked: how was it possible that one of the founders of neoclassical economics and what is commonly called the Keynesian revolution, an advocate of market socialism with a highly limited role for the socialized sector, a socialist who strongly emphasized the need for, and the dangers to, freedom, could return to a country governed by Communists who wielded power on behalf of Moscow? Why did this liberal socialist support a Communist regime, why did he contribute to the creation of central planning in its Soviet version, why did he become one of its theoreticians, and why did he subsequently try to reform it, albeit in a direction far removed from his earlier radical ideas?

Without considering all aspects of this question, I would draw attention to the most important ideas that inclined Lange to such cooperation. Let us try to answer the question of how he reconciled his economic views with his participation in a Communist system.

There are grounds for believing that, initially at least, Lange was convinced that Soviet communism was undergoing a profound transformation toward the kind of system that he advocated. To use the language of today, it could be said that Lange already then perceived the social-democratization of Communism. He expressed such views in the course of a dispute with Paul Sweezy in 1943 (Lange's letters to Sweezy were published only in Polish translation in the seventies, in his *Works*). Lange wrote that the program of the Union of Polish Patriots in the USSR (which subsequently created the postwar Communist regime in Poland) had abandoned all Marxist terminology. The program attacked monopolies rather than private property as such, it demanded the transfer of power to "the people" rather than the working class, it stressed the need for continuity in culture, and so on. In the Soviet Union itself, the war was leading to similar processes. In Lange's view, these corresponded to the changes taking place in the West, where fascism and monopoly capitalism had eliminated the division between the working class and the peasantry on the one hand and the lower strata of the middle classes on the other and where all were now united in the struggle against imperialism.

Lange viewed the administrative system of economic planning and management in the Soviet Union as the result of the economy's subordination to political goals—the waging of war on two fronts: war against imperialism and civil war against technological and economic backwardness. Defining the Soviet economy as a kind of war economy, Lange believed that after winning both wars, and given conditions of international peace and cooperation, the Soviet Union would abandon administrative coercion in favor of an economy based on market mechanisms.

It was this conviction that determined his attitude toward the Soviet Union. Lange liked to say that he had never been a Communist and that, like the Mensheviks, he had no illusions that the Bolsheviks would construct socialism. But this did not prevent him from recognizing that the Soviet Union might develop toward democracy and socialism in the future.

Lange did not exclude the possibility that the Stalinist regime would degenerate further if the international situation obliged the Soviet Union to continue arming itself and to engage in forced industrialization based entirely on its own resources. Nevertheless, he saw his mission as being to promote rapprochement in the postwar era and thus to increase the possibilities for democratic development in the Soviet Union. This is what he told his colleagues at the University of Chicago when they urged him not to abandon his academic career for a diplomatic one. He added that he knew both worlds better than most people and could help to build bridges in troubled times. Of course, he was not certain that he was right. Sometimes he linked his fate to socialist revolution in the West. (When Lange returned to Poland he is supposed to have told a friend: "Either there will be revolution in the West or I shall end up in Siberia.")

More often, however, Lange expressed the hope that restrictions on Poland's independence imposed by Moscow would be confined largely to foreign policy and that the country would have substantial freedom in domestic affairs. He took at face value Stalin's assurance that he wanted a strong and independent Poland. In the immediate postwar period, a number of factors seemed to confirm such hopes. The Polish road to socialism, proclaimed by the Communists, involved a limited political pluralism. Other political parties were allowed to function, including the Polish Socialist party, with Lange as one of its ideologists. Lange entertained similar hopes in 1946–47, although by then such hopes were certainly growing fainter. He published his antistatist program for a mixed economy with limited socialization of industry, and he cooperated in preparing for publication a Polish version of his book *On the Economic Theory of Socialism* (which did not actually appear until the beginning of the 1960s).

Lange's real drama began (or perhaps only then revealed itself) in 1948 several months after his return to Poland from New York where he had served as Poland's temporary representative to the United Nations Security Council. This was a year in which there was mounting evidence of the increasing Sovietization and Stalinization of Eastern and Central Europe. In the economy, this was signalled by the program of forced industrialization and militarization, by the collectivization of agriculture, and by the shift to highly centralized planning. All possibilities for a mixed economy with a limited role for central planning were eradicated. For Lange this was undoubtedly a personal catastrophe. But he continued to cooperate with the Communists; he was a member of the party leadership, a member of parliament, and the rector of the most important higher educational institution in the field of economics. In all these positions, however, "he ruled but did not govern." This was the case, for example, with his presidency of the Central Cooperative Union, a position that he held at a time when the cooperative movement was completely subordinate to the state administration.

The Communists frequently made use of Lange's international prestige to lend luster to various propaganda exercises. The greatest of these was the International Conference on Economic Cooperation, which Lange organized in Moscow in 1952, at the height of the cold war. One of the strangest of Lange's acts, and one of the hardest to explain, was his apologetic writing about Stalin's pamphlet, *On the Economic Problems of Socialism in the USSR.*

It is difficult to explain Lange's cooperation with the Communists during their worst period. Numerous factors were at work. One of these was purely human—Lange's fear for his own life. When I asked him once why he had written those apologias for Stalin, Lange replied indirectly: in 1953 he had sent greetings to a foreign friend who had inquired through an intermediary, "Is Lange still alive?" But this was clearly only part of the explanation. Lange had certain intellectual reasons for considering cooperation with the Communists worthwhile.

Lange thought that the Soviet Union, although politically repugnant, constituted an effective system for economic modernization. Eventually there would emerge a modern society with a rapidly changing social structure. Stalinism would thus dig its own grave by giving birth to social forces that would destroy the dictatorship of the bureaucracy and democratize the system. Forced industrialization, together with the revolution in education, would create a new working class and "socialist intelligentsia." These two social forces would adapt the authoritarian superstructure to the demands of modern forces of production. Events in the Soviet Union following the death of Stalin and in Poland after 1956 seemed to confirm Lange's theory (which he derived from the work of the Austrian social democrat Otto Bauer). Thus, shortly after Khrushchev's speech denouncing Stalin and the workers' revolt in Poznan, Lange began to play a major role in the reform movement. He became the revisionists' idol, proclaiming the need for democratization and economic decentralization. It is interesting that he did not, however, return to his idea of market socialism. In renouncing his earlier work, he went so far as to forbid its publication in Polish. In private conversations he justified this on the grounds that he did not want to lend his support to proponents of "socialist laissez-faire."

It seems to me that there were two major reasons for his rejection of his previous model. First, Lange had come to the conclusion that the visions of would-be reformers are worth little when compared with social experience. Asked in 1956 to say "How I See the Polish Economic Model" (the title of one of his most programmatic statements during this period), he stated:

> It cannot be formulated from above or worked out at a conference table. It stems from the great movement toward socialist democracy, which has permeated the country, from the setting up of workers' self-management, from the renewal of the self-governing cooperative movement, from the search for new forms of self-management and of social initiative among farmers.[10]

Second, there was a theoretical reason for Lange's change of mind. His own observations and studies had brought him to the belief that the market should be subject to debureaucratized scientifically based central planning; that market mechanisms ought to be a tool in the hands of central planners and that their operation should be subordinated to the need to determine consciously the direction of economic development; that decisions concerning the scale of investment and even the level of many prices ought to belong to the central planners. Lange's proposals for economic reform can be summed up as central planning plus decentralized management.

In line with this approach, Lange's chief concern became to "enlighten" central planners, to equip them with modern tools of analysis, forecasting, and planning. This was the main thrust of all his works at this time (with the exception of his *Ekonomia polityczna* [*Political Economy*]), such as *Wstep do ekonometrii (Introduction to Econometrics), Optymalne decyze (Optimal Decision Making),* and *Wstep do cybernetki eknomicznej (An Introduction to Economic Cybernetics).* In the last ten years of his life, Lange was fascinated by what Benjamin Ward has so accurately termed the "formalist revolution" and Egon

Neuberger, "computopia." This fascination, expressed in his definition of the market as a calculating machine of the pre-electronic era, was all the stranger in that Lange perceived with ever-increasing clarity the emergence of social processes leading to long-term stagnation. He attributed these, however, to the backwardness of the Polish ruling group and not to deeper systemic factors inherent in the very concept of central planning in conditions of a highly developed system of needs and division of labor.

## Market Socialism: Utopia or Missed Opportunity?

Let us try to answer this question as briefly as possible. With one exception (about which more below), none of the countries in Eastern Europe adopted the model of market socialism to the extent necessary to allow us to say that it has been tested in practice. Hungarian economists (especially János Kornai) have shown that even in the best period of the Hungarian reform of 1968, market mechanisms were more a passive than an active tool of the central planning agency and were subordinated to its preferences. Polish reform efforts were even further removed from Lange's model.

Some people consider the Yugoslav model an exception (although Yugoslav economists claim that it was conceived without reference or even knowledge of Lange's model and others similar to it). There is some truth to this assertion, given the Yugoslavs' far-reaching decentralization, reduction in the role of central planning, and reliance on self-management, to which Lange attached great importance.

In my opinion, the failure of the Yugoslav model cannot be taken as proof of the failure of the very concept of market socialism. The model contains many other defects of far greater significance than the conceptual defects of Lange's model, and it was these that led to the failure of this system. Two of them are of particular significance. After 1965, economic decentralization and the abandonment of macroeconomic policy went beyond the bounds of rationality in Yugoslavia. To many Western specialists, Yugoslavia is more reminiscent of "the type of liberal market economy envisioned by Adam Smith than is the case in any country of Western Europe."[11] This is inconsistent with

Lange's model, which is based, as we have seen, on a combination of "visible and invisible hands."

Second, it is difficult to reconcile either market mechanisms or self-management with the leading role of the Communist Party. Party officials have intervened in both these institutions so frequently and to such a degree that "political investment" and "political prices" have become common phenomena. Lange, on the other hand, demanded a strict division between the system of economic planning and management and the political system in the narrow sense of the term. Even if his model contained a clearly utopian (unrealistic) element, the Yugoslav model went to the other extreme in its politicization of the economy. Between the two there is room for a whole range of less extreme possibilities.

In general, then, I do not think that the Yugoslav experience offers conclusive evidence regarding the viability of market socialism.

Thus, a more fundamental question arises: why has not a single country in Eastern Europe succeeded in introducing a form of market socialism that would have worked? One possible answer is that bureaucratic power elites, protecting their vested interests, have successfully opposed such a system. If this is the case, however, why has market socialism not been advanced as an alternative to the Communist systems that have been collapsing all around us during the past year?

A complete answer to this question would demand a separate article, if not an entire book. All I can do here is express a general opinion. The current convulsions in Eastern and Central Europe are, above all, of a negative kind. Their aim is to bring about the most radical possible rejection of the universally hated Communist system. The craze for Thatcherism and Reaganomics is based largely on the fact that they appear to be at the opposite end of the political and economic spectrum from this system. Their popularity can also be attributed in part to the fact that the Communists have destroyed the noncommunist socialist and social democratic left. A more sober assessment of the social and economic cost of the therapy adopted from the West will come only when we have mass unemployment and slums, when we have shocking inequalities in incomes and in access to education and health care. From a purely pragmatic point of view, the evolution of Communist systems toward some form of market socialism (with much greater pluralism of forms of ownership than envisaged in Lange's classical model) would be the easiest and least destabilizing path to take. For political reasons, however, such a choice is unlikely to be made in the near future.

Translated from the Polish by Jane Cave.

## Notes

1. János Kornai, "The Hungarian Reform Process: Visions, Hopes, and Reality," *Journal of Economic Literature* 24, no. 4 (December 1986), p. 1727.

2. Oskar Lange and Fred M. Taylor, *On the Economic Theory of Socialism,* ed. B. E. Lippincott (New York: McGraw-Hill, 1964), p. 109.

3. Kornai, "The Hungarian Reform Process," p. 1727.

4. Joseph Schumpeter, *Capitalism, Socialism, and Democracy* (New York: Harper and Row, 1962), p. 83.

5. Ibid., p. 84.

6. Oskar Lange and Fred M. Taylor, *On the Economic Theory of Socialism,* p. 110.

7. Oskar Lange, *Dziela*, Vol. 2 (Warsaw, 1973), p. 553.

8. Oskar Lange, "Ekonomiczne podstawy demokracji w Polsce," in *Dziela,* Vol. 2, p. 472.

9. *Contributions to Political Economy* 6 (1987), p. 324.

10. Oskar Lange, *Papers in Economics and Sociology* (Warsaw, 1970), p. 439.

11. David Granick, *Enterprise Guidance in Eastern Europe* (Princeton: Princeton University Press, 1975), p. 25.

# The Turning Point: A Review of Brus and Laski, *From Marx to the Market*\*

## (Winter 1991)

## *David Belkin*

American socialism has endured many crises. But these have mostly been, or appeared to be, crises of agency and strategy, brought on by repeated failures to build the movement or by capitalism's disconcerting capacity to emerge strengthened from depression and war. However, if we couldn't find our way, at least we remained sure of our goal: a democratically controlled economy that either eliminated or subdued production for private gain. It was just—just!—a matter of getting there, not whether there *is* a "there."

In 1983 Alec Nove's *The Economics of Feasible Socialism* set off some alarm bells. For it was the work of an avowed socialist, and it went beyond the usual criticisms of Stalinist "deformations" and laid a significant part of the blame for the problems of the command planning model on Marx himself. And the Marxist axioms that Nove methodically dismantled—long sacrosanct beliefs concerning the feasibility of *ex ante* economic coordination and "produc-

---

\*Wlodzimierz Brus and Kazimierz Laski, *From Marx to the Market: Socialism in Search of an Economic System* (Oxford: Oxford University Press, 1989).

tion for use"—had in part animated *our* democratic planning schemes as well as *their* centralized bureaucratic approach.

The main target of Nove's attack was the Soviet system. He sketched out an alternative that, although including product and labor markets and even production for profit, also featured large measures of public and cooperative ownership and severely restricted private capitalist accumulation. Capital markets were excluded, and it could be reasonably argued that the principle of social determination of the basic contours of the economy was preserved. In the end, democratic socialists could take heart.

Nove's prescription reflected in part the work of a number of economists in Poland, Hungary, and Czechoslovakia who developed reform socialist models in the 1950s and 1960s. One of the most influential of these reformers was Wlodzimierz Brus, whose major works *(The Market in a Socialist Economy, Socialist Ownership and Political Systems,* and *The Economics and Politics of Socialism)* were translated and gained some currency in the West in the mid-1970s.

Brus was a committed Marxist who took the goal of socialization of production very seriously. In this respect, he found both the *étatist* planning practices of the Soviet Union and its satellites and the radical self-management approach of Yugoslavia wanting. Brus proposed another way, a combination of "central planning with regulated markets," with the plan's dominance secured through public ownership of the means of production and central allocation of capital. Genuine socialization would be attained "by ensuring the real participation of society in the taking of decisions at the center, that is, by a genuine democratization of the system for the exercise of state power."

Brus's model was based on the theoretical solution provided by Oskar Lange during the "socialist calculation" debates of the 1930s. Lange had set out to show that central planners in an economy without capital markets could correctly determine the prices of capital goods and that they could use these prices and a few simple "rules" effectively and unobtrusively to direct the activities of socialist enterprises into "optimal" channels.

What distinguished Brus's approach was his exceptional thoroughness in mapping out the conditions for realizing socialist values in an economic system. His model influenced the construction of the New

Economic Mechanism (NEM) in Hungary. It also fell within the mainstream of democratic socialist thinking in the West, although many Western leftists remained (and, of course, remain) suspicious of the market socialist label. So now, when Brus and his frequent collaborator, Kazimierz Laski, write a book that focuses intensively on the Hungarian and Yugoslav reforms and their theoretical underpinnings, we might expect the results to be of particular concern to democratic socialists everywhere.

And so they are. *From Marx to the Market* raises fundamental doubts about the premises of the regulated market and self-management alternatives that have been the basis for democratic socialism's rejection of both capitalist and "bureaucratic collectivist" economics. The book covers many critical questions concerning the scope for socialist economic policy; in this review I shall focus on the two that I think Brus and Laski regard as the most crucial: the question of the capital market and the question of ownership.

To remind us where we are coming from, Brus and Laski observe that

> whatever the strength of the negative position with regard to the market in general in orthodox Marxist theory, *the attitude towards the capital market must be that of outright and uncompromising rejection.* This is understandable enough, and obtains not merely on doctrinal grounds (the capital market, even limited to nonprivate participants, denies labor the alleged role of the ultimately single factor of production and the only legitimate nonexploitative source of income) but also because *socialization of capital, its allocation on behalf and in the interests of the community as a whole, represents the mainstay of the postulated economic superiority of socialism over capitalism.* [Emphasis added.]

Lange's solution in the 1930s debates, the East European reform models of Brus and others in the 1950s and 1960s, the Hungarian NEM after 1968, and Nove's proposal in *Feasible Socialism* all remained faithful to this most basic of socialist tenets: All postulated some sort of overt political control of at least the major investment flows of the economy, with individual enterprises retaining sovereignty only over decisions adjusting levels (not types) of current output and capacity.

On the other hand, the planning authorities were supposed to restrict their own activities to strategic investment decisions, selective price fixing, and determination of overall accumulation rates; they were to keep their noses out of the day-to-day operations of the firms—this was the major departure from the command approach—leaving the latter free to work out the most efficient responses to (plan-mediated) consumer demand, or to suffer the consequences if they did not. Brus and Laski argue in the most forceful terms that this envisioned (and in Hungary attempted) division of responsibility does not and cannot work.

This arrangement breaks down essentially because it blurs the responsibility for enterprise performance. First, an enterprise may do well or poorly financially because of distortions in prices fixed by the state. Second, if an enterprise is doing poorly but—having no access to a capital market—is unable to branch out on its own into new activities or otherwise redeploy its resources, it is hard to argue that this enterprise should be punished for its performance, that is, threatened with bankruptcy. Moreover, the threat of bankruptcy becomes moot because (again because of the absence of a capital market) there are no "free capitals" around to take over failed enterprises.

Under these circumstances, it really does not make much sense for the enterprise to pay too much attention to product quality, consumer demand, prospects for innovation, and the like. Instead, the enterprise winds up devoting most of its energy to securing the state dispensations (soft loans, price changes, tax exemptions, and so on) required to keep going regardless of its immediate financial condition; and the state, with little other real alternative, winds up granting most of what the firm is bargaining for. But usually, to protect its own interests, the state issues new instructions and restrictions which make the enterprise even less responsible for its own performance!

Thus Brus and Laski emphasize that it is not merely poor policy decisions or the twisted legacy of Stalinism, but *flaws in the basic design of the system* of "central planning with regulated markets," in particular its exclusion of a capital market, that perpetuate what Janos Kornai calls the "soft budget constraint" with all its debilitating effects.

In theory, Yugoslavia following the 1965 reforms was to have been different. As befits a full-fledged "labor-managed market economy," the responsibility for resource allocation and for determining the proportions of accumulation and personal consumption was to be shifted from the state to the self-managed firms. This implied a capital market (though only by any other name).

In reality, however, Yugoslavia's twin commitments to "societal" ownership of capital and direct labor as the only proper source of earnings made it hard to impose hard budget constraints and at the same time did not allow much latitude for investments by either the enterprises or their members. This resulted in chronic underinvestment, contributing to the relatively poor performance of the Yugoslav economy in the post-1965 market socialist period, and after a few years there was a turn toward more bureaucratic mechanisms of economic coordination.

As for the period of Yugoslav market socialism itself, Brus and Laski conclude that it "presents a case of an abortive attempt at introducing a limited capital market . . . rather than a case of deteriorating performance as a consequence of institutionalization of such a market."

Nowadays one doesn't hear too much talk about undivided public or state ownership of the means of production being a prerequisite for socialism. Instead, Western socialists tend to argue more in terms of public controls selectively aimed at the essential sectors (sometimes depicted as the "commanding heights") of the economy—but with the same object of effectively subordinating the whole to conscious planning. Brus and Laski remind us that the old preoccupation with nationalization was not just some accidental alien graft onto the body of socialism. On the contrary, it flowed immediately

> from the original socialist idea of "directly social labor," with its powerful stress on integration and cooperation as against separation and rivalry. . . . The formula of state ownership of the means of production as "ownership of the whole people" may have been used widely for propaganda purposes, but it reflected also the substantive concept of indivisibility of the object of public ownership, at least on a national scale. . . . The indivisibility of public ownership underlay the claim to the superior rationality of socialism.

The incorporation of capital markets (which, by the way, Nove now also endorses) threatens to breach this concept of indivisible public or social ownership in two ways. First, it requires that the state effectively separate itself from the economy, so that it is no more than "one of the actors"—rather than *the* actor—on the economic stage. This means a substantial transfer of the prerogatives of ownership to the individual enterprises.

Second, even supposing that it is possible to reconcile some notion of public ownership with enterprise independence, it remains an open question for Brus and Laski as to whether this can be the basis for bolstering *entrepreneurship* in the socialist economy. The essence of entrepreneurship is risk-taking, "the grasping of new opportunities," the deliberate creation of *dis*equilibrium—a facility the importance of which Lange never grasped. Entrepreneurial behavior has always been grounded in a sense of personal material risk, even, the authors argue, in the so-called managerial corporation of modern capitalism. This is precisely what is ultimately lacking in a system of public ownership where both the enterprise directors *and* their superiors in the state administration are agents rather than principals: where in the final analysis there are *no* personal principals. (There is a comparable dilution of personal responsibility under the Yugoslav system of "societal" ownership.)

The authors are not arguing that managers and workers in state-owned enterprises are never personally motivated to be innovative; they believe rather that a system of extensive state ownership doesn't adequately support such motives. They hold out more hope for a mixed system whose nonstate sector is large enough to provide meaningful competition for state-owned enterprises. Brus and Laski don't entirely abandon the concept of social ownership, but they suggest that socialism will require a "renunciation of any sort of ownership doctrinairism."

Twenty years ago, Brus asserted that "the question of socialization is decided not on the plane of 'depoliticization of the economy' but of 'democratization of politics.' " Similar formulations are indeed still recited by democratic socialists in the West. Now he and Laski declare that "the economy has to become depoliticized," and they support democratization "because no other guarantee can meaningfully exist for the maintenance of the depoliticization of the economy."

Depoliticization has a very specific meaning for Brus and Laski. It does not mean laissez-faire. It does not preclude enforcing environmental and safety standards for industry, remedying market failures by providing public goods (education, health, infrastructure, and so on), assuming responsibility for poverty, or conducting monetary and fiscal policies to stabilize employment. Depoliticization simply means that, given all of the above, the business of resource reallocation is for the most part conducted by relatively independent entrepreneurs through relatively competitive markets rather than by agents of an overriding state.

But what about economies that have never been, in the special sense given, politicized? Perhaps one could argue that the lessons drawn from the struggle for economic reform in Eastern Europe don't apply here, since the United States suffers from too much market, not too much state planning. It is clear, however, that Brus and Laski are addressing not just specific failures but underlying models of democratic socialism (note the subtitle of their book). The authors' prescription for enlarging the scope of marketization in the East is at the same time a warning to define better the limits of prospective extensions of state power over markets and enterprises in the West.

This applies in particular to the commonplace belief that the growth of the great multinationals and the widening scope of state interventions in the capitalist economy demonstrates an objective tendency toward the subordination of markets by rational control on a continuously expanding scale, so that it is only a question now of whether we will have corporatist or democratic control. This line of reasoning is confuted by one of the pivotal conclusions of Brus and Laski's analysis—that a critical threshold is crossed when planning seeks to broadly supplant, rather than selectively complement, markets as a means for resource reallocation.

On one side of this threshold is the large, multidivision private corporation. True, within such an organization vast numbers of economic transactions are shielded from the direct glare of the market. Nevertheless, "[E]ven under conditions of oligopolistic competition a large corporation still acts in a market environment and *cannot destroy the principal rules of the game.*" [Emphasis added.]

On the other side of this threshold would be a socialized state sector whose weight within the overall economy is so great that concerted action by this sector "would actually destroy the market and let in the command system by the back door." This sector, in other words, would ultimately lack what even imperfectly competitive markets provide, external reference points for judging the effectiveness of its actions. As the price for being "at the wheel" of the economy, the directors of the state sector would be forced to drive blindfolded.

Brus and Laski seem to leave us with no alternative but to try to specify a socialism that can be identified with, or at any rate accepts, substantial private (individual, share, or cooperative) ownership rights, real competition, and capital markets—in the authors' words, a genuine market socialism. But this requires a wrenching reorientation, for

> the distinctions between capitalist and socialist economic systems, as hitherto perceived, become under MS [market socialism] thoroughly blurred. If therefore marketization is accepted as the cure for the economic ills of "real socialism," not only the original Marxist promise has to be cast aside as anachronistic, but also the very concept of transition from capitalism to socialism. . . . The recourse to MS means that *socialism should actually cease to be perceived at all as a bounded system,* transcending the institutional framework developed in the past, and hence by definition postulating its total replacement by new institutional foundations, if not immediately so then in a longer perspective. The recourse to MS means, on the contrary, that the very idea of the grand design of a supremely rational economy has been acknowledged as utterly fallacious. [Emphasis added.]

It is evident that what the authors call market socialism bears a great resemblance to, and may be no more than, social democracy. But perhaps not. Without straying over the threshold discussed above, there are at least three initiatives that can be considered that might advance socialist values beyond the level proverbially realized in Sweden.

First, the state could establish a capacity for indicative planning (or industrial policy) that is democratic and inclusive. Under indicative planning, the state does not own or "run" the economy, but uses a variety of incentives to promote particular priorities. Perhaps paradoxically, such an approach may be more amenable to efforts to make economic policy democratically accountable than one in which direct public ownership is dominant and individual production decisions are politicized. But politicization presents problems even when the state is not burdened with a Sisyphean responsibility for directly or indirectly coordinating all economic activity. It is important to note that up till now the *absence* of public accountability, the clubby insulation of planners from conflicting pressures concerning the distributional implications of their schemes, has more often than not been deemed essential in conducting successful industrial policy (as in France or Japan). Establishing genuine public participation in this area would be an important breakthrough.

Second, the state could cultivate a delimited but vigorous role as *an* economic actor in its own right, not large enough to "destroy the rules of the game," but capable of mounting projects that the private sector can't or won't pursue.

Third, there could be a drive to support and extend the emerging tendency toward wider worker participation in decision making and ownership rights within enterprises. While a transition from state or "societal" ownership to cooperatives is a form of privatization (breaching the concept of "ownership of the whole people"), a transition from capitalist corporate ownership to cooperatives still embodies significant elements of socialization.

Together, these kinds of initiatives (and no doubt others) might point toward a socialism that doesn't need to be realized as "a bounded system," but which can abide as a perpetual restless "movement toward" rather than as a consummated end, with its aspirations for solidarity and participation and justice existing in ongoing, fruitful tension with the elements of competitive self-interest that also drive society.

*From Marx to the Market* is an unsparing portrayal of a socialism held spellbound by the "idea of the grand design of a supremely rational economy" in its many guises. What Brus and Laski demand and provide is, in the double sense of the word, a disenchantment, and for this they will not be much loved. Yet this book asks the reader to abandon only socialism's illusions, not its ideals. It points not to the certain end of our quest, but to an uncertain beginning.

# 8

# Socialism and Planning: Beyond the Soviet Economic Crisis

## (Winter 1991)

### Daniel Bell

Was the Soviet Union's a planned economy? The simple answer is no. Is a planned economy possible? That is a more difficult question to answer. Marx never had a theory of a planned economy, for he thought—from *The Communist Manifesto* to the penultimate chapter of Volume One of *Capital*—that capitalism would solve the problem of "production," that is, overcome scarcity through the "forces of production," restrained only by the private property "social relations of production," and that socialism was essentially a distributive problem to be solved cooperatively by the new, socialized owners of the means of production.

We now know that the issue of "production" may never be solved. There will probably always be more demand—new needs, new wants—for a limited amount of goods. Even if one distinguishes, as the late Fred Hirsch did, between "distributional" goods (those that can be multiplied easily) and "positional" goods (those that are intrinsically scarce, such as the number of houses on the top of a mountain), the allocative problem remains. And if scarce resources among competing individuals remain the issue, the question is whether a market system or a command system is to be preferred.

Historically, most goods were allocated by command, the distributions made by a Lord or the benefices (food and lodging) received by the monks. Money and the market (as Georg Simmel pointed out long ago) were the means of freedom because, with money, one could choose where to live and buy what one preferred. But if there is to be a market economy, then social justice requires a fair, not unequally skewed distribution of *income,* so that individuals can bid evenly against one another for the goods they desire. Within a highly skewed income distribution, the market allocates goods on the "weighted average" of money, which may be unjust, especially if the money is not earned. So if we are to have a market economy, we also need a definition of citizenship (what I have called "the public household") that permits individuals to participate fully, in the market as well as the polity, as members of a civil society. A market economy without a civil society is an individualistic monstrosity.

To return to the question, at least in principle, of a planned economy. If one accepts the fact that the problems of production and allocation remain, then it is also clear that such an economy can only be coordinated through a price system that accurately reflects the costs of resources both with respect to a "production function" (that is, the relative mix of capital and labor) and the supply and demand of consumer items at relative prices.

In the "pure" market system, these decisions are guided by consumers with respect to their preferences and by producers who provide supply in response to such demand. But what if these *markets* are skewed or rigid? Socialists put forth the proposal for planning from two theorems, one of which was patently wrong. The first was the idea of the "anarchy of the market." In his little book *The Living Thoughts of Marx,* Trotsky, in one of his characteristic aphorisms, advanced the argument that under capitalism each man thinks for himself, and no one thinks for all. But who is the "one" who could think for all? (We have here a curious economistic version of Rousseau's "general will.") No one.

But the second, more compelling argument was that under capitalism major industries tended toward monopoly or oligopoly and distorted prices or restricted production through administered controls, or that capitalist firms sought to exempt themselves from the hazards of the market through cartels or price-fixing rings. The curious fact is that before World War II few capitalists used the phrase "free enterprise." Most capitalists wanted planning of a corporatist kind. As Werner Sombart wrote of the period of "late capitalism" (in 1930!):

> The entrepreneurial group has been consciously striving for stability as in the cartels and trade associations. Public authorities have intervened to offset business fluctuations by withholding orders in periods of prosperity and granting them more generously in periods of depression; this policy will play an increasingly important role. "Stabilization of business" seems to be both the slogan and the accomplishment of this period.[1]

In the United States, during the depression in 1931, the head of General Electric, Gerard Swope, proposed "The Swope Plan," a corporatist model of the economy to provide a price floor for industry and to allocate market shares of production. This was taken over almost completely in the first days of the Roosevelt administration through the National Recovery Act (NRA), which set up industry codes and price fixing to provide stability for the system. The NRA was not opposed by the large capitalist firms; it was declared unconstitutional by the Supreme Court. Yet in particular industries this "cartelization" continued, such as with the famous "Pittsburgh Plus" system in the steel industry. Under this arrangement, a nationwide uniform price system was maintained throughout the country, so that even if a firm in Chicago ordered steel from a nearby mill, the price was based not on local costs but as from Pittsburgh plus transportation. So there was no economic advantage in ordering locally, and the large oligopolistic firms, such as U.S. Steel and Bethlehem, could dominate the industry. Again, it was the Supreme Court that declared the practice illegal. There are still today price floors for farmers in milk and agricultural products maintained by huge government subsidies. And while Jesse Helms may not like rent control, he does want price supports for tobacco.

The point of all this history is that socialists, such as Oskar Lange and A. P. Lerner, argued that distortions of production were inevitable under capitalism and that only under socialism could one have free markets and "consumer sovereignty"! But how is "economic calculation" possible in a socialist economy, as Ludwig von Mises set the challenge? Lange's answer, briefly put, is that "socialist administrators" would have the same information as "capitalist managers" and could "solve" the price equations on the basis of market-clearing trial-and-error adjustments. The implicit premise was that one set of coordinators was replacing another, but the socialist managers would be more "socially minded" than the capitalist ones and thus be more responsive to the commonweal. The technical economic issues apart, what Lange and other socialist economists ignored is what Max Weber stated in 1920: that a socialist society would be more bureaucratized than a capitalist one; and, as socialist "practice" showed, government bureaucrats and socialist factory managers were more mindful of their own interests—the pollution of the environment is the gravest illustration of all—than of the commonweal.[2]

To return to the Soviet economy. As I have indicated, the Soviet economy was never a planned economy but a mobilized economy with two fundamental deficiencies. It targeted physical outputs (for example, tonnage of steel) and used a system of material balances to measure the success of achievement with no measure of actual costs. And the lack of an interest-rate mechanism (because of dogma, derived from Marx, that interest was usurous and exploitative) meant that it could not measure the true costs of capital and make allocations efficiently.[3]

In principle, the mobilized economy was little different from the wartime economy of the War Production Board in the United States and the Ministry of Supply in the United Kingdom. What one also had was planning by physical targets—the number of planes, ships, tanks required—and the control and allocation of key materials (such as steel, copper, tin) to designated factories along with the control of wages and prices. In wartime there is a recognition of the role of the government as the major "consumer" shaping production for some specified needs. But there is also the recognition that such a centralized system would be impossible in a diverse and free economy that would be responsive to individual "consumer sovereignty."

In Soviet history there are some important lessons, as much for the idea of planning as for the necessity of markets. They are the lessons of complexity and growth.

In retrospect, it is extraordinary how simple-minded were the notions of planning that first guided the Soviet economy. In December 1920, "Goelro," the State Commission for the Electrification of Russia ("Communism," said Lenin in a famous phrase, "is the Soviet power plus the electrification of the whole country"), set forth the first, single economic plan for the country. It is "a genuinely scientific plan," wrote Lenin:

> We have the precise calculation of the experts ... for every branch of industry. We have—one small example—a calculation of the production of footwear at the rate of two pairs per person (300,000,000 pairs). ... We have a material and financial (in gold rubles) balance sheet of electrification (about 370,000,000 working days, so many barrels of cement, so many bricks, so many poods of iron, copper, etc., the power of the turbogenerators, etc.).

The "precise calculations" were, of course, wild guesses based on a primitive kind of economic arithmetic, a point of view as "sophisticated" as the statement of Lenin earlier in *State and Revolution* that running the administration of the state was as complex as running the post office!

By 1921 the Soviet economy was in chaos and on the brink of disintegration, and Lenin realistically retreated to the New Economic Policy (NEP). The indiscriminate requisitioning of peasant produce was abolished, and peasants were allowed to sell freely part of their surplus; small-scale and medium-scale industry and trade were denationalized, and the bulk of the nationalized large-scale enterprises was put on the basis of "cost accounting." The measures worked. The marketable output of agriculture rose 65 percent from 1922 to 1925. The output of large-scale industry, which had fallen to 14 percent of its prewar level by 1920, rose to 75 percent by 1925, and so on. Yet there were problems as well, notably a "repressed inflation" by 1925 that was threatening to tear the economy apart. And the slackening of industrial output was leading to the argument that new measures for industrialization were necessary. In Soviet parlance there was the need for transition from "restoration" (which was NEP) to "reconstruction"—*perestroika;* the word was used at the time.

From 1925 to 1928 the great Soviet industrialization debate took place in the Soviet Union. What is remarkable is how clearly each side understood the consequences of its positions. One argument, advanced by Bukharin (designated as "the right"), was to mollify the peasants ("Enrichissez-vous," he said, consciously echoing Guizot's famous remark—revolutionists always used metaphors from the past), who would be encouraged by economic incentives to "grow into social-ism." Capital investment in industry had to be limited to what the peasantry would tolerate, if Soviet power was to be consolidated. The "left" point of view, advanced by Preobrazhensky (supported covertly by Trotsky), self-consciously advanced the formula of "primitive so-cialist accumulation," on the model of Marx's "primitive capitalist accumulation," as described in Part VIII of Volume One of *Capital*: breaking peasant "autarky," squeezing out the small traders, raising capital by state manipulation of prices, and funneling all investment into heavy industry and electrical energy.[*4]

Stalin, at first, for political reasons, sided with Bukharin against Trotsky and, following that victory, turned against Bukharin. The crux of the turn, for Stalin knew how recalcitrant the wily peasant could be, was the forced collectivization of agriculture, the famine in the Ukraine, and the deportation and murder of tens of thousands of "kulaks." The forced industrialization had begun its long march. But industrialization, driven from a center, has its limits, and by the 1960s the Soviet economy had begun its long period of deceleration and stagnation.

Curiously, in the United States, twenty-five years before, there had been a theory of maturity and stagnation. These were the pronounce-ments of Alvin Hansen of Harvard, building on the TNEC mono-graphs of the late 1930s (mostly written by left-wing economists led by Paul Sweezy) and the theory of oversavings of Keynes. In his 1941 work, *Fiscal Policies and Business Cycles*, Hansen argued that we

---

[*]As Preobrazhensky admitted, the "law of value," which governs the operation of the competitive market and makes the exchange ratio between goods depend upon the relative amounts of "socially necessary labor" contained in them, had to be suppressed as far as possible. What it meant was a shift of resources to the state sector, by manipulation and compulsion, over and above what the latter could obtain as a result of the operation of the law of value in a competitive market. This, as Alexander Erlich points out, "was what the famous 'law of primitive socialist accumulation' actually amounted to."

were beached at the end of a series of long waves, as well as a decline in population growth, the disappearance of new territory for expansion, and the growth of monopoly, which inhibited the introduction of new machinery and investment.

The man who broke the back of that argument was Joseph Schumpeter, also at Harvard. For Schumpeter, economic growth was a function of two forces, neither of which was integral to neoclassic economic theory: technology and the role of the entrepreneur. In *Capitalism, Socialism and Democracy,* written in 1942 but receiving critical attention only four years later with a new edition, Schumpeter wrote that "technological possibilities are an uncharted sea," and it is technology, as utilized by the entrepreneur, that prompts economic growth. Keynes, said Schumpeter, dealt with "phenomena whose range was limited by his assumption that techniques of production remain unchanged." But it was just the fact that techniques of production do change rapidly under capitalism that was decisive for Schumpeter.[*5]

If anyone had located the "secret" of growth, it was Schumpeter in his emphasis on the need of an economic system flexibly combining technological and market forces to shift capital and resources into the more productive sectors generated by the new technologies—as amply demonstrated by Japan in the past thirty years in moving successively from light industry (textiles and apparel) to heavy industry (steel, auto, shipbuilding) to instruments (optical goods) and, in the last decade and a half, into knowledge-intensive electronics, computer, and telecommunications sectors.

What, then, if any, is the role of planning? The price system is a mechanism for the relative allocation of goods and services within the framework of the existing distribution of income and the cultural patterns of socially shaped monetary demands. What ultimately provides the direction for the economy, as Veblen pointed out long ago, is not the price system but the value system in which the economy is embedded.

---

[*]Yet Schumpeter, with typical Central European *weltschmerz,* felt that capitalism was doomed—doomed by the hostility of the intellectuals, "the new class," and by the bureaucratization of business, what J. K. Galbraith later called the "technostructure" that would atrophy the entrepreneurial function.

How can one establish the parameters of an economy if one wishes to see what *other* patterns may prevail with *other* values? In 1959, the Russian mathematical economist Leonid Kantorovich (who in the 1940s worked out a technique of linear programming that, independently, was also worked out by George Dantzig at the Rand Corporation) wrote a volume, *The Best Use of Economic Resources* (published in English in 1964 by Harvard University Press), in which he sought to show that with mathematical models and high-speed computers, one could write a single economic plan for the country that would, through Leontieff input-output matrices, provide the optimal distribution of economic resources with valuations of production corresponding to full economic costs. But as we now know, given the nature of bureaucracies, the administrative difficulties in implementing it would probably be insuperable, and in practice the market would have to be the mechanism whereby the economy would run.

Yet "planning" could remain as a *normative economic tool,* a shadow *"tableau economique"* to model different paths of growth and different assumptions of optimality and cost, against which the actual economy could be judged. One could play, in the planning models, different kinds of non-zero-sum games to see the different outcomes in the distribution of goods and services and different growth paths in the economy.[6]

Planning thus becomes a series of *what ifs,* a set of different "games" to judge and debate different policy actions and their consequences. Much as "perfect competition" and "general equilibrium" become heuristic tools to measure the adequacy of economic efficiency as means, so planning models become a tool of "utopia," a way of setting forth different assumptions of distributive justice—from Rawlsian maximin to Pareto-optimalities—and seeing how far the existing economies, based on the power and income relations that exist, depart from those assumptions.

A modest role, perhaps. But we need to live in modest times.[7]

## Notes

1. Werner Sombart, "Capitalism," in the *Encyclopedia of the Social Sciences* (New York: The Macmillan Company, 1930), p. 208. A more telling indictment of capitalism, now familiar today under the rubric of market imperfections, was the argument put forth by Oskar Lange (building on the work of A. C. Pigou) that private enterprise does not pay the social costs generated by its activities. As Lange wrote:

An economic system based on private enterprise can take but very imperfect account of the alternatives sacrificed and realized in production. . . . A socialist economy would be able to put *all* the alternatives into its economic accounting . . . it would be able to convert its social overhead costs into prime costs. By doing so it would avoid much of the social waste connected with private enterprise. [On the Economic Theory of Socialism, Minneapolis: University of Minnesota Press, 1938, p. 104.]

Lange is right, but what we have learned, as in the costs of the environment and pollution, is that corrections can be undertaken in a *democratic* society through legislative intervention.

2. For a recent reprise of the Lange-von Mises debate, see Robert Heilbroner, "Analysis and Vision in the History of Modern Economic Thought," *Journal of Economic Literature* 28, no. 3 (September 1990), pp. 1097–1114.

3. Marx was aware of the problems of allocation of resources in a socialist economy (as is evident in a letter to Kugelmann in 1868). But he thought of *labor* as the only kind of scarce resource to be distributed between different uses and wanted to solve the problem by the labor theory of value. Clearly, this is wrong. And in Soviet planning, as I have indicated in the footnote reference to Preobrazhensky, even the "law of value" was "suspended" in order to exploit labor for the purposes of "primitive accumulation."

4. For a comprehensive review of this crucial controversy, see Alexander Erlich, *The Soviet Industrialization Debate, 1924–1928* (Cambridge: Harvard University Press, 1960).

5. For an early discussion of Schumpeter's themes, see my essay "The Prospects of American Capitalism," in *The End of Ideology* (New York: The Free Press, 1960; reprinted with an Afterword, Cambridge: Harvard University Press, 1988), especially pp. 80–85. See, too, the appreciation by Robert Heilbroner in "Analysis and Vision in the History of Modern Economic Thought."

6. In a recent, unpublished paper on "Growth Theory," Robert M. Solow recalls the idea of planning as a normative idea. He writes:

There was an alternative, frankly normative tradition, dating back to Frank Ramsey [the famous Cambridge University logician and mathematician, 1903–30]. Instead of asking how such and such an economy *would* behave, one asked how it *should* behave if its goal were to maximize a time-additive utility functional dependence only on the time-path of consumption per person. This "optimal growth" problem was generally treated as a planning exercise. The possibility of decentralizing it through the operation of intertemporal prices occurred naturally to modern economists, though it had not been part of Ramsey's mental furniture. Even with this refinement, it remained a planning exercise.

I am grateful to Mr. Solow for permission to quote this pregnant paragraph.

7. For a discussion of economic theory as a normative device, see my essay "Models and Reality in Economic Discourse," in Daniel Bell and Irving Kristol, eds., *The Crisis in Economic Theory* (New York: Basic Books, 1981), pp. 46–80.

# 9

# From Sweden to Socialism?
# An Exchange

## (Winter 1991)

### Robert Heilbroner and Joanne Barkan

**Robert Heilbroner**

I have recently posed a question to which I have no answer, but which seems to me to go to the heart of the outlook for democratic socialism, at least in the advanced capitalist countries. The question is: how far beyond the borders of what I call "real but slightly imaginary Sweden" would we have to go before a visitor to that land knew that he or she was in a socialist, not a capitalist, country?

Let me suggest some of the more obvious answers—and the problems they raise:

1. A small number of large corporations constitute the dynamic core of the Swedish economy. Would these corporations have to go? With what would they be replaced? The one thing we know is that they should not be nationalized. Then how governed? Or if dismantled, into what sorts of units, themselves how governed?

2. Sweden has a large and generous public sector. Its purpose, however, is to provide the amenities needed in a capitalist economy, not those of a socialist society. The difference, I should think, is

that a socialist public sector would aim at "decommodifying" labor—removing the necessity for performing unwelcome work. If so, how would these wide-ranging entitlements be provided? What would be their effect on economic and social life?

3. Sweden is closely entwined in the world capitalist market. To extricate itself would require an extensive change—I will not say "fall"—in its living standards. Wasteful private consumption would have to yield to economical public consumption, automobiles making way for busses and trains, washing machines for laundromats. How can a population that clearly enjoys its wasteful standard way of life be persuaded to make such a change?

4. Bourgeois life itself may be a matter of concern. Sweden is a highly pragmatic, comfort-minded, nonideological place. Is that a culture that socialism would seek? What other?

There are no doubt many ways in which Sweden would have to change before the imaginary land to which we refer was unmistakably socialist. To indicate those ways, and to consider their economic and political costs, seems to me the manner in which democratic socialists should measure the challenge of the coming decades.

Irving Howe adds: *Let me supplement Bob Heilbroner's cogent questions with another, perhaps preliminary to his, which our critics, and perhaps some friends, would ask: if we imagine so advanced and attractive a welfare state as the "Sweden-plus" that he postulates, would there be any reasons still to wish to move further toward a socialist society? If so, what would those reasons be?*

**Joanne Barkan**

Poking around Slightly-Imaginary-Sweden (SIS), even the skeptical socialist is impressed. A solidaristic wage policy (centralized bargaining to achieve equal pay for equal work nationwide) forces unproductive enterprises to shape up or go under. This boosts overall economic efficiency. Strong tax incentives pull profits into reinvestment, further raising productivity and creating jobs. Intelligent labor market policies (job training and placement, subsidies for worker relocation, and so on) hold unemployment down to statistically irrelevant levels.

Because the transition to new jobs is eased, a powerful democratic labor movement cooperates in industrial rationalization, once again increasing efficiency and growth. Surplus from this dynamic economy is used to protect the environment. The surplus also supports a system of universal, high quality social welfare programs that are decentralized enough to be "user-friendly." Good education builds a skilled work force. Progressive tax policies shrink income inequalities, which keeps the market from listing too heavily toward luxury goods. Public agencies oversee the immense pension funds, thereby exercising some democratic control over investment.

National legislation prevents arbitrary firings, requires worker representation on the boards of directors of all firms, allows workers to halt production if they find unsafe conditions, and obliges employers to negotiate with local unions before implementing major changes.

After living under this system for some decades, most SIS citizens hold dear the values of equality, social justice, solidarity, democracy, and freedom. Images of the homeless on the streets of New York shock them. They pressure their government to increase aid to the Third World. They point with pride to the fact that the overall health of SIS children in the bottom 10 percent income group is identical to that in the top 10 percent. During their six weeks of vacation each year, SISers love to travel abroad. But they return convinced that their system best implements basic values.

Life is sweet in SIS. Why go beyond? The socialist points out that because most industry is privately owned, the system is vulnerable. The left government and unions try endlessly to accommodate private capital. Not only must profits be high, private owners and investors must be persuaded that they will benefit more by staying in SIS than by moving. This gives them excessive economic power and political leverage. But no matter how well the SIS system performs, private capital will defect if it perceives significant advantage elsewhere. National loyalty is a myth. (The current flight of capital from real Sweden into the EEC countries is sad proof.) The gains made in SIS remain precarious.

The socialist has other reasons for wanting to move beyond SIS. First, she would like to break up concentrations of wealth and power in order to promote democracy. Second, she believes that people can have substantial control over their work life only if the workplace belongs to them. Third, although SIS wins high marks for equalizing life opportunity, redistributing wealth, and fostering fine (socialist) values, the socialist thinks even more could be done.

What structural changes does the socialist propose? The innovations must do more than upgrade SIS (more than, say, improve day care or make taxes more steeply progressive); they must transform capitalist SIS into a socialist country. Forms of ownership must change, and the scope of markets be reduced.

The socialist recommends enlarging SIS's small socialized sector. Under the new system, the state would own enterprises in key industries as well as natural monopolies (the telephone system, power companies, railroads, and so on). Socialization would keep concentrations of power and wealth out of private hands, give the government and labor movement more control over the economy, and prevent capital flight.

But the skeptical socialist acknowledges serious problems. The inevitable oversight agencies can undermine freedom of initiative for the managers of socialized firms. Assessment of responsibility becomes difficult. Even if a good managerial culture develops in the socialized sector, the entrepreneurial function, essential to a dynamic economy, may be lost. The socialist doesn't value efficiency, competitiveness, and economic growth for themselves, but rather wants enough of these to fund the institutions that make social justice and equality possible. No socialist party wins a free election with a program of enforced autarky for a state-controlled economy.

So the socialist suggests an alternative form of ownership— workers' cooperatives. Cooperatives, too, break up concentrations of power and wealth and prevent capital flight. They give people the greatest control over their work life, eliminate unearned income, and encourage participation. The decision is made to expand SIS's existing cooperative sector until co-ops are the dominant form of ownership.

Unfortunately, new difficulties develop. Co-ops within an industry can compete ruthlessly; some knock out others, leading to new concentrations of wealth and power; some worker-members may resort to extreme self-exploitation. The socialist proposes laws to counter monopolization and to protect workers from themselves. But more serious imbalances emerge: cooperatives resist taking in new members in order to keep profits per member as high as possible. Labor mobility decreases throughout the economy. Co-ops also resist labor-saving technology, undermining overall efficiency.

Then Co-op A decides to invest its surplus in Co-op B, turning Co-op A members into capitalists. Co-op A has the possibility of becoming a powerful conglomerate. Laws are passed to prevent one co-op from investing in another. But this immobilizes capital, and the economy may lose its dynamism. Finally, an economy dominated by cooperatives doesn't have labor unions uniting workers both industry wide and throughout the economy. There is no solidaristic wage policy and therefore none of its far-reaching benefits.

Needing respite from the ownership question, the socialist considers the market and its noncapitalist alternative, planning. Comprehensive planning—including price setting, production quotas, and the allocation of capital, raw materials, and intermediate goods between firms— is rejected. No one can fathom how to make such a system work, with its built-in inefficiencies, shortages, impossible data requirements, arbitrary prices, and inadequate criteria for evaluation.

The socialist advocates a lighter touch. The government will shape economic development by phasing out declining industries and promoting new ones with tax credits, discounted interest rates, and direct subsidies. The socialist keeps in mind that too much intervention will undercut market discipline and the economy will be dragged down by inefficient firms that don't cover their costs.

Until convinced that something else will work, the socialist opts for a level of planning and an economy of mixed ownership that resembles more than anything else ... well ... SIS. The socialized sector has been enlarged a little to ensure socially useful production that the market neglects. Rigorous legislation promotes small businesses and disperses large concentrations of economic power. The co-op sector might be somewhat larger. And perhaps ways are found to root socialist values more deeply.

Our socialist is anything but satisfied. The fundamental contradiction of the system hasn't been resolved. Improved SIS is still vulnerable to capital flight. Investors might cut out anytime for places where the wages are lower, the regulations fewer, and the ethos less egalitarian—thus confirming the dictum that it's difficult to maintain SIS in just one country. The only solution is to operate in an international market where SIS conditions predominate. What SIS needs is Very-Imaginary-Europe (VIE).

So the socialist joins the movement to build VIE—yet all the while is plagued by doubt: If an ever-improved SIS depends on the dynamism of private enterprise, how can the system ever be called socialism? The response for now is another question: If the system is equally characterized by the decommodification of human needs, market regulation, and the redistribution of wealth and power, can it still be called capitalism?

# PART IV

---

# Visions, Models, and Blueprints

# 10

# Feasible Socialism? Some Social-Political Assumptions*

## (Summer 1985)

## *Alec Nove*

By possible or feasible socialism I mean a state of affairs that could exist in some major part of the developed world within the lifetime of a child already conceived, without our having to make or accept implausible or farfetched assumptions about society, human beings, and the economy. This means that we exclude abundance (in the sense of supply balancing demand at zero price, the disappearance of opportunity cost).

We naturally assume that the state will exist; indeed it will have major politico-economic functions. The state cannot be run meaningfully by all its citizens, and so there is bound to be a division between governors and governed. Ships will have captains, newspapers will have editors, factories will have managers, planning offices will have chiefs, and so there is bound to be the possibility of abuse of power, and therefore a necessity to devise institutions that minimize this danger.

---

*Editors' note: This chapter is adapted from Alec Nove, *The Economics of Feasible Socialism* (London: George Allen & Unwin, 1983), Part 5. A second edition of Nove's book was published in 1991 as *The Economics of Feasible Socialism Revisited* (London: Routledge). This essay is reprinted as it appeared in *Dissent* (Summer 1985) with permission of the author and the publisher.

Political assumption: a multiparty democracy, with periodic elections to a parliament. The only known way to prevent the formation of parties is to ban them. The notion that several parties are needed only when there are separate social classes is clearly false. On the evils of an imposed one-party system it is hardly necessary to comment. Except in moments of crisis or civil war, parties must not be banned. If parties are not needed or wanted, they will wither away, and individual "independents" will be elected on personal merit. But this is not likely. The electorate needs to be presented with alternatives, including different economic policies, priorities, strategies, in an organized way. How else, except through parties, with perhaps occasional referenda on issues that lend themselves to this procedure.

Should the parliament consist of professional politicians, or part-timers who have normal jobs in factory, office, or farm? The choice depends on what functions the parliament is to perform. Dogmatists unthinkingly opt for the "worker from the bench," with frequent rotation and recall, and then imagine the elected assembly exercising the tightest control over everyday affairs, which is plainly impossible if its members' main occupations are outside the assembly. Or there could be a mixture, with a core of "professionals" who are members of standing committees and report to plenary sessions.

## Enterprises, Markets, and Competition

There have been surprisingly few attempts to sketch out a model of the kind that is being attempted here. . . . So let us start, so to speak, from scratch, by asking some elementary and fundamental questions. How should production be organized? First of all, what *categories of producers* of goods and services should exist, what forms of property in means of production?

Several ideas come together here. The first is the need for variety, and for opportunities for individual and group initiative. We must bear in mind the need to avoid or minimize the feeling of alienation, and take into account *producers' preferences*. While consumer preferences, user needs, should certainly predominate in determining what to produce, the preferences of the work force should play a major role in determining how it should be produced, bearing in mind the need for economy of resources and the technology available. Of course, in the real world "how" and "what" can overlap. Thus railwaymen may prefer not to run a late-night train, to the detriment of suburban theatergoers, and one then needs to reconcile conflicting interests.

An important and highly relevant point was made by André Gorz. This relates to diseconomies of scale, from the standpoint of the producer, the worker. The bigger the unit in which he is working, the more he is likely to feel alienated, remote from management decisions, a minor cog in a big machine. Gorz surely is right that this question of scale, rather than just ownership, can be decisive. From this standpoint, "small is beautiful." (Gorz, in his French book, quotes these words in English; they come, of course, from Schumacher.) Gorz goes a little too far, perhaps influenced by Ivan Illich, in his belief in do-it-yourself as the basis of producers' satisfaction; in his version, the state's industries should aim at providing the means for all kinds of domestic production for use, such as parts for home assembly of radios. No doubt, such things are desirable, but many citizens are both unattracted by and incapable of handling technology in the home, so this can be only one of the wide range of possibilities.

Gorz is no fanatic; he realizes that economies of scale exist too and cannot, for certain productive activities, be ignored save at prohibitive cost. He therefore accepts that some branches must continue to produce on a large scale: electricity generation, heavy chemicals, steel, oil, to name a few. His idea is that workers should take turns to work in such industries as these, and devote to them as few hours as modern technology makes possible, so as to fulfill themselves in small-scale activities. He does not make it clear how the small units are to interrelate. His approach implies a market, but he does not spell this out. (I wrote to him to ask, but he did not reply.)[1]

Human beings vary greatly in the way they like to work. Some seek responsibility and are good organizers, others work better as individuals, still others are happiest in a small team, and so on. Technological economies of scale do indeed differ widely in various activities. Everyone benefits from large-scale generation of electricity; it would be idiotic to decree that every household fetch water from wells, or that pipelines be condemned as inappropriate labor-saving technology when the only alternative is little men with buckets running across the desert.

Gorz is right in his formulation: if large scale offers only a modest saving in costs, one's predisposition should be to opt for small scale, on just the grounds that he advances. Let "small is beautiful" be an operational guideline in choice of techniques, to be preferred if other things are almost equal. But be it noted that "small" means a small number of workers, which may not imply labor-intensive techniques. Sometimes a small number can do the job only if highly labor-saving technology is used. The choice must depend on whether shortage of labor or unemployment is the main problem, and whether the labor that is saved is agreeable or disagreeable, skilled or repetitively boring. . . .

Radoslav Selucky opts for what he calls "social ownership," with "means of production managed by those who make use of them," separated from the state. He does refer to "the remnants of the yet nonsocialized," which would be "fully compatible with the socialist nature of the model."[2] But this seems to him to be a temporary, transitional arrangement. Selucky appears to envisage an evolution moving toward one type of producing unit. In my view it is possible and desirable to have several.

In these and in other respects, it is essential to recall the assumptions of political democracy. The citizens can choose, for example, what sorts of private initiatives to encourage or to tolerate, the desirable forms of cooperatives, the extent of workers' participation in management, and much else besides. They can experiment, learn from experience, commit and correct errors. Successive generations may shift their predominant opinions and objectives. Nothing need be unchanging. Certainly nothing will be.

## A Legal Structure for Enterprises

Suppose we have a legal structure that permits the following species:

1. State enterprises, centrally controlled and administered, hereafter called *centralized state corporations*.
2. State-owned (or socially owned) enterprises with full autonomy and a management responsible to the work force, hereafter called *socialized enterprises*.
3. *Cooperative enterprises*.
4. *Small-scale private enterprises*, subject to clearly defined limits.
5. *Individuals* (for instance, free-lance journalists, plumbers, artists).

The first group would include banks and other credit institutions, and sectors that operate in very large, closely interrelated units, or have a monopoly position, or both. The most obvious example is the electricity network: Wherever the actual power stations are located, it can only be the center that knows how much current is needed and which power stations should be feeding kilowatt-hours of electricity into the national grid. Neither the manager of one power station nor its workers should have any decision-making authority over electric power generation.

Similarly, a rail network, large integrated steelworks, oil, and petrochemical complexes would seem functionally to be large *and* hierarchical. For example, North Sea and Alaskan oil enterprises require closely coordinated investment and production activities, involving a large number of different units (engaged in drilling, laying pipelines, pumping, maintaining oil rigs, erecting refineries, operating tankers, and so on). Typically these are activities that, even in a capitalist market economy, are *administered* by large corporations, within which the links are those of subordination-coordination, that is, vertical and not (or as well as) horizontal.

In most instances of this sort, it must be supposed that organizational and informational economies of scale are of great significance, offsetting the extra cost of corporate bureaucracies. As techniques and computational methods alter rapidly [this may not] necessarily be so tomorrow. We also must bear in mind that some corporations are large because of the power it gives them over the market and not because of efficiency considerations. They sometimes take over smaller units that operate quite efficiently. Nonetheless, it seems clear that in my model of "feasible socialism" there will be some very large corporations of this sort.

Some of these corporations will have a strong monopoly position—caused by the effects of technological economies of scale, or because they are public utilities (supplying electricity, telephones, mail, public transport, and so on), which by their nature tend toward monopoly. . . . The relative absence of competition opens the possibility of "improving" performance at the customer's expense, and this could be achieved just as well within a self-management model as by an "autocratic" director appointed from above. Selucky quite rightly stresses in his book the need for special arrangements in such cases. He recommends tripartite supervision, with management responsible to the state, the users, *and* the work force. This seems an eminently sensible approach. Clearly, there would have to be devised criteria of efficiency that take into full account social and economic externalities, systemic elements, as well as duty and purpose.

Let no one suppose that this will be simple, or can be made simpler by some kind of socialist magic wand. . . .

Cost-benefit analysis will help, but predictably not everyone will agree on the evaluation of cost or (especially) benefit. Thus I am writing these lines on a Hebridean island. The ship that serves the island operates at a loss. The islanders complain bitterly of heavy freight charges, and make the point that for them the ship is the equivalent of a road, or a bridge, on which profit-and-loss accounting should not (or need not) be applied. Those (like myself) who wish to preserve the viability of life in remote islands wholeheartedly concur. However, this implies a much larger transport subsidy, which has an opportunity cost. Other claimants on limited resources will be less sympathetic.

In the end the decision will be political, and will not depend on the "commercial" judgment of the shipping line or the votes of the seamen who run the ships. As noted earlier, shipping to remote small islands is almost inevitably a monopoly, since a ship large enough to brave Atlantic storms cannot be profitably duplicated (whereas the innumerable ferries that cross the English Channel can be separately and competitively operated; there is plenty of traffic).

## More Notes on Categories of Producers

Let us return now to the list of categories of producers. The big state-owned units could be described as constituting the "commanding heights" of large-scale industry and public utilities, plus finance. Some will be monopolists in their sphere, but it should not be an imposed monopoly. Thus, if for any reason the state electricity grid fails in its duty to supply power at reasonable cost to all users, then it should be open to any group that thinks it can do better to generate its own.

But even when there is no monopoly, it is hard to envisage giants of the size of a socialist Du Pont, or Shell, being meaningfully "self-managed" by the work force. Perhaps the best way to define a dividing line between the state-centralized and the autonomous categories is by reference to the range of decisions on production that "belong" at the level of the production unit, as distinct from corporation headquarters.

It is worth dwelling on this point, which, at long last, is being seriously tackled in Western theory, for instance by O. Williamson (it is enough to quote the title of his book, *Markets and Hierarchies*), and one should also recall the pioneering work of R. H. Coase and G. B. Richardson.[3] Western orthodox "theories of the firm" in fact provided no reason for the firm, as an organizing entity, to exist at all. To cite the words of Shubik, no difference was seen between General Motors and the corner ice-cream store (or indeed between corporations and individuals). Very valuable ideas on this topic can also be gleaned from J. Kornai's book, *Anti-Equilibrium,* and from the ideas of G. L. S. Shackle and B. Loasby.[4]

There are good, solid reasons why certain productive activities are very large-scale, and centralized. The manager of one factory within Du Pont, or Imperial Chemical Industries, or Shell may have little or no more autonomy in decision-making than his equivalent in the Soviet centralized planning system. Why? And how many of the reasons would apply also to a realistically conceived socialist industrial economy? One, applying particularly to investments, may be the huge initial cost, which is only worth paying if there is some assurance that there will be no "duplicatory" competitive investment. The high cost of R & D is a similar point. In both, the firm is seeking to limit uncertainty, to be able to approach what amounts to *ex ante* planning.

Another reason, related to the above, is informational; to know what investments or output are needed may require the decision-maker to be at the center. In some instances—oil and chemicals are obvious examples—the large firms are providing the inputs for their own processing and manufacturing, so that vertical integration is the best way to ensure the smooth provision of the necessary supplies. The above points must be distinguished from purely technological economies of scale. Obviously, if Du Pont (for example) owns almost a hundred factories and plants, its size cannot be ascribed to the need to produce its (very varied) output under one roof. To reduce uncertainty, to avoid wasteful duplication, to know in advance the user's requirements, to be confident of obtaining supplies of the needed specification are also reasonable objectives for socialist planning.

We have seen that to try to include the *whole* economy in an all-embracing disaggregated central plan is impossible, self-defeating, inefficient, and also in my view undesirable on social and political grounds. ... One can only seek to identify sectors and types of decision in which external effects are likely to be substantial, so as to make the task of taking them into account administratively manageable without requiring the creation of a vast bureaucracy. Similarly, analysis of organizational alternatives can show us which are the sectors, industries, types of decision where the cost of centralization exceeds the benefits (and "cost" here includes the alienation and frustration caused by remoteness of control), or where the cost of *not* decentralizing can be excessive—all this with a built-in preference for small scale. Such a preference, be it noted, is quite contrary to the Marxist tradition, as Gorz has correctly pointed out.

### Competition: Will It Have a Place?

If competition is present, and production decisions "belong" at the level at which production takes place, then there could be *socialized enterprises* with a major role in management for representatives of the work force (cooperative property and private property will be considered later). Before discussing the forms this could take, let us consider the role of competition in a model of socialism. The word has undesirable connotations to many a socialist, yet it is inconceivable to imagine choice without competition among suppliers of goods and services. ...

Let us take an example from culture and education. Only wild-eyed dogmatists (they exist, alas!) can exclude it. Not every competent violinist will succeed in being accepted by the Scottish National Orchestra. It is inconceivable, outside fairy tales, that every university will be equally prestigious in all subjects, and so there will be competition to get in. Not everyone will win the school 1,500-meter race. Only a few of those who graduate in any subject will be found competent to teach it to students—and students need to be protected from incompetent would-be teachers. A theater competes for an audience with other theaters by trying to be better. A scientific research team will seek to attract funds that might be allocated to rival teams. It seems to me that all this, *within reason,* is benign. But it can become vicious: thus we read of the Japanese children's educational rat race, which creates misery and drives some to suicide. It was reported that in an American medical school some students deliberately sabotaged experiments by other students, so as to surpass them in the highly competitive examinations. One cannot define the difference in law but, plainly, it exists. A soccer team must strive to win, but to set out to cause serious injury to the opponent's center forward is, to put it mildly, improper. All this has its economic and commercial parallels.

In the Soviet Russian language a distinction is made between "competition" *(konkurentsiya),* bad, and "emulation" *(sorevnovaniye),* good. This does not correspond at all to the distinction that I am trying to make. One can cheat and perform vicious acts in the process of "emulation" as well as in "competition," and competition for the favor of customers is most definitely *konkurentsiya.*

Suppose there are sixteen or more (socialized and cooperative) firms engaged in providing some one good or service. Let it be wool cloth, toothpaste, ball bearings, holiday hotels, or whatever. They base their productive activities on negotiations with their customers. The latter can choose from whom to obtain the goods or services they require. All can obtain from *their* suppliers, whom *they* can choose, the inputs needed to make production possible. Suppliers have a built-in interest in satisfying the customer, and so no special measures are required to ensure this (apart from ensuring also that both parties adhere to the "normal" regulations about pure food, correct labeling, and so on). All benefit from this situation as customers (and users). Few producers willingly suffer the consequences of competition. Ideally, we want people to seek our services . . . and freely choose our own suppliers. However, having your cake and eating it is excluded by our realistic assumptions. It may be that most citizens will appreciate that the choices of others are a precondition for their own. . . .

What, then, is undesirable, "wasteful" competition, which socialists would wish to prevent, or at least to minimize? A whole number of examples can be cited. There are certain areas in which competition can have paradoxical, negative results. Thus if there were three TV programs run by the same public-service-oriented organization, there would be more choice for the viewer than if there were three competing networks, which tend to put on similar programs at peak hours. A single integrated service of public transport may make more sense than separate competing units. But what most socialists regard with distaste, and with reason, are massive advertising campaigns, especially for products almost indistinguishable except for name and label, where the advertising costs become a high proportion of the final selling price.

What can be done about this? If it is easy to dispose of one's product, advertising is pointless; but then one does not have to bother about the customer either, as in all sellers' markets. Kornai has rightly stressed the desirability of a degree of difficulty in selling. Then the autonomous and competing firms will wish to persuade the customers to buy, to win goodwill by quality and reliability, and to send round brightly produced catalogues suggesting that BLOGGS' WIDGETS are just what is needed. Newspapers would seek to attract readers by publicly suggesting that *this* one should be read, naturally in the conviction that it is a good newspaper. It seems as impossible to ban this as to prevent a theater from putting up posters advertising its next play. It can be called "informational" advertising, and in part it is that. But it can degenerate into the more undesirable and wasteful phenomena: pseudoproduct innovation and differentiation, excessive expenditure on garish packaging, and so on.

Perhaps one could devise a regulation limiting such outlays, along the lines of limits on election expenses imposed by a number of countries (and perhaps newspapers should be prevented from attracting readers by printing pictures of unclad blondes on page 3; or maybe socialist readers will have no need or desire for such pictures, who knows?). Soccer teams will compete too, and again we must hope that they will do so without money prizes. We all know players who play their hearts out without expecting financial reward, but Soviet experience shows that soccer competitiveness, which cannot be rewarded by open payment ("there is no professionalism"), is rewarded on the side by highly paid part-time "work."

Finally, there is competition for high political positions. Here again, the Soviet "Stalinist" experience shows that it is possible to "succeed" by having your rivals executed on false charges, just as at a lower level ordinary citizens would denounce their neighbors to the secret police in the hope of acquiring their housing space. All this shows how the evil side of "competition" can show itself in all spheres, economic and noneconomic, with or without a market. It also reminds us how difficult it is to adopt rules that securely prevent the wrong sort from emerging. It will be necessary to try.

It is worth quoting an example that seems at first sight to be an argument *against* me. What of patents, inventions, technical progress? At least, so it will be said, where there is mutual cooperation there will be no commercial secrecy, all ideas will be freely available for use throughout the economy. If one has a market, with sectional interest prevailing over the general interest, then once again there will be obstacles erected to the diffusion of technology.

There are two counterarguments. One is the familiar one that, without the spur of competition, new technology might simply not be adopted, owing to routine and inertia (and because of the other reasons advanced in discussing Soviet experience). The other is that to make technological information available is costly; if it is free, this means one is forbidden to charge for it, and so one does not bother to provide it. It turned out, in the Hungarian experience, that such information circulated more freely if it *could* command a price. The dogmatist would reply: Under a "real" socialism, everyone would pass on useful information for love of his fellows. Again, let us hope so. (The inventor of, say, penicillin would not restrict its use by patent.) But let us not build an economic system on the assumption of high-minded altruism; no more than, in devising a constitutional structure, should we assume that no one would wish to abuse authority. Never let us forget that people have an almost infinite capacity for identifying the (never-too-clearly-defined) general interest with their own.

Socialized and cooperative enterprises would have managers appointed by an elected committee, responsible to this committee—or to a plenary meeting of the work force if the numbers are small enough to make this possible. The division of functions between professional management, the committee, and the plenary sessions can be determined democratically by each unit in the light of its own experience, and its own mistakes.

The principal differences between socialized and cooperative enterprises in a competitive environment would derive from the difference in property relations. In the former the means of production would not belong to the workers, and the state would have a residual responsibility for their use or misuse, or for debts incurred. (We will discuss the problem of failures in a moment.) [However,] a cooperative could freely dispose of its property, and freely decide to wind itself up. There would also be a difference in income distribution and in tax liability; of this too more in a moment. In general, one would suppose that cooperatives in manufacturing would tend to be relatively small.

**The Subject of Free Enterprise**

Presumably even the fanatical dogmatist would accept the existence of free-lance writers, painters, and dressmakers. My own list would be longer. Indeed, there should be no list. If any activity (not actually a "social bad" in itself) can be fruitfully and profitably undertaken by any individual, this sets up the presumption of its legitimacy. Perhaps an earlier example could be reused here to illustrate the point.

Water supply is a "natural" monopoly. If water flows from taps, private water carriers are an absurdity. So no law is needed to forbid them. But if for some reason the water supply becomes unreliable, this can create a situation in which private water carriers can make a living. This is indeed far-fetched (the example, not the water!) but innumerable instances of a much more realistic character can be cited.

Suppose that there appears to be an unsatisfied demand for a Peking-cuisine restaurant, Fair-Isle sweaters, a holiday booking agency, wedding dresses, car repairs, mushrooms, sailing dinghies, house-decorating, barley, chocolate cake, or string quartets. Large, state-managed undertakings are otherwise engaged. The smaller, socialized or cooperative enterprises may or may not act; after all, it is absurd to assume that all opportunities are always taken or that lack of enterprise cannot occur even in a competitive environment. (Mistakes can take the form of inaction as well as incorrect action.) Or perhaps an individual has devised some new and economic design or method of production. Why not let him or her go ahead, and produce privately for sale?

So long as it is one individual, there would probably be no objection, except from dogmatists so extreme that they are out of sight, away on the extreme far left. (They may be blandly assuming that under their perfect socialism the "associated producers" will always provide whatever is needed in whatever are the needed quantities.) But there would also be the possibility of a private entrepreneur actually employing a few people, which makes him an "exploiter," insofar as he makes a profit out of their work. This is illegal in the Soviet Union today. It is tolerated within defined limits in Hungary and Yugoslavia.

I would suggest that, subject to limits, this should be allowed. Once again it must be stressed that Marx believed that petty producers would become unnecessary in a socialist commonwealth, not that they be compulsorily liquidated by the police. Thus a family farm that may be producing efficiently could employ a few laborers, a restaurant might hire a cook and/or some waiters, a couple of clerks could type letters for a holiday agency, a promoter could hire a hall and a string quartet, a repairman may prefer to work for a private garage, and so on. In each case, the "entrepreneur" *works,* organizes.

Subject to what limits? As earlier suggested, this could be decided democratically in the light of circumstances and experience. The limit could be on numbers employed, or on the value of capital assets, and could be varied by sector. One possible rule might be that above this limit there be a choice, either to convert into a cooperative or to become a socialized enterprise, with proper compensation for the original entrepreneur.

Is this a dangerous loophole for the "restoration of capitalism"? Not if the limits are observed. Is it a means of illegitimate enrichment? Not if the market and price mechanism are in working order. Obviously, if prices fixed by the state were too low, and shortages were endemic, the private sector could become excessively remunerative. Presumably a wise government would avoid this. But more later on prices, taxes, and incomes. Be it noted that there is no provision for any class of capitalists; our small private entrepreneur *works,* even when employing a few others. There is then no *unearned* income, arising simply from *ownership* of capital or land.

Marx justly noted that competition is apt to destroy competition.

Adam Smith had observed a century earlier that businessmen may conspire together for their own benefit. It is by no means excluded that self-managed enterprises can form rings or cartels. Both under modern capitalism *and* in the contemporary Soviet system there is a strong tendency toward mergers. This would have to be resisted, save where the economies of scale are substantial, whereupon the sector might have to be added to the list of those centrally controlled and administered, to prevent misuse of monopoly power.

**Functions of the Center: Planning**

What, then, of planning? The center, in this model, would have a number of vital functions. *First,* major investments would be its responsibility. *Second,* directly or through the banking system, the planners would endeavor to monitor decentralized investments, conscious of the need to avoid duplication and the financing of plainly unsound projects initiated locally. *Third,* the center would play a direct and major role in administering such "naturally" central productive activities as electricity, oil, railways. *Fourth,* there would be the vital task of setting the ground rules for the autonomous and free sectors, with reserve powers of intervention when things got out of balance, or socially undesirable developments were seen to occur.

There would plainly also be functions connected with foreign trade. There would be drafts of longer-term plans, incorporating changes and improvements in techniques, working practices, living standards, which would be submitted to the elected assembly. It appears to me that the extent of the necessary planning would be greater than is allowed for by Selucky in his model; the difference is doubtless explained by his experiences in Czechoslovakia, and by his anxiety to reduce the powers of the state to a minimum.

Another way of defining the functions of the center would be as follows. In those sectors where externalities are likely to be significant, intervention is essential; it can take the form of regulations (such as measures to protect the environment from pollution), and subsidies (such as for public transport, research), the correction of regional imbalances, and so on. [Also] there will be the quite basic task of determining the share of total GNP devoted to investment, as distinct from current consumption, and this in turn would affect the rules that are made to ensure adequate savings (either by way of taxation or through the use of [reinvested] profits, or both).

There will also be the far-from-easy task of combating inflationary excesses in distribution of personal income and in investments, ensuring as far as possible that the major investments that are made correspond to the expected future pattern of demand, so that the prospective plans are balanced. The center would also have a vital role in ensuring a balance between present and future where the time horizon of both management and labor is too short, as well it may be: the theory and practice of "self-management" suggest the danger of overemphasis on short-term gains [on behalf of] the "time preference of the community. . . ."

Finally, democratic vote could decide the boundary between the commercial or market sectors and those where goods and services could be provided free. Education, health, social security (including retraining grants for those made redundant by technical change), amenities of various kinds (public parks, museums)—the list can be a long one. I suspect the voters of a future socialist society would not wish to make it too long, as they (unlike some people today) would appreciate that free goods and services need to be paid for, and that the longer the list the smaller can be the level of personal disposable income. If people like it that way, they could form latter-day communes, and pay each other just pocket money.

In a less romantic context, when I joined the British army I was issued a uniform, mess tin, blankets, paillasse [a sort of straw mattress or pallet], dinners, a tent (shared with seven others) to sleep in, and one shilling a day (after deductions). This was 1939, and I would have change from a bag of fish and chips and a half-pint of beer. My French fellow soldiers thought we were rather scandalously overpaid. . . . I know the army is not a commune or a kibbutz. A minority, nonetheless, joins it voluntarily in peacetime; they like having virtually all basic consumer goods and services issued to them free. Another minority joins kibbutzim and communes. Let these people do so by all means. But it is unrealistic to build a model in which it is the majority that wishes to live this way. So it must be supposed that the bulk of goods and services will be bought and sold.

The bulk of current production and distribution would be within the decision-making competence of the producing units that negotiate contracts with each other. These would naturally have to be enforceable. It cannot be open to a meeting of the work force to decide by a majority not to observe delivery obligations; there would have to be a penalty.

## And What of Failure?

Mention of penalty leads us into a much-needed discussion of failure. In the Soviet system, one of the many difficulties in the way of enforcing obligations lies in the fact that fines, when levied, are paid out of public funds, penalize no individual, and represent a transfer of state money from one pocket to another. Then there is the equally familiar problem of "socialist bankruptcy," or lack of it. Suppose investments made on credit from the state bank cannot be repaid because of a change in market conditions, inefficient operation, errors of judgment. Who is to be penalized, and how? In the utopian-Marxist vision all is clear *ex ante:* The plan is faultless through perfect knowledge. In the real world, too, many decisions are meaningfully taken *ex ante,* as when one decides to build additional power stations or signs a long-term contract for the supply of iron ore, based very largely on quantitative, input-output calculations. (These may prove mistaken, but infallibility is not a typical human characteristic.)

However, the problem is more serious when autonomous units orientate themselves in a market environment. When groups of people are free to respond in a decentralized way to necessarily imperfect market signals, errors must happen quite frequently. Furthermore, competition implies not only winners but also losers. For competition to be possible at all there has to be spare capacity. The unsuccessful will be unable to ensure full employment of their material and human resources; they will have an excess of expenditure over receipts.

Clearly, this is an inescapable consequence of freedom to act. Equally clearly, the "punishment" of error (and the reward of risk) will be major problems, major sources of controversy. Inevitably there will be claims for subsidies, sometimes justified. A procedure will have to be devised for winding up the outright failures, or for imposing a change of management as a precondition of meeting the debts. Procedures will naturally vary according to the different categories of ownership. Cooperative and private activities must be expected to bear the cost of their own mistakes. At the other end of the scale, the centrally run state sector is plainly the responsibility of government, which would determine the price policy to be followed (which could involve, for instance, large subsidies for [low-cost] public transport, or prices far in excess of costs for cigarettes). There is no reason whatever why the workers in these sectors should either gain or suffer from the condition of the profit-and-loss account.

Efficiency criteria will not be easy to define, but we have seen that these difficulties already exist. The most awkward problem will arise in the case of those socialized enterprises in which management is responsible to the work force. Let us consider two likely sets of circumstances. In one, management initiates a production and sales policy that turns out to be a failure; why, the workers may well ask, should they suffer for this, are they not entitled to the pay rate for the job? Alternatively, management's proposals are rejected by the work force, which votes for an alternative, and *this* is the cause of loss. Should not the workers then shoulder some of this loss? This raises important questions of income distribution and incomes policy, to be discussed in a moment. The Yugoslav experience is very much to the point.

**Profits, Prices—and the Theory of Value**

The logic of the proposed system naturally requires prices that balance supply and demand, reflect cost and use-value. This does *not* exclude subsidies whenever these are considered to be socially desirable, or where external economies are significant (public transport, vitamins for nursing mothers, perhaps housing, and so on) and, of course, some items ought not to be "priced" at all: education, hospitals, parks, and so on. Just what is to be available free of charge is a matter of democratic political decision. As already suggested, it is likely that a large majority would not wish (for instance) to be fed free, suspecting that this would mean that they will be unable to choose the menu.

Soviet and other experience proves conclusively that comprehensive price control is impossible to administer, that there are too many
prices, many millions, as we have seen. To abandon price control
altogether would plainly be wrong, given that some industries will be
centrally managed and in a semimonopoly position. We return to the
examples of electricity, oil, telephones, steel, railways, and others in
the category of centralized state enterprises. Some basic agricultural
products should also be on the list of those prices subject to central
control; it is surely no accident that this is the case in virtually every
country today, regardless of system.

The large majority of goods and services can, however, only be
effectively priced in the process of negotiation between supplier and
customer, the bargain including detailed specifications, delivery dates,
quality. We must naturally expect the producing enterprises to try to
"administer" prices, and wholesale and retail organs would seek to
obtain the "mark-up" they regard as proper, but in the absence of
shortages and the presence of choice the buyers can refuse, can go
elsewhere, can bargain. In other words, competition should prevent
abuse of producers' powers.

The word "profit" is not always popular in socialist circles. Yet, if
prices are economically meaningful, profits at the micro level represent the difference between cost and result, between the efforts of the
producers and the evaluation of this effort by the users. It is evident
that, on balance, this difference should be larger rather than smaller, so
long as the profit is not the result of monopolistic price-fixing, though
of course in no economy is this a perfect measure. It is the appropriation of profits by capitalists that offends, not profit as such. (Similarly,
rent as an unearned income of landlords is objectionable, but differential rent must—as we shall see—enter into economic calculations also
in a socialist economy.)

If profits appear to be "excessive" where there is no monopoly
power, this may well be a reward for enterprise, efficiency, and anticipation, and the entry of other producers can force down the price by
expanding supply. . . .

Marx, in his formulation of the law of value, related it to productive
labor, and related productive labor to exploitation: that is, anyone
exploited by a capitalist is "productive" (of surplus value). However,

he made an exception for the sphere of circulation, buying and selling, which adds nothing to value. These distinctions would plainly be inappropriate for a socialist economy. Surely it would treat all socially useful human effort as productive labor, making an exception perhaps for those items (such as public administration, police) that could be regarded as a social cost, albeit a necessary one.

A *labor theory of value* would be appropriate, in the general sense that, all other things being equal, goods would exchange in rough proportion to the effort required to produce them, with market forces acting to connect use-value, exchange-value, and the expenditure of human labor. Physical capital assets would, of course, be seen as contributing to the process of production, but there would be no legitimation of income arising from owning them.

The reward of labor would be seen to relate closely to its average productivity, and the degree of income differentiation would be properly regarded as a consequence of several factors: supply and demand for different kinds of labor, social policy, the need for incentives, compensation for heavy or disagreeable work. Someone might remember what Marx, and Mao, said about "bourgeois rights," and one must expect disputes on the subject of what constitutes excessive inequality.

The "transformation problem" (of labor value into "prices of production") would disappear, as an unnecessary and pointless detour. Obviously, labor itself would not be paid its "value," in the sense of the amount necessary to cover the labor cost of its own production and reproduction. The amount it would be paid would be a function of the general level of productivity, with deductions (decided on by democratic means) for social services, pensions, investments, and so on.

Such factors as scarce natural resources, fertile land, and land in the center of cities would be given the valuation appropriate to the process of calculating their most effective use. Whether oil-bearing land has "value," or is a gift of nature, and whether a gift of nature can have "value," is a point that is more metaphysical than real. Marx was concerned most of all with demonstrating the existence of exploitation, the nature of the surplus, and its appropriation by owners of land and capital. Economics in the "feasible socialism" envisaged here would be much more concerned than was Marx with defining and discussing efficient allocation, calculation, and valuation. For purposes of efficient use of resources, it is evident that their relative scarcity is a relevant factor, most obviously so when the resources are nonreproducible—as in the case of oil-bearing land.

Time, too, would have to be taken explicitly into account. Clearly, a project completed in five years is preferable, all other things being equal, to one completed in eight years, even if the direct costs of the two are identical. So there would be interest rates as well as rent, but these would be payments to the state, not to private individuals (with exceptions, of course, such as renting a room in an apartment, or interest on private savings).

The history of economic thought would explain to puzzled citizens that there was a time when the very rich did no work, and that most economists found this quite natural and built their theories on such a basis. It would sound quite irrational to these citizens that the owners of, say, twenty-five acres of London's West End could live a life of luxury and ease, and bequeath the same to their children, merely for authorizing (that is, not preventing) more construction on these acres. However, the twenty-five acres would remain very valuable, and an appropriate rental should enter into any economic calculation involving their use.

Let me give another example. Suppose the number of people in Scotland wishing to fish for salmon in the rivers grossly exceeds the number of rivers and salmon available. At present (let us say) payment must be made to a duke for permission to fish, and this helps the said duke to be rich. Suppose one eliminates the duke. This makes no difference either to the desire of the citizens to fish or to the number of rivers and salmon in Scotland. So either the numbers who fish will be limited by a permit system (therefore there will be queues, influence- and string-pulling, and so on), or a charge will be made. The charge may even be identical to that levied by the duke—only now it is a rent that is used to cover social expenditures, not an individual's unearned income. . . .

## Division of Labor, Wage Differentials, and Self-Management

The utopian nature of Marx's vision of a universal man has been expounded and rejected earlier in this essay. However, underlying it are some ideas important for any socialist. No doubt specialists will continue to exist. The lecturer in Italian is unlikely to be able to teach Spanish, let alone repair teeth, drive heavy lorries, maintain jet engines, be a part-time architect, or milk cows.

We must abandon any idea of doing without a horizontal division of labor. However, there must be an attempt to widen opportunities for change of jobs or specialization; boredom and routine surely are not social "goods." The fullest educational opportunities for youth must be accompanied by generous retraining schemes, including higher education for mature students who have previously repaired teeth or driven heavy lorries. People vary widely in aptitude, ambition, and talents. Activities that I would find boring give others great satisfaction, and vice versa. One can and should encourage changes of job and career, but these are bound to have their limits.

More difficult is the problem of the vertical division of labor. One must first of all identify the functional necessities of subordination, in industry and elsewhere. Why must a ship have a captain, a newspaper an editor, a steelworks a manager? Why must someone be in charge of a building site, an airport, a school, a planning office? Which of these functions require special qualifications and experience? As anyone who has ever worked under inefficient superiors will bear witness, there is such a thing as managerial, controlling *skill,* a knack for personal relationship as well as specialized knowledge, a desire for and ability to carry responsibility. How far is this consistent with rotation? Which should be the elective jobs?

On balance, it does seem likely that most human beings will continue to prefer to avoid responsibility and be glad to accept (appoint, elect) others to take it. (How many university professors wish to be vice-chancellors?) The likelihood of a shorter working week, and the widespread encouragement of technical and cultural hobbies ("do-it-yourself"), may well incline many workers to devote their surplus energy to tasks outside the job rather than to "participate" actively in it, especially if to do so requires hours of "homework," familiarity with accounts, and so on. So the most likely outcome is a mixture of election and appointment, with the objective necessity of hierarchy duly reflected in the existence of hierarchy. There will be government; there will be managers in charge of electricity, oil, steel, and railways; the state planning office will have a chief, who will have deputies, and so on. It will be of vital importance to limit official powers and prevent abuses. The elected assembly would have a key function here, as would a free press.

How much inequality should be tolerated, and how should this be related to hierarchical position? The first point to make is that income differentials (a species of labor market) are the only known alternative to direction of labor. Here it is essential to avoid a mental muddle: some might say that within a commune, or a good kibbutz, one can have full equality and rotation in jobs (everyone takes a turn at unskilled work such as washing dishes). But this cannot be generalized over the whole of society, partly because it is only workable with small numbers of people who know each other and can meet daily, and partly because such communes would attract only the enthusiasts who like this sort of life. Trotsky in 1920 envisaged the necessity of direction of labor until a time when people achieved such a high level of social consciousness that they would voluntarily go where society needed them. This is far-fetched indeed, being based not only on the totally unselfish man and woman, but also on the naive notion that the good of society can be so defined that any citizen can identify it and identify his or her own role within it. A complex, large society with a division of labor makes this impossible.

So we should envisage the degree of inequality that is needed to elicit the necessary effort by free human beings. Actual wage scales would therefore be influenced by supply of, and demand for, specific kinds of labor. How much differentiation would this require? A great deal must depend on relative scarcities in relation to need, on the general standard of living, and on human attitudes. There seems no good reason to make some individuals many times richer than others in order to obtain the necessary incentive effect. In our societies today some pleasant and honorable jobs are, by convention, paid very well. There is no reason why a university professor should necessarily earn more than a garbage collector. Few professors indeed would wish to earn more by turning their efforts into garbage collection! (Adam Smith noted, 200 years ago, that curates have an expensive education, but earn "less than a journeyman stonemason"!) We must take into account the belief of most workers in income differentials, and also the almost universal view that a senior officer in any field should earn more than his juniors.

Again, we cannot and should not anticipate the extent of the need for differentials or the state of democratic opinion on the subject. What we should anticipate is the requirement of an incomes policy with appropriate wage and salary scales, and that this will be a thorny and difficult subject because of the absence of any objective point of reference (other than a labor market).

Would a 2:1 or a 3:1 ratio between highest and lowest paid adults be sufficient? In a relatively prosperous society in which the minimum wage assures a reasonable standard of comfort, this does not seem a fantastic prospect. One can also envisage that piece-rate payments would be reduced to a minimum: even in today's U.S.A., they are largely unnecessary to ensure reasonable effort.

To secure acceptance of an incomes policy, of limits on incomes, has proved to be very difficult, especially where trade unions, pursuing sectional interests, make it their business to demand higher incomes and threaten a strike to enforce an incomes policy. There would be no large fortunes obtained by those not working. Indeed, there would be no large fortunes at all.

A limited bonus scheme linked with profit would be desirable in the socialized (competitive) sector, to provide a material interest for participation in management, despite the probability that this would cause friction. There would, however, be some individuals whose incomes would be in effect uncontrolled: members of cooperatives of all kinds, in town and country, and the small private farmers and other "entrepreneurs," plus individual craftsmen and professionals. However, the cooperative and small private enterprises take greater risks, can lose as well as win, and in any event it should be possible to limit their take-home pay through the use of the market mechanism, and also by progressive taxation. Would this be sufficient to keep trade union militancy within bounds? It is by no means certain.

There would be danger of inflationary wage claims, especially given the commitment to reasonably full employment. There would also be the problem posed by the external world, with comparisons made: some group might find that similar people were better off in another country. However, identification of possible sources of conflict does not imply that they are incapable of resolution.

### The Unions' and Workers' Role in Managerial Decisions

A question mark will stand before the role of trade unions. Where virtually everyone is working, where there are no capitalist employers, what tasks are they to perform? Living standards will not rise through militant wage demands; the distribution of the GNP between individual consumption and various other purposes (investment, social services, and so on) will be for the elected assembly to decide. Yet the freedom to organize, and in the last resort the right to strike, are human freedoms that matter. There would no doubt be some extremists who would be encouraging strikes in the name of an imaginary "real" socialism, labeling the mixture recommended here as "state capitalism" or worse. One hopes that good sense will prevail.

The right to have *free* trade unions is an indispensable part of the precautions against abuse of power and illegitimate privilege. But in the modern complex world, the ruthless use of union power can do very serious damage to [the unionists'] fellow citizens. Among the important innovations to which they, and the management, will have to adjust is work-sharing, if technical progress is of a massively labor-saving kind.

Reverting to labor's role in managerial decisions in socialized enterprises, one must recall two negative aspects of the Yugoslav experience. One is the interest of the workers in not expanding the labor force, at a time of serious unemployment, because to do so could reduce their incomes. The other is the workers' lack of long-term interest in "their" enterprise, because it is in fact not theirs: they derive no benefit from working for it once they leave it, having no shares to sell.

There are possible remedies. One is to have a clearly determined wage rate for the job, this not being a function (as it is in Yugoslavia) of the net revenue of the firm. A modest bonus based on profits should then reduce or eliminate the opposition to additions to the labor force. The second problem is more difficult; the word "shareholder" would cause hackles to rise. Yet some kind of length-of-service bonus, linked with the long-term level of profits or the value of basic assets, could be paid to a worker who retires or transfers elsewhere. (See the example of Mondragon, pp. 210–11.) The important point is by trial and error to devise a pattern of personal interest that would incline the work force to support economically (and socially) efficient decisions.

The question then arises (again) of how to penalize those who consciously and democratically take wrong decisions. Several possibilities occur. One is to provide that if the elected committee overrules the management and a loss results, the members of the work force suffer a (limited) deduction from their pay envelopes, proportionate to the (limited) bonus to which they would be entitled in the event of success. How large should *this* be? Would what is called in Russian "the thirteenth month" be sufficient? Is more needed to overcome risk aversion?

Of course, ideally one wishes to create a model in which the material and moral interest of the sub-unit is always in conformity with the interest of all of society but, in a complex and interrelated economy, this must be seen as an *optimum optimorum*, devoutly to be wished but seldom attainable. We know from Soviet (and indeed all other) experience how easy it is inadvertently to create situations in which the pursuit of local interest by labor and management causes conflicts and contradictions.

### Procedures, and Problems, of Self-Management

Cooperatives would, being genuine, be managed by the members. As already indicated, losses or windfall gains would be borne or enjoyed by them, subject to tax or (where socially desirable) a subsidy.

Intermediate categories are also possible: for example, in Hungary today small shops and cafés that belong to the state are leased to private operators. Obviously, in these instances the revenue of the leaseholder depends on what remains after payment of the lease and other costs, and, if this amount proves excessive, the charge can be increased.

This is a possible approach to agriculture in a country without an established small peasant class. For example, in Great Britain the large majority of farmers pay rent to landlords. If the land were nationalized, the state would levy a charge (rental, lease) on the family or the cooperative that would operate the farm. This rental could be differentiated in accordance with the fertility and situation of the land. This would be essential to avoid giving an undeserved bonus to whoever happened to be operating in a geographically favorable environment. (Where peasants actually own the land, their expropriation would present acute political problems, and the problem would need to be dealt with by differential taxation.). . .

Some of the work on this subject is done at a high level of abstraction. It is none the worse for that, of course. A certain lack of realism is a legitimate price to pay for theoretical rigor. But one must never forget the extent of the abstraction that has been made from a necessarily complex reality. To give one relevant example, E. Domar has shown that a change in the assumptions concerning supply of labor to a self-managed cooperative totally alters its (formal, theoretical) response to a rise in price and/or a change in tax. He was referring to Ward's perfectly logical conclusion, based on *his* assumptions, that a price rise could lead to the paradoxical effect of making a self-managed enterprise reduce employment and output.[5]

There are other reasons why this outcome is improbable. One is the effect of competition. (*Real,* not "perfect," competition!) Imagine, for instance, ten self-managed enterprises, all producing only widgets, all trying to expand their share of the market—that is, they have the possibility to produce more than they are actually able to sell, a not unrealistic assumption that *must* underlie genuine competition; and suppose the price of widgets rises.

While it is possible that in the very short run the "dividend" for working members could rise if a given firm produced less with fewer workers, is this likely, bearing in mind the following points?

1. There are indivisibilities in processes of production—process specialization, and so on. Labor is not homogeneous.
2. Self-managed units are usually unwilling (sometimes by their rules unable) to dismiss fellow workers.
3. More important, what of *goodwill?* Customers once lost may never be regained and, after all, prices that rise today may fall tomorrow. Some of the nine assumed competitors will not be so foolish as to

miss the opportunity. Some, having spare capacity, may be at the stage of increasing returns (falling costs per unit).

4. In the unlikely event of all ten producers deciding to increase net revenue per worker by reducing output when prices rise, what is to prevent new entrants from starting to produce widgets? Of course, the existing producers know this and would wish to avoid it, which would affect their actions.

The possibility that existing firms would fail to respond to a price rise, and simply add to their net revenues, cannot be ruled out, even in real capitalism, given the existence of human inertia and informal rings of various kinds. Entry of new firms is an important corrective to such practices, and will be important also in the sort of socialism here envisaged. It would also play a role in reducing the danger of unemployment. Procedures for the setting up of new social and cooperative enterprises must therefore be devised. Bank credits would play a major role in financing these "starts," and here the state plan can exercise an important influence: regional problems, labor supply, forecast of future requirements, environmental considerations can and should influence the decisions.

But this still leaves unsettled the issue of *who* actually undertakes the task of starting a new firm. For the centralized state sector, the picture is clear enough: the central planners, the central body that runs the industry (corresponding to the National Coal Board in Britain, or the Ministry of Electric Power Stations in the Soviet Union), make the calculations, take the initiative, create the enterprise. At the other end, so to speak, the picture is also fairly clear: cooperative enterprises, or petty private businesses, are set up on the initiative of the individuals or groups concerned, with or without direct encouragement from the public authorities. But what of socialized enterprises? One can imagine a range of possibilities. One is "conversion" of some of the larger cooperative enterprises.

Other initiatives should be encouraged. According to the Yugoslav rules, "any public body, institution, social organization or group of citizens" may take the initiative. Enterprises can also merge and divide. Central planners might also act, and have the choice of granting credits for the expansion of an existing firm or for setting up a new one. Mindful of the need for competition, they might prefer the latter. A manager would have to be appointed *pro tem,* and contracts signed with building firms, suppliers of machinery, and so on. These procedural problems seem unlikely to be insuperable and need not detain us. . . .

To discuss all this in full requires a book, not a few paragraphs, so what follows must be seen as no more than a few thoughts, in a constructive spirit, on a difficult subject.

How can one combine self-management with efficient use of resources, while avoiding excesses of inequality? An interesting case is Mondragon, in Spain.[6] This is a very large cooperative "conglomerate," and worker-members who join must make a sizable capital contribution, which earns a rate of interest and is repayable when they leave (subject to a modest deduction, but indexed to the rate of inflation). Management is elected. Income differentials are decided by the work force (apparently after much argument). Interestingly enough, there are wage and salary scales (the reward of labor is not a residual); there is, therefore, a profit margin. The major part of the profits is used for investment and reserves, but a portion is shared out among the work force. We cannot concern ourselves here with the detailed history and problems of Mondragon; it may be that it has become too big to be an effective cooperative.

However, [the Mondragon experience] suggests certain possibilities. Thus a contribution to capital from each worker member (in Mondragon a major part of this may be lent to the worker by the cooperative itself, to be repaid out of earnings) makes the member materially interested in the longer-term welfare of the firm; the amount returned to the worker when leaving the firm could be varied by length of service and include an extra amount related to the profits made. Equality in this respect is assured at Mondragon by making every worker's contribution equal—that is, the minimum is also the maximum. (Of course, some capital is raised externally, through credits from the banks.) Such an arrangement best suits cooperative enterprises, but in socialized, self-managed enterprises, too, there could be some scheme that makes reward for long service relate to accumulated profits and/or increase in the value of the enterprise's capital.

The essential points seem to me to be the need to link the worker's material incentives with the longer-term health of the enterprise (making the worker interested also in investment and providing a stake in the future). And this is integrally linked with the existence of a wage, that is, a rate for the job, without which the very concept of "profit" ceases to have a statistical meaning: if the entire net income (after paying for inputs, taxes, and so on) is divided among the work force, there is no "profit" as such; yet there ought to be. Which in no way prevents the existence of profit-related bonuses.

In Mondragon, according to a friendly but critical survey,

> the combination of participation in decision-making with respect to organization of work and the distribution of earnings; to narrow differences and fixed wages; to an extensive program of education and on-the-job training; to a high degree of security of employment; and to a financial stake in the ownership of their own cooperative factory, adds up to a system of collective incentives that is not found in private enterprise, which partly explains why performance in the cooperatives has achieved such a high degree of efficiency.[7]

True, the evidence shows that only a small minority actively participates, but it also shows that the bulk of the work force appreciates the right to participate. Let us be realistic: if everyone wanted to speak at general meetings, there would be no time available for anything else! Nonetheless, we should also heed the warning of Mihajlo Marković: "One of the greatest dangers for self-management is the formation of a small oligarchic group made up of managers, heads of administration, and political functionaries, which tends to assume full control over the workers' council."[8]

It is noteworthy that the large Mondragon complex is divided up for effective management purposes into smaller units, thus avoiding or reducing the danger of alienation of the work force through scale and remoteness. The manufacturing units operate in a competitive market environment, and the wage rates are based upon those in existence in analogous private industry in that part of Spain. Evidently, this experience is worth very careful study. . . .

The level of incomes in state, socialized, and cooperative enterprises should not vary greatly, to avoid social stress. In Hungary the higher incomes earned in cooperatives did cause friction. It seems reasonable to expect national wage negotiations and a national wage scale for the state and socialized sectors, but cooperatives of this nature must have greater freedom to make their own decisions in this respect.

Excessive differentiation could be reduced by a progressive tax (on individuals or on enterprises). There could be rental, lease, or lump-sum payments designed to avoid differentiation because of natural advantages. This could apply particularly to land and minerals. For example, rent or tax levied on farms (whether state, cooperative, or individual) would be varied in accordance with a land valuation survey *(cadastre)*, as indeed is now the case in several countries. The same could apply to shops favorably located in a central area. There would be much room for experiment. The problem, of course, would be to avoid discouraging efficiency and enterprise, which would certainly occur if taxes, leases, [and] rents were such as to penalize success. But this can hardly be said to be insuperable.

Finally, we must expect any meaningful self-management to alter the worker's frequently passive or negative attitude toward work. Textbooks on economics usually ignore this factor. Labor, if not treated as homogeneous, is distinguished only by specialty. Yet men and women can work well or badly, can try consciously to minimize effort or take pride in their work. In arguing that "the labor-managed system appears . . . to be superior by far, judged on strictly economic criteria, to any other economic system in existence,"[9] Jaroslav Vanek makes many points, but the one concerning attitudes, morale, and avoidance of conflict seems to me particularly important.

In this connection, it seems necessary again to stress the importance of *scale* ("small is beautiful"). A recent illustration of this from Soviet agricultural experience is the so-called *beznaryadnoye zveno,* or autonomous work team. It turns out that a group of seven or eight peasants, left to themselves to organize their own work, can greatly increase productivity, and need not be supervised, in contrast with much larger units. There is a moral here. Of course, I do not suggest that seven or eight is some optimal magic number. But it may well be found that even a good organizational scheme with a cast of thousands would produce disappointing results.

## Investments and Growth

Investments would be divided into two parts: those of structural signif-icance, usually involving either the creation of new productive units or the very substantial expansion of existing ones, and those that repre-sent an adjustment to changing demand (or to new techniques). The latter would be the responsibility of management (cleared as required with the elected committee), and the necessary finance would be ob-tained either from retained profits (and reserves based upon past prof-its) or credits from the state banking system. Exceptionally there could be a budgetary grant, where the activity carries with it large external economies or is seen as a social "must." It would be the task of the bank, in conjunction with the central planners, to keep watch on the level of credits and on their destination.

One must avoid generating inflationary excess demand for invest-ment goods and building labor, and avoid also a situation in which the same investment opportunity is perceived by many managements. For example, suppose there is a clear need for expanding the output of typewriters. Wasteful duplication and triplication of this apparently profitable investment could result, and it might be necessary to grant the credit to the firm that promised to be most efficient and refuse it to other applicants. As for big, structurally significant investments, these would be the major responsibility of the central planners.

As we are discussing an industrialized, developed country, there is no need to assume that *high* growth rates would be a high priority. Since scarcity will be a fact, there will be pressure to provide more material goods, housing, social services, and so on, but that is not the same as a drive to achieve a radical structural transformation in a short span of time. Such a drive may indeed prove inconsistent with reliance on the market mechanism. A large part of investments would therefore be of the "adjustment-to-demand" sort. It is plainly essential, within a controlled market environment, that firms (state, social, cooperative) have the means to make such adjustments, for otherwise the profits they make would serve no rational purpose.

If, for example, demand increases for anything from microchips to potato chips, the price will rise and so will profits. The function of this rise in price and profits in a market economy is to stimulate additional production, which, unless there is already spare capacity, requires additional investment. If this result (additional production) does not follow, the mechanism fails to work, and the enterprise thus will make excess profits to no social or economic purpose. And this, indeed, would require a species of socialist antitrust legislation. In the sectors in which competition is desired and desirable, a watch would have to be kept to prevent the creation of informal rings or cartels that would agree not to expand or compete. One way of combating this tendency is to encourage the creation of new productive units in the sector concerned (by credits on favorable terms, and so on), which would be another important function of central planners in a "socialist market."

Experience points to the danger of investment cycles. A fundamentalist objection to the conception advanced in the preceding pages would stress this. The absence of comprehensive planning and the role of market forces would introduce elements of "anarchy," of uncontrollable zigzags, booms and slumps. Markets provide (imperfect) information about what has already happened. Did not someone use, as a parallel, a driver who looks out of the rear window at the road behind him?

The criticism has a point. However, imperfect information can also not be ruled out where planning is highly centralized, and the model put forward here places in the centrally planned categories those large investments (in such sectors as energy, steel, heavy chemicals) for which information about future requirements is best collected and analyzed at the center. Besides, as we have seen, investment cycles also occur in centralized, nonmarket economies. It will indeed be a difficult task for the center to steer the rest of the economy by remote control, without detailed orders, avoiding mass unemployment and inflation—difficult, but surely not impossible. The center will have at its disposal such weapons as credit policy; licenses to set up (or to encourage the setting-up of) production units; control over prices in the centrally managed sectors; the drawing-up and enforcement of ground rules on profit disposal, income distribution, and taxation.

True, the greater the freedom allowed to enterprises or to individual citizens, the greater the risk that some undesirable act might be committed. Thus it seems easier to control incomes if the state and only the state employs labor than if the worker can choose to work for a cooperative or for himself. It may also seem easier to avoid duplication, to ensure economies of scale, if there are no separate autonomous production units with the right to decide what they should be producing and how. Yet Soviet experience does not altogether support these assertions. Even if the state is the only employer, different state institutions can compete for labor in a sellers' market and lure away good workers from each other. And uncertainty of supply leads to self-supply, to duplication on a quite massive scale, to the detriment of economies of scale based on specialization. There is no magic wand. Total control is impossible; the effort to achieve universal planning by an all-knowing center produces results that no one actually desires (not even the center). Total decontrol is also unworkable, and certainly cannot be seen as a socialist solution.

One must agree with Thomas and Logan when, writing in the context of the Mondragon experiment, they argue that

> . . . at the meso- and macro-levels, a strong planning agency is essential as otherwise a self-managed economy could not function. Phenomena such as the entrance and exit of firms, and the adjustment process of capital intensity, can only be realized by careful planning and institutional support.[10]

Also correct is the following opinion of Tinbergen:

> It is highly improbable that the proponents of a "laissez-faire theory" of self-management are right. It can be convincingly shown that in an optimum order some tasks must be performed in a centralized way and cannot therefore be left to the lowest levels. . . . One should seek the level that "minimizes external effects."[11]

So what must be sought is a workable compromise between centralization, self-management, and local initiative. Some Soviet economists, in examining critically their own system, have written intelligently on theories of complex organizations, within which the sub-units are free to take certain categories of decisions. They seek to devise an optimal decision-making structure. Ideally, one wishes to have a situation in which the perceived interest of individuals and groups always conforms to the general interest. For reasons we have discussed earlier, this is an unattainable ideal—just as it is impossible for some central body to examine every decision in the light of the general interest, that is, to internalize all externalities. The complications are just too great, the possibilities to consider far too numerous, and the perception of interest is inevitably affected by the situation within a complex society of various individuals and groups.

The best that can be done, in the field of investment as in others, is to identify in advance the kind of problem or decision that will have significant external effects, that is, effects (positive or negative) beyond the knowledge or responsibility of those directly involved. Where the cost of internalizing (that is, reference to a higher authority within the firm) is unlikely to result in benefits that will outweigh the entailed cost in frustration and delay, freedom to decide on the spot should not be limited.

### Foreign Trade—in Brief . . .

There will be, of course, foreign trade. Either some of the world will not be socialist or there will be separate socialist countries, though naturally a union of several socialist countries would be both possible and desirable, and/or a socialist "common market" with close cooperation and perhaps a common currency. . . .

The dogmatists' "alternative" would be either a world socialist commonwealth with production "directly for use," which implies a degree of centralization that surely is both undesirable and impracticable, or perhaps some quite imaginary model of abundance, in which the comrades in West Africa freely decide to supply cocoa and bananas in just the right quantities to the comrades in Western Europe for sheer love of humanity, without the requirement of any *quid pro quo*. No unequal exchange, because no exchange! Not a very likely story, to put it mildly.

### The Economic Role of Democratic Politics

It is an essential part of socialist beliefs that there be a real form of economic democracy, that people can influence affairs in their capacities as producers and consumers. It is by this standard, among others, that the Soviet model can be judged and found wanting.

To influence the pattern of production by their behavior as buyers is surely the most genuinely democratic way to give power to consumers. There is no direct "political" alternative. There being hundreds of thousands of different kinds of goods and services in infinite permutations and combinations, a political voting process is impracticable, a ballot paper incorporating microeconomic consumer choice unthinkable. Majority votes are in any event undesirable as well as unsuitable. What of minority rights in matters of consumption? Is it proper for the citizens of a town or a country to vote by a 3:1 majority in favor of *not* providing anything—from string quartets to pumpernickel—which happens to be a minority taste? How can we measure the intensity of desire for anything other than by discovering how many things one is prepared to give up to obtain it (what *price* one is prepared to pay)?

With an acceptable distribution of income, and in the absence of large unearned incomes, no better method for arriving at consumer choice is known than that of allowing the consumer to choose, and (save on far-fetched assumptions of "abundance") this means choosing by using his or her purchasing power, by buying in shops—what Soviet reformers call "voting with the ruble." The shops, in turn, must then have the means of obtaining the goods their customers wish to purchase. There is not and cannot be anything antisocialist in the notion that the citizens should seek to satisfy their varied needs and tastes to the fullest extent consistent with the productive capacity of society and the welfare of their fellow citizens (for instance, avoiding pollution). . . .

Earlier on, we have tried to draw the distinction between relative and absolute scarcity. Higher prices and other material stimuli can elicit additional supplies of reproducible goods. However, if what the future holds is an extension of the experience of absolute shortage (as exemplified by fish in the North Sea), then society, by its votes, could opt for a rationing scheme of such products, as a temporary measure at least. This would be a restriction of choice, of course, but might find its justification in the principle of fairness in distribution under conditions when the supply effect of higher prices would be insignificant. One has reasonable hopes that such conditions would not be frequently encountered.

Democratic votes, including referenda, could be utilized to determine (or choose between) broad priorities; to devote more investment resources to, say, retail distribution, public transport, rural clinics, nursery schools, the mass production of deep freezers; or to launch an investigation into the malfunctioning of any branch of the economy. Representatives of users would be given an important function, alongside those of the producers and the state, in the top-management echelon of the centralized nationalized industries. These measures are quite different from imagining a "democratic" vote to reduce (or increase) the output of brown boots or to allocate (or not allocate) sulfuric acid to a given user.

The democratically elected assembly would adopt, amend, and choose between internally consistent plans for the economy as a whole when these were laid before it. Such plans would, of course, be at a high level of aggregation, and would have their primary effect on the pattern of major investments in the next plan period.

Such high-level discussions and decisions would directly touch only a small proportion of the work force. Participation is most meaningful at a much "lower" level—at the workplace. It is useful to recall W. Brus's correct argument (in *The Economics and Politics of Socialism,* London: Routledge & Kegan Paul, 1973) that workers can hope to participate effectively only at the level at which effective decisions are taken, and that a centralized or marketless planning model leaves little to be decided at the level of the enterprise. "The larger the group, the more difficult it will be for individuals to identify with distant structures that transcend the horizon of their own work organization," to quote Thomas and Logan.[12]

Vertical subordination must, where possible, be replaced by horizontal links—by negotiated contracts, agreements with suppliers and customers. This, it must be insisted, is a precondition for the satisfaction of both consumers' and producers' preferences—assuming that customers and producers both wish to have some effective influence on their everyday lives.

The dogmatist evades this issue by seeking a nonexistent species of direct economic-political democracy, in which "society" decides, in which labor is directly social (labor is consciously applied by society for the satisfaction of its wants, without the "detour" of market and value relations). . . .

In the competitive socialized ownership sector and in cooperatives the work force would receive encouragement to participate: to attend meetings, to stand for committees, to put forward proposals, to help elect the working management. Not all would be interested, since some would pay greater attention to hobbies outside the work process, and have every right to do so.

The smaller the numbers engaged in a given productive unit, the more likely would be the effective feeling of participation, of "belonging." Intuitively we surely would all agree that it would be far easier in a group of 50 than in one of 5,000. Individuals would be free to change their jobs, acquire a different specialization, switch from working for the state to working in a cooperative or on their own account. The concept of producers' preferences is a useful one to keep in mind, alongside that of consumers' preferences.

## Is It Socialism?

Let me recapitulate. The society outlined in the preceding pages has the following features:

(a) The predominance of state, social, and cooperative property, and the absence of any large-scale private ownership of the means of production.

(b) Conscious planning, by an authority responsible to an elected assembly, of major investments of structural significance.

(c) Central management of current microeconomic affairs confined to sectors (and to types of decision) where informational, technological, and organizational economies of scale, and the presence of major externalities render this indispensable.

(d) A preference for small scale, as a means of maximizing participation and a sense of "belonging." Apart from centralized or monopolized sectors, and the limited area of private enterprise, management should be responsible to the work force.

(e) Current output and distribution of goods and services should, whenever possible, be determined by negotiations between the parties concerned. There should be explicit recognition that this implies and requires competition, a precondition for choice.

(f) Workers should be free to choose the nature of their employment and given every opportunity to change their specialization. If they prefer it, they could opt for work in cooperatives, or on their own account (for instance, on a family farm, in a family workshop, or a service agency).

(g) As an unlimited market mechanism would in due course destroy itself, and create intolerable social inequalities, the state would have vital functions in determining income policies, levying taxes (and differential rents), intervening to restrain monopoly power, and generally setting the ground rules and limits of a competitive market. Some sectors (such as education and health) would naturally be exempt from market-type criteria.

(h) It is recognized that a degree of material inequality is a precondition for avoiding administrative direction of labor, but moral incentives would be encouraged and inequalities consciously limited. The duty to provide work would override considerations of microprofitability.

(i) The distinction between governors and governed, managers and managed cannot realistically be eliminated, but great care must be taken to devise barriers to abuse of power and the maximum possible democratic consultation.

The most serious problem, observed R. Bahro in his writing on socialism, is the reconciliation of partial and general interest.[13] This is correct, and applies also to the model outlined here. It is only in fairy tales that people live happily ever after; it is only in utopia that all agree (in a pseudo-utopia all are *made* to agree). It is nonsense to assert that fundamental disagreements occur only because of private ownership of the means of production. The assumption of relative scarcity, and thus of opportunity-cost, is enough to ensure the certainty of some conflict.

The state, its democratic institutions, will be there to resolve disputes, to settle competing claims on resources, but trade-union and other interest groups (regional, or national in a socialist federation of several nations) could make trouble, and cause an overcommitment of resources, excessive incomes, inflation.

Some may regard all this, and the presence of markets and competition, as showing that the proposed model is not viable, or not socialist, or both at once. They would doubtless wax sarcastic about "socialism in one country." On this last point, I would again stress that a socialist federation, common market, economic community would be highly desirable (perhaps even essential, certainly for medium-sized, let alone small, countries). But to define "socialism" as necessarily worldwide, to dismiss any other kind, is to depart from the realm of the feasible within the time scale of the present exercise. In the longer run, "one world" is a possibility, and it may be that the destructive powers of nuclear weapons are such that the survival into the next century of sovereign states makes the survival into the next century of the human race somewhat less than probable. Let us, however, put forward here the notion that a state or group of states with a legitimate claim to call themselves socialist will undertake foreign trade.

**Conclusion**

I hope that, in presenting a feasible form of socialism, I have nowhere slipped into romantic utopianism, have made no far-fetched economic or psychological assumptions. Is the resulting picture attractive? Is it desirable? This is very much a matter of opinion. For some, its lack of romanticism is a serious defect. Socialism is for them a substitute religion, worth dying for. The picture presented here is prosaic, with an emphasis on practical matters. Outside one of Paris's numerous universities, among the graffiti, was one that read: *"À BAS LA VIE QUOTIDIENNE"* which could be translated as "Down with Week-days!" Obviously my doctrines could not satisfy its author. But then nothing practical could. People will still be buying and selling, and "consumerism" is not excluded; I share with the millennarians a distaste for the excesses of conspicuous consumption (or keeping up with the Joneses), but this is not an attitude that outsiders can impose, either by decree or assumption.

We all hope that thievery and fraud will wither away, but we should realistically assume that locksmiths and auditors will still have functions to perform, and police, too. Jealousy is not a noble virtue, but some individuals will probably be jealous of the achievements of others, whether in bed or in the council chamber. Unless one naively supposes that drunkenness is caused by private ownership of the means of production and advertising by the liquor trade, some individuals will presumably continue to drink to excess (to mark success or to console themselves for failure), much though I regret this. An imperfect world cannot be rendered perfect because we wish it so, and the assumption of original sin is (alas) a more realistic basis for organizing society than the assumption of a noble savage deformed by the institutions of capitalism and the state.

It is clear that the role of the state will be very great, as owner, as planner, as enforcer of social and economic priorities. The assumption of democracy makes its task more difficult, not easier, since a variety of inconsistent objectives will be reflected in political parties and the propaganda they will undertake. One hopes that an educated and mature electorate will support governments that will keep the economy in balance, avoiding inflationary excess and unemployment, allowing the market to function but not letting it get out of hand. The danger one foresees is not one of a vote to "restore capitalism." There was no mass movement of this sort even in countries where the Soviet-type system was intensely unpopular—for instance, in Poland or Czechoslovakia. The danger is more one of so "political" an economy, especially in income and price policy and investment, that the resultant stresses and strains will lead to economic crisis, which could disrupt both the economic and the political balance.

However, both in the economy and in politics there is an inescapable price to pay for freedom to act: people may act wrongly; just as, if there is no censorship, we may be sure that some false, objectionable, and misleading matter will get published, and our hope that the citizens will be adult enough to reject rubbish may or may not be disappointed.

Is the "socialism" here pictured preferable to capitalism, or to the imperfect and mixed "system" that now exists? Would it attract the opprobrium of critics such as Hayek or Friedman? Is it a stage on the "road to serfdom"? In my view it would provide better opportunities for more people to influence their own lives and working conditions, reduce the dangers of unemployment and of civil strife, provide sufficient encouragement to enterprise and innovation, and give some attention to the quality of life.

Of course, it *guarantees* none of these things. Nothing can. People can vote for triviality, watch soap operas on television, leave litter at scenic spots. Conflicts of interest can go too far and threaten stability. But at least the socialism here presented should minimize class struggle, provide the institutional setting for tolerable and tolerant living at reasonable material standards, with a feasible degree of consumer sovereignty and a wide choice of activities for the citizens. Would an economic optimum be assured? Of course not! The possibility of economic calculation will be present, but freedom of choice involves both uncertainty and the risk of error. Compared with the inflation, exchange-rate fluctuations, zigzags in interest rates, and unemployment, in what passes today for capitalism, decision-makers might well have better means for being right more often.

Mistakes will happen, contradictions will show themselves, rebels will demand change, conservatives will resist, history will neither end nor begin. Economists, philosophers, social scientists of different schools will be assured of full employment. Unless, of course, a nuclear holocaust puts a stop to it all, and to us all, too.

"Permanent revolution" can be a disaster, as China's Cultural Revolution has shown. It disorganizes, impoverishes, confuses. But permanent vigilance, *permanent reform,* will surely be a "must."

On this happy(?) note it is appropriate to end this excursion into a feasible, possible future. Many of the propositions put forward here are open to challenge, and I hope they *will* be challenged. This is a kind of long (too long?) discussion paper, intended to provoke both socialists and antisocialists, provoke them into some hard thinking about the possible, about alternatives. If it succeeds in this, the author will be satisfied.

## Notes

1. See A. Gorz, *Adieux au prolétariat* (Paris: Editions du Seuil, 1980).
2. R. Selucky, *Marxism, Socialism, Freedom* (New York: St. Martin's Press, 1979), pp. 179, 181.
3. R. H. Coase, "The Nature of the Firm," *Economica* 6 (November 1937), pp. 386–405; G. B. Richardson, *Information and Investment* (London: Oxford University Press, 1960).
4. J. Kornai, *Anti-Equilibrium* (Amsterdam: North-Holland, 1971); G. L. S. Shackle, *Decision, Order, and Time in Human Affairs* (Cambridge: Cambridge Uni-

versity Press, 1961); B. Loasby, *Choice, Complexity, and Ignorance* (Cambridge: Cambridge University Press, 1975).

5. See E. Domar, "The Soviet Collective Farm as a Producers' Cooperative," *American Economic Review* 56 (September 1966), pp. 734–57.

6. For a good brief description, see R. Oakeshott, "Mondragon: Spain's Oasis of Democracy," in *Self-Management: Economic Liberation of Man,* J. Vanek, ed. (Harmondsworth: Penguin, 1975), pp. 290–96. A valuable longer study is: H. Thomas and C. Logan, *Mondragon* (London: George Allen & Unwin, Ltd., 1982).

7. Thomas and Logan, *Mondragon*, p. 161.

8. M. Markovič, *From Affluence to Praxis* (Ann Arbor: University of Michigan Press, 1974).

9. J. Vanek, "Decentralization Under Workers' Management: A Theoretical Appraisal," in *Self-Management: Economic Liberation of Man,* p. 364.

10. Thomas and Logan, *Mondragon,* p. 187.

11. J. Tinbergen, in *Self-Governing Socialism: A Reader*; B. Horvat, M. Markovič, R. Supek, and H. Kramer, eds. (Armonk, N.Y.: M. E. Sharpe, 1975), p. 226. The same point about the contradictions "between the interests of self-managing bodies and the demands of the national economy" is made by W. Bienkowski, *Theory and Reality* (London: Allison & Busby, 1981), p. 269.

12. Thomas and Logan, *Mondragon,* p. 187.

13. R. Bahro, *Die Alternative* (Cologne: Europäische Verlagsanstalt, 1977), p. 537.

# 11

# A Case for Market Socialism: What Does It Mean? Why Should We Favor It?

## (Summer 1987)

### *David Miller and Saul Estrin*

The term "market socialism" has no unique reference. It is a blanket term that has emerged to cover all versions of socialism in which markets are given a significant role to play. If there is any community of view among market socialists, it is simply that markets are not automatically to be identified with capitalist markets, and may have a number of properties that all socialists should be willing to find attractive. Since this bare assertion still provokes dissent in some quarters, we will begin by outlining the essential case *for* markets before going on to look at many of the qualifications that have to be entered.

**What Is the Market?**

It is necessary first to dispense with the fiction of "the market" as a single entity. Many separate markets interact with each other, and the operation of each depends on a variety of background conditions; institutional factors such as government regulation and the specification of property rights; empirical factors, like the number of buyers and sellers and the degree of their organization; normative factors, the customs and conventions governing exchanges in that particular area. It is equally wrong to think of "market" and "planning" as diametrically opposed processes. Forms of planning may be as numerous as kinds of markets, and there are many possible ways in which planning decisions can be linked to the operation of markets. By setting the parameters of diverse markets, they can be made to advance various public interests yet still cater to different individual tastes.

A second consideration is the *legitimacy* of markets. A socialist will not see this as a corollary of the property rights of individuals, as some individualists would. Even if certain personal rights are indeed sacrosanct, these will not include the unrestricted right to sell and acquire possessions, a right which is liable to have social consequences of serious concern to socialists. So the case for markets must be made in terms of their general consequences. Here there are broadly speaking three considerations.

- Markets are an efficient way of producing and distributing a very large number of mundane items, from tomatoes to transistor radios. In fact, no complex society dispenses with markets as means to allocate goods to consumers. The variations occur in the extent to which producers face market incentives in deciding what to produce. The familiar Smithian point, that market incentives are a dependable way of getting our bread baked, should be taken seriously. And as Hayek points out, markets allow us collectively to make the best use of the information dispersed throughout a society, though one does not have to elevate this proposition to the status of a universal truth. It just does not make sense for a central planning board to make decisions about the relative quantities of salami and garlic sausage that its citizens need; nor would such issues enhance the tone of debate in the democratic assemblies arising in a socialist society. One of the virtues of markets is that, by transferring these decisions to a small group of sausage makers, it clears the decks for more important discussions.

- Markets give their participants a certain kind of freedom. They tend to expand the range of choices that may be made, and they give each person a variety of partners with whom to deal, so that no one is forced to interact with people who cause problems of one kind or another. This is most obviously the case where the items in question have a direct political content. Few socialists can now fail to see the attraction of some kind of market in newspapers, books and so forth, even if they are profoundly skeptical about the existing market structure in this area. However, the point can be broadened: if I am buying for cash, I have no need to explain or justify a request for a large consignment of salami, and this freedom to arrange my personal life in the way that I happen to prefer is one whose value should not be underestimated.

- Markets tend to dissolve personal power. Although they certainly place constraints on people's behavior ("market forces"), they free people from dependence on particular individuals such as petty bureaucrats. This is not because markets have a directly ennobling effect on human nature, but because obstructive individuals can be circumvented, and because competitive pressures tend in the long run to favor the survival of the helpful.

None of this is intended as a blanket endorsement of market mechanisms. It is meant to show that, where markets can be expected to work effectively, there are good reasons for allowing them to operate. Socialists ought not to despise efficiency and freedom of choice, and they ought to be fully aware of the defects of officialdom. At the same time, they ought to be alive to the wide variety of circumstances affecting the operation of markets.

In some areas, markets will not work at all, for example where the product is such that two or more competitors cannot remain in equilibrium, and one productive unit tends to establish a dominant position from which it cannot then be dislodged by new entrants. Such cases may be comparatively rare. Far more common are markets in which competition benefits those immediately involved in it but has adverse consequences for a wider constituency or broader social interests. The concepts of externalities and public goods currently underpin a large amount of state activity aimed either at regulating markets to prevent damaging side effects or at providing goods and services that private individuals have inadequate incentive to produce. The state will continue to play such a role under market socialism, as indeed it must under all forms of socialism.

From a socialist point of view, however, externalities and public goods have a deeper significance. Socialists are concerned not only with economically calculable losses, but also with effects on the general quality of life in a society. We will want to ask, for example, about the effect that particular markets have on local communities: do they create incentives that will lead, as a byproduct, to the breakup of living patterns that are valued by those who participate in them? We will also want to look at the distributive results of various markets in terms of ideals of fairness and equality. If the results of those inquiries reveal market failures in the broader sense, we will begin to search for ways either of replacing the market entirely or of intervening to correct undesirable tendencies.

**Capital and Labor**

Drawing the boundaries between market and nonmarket provision is therefore a matter for empirical investigation, and the boundaries themselves may be expected to shift over time. There is, however, one general point that market socialists need to insist upon in their response to neoliberalism. This is that markets in *capital* and *labor* are very different in their implications from markets in most *products*.

The neoliberal case looks most convincing when applied to markets in ordinary consumer goods. In these cases consumer sovereignty can normally be expected to work effectively, and socially damaging side effects will only occur in special cases. The neoliberal strategy is to try to assimilate all markets to these intuitively appealing cases. However, capital and labor both have special features that make the assimilation highly problematic. Take capital first, and consider decisions to invest in this or that productive enterprise. Such decisions are of their nature harder to make than (typical) decisions about consumer goods; to be rational they need to be based on complex judgments about the future performance of enterprises. Thus there is a powerful tendency for these decisions to gravitate in practice into the hands of experts who are able to spend time acquiring the necessary information, and so control of capital passes effectively into the hands of a small elite.

Furthermore, the social repercussions of investment decisions are likely to be substantial. Whereas my decision to buy salami rather than garlic sausage has at most a marginal effect on anyone else's life, a decision to build or not build a factory in a particular location may have enormous consequences for the local community, and for a future generation. The shape of the capital stock accumulated in one period creates the world in which succeeding generations have to make their way; investment in housing is an obvious example here. An elite makes the decisions which significantly affect a large number of lives; which is to say that it exercises *power*. It does not follow immediately, of course, that capital markets should be abolished. There is still a choice to be made between diffusing power as far as possible through competition, and regulating it through public authority. But it is misleading to pretend that capital poses no special problems for the theory of markets.

Labor poses problems of a different kind. To begin with, it is usually impossible for workers to spread their labor among a number of alternatives, as if they were mere commodities. That is, a worker acquires a particular skill and works full-time for a single employer, not many different firms. This makes workers highly vulnerable; if their decision turns out to be mistaken (the firm lays off employees or goes bankrupt) the costs are very large indeed. Thus there is a strong *prima facie* case for special protection that does not hold in ordinary market contracts where *caveat emptor* is the rule.

Second, the worker in supplying labor also hands over a large segment of his or her *life* to the employer. This will to some extent be reflected in the operation of labor markets, where working conditions as well as pay can be expected to affect the choice of work, but it is unreasonable to expect all the consequences of labor to be taken into account in this way. There may be, for instance, long-term health implications whose seriousness is hard to judge. More controversially, the environment in which people work may affect their personalities and future preferences. Occupying a subordinate role at work lessens the ability to participate effectively in political arenas, for instance. A socialist, having a general view about the shape of the society she or he would like brought into existence, cannot remain indifferent to such effects even if the individuals in question do not actively resist them. This raises questions about the extent to which socialists should regard people's present preferences as having canonical status in decisions about the allocations of goods and services.

Nevertheless, it is clear that capital and labor must be treated differently from ordinary consumer goods. In broad outline, market socialists want to have a free market in products, and either no market at all, or a well-regulated market, in labor and capital. This position is less absurd than those standing both to the left and to the right would like to make it seem.

## The Structures of Enterprises

If product markets are to be retained under socialism, but capital and labor markets abolished or at least transformed, what ought the structure of enterprises to be? At the libertarian end of the spectrum, socialism implies no more than equal entitlement to the means of production, with the question of how people choose to use their endowments (whether in capitalist enterprises, cooperatives, etc.) left entirely open. Second, there is the Croslandite* view that capitalist firms are an acceptable component in socialism (perhaps alongside other components) provided that the state uses its powers of taxation and regulation to correct income deficiencies and so forth. Third, the respective rights of capital and labor in the enterprise should be redefined in the form of a capital-labor partnership, with each party being allocated a predetermined share of profit. Fourth, enterprises in market socialism should normally take the form of workers' cooperatives, with capital supplied externally and entitled only to receive interest. Since the fourth view is at first glance the most congenial from a socialist point of view, we will begin by examining its strengths and weaknesses.

The attractions of workers' self-management are easy to see. Power is spread throughout the enterprise, with each member formally having equal voting rights, and a chance to share in managerial functions (e.g., through a rotating committee system). The organization of work (hours, conditions, etc.) can be altered to suit members' preferences. Since each member has a stake in the profit of the enterprise, there are likely to be substantial gains in productive efficiency. Finally, the

---

*Editors' note: See Anthony Crosland, *The Future of Socialism* (London: Jonathan Cape, 1961).

distribution of income, although it must to some extent reflect the market position of those with special skills, is likely to be considerably more egalitarian than in the alternative forms of enterprise canvassed above. On the other hand, there is now abundant literature, both theoretical and empirical, on the functioning of cooperatives, suggesting some significant limits on the potential scope of a self-managed sector.

The economic analysis shows above all that producer cooperatives react sluggishly to changes in market conditions. The capitalist system is highly responsive to changes in market conditions from both the cost and demand side, whereas cooperatives are interested in the collective welfare of their members, which will include their pay, conditions, hours of work, and size of the group with whom they are employed. Improved market conditions permit cooperatives to gratify more fully their collective goals, but to the extent that these conflict with increased production, the effect on output will be dampened relative to that of capitalist firms.

Many analysts have seen this as a source of unemployment under market socialism, but cooperatives are unlikely to fire members in order to increase collective welfare. It is an appropriate macroeconomic policy on the demand side that is needed for full employment, matched if necessary by government creation of the additional cooperatives required to mop up surplus labor. The moral is surely that the cooperative form may be inappropriate if we want to exploit social opportunities in sectors with rapidly changing demand, technological or cost conditions. In good times, cooperatives will not adapt sufficiently to high demand or technological changes. In bad times, cooperatives are ill-suited to the hard decisions involved in fundamental capital and labor restructuring. If the economy is open, domestic cooperatives will be squeezed out of foreign and home markets by more flexible international competitors. If the economy is closed, the welfare burden will fall on domestic consumers.

## Investment

This brings us to the second issue: investment. Left to themselves, cooperatives tend to invest less than capitalist firms in the same situation would have done. There is likely to be a bias within conventional capital markets against the cooperative mode of production which leads to restrictions on the provision of external funds. This could be eliminated by the creation of a cooperative bank to act both as a source of saving and a broader supporting institution for the self-managed sector along the lines proposed by Vanek and to some extent undertaken by the Caja Laboral Popular for the Mondragon group of cooperatives.[1]

But there could still be problems for investment on the demand side. If we accept that cooperative entrepreneurs will be relatively more risk-averse than their capitalist counterparts, they will require a risk premium from projects over and above the market rate of return that would choke off the volume of investment undertaken. Moreover, all the discursive evidence suggests that cooperatives are unhappy about accepting "excessive" external financing because of the consequential loss of control over the future of the firm. One can view this as placing a limit on investment demand at a quantity multiplied up from internal financial sources by a ratio which the membership determines to be consistent with retaining control over the destiny of the cooperative.

For some or all of these reasons, cooperatives are prone to invest at a lower rate than their capitalist counterparts. This strongly suggests that cooperatives are also inappropriate for the production of goods that require capital-intensive techniques. Unless some solution to the underinvestment problem is found, for example via the central direction of fixed capital accumulation through cooperative banks, this seems to rule out self-management for the heavy industrial sectors—steel, chemicals, metal-working—sometimes referred to as the "commanding heights."

Other reasons argue against a significant role for self-management in highly capital-intensive large-scale plants or indeed any sectors with major economies of scale in production. Self-management is not impossible in large, multi-plant diversified corporations—the Yugoslavs approach the problem by breaking the firm up into a loose coalition of self-managing sub-units—but the costs of democratic management rise while the benefits for the work force diminish. Co-operatives in such sectors could actually lead to significant welfare losses, since the collective membership might choose to sacrifice economies of scale for retaining relatively small size and effective work force control over the firm. This is another example of potential conflict between the interests of the cooperative members and those of the consumer, who gains from the lower prices arising from the larger scale of production.

## Skills

Related to size is the nature of skills required in the production process. Self-management involves the democratic control of the firm by its labor force and its success will hinge on the relevance and capacity of the entrepreneurial group's innate skills. Cooperatives will be most effective where the labor force as a whole, rather than some tiny proportion, has significant contributions to make on the managerial side and least where it does not. This does not augur well for self-management in sectors in which the production process itself is relatively mechanical and enterprise success instead hinges on the highly specific talents of a small group of workers: in design, in finance, in marketing, or in foreign sales. When combined with the probable limitations by cooperatives of their size, which will restrict the spreading of risks through diversification, this criterion rules out sectors such as banking, finance, and insurance.

The cooperative form may also be inappropriate in high-risk industries and industries subject to rapid technological change. It is more likely to succeed in areas with relatively small-scale production processes that rely disproportionately on the skills of the entire labor force (rather than on capital or the talents of a small subgroup), and in relatively well-established markets and product lines.

Capital-labor partnerships may be a way of combining the benefits of self-management with some of the economic advantages of the orthodox capitalist firm. These operate on the basis of an agreed division of rights and responsibilities between the two sides, and a corresponding division of profits. Since capital is now a risk-bearing factor, there is room for a more conventional capital market; and the need to compete in such a market for continuing investment obliges the labor force in each enterprise to pursue overall profit (rather than profit per worker) as its goal. Partnerships of this kind will be more inclined to expand employment in the face of market opportunities since employment levels will be decided by the representatives of capital.

## Difficulties

There are, however, at least two difficulties with the partnership idea. One is that it reintroduces the possibility of conflict between one party whose interests are solely in levels of profit and a second party whose interests are more diverse. To avoid this kind of conflict, the partnership agreement may need to be quite detailed (otherwise potential investors will be deterred). But self-management is not *merely* a matter of giving workers an economic stake in their enterprise, desirable though that may be from the point of view of performance. It is also a matter of encouraging active decision-making in an area of daily life that is centrally important to most people. Clearly such participation only makes sense where there are real decisions to be made.

A second difficulty is that the effects of the partnership system on the distribution of income may in the long-term be less desirable than those of the cooperative system. As people invest in more or less successful partnerships, any initial equality in the distribution of investment capital is likely to give way to a cumulative advantage for the shrewd investors. Why should this matter? Socialists are likely to believe that income inequalities above a certain point, however they are generated, are socially damaging, and that skill at investment, though certainly a socially useful talent, is not the kind of skill that should command very large rewards.

In general terms, a feasible socialist market economy would have to be institutionally pluralistic. There would be a large cooperative sector, perhaps a sector in which capital-labor partnerships were formed, perhaps a sector of very small enterprises (restaurants and so forth) taking a conventional capitalist form. It seems overwhelmingly likely that basic industries requiring massive levels of investment (oil, coal, steel) would be state managed, even though subject to (mainly international) market competition. Such diversity would be a realistic reflection of the varied types of production that exist in a modern economy. Such pluralism would have to be cultivated as a matter of policy, and supported by the appropriate regulatory and investment agencies. Thus the confluence of plan and market, referred to at the beginning, would reappear here as a deliberate structuring of the institutions of the market.

Yet we do not envisage the market sector in a socialist society as being all-embracing. Clearly there will still be a place for industries that are run as public services under government control—the railways, for example. Lack of direct competition and the potential social costs of a market-based service together provide a strong reason for taking these services out of the market sector. Different reasons support the same conclusion in the case of several of the welfare services. It should therefore be apparent that government continues to have a major policy role in our version of market socialism. In some areas its role will be direct, in the sense that an arm of government will administer services directly; in other areas its role will be a supervisory one—structuring and then regulating the working of a market. Market socialism is therefore not about "rolling back the state" in a blanket sense, though it is possible that in some particular areas market socialists would wish to see the role of the state diminished. It is rather about using the power of government intelligently, to carry out those tasks which the state alone can perform.

From a certain point of view, the picture we have painted is anti-utopian and may not seem to differ much from the mixed economy favored by social democrats (of whatever party). Why, then, should it be considered as a significant socialist advance? The major gains lie in three areas. First, it promises a much greater involvement for ordinary people in the running of their enterprises. Second, as a result, the distribution of income is likely to be very considerably more egalitarian than under the modified version of capitalism that we enjoy at present. Third, our proposals would amount to a socialization of capital, and thus to bringing under popular control a major source of power in the present system. We have not taken a dogmatic line on the extent to which this means placing capital under public control (say through a publicly managed investment bank) or on the other hand dispersing capital ownership far more widely in the form of individual holdings. In either case (or with a mixed system), large concentrations of capital in private hands are broken up, and power is diffused.

## Criticisms

Showing that a feasible institutional structure can be devised for the economy is, however, not the only task facing market socialists. They must also show that their proposals can be reconciled with the core ideals of socialism itself. In the first part of the chapter we outlined arguments *for* markets that we thought socialists should take to heart; and at the same time indicated where the socialist view on these questions would differ from the neoliberal view. But we have not yet attempted to respond to some basic criticisms that may be launched against our proposals from what might be called the "fundamentalist" position. These criticisms come in various shapes and forms, revealing three major strands in the antimarket case.

• The argument for markets falsely assumes that consumers are sovereign. In fact, the desires that markets respond to are very largely created by the market itself, and they are in that sense inauthentic. The object of production should rather be to meet human *needs*.

• The market distributes goods and services in a way that is, from a socialist point of view, inappropriate. It rewards merit and luck rather than need.

• The market breeds competition and destroys community. It encourages people to think of themselves as isolated individuals and to neglect the ties that bind them together. The economic incentives it provides tend to break down communal relationships.

All of these arguments have force; but they tell far more strongly against libertarian visions of an all-encompassing market economy than against the circumscribed use of market mechanisms that we have been proposing. We have stressed throughout that, for socialists, markets must be offset by government planning, and also by a public sector in which services are provided on a nonmarket basis. A mixed system of this type can be defended against the challenges listed above.

### *Consumer sovereignty*

It is certainly true that many consumer demands are stimulated by producers who have an interest in satisfying them, but it is not clear why this should give grounds for objection. Most of our desires are in any case socially produced, as Marx himself was eager to point out. Why should this origin be worse than any other? There seem in fact to be only two broad instances in which the case for consumer sovereignty breaks down:

(a) What the consumer is aiming at is beneficial to her or him, but she or he lacks the expertise to make an intelligent judgment about how to obtain it.
(b) What the consumer is aiming at is, in fact, detrimental to his or her own best interests.

We should be wary of making too much of case (a). There will be many instances where consumers indeed make erroneous choices, but these choices are self-correcting in the sense that, next time around, a better decision will be made. The exceptions are cases in which a particular choice is unrepeatable and/or the costs of making a bad decision are very high. Both features are often present in the case of medical treatment, for example, and are good reasons for disallowing a free market in medical services. Patients should be protected at least by a state licensing system and possibly by state funding of doctors.

This does, of course, have a paternalist ring to it, and socialists may differ in the extent to which they wish to see people safeguarded against making harmful market choices. It is worth bearing in mind, however, that, first, people may positively welcome such safeguards as ways of avoiding onerous decisions; second, a community that recognizes a responsibility for the welfare of its members cannot remain indifferent if they embark on courses of action whose effects eventually drain the community's resources (e.g., if the victims of irresponsible private medical treatment have later to be looked after at the community's expense).

Case (b) takes us into more debatable territory. Some socialists would want to deploy a strong theory of human needs, in terms of which felt desires are to be critically assessed. We would, on the contrary, endorse the presumption that the individual is the best judge of his or her own interests unless there are special factors present that make this implausible. The clearest cases will be those in which choices when acted upon change the agent's preferences in a way that is, on balance, undesirable in the light of his or her overall system of desires. A familiar example is addiction, where exposure to a substance or experience has the effect that the person comes to need increasingly large doses to maintain a minimum level of satisfaction; with limited resources, she or he is less able to pursue other plans and projects. Other examples can be cited. The onus, however, is on the critic of market provision to show that one or another of these factors is liable to be present in the case of a particular good and service; one cannot build a general argument against the market on the basis of a series of special cases.

### *Distributive justice*

We assume that the idea of distribution according to need will feature prominently in the thinking of almost all socialists. Two questions then immediately arise. First, are needs to be defined so extensively that all resources will have to be allocated on this basis? Second, does distribution according to need imply the abandonment of markets, or might the principle be met by retaining markets but redistributing purchasing power, say through the tax system? On most understandings of "need," the answer to the first question is "No." Needs cannot be defined in an ahistorical, quasibiological way; on the contrary, they are socially defined, on the basis of standards of living that are regarded as "normal" in a particular context. It does not follow that needs, so defined, are infinitely expandable. It is quite feasible to think of a division of social resources between those earmarked to satisfy needs and those serving to reward merit, and to provide the incentives that are required to make a market sector function effectively.

The second question is less easy to answer. Where needs are largely similar, or where differences in need can easily be estimated by simple observation, it may be possible to respond to them by cash transfers. Where, on the other hand, the extent of need cannot be accurately judged in advance of the treatment that meets it, the only effective policy will be provision in kind. Since some needs are always likely to fall into the latter category, there will be a good case for nonmarket provision in these instances. Compare, for example, the need for food with the need for medical treatment. So on this ground, too, the market socialist ought to concede that the scope of the market should be circumscribed. On the other side, there is no case for a general veto on market mechanisms.

## Community

For a community to exist, two conditions appear to be necessary. First, the members must regard themselves as belonging to such a community. Second, this shared attitude must be expressed in the way that people behave to one another, including here the institutions that they establish to govern their formal relationships, as well as aspects like solidarity and mutual aid among equals. The internal and external conditions seem naturally to reinforce one another: that is, a communal identity encourages people to practice and support institutions of mutual aid, while on the other hand the practice itself tends to strengthen that identity. Nonetheless, it is clearly impossible to create a community *ex nihilo* simply by institutional change, and to that extent all socialists must recognize the practical limits of their proposals in this area.

Constraints on the market can be seen as contributing to the realization of this communitarian ideal. Protecting people against making damaging choices as consumers and providing for needs outside of market mechanisms can both be regarded as manifestations of a caring society. Assuming that these policies are popularly supported, people are giving up some fraction of their income to protect the vulnerable. There is of course an element of insurance as well, in the sense that each person is a potential beneficiary at some point in his or her life, but the idea of mutual aid does not exclude this possibility.

Some questions remain. Are these communitarian elements strong enough to offset the individualism that appears to be inherent in market relationships? Won't the effect of market competition be to break down communal ties and set people against one another? Can this be avoided without a complete transcendence of markets?

This issue cannot be definitely resolved here, but it is relevant that people seem able to stand in multiple relationships to one another depending on the various roles that they occupy from time to time. For instance, two people might be, simultaneously, friends, competitors on the tennis court, political allies, and rivals in the marketplace. Provided that they can keep those roles distinct—that is, they have ways of preventing their economic interests from intruding on their political aims, and so forth—there seems no reason why such a complex relationship should not be stable. Contrary to the view that economic markets, once established, necessarily pervade all aspects of existence, it is possible to point to many areas of life, even under capitalism, from which economic considerations are successfully barred. Socialists should look for ways of strengthening these areas; in particular, political participation should become a more significant aspect of life under socialism, and a major counterbalance to the economic sphere.

There is, however, a tradition of socialist thought that emphasizes the *simplicity* and *transparency* of social relations under socialism, and from this point of view the idea of role-playing, with its suggestion of artifice, may seem alien. Such a view is most eloquently expressed in William Morris's utopian fable *News From Nowhere*.[2] His vision of human fulfillment has its charms, but it is by no means self-evidently true. Here people seem one-dimensional just because of their simplicity. Missing is the creative tension that most actual people experience between the need for self-assertion and the moral demands of their community. Clearly the tendency of capitalism (and of unrestricted market relations in general) is to foster self-assertion at the expense of social loyalties. On the other hand, people in the Marx/Morris view of things seem over-socialized to the point at which their individuality is in danger of disappearing altogether. Perhaps, then, the idea of role-playing, and of coping with the dilemmas that arise when role requirements appear to conflict, will seem on reflection to be integral to our idea of a developed human being.

The remarks in the last paragraph fall far short of a properly worked-out philosophical basis for market socialism. They are meant to suggest only that it may be possible to find a principled grounding for the institutionally pluralistic system that we sketched earlier. Market socialism as we understand it combines market and nonmarket elements in a way that allows for the expression both of individual desires and of communal loyalties. Communitarian ideals find their practical expression in the shaping of markets to meet social objectives and in social policies which aim to satisfy a range of needs. The sense of community would be fostered through participation at work, and through nonmarket forms of association, especially political assemblies. It is not clear that a stronger form of community than this implies would be desirable. Ultimately socialists must decide how far their communitarian commitments can be taken, in view of their equally strong commitments to individuality and freedom.

## Notes

1. See J. Vanek, ed., *Self-Management: Economic Liberation of Man* (London: Penguin, 1975).
2. William Morris, *News From Nowhere* (London: Routledge & Kegan Paul, 1970).

## COMMENT

### by Robert Blair

The essay by David Miller and Saul Estrin, "A Case for Market Socialism: What Does It Mean? Why Should We Favor It?" is a valuable contribution to the discussion of alternative economic systems. Its discussion of workers' self-management is excellent, and its review of the role of the market process is intelligent and—as far as it goes— fairly convincing. The major problem is that the latter discussion doesn't go very far at all.

Miller and Estrin express a preference for "a free market in products, and either no market at all, or a well-regulated market in labor or capital." But by asserting that the market process when applied to consumer goods leads to (1) efficient production and distribution, (2) the best use of socially decentralized information, (3) increased personal freedom of choice, and (4) decreased bureaucratic power, the authors have *necessarily,* if indirectly, raised the question of whether these benefits would not also apply to capital markets and labor markets.

While pointing out the special circumstances that they see in capital markets and labor markets, Miller and Estrin neglect the other half of the equation: Do the problems cited fully or only partially offset the benefits (efficiency, information, freedom, and power) of markets? Could the special circumstances be dealt with by supplementing the market process with limited social legislation rather than by abolishing markets? Would the likely alternatives to capital and labor markets (presumably various forms of central planning) lead to a curtailment of these market-based benefits? What trade-offs might be faced under each system?

There are other points at which their arguments for market socialism seem vulnerable. When discussing the "special features" of capital markets, for instance, Miller and Estrin argue that investment decisions (1) are particularly complex and (2) may have substantial social repercussions. The first condition means that investment decisions tend "to gravitate in practice into the hands of experts who are able to spend time acquiring the necessary information . . . a small elite." The second condition means that the decisions of that "elite" give them a "power" over the majority of citizens whose lives are affected by private investment decisions.

It is clear that Miller and Estrin are not offering any formula for making investment decisions less complex. The small "elite" of investment "experts" will remain with us. The difference between a market process and a nonmarket process in this case is simple: Under a market regime the investment "experts" are constrained by the need to earn profits for the investors whose capital they employ and by the competition they face from other investment "experts." Under the most obvious alternative—state planning of capital investments— the "experts" will be constrained by the need to please their political and bureaucratic superiors. They, in turn, must please the politically significant players in the given political system (the Politburo, for example, or core constituent groups in a democratic system). An examination of recent performances by Congress and the president in preparing the federal budget suggests that nonmarket approaches have significant limitations of their own. As between a congressional subcommittee and the strategic planning staff of IBM, I am not as sure as Miller and Estrin that I'd be happier to have my investment dollars looked after by the public sector. Letting the state, even a democratic state, control or closely regulate investment is not likely to produce results clearly superior to those achieved by a market process. Miller and Estrin need to address such issues.

I see no reason to assume that a free market in labor—supplemented with adequately designed and funded education and job-training programs—would be unacceptable to intelligent socialists. Given the virtues that Miller and Estrin attribute to the market process, I can see why it might in fact be the *preferred* approach. And if critics answer that the government never does adequately design and fund such programs, I would have to inquire why such critics would therefore expect the government to do a better job designing and maintaining job-allocation programs.

It is clear from the opening of their article that Miller and Estrin have a good grasp of the benefits and limitations of market processes. They seem to have a much less clear picture of the limitations of governmental efficiency, wisdom, and benevolence. Nor do they seem to grasp the fact that consumer goods markets are tied, through the production process, to capital markets and labor markets and that to do away with the markets in the latter categories effectively cripples the markets in consumer goods.

On the plus side, Miller and Estrin are headed in the right direction: away from dogmatic demands for comprehensive state planning. And for the right reasons: greater economic efficiency and individual freedom of choice.

## REPLY

### by Saul Estrin and David Miller

Robert Blair attributes to our essay "A Case for Market Socialism" more definite intentions than its authors had. Our aim was not to provide a blueprint for a society organized on market socialist lines but to present some underlying principles and canvass some practical options—chiefly on the question of the preferred structure of economic enterprises. The intention was to persuade those on the left committed to a vision of socialism built on centralization, bureaucracy, and planning that a decentralized solution through markets was not merely feasible but attractive. We therefore sought to explain and defend market socialism in a broad way, rather than to peddle a particular vision.

Blair focuses on our claim that labor and capital markets have special features that set them apart from ordinary commodity markets. He infers that we favor nonmarket allocative procedures for labor and capital. But this inference is mistaken. Our point was simply that whereas with most ordinary commodities the case for allowing markets to operate freely as mechanisms of exchange is overwhelmingly strong, with labor and capital other factors—social costs, in a broad sense—enter the equation. The most committed free marketeer would not permit the invisible hand always to reign supreme in these areas, nor would we. In what ways, then, would labor and capital markets be differently organized under market socialism?

Take labor first. For the most part, we envisage that the labor market would operate freely. Workers would choose which skills to cultivate and which enterprises to apply to join. Quitting would be equally voluntary. There is nothing resembling labor direction in this model of socialism. But market socialists must ensure that when market forces take equilibrium real wages for some groups below the socially defined level of subsistence, for example, because of a serious downturn in world trade, workers' incomes do not actually fall to this level. There must be a floor to levels of pay for all groups, whatever their special situation in the economy. Moreover, the government must intervene to prevent the emergence of the unemployment that would otherwise result. Within limits, we would be less concerned about the free operation of market forces determining pay at the top end of the scale, provided that high salaries reflected the intelligent use of real skills, rather than the exploitation of monopoly power in the labor market.

A second constraint on the labor market derives from our concern with enterprise structure. Although we do not wish to rule out private activity on a small scale, we believe it is essential to the survival of market socialism that large-scale privately owned enterprises not be permitted to emerge. Above a certain size, all productive companies must therefore become either publicly owned corporations or producer cooperatives. It is our view that for most productive activities co-ops should be the predominant form. Public corporations should be restricted to the utility sector and other natural monopolies. But wherever the dividing line is finally drawn, our concern about the reemergence of capitalist ownership arrangements implies an additional labor market rule precluding voluntary employment contracts between workers and a private owner in organizations above a certain size.

Capital allocation raises more complex questions. They are not so much questions of principle: We can set out the desiderata for an investment system without great difficulty. There are three main requirements: (1) It should operate efficiently, in the sense that capital is allocated to the enterprises where it will be used most productively; (2) It should preserve the autonomy of the enterprises that receive the capital; (3) It should not generate very large inequalities of wealth among those responsible for the investment decisions. (1) and (2) together strongly suggest that there should be market competition between the investment agencies, so that the agencies bear the gains and losses of their decisions and so that cooperatives and other enterprises can use the option of switching from one agency to another to protect themselves from unwarranted interference. (3) suggests that privately owned banks of the traditional sort would not be appropriate to market socialism.

In addition, investment choices can have important effects spilling over to individuals other than those responsible for the decisions. An obvious example is pollution, but of equal social importance might be the special employment needs of particular areas. It then becomes hard to balance the market elements of allocation against the necessity for some sort of political regulation. Contemporary capitalist economies face similar problems and tend to resolve them in an ad hoc way, with nonintervention the norm and sporadic, but dramatic, government involvement in cases where public opinion or interest is strong. Our preferred solution would be to place the problem in a permanent institutional framework—a forum in which the competing claims of market and social returns could be fought out, case by case. This indicative planning framework would not, in itself, ensure public intervention in the accumulation process. Our predisposition remains for free-market outcomes whenever possible. But it ensures that investment takes place after the maximum feasible exchange of information, with government intervention triggered by predetermined criteria.

The most difficult issue is choosing between the options that remain for running a market-socialist capital market. On the one hand, we might envisage an array of public bodies, legally constituted and operating independently of one another—several national investment banks and a plethora of local and regional agencies mandated to foster investment in their particular areas. On the other hand, the investment banks might be constituted as private companies, with their shares owned (for instance) by the enterprises to which they lent their capital and raising their money from private as well as public sources. Note that in either case it would be possible to assess the investment managers according to the economic success of their decisions, and to work out appropriate reward schedules. Further refinements on these options can be devised and are discussed in our forthcoming book on market socialism (see J. Le Grand and S. Estrin, eds., *Market Socialism,* Oxford University Press, 1989). It probably does not make sense to state an absolute preference between them regardless of the historical circumstances of particular countries.

We would stress in conclusion that we certainly do not have a naive faith in the benevolence or omniscience of civil servants. Our predilection is for decentralized solutions wherever possible, and our aim is to find ways of combining these with long-standing socialist commitments to distributive justice and aspects of welfare that conventional markets tend not to accommodate. Of particular importance here are the benefits of workers' self-management and a distribution of income that is closely aligned with productive contribution. These commitments militate against the private ownership of enterprises and take us beyond the "mixed economy" if it means a system that preserves private ownership of capital in all essential respects but tries to offset its effect by political means. In another sense, our solution is a "mixed" one, inasmuch as we try to combine markets with planning in a way that makes best use of both of these (fallible) instruments.

# 12

# A Vision of Market Socialism: How It Might Work—And Its Problems

## (Summer 1991)

### David Miller

The collapse of communist regimes in Eastern Europe reopens the question whether there is any form of socialism that might be adopted, with popular support, in the advanced societies. The experience of communism suggests, fairly unequivocally, that such a system must rely mainly on market mechanisms. Mikhail Gorbachev has gone on record as saying that markets and capitalism are not to be confused, that one predates the other by many millennia and, by implication, may postdate it too. But proposals for a socialist market economy, aiming to combine the efficiency advantages of markets with the humane and egalitarian goals of socialism, still meet with fierce resistance on both sides. Defenders of orthodox capitalism claim that you cannot reap the economic benefits of markets without private property in the means of production, whereas some socialists continue to argue that market socialism represents a capitulation to the enemy. My main purpose here is to show that market socialism remains true to basic socialist aims, but I shall also try to dispel some frequently expressed doubts about its practical viability.

If we are rethinking socialism in the light of twentieth-century experience, we must begin by identifying clearly the basic goals that animate the socialist tradition. There are several such goals, whose relationship to one another is neither obvious nor straightforward. First, there is the conscious direction of social activities toward common purposes: Socialists have opposed the anarchy, so-called, of market capitalism, in which overall outcomes are simply a by-product of the pursuit of private interests by uncoordinated actors. Second, there is democracy, understood not simply as formal, parliamentary democracy but also as social democracy, democratic control of a much wider area of social and economic life. Third, there is material equality in the conditions of life. For a few socialists this has meant absolute equality; for rather more, it means a limit to inequality, with some disparities in living standards acceptable on grounds of justice. All, however, oppose what are seen as the excessive inequalities of a capitalist society. Fourth, there is freedom, understood as the opportunity for each person to develop his or her latent potential, and often contrasted with the narrow "negative" freedom of liberal society. Fifth, there is community, the idea that social relations should be characterized by cooperation and a sense of collective belonging rather than by conflict and competition.

It is worth noticing that there are possible tensions among these values. The aspiration to consciously direct social activities suggests the need for a single directing center, and this might well conflict with the socialist commitment to a widening of democracy. Again, the socialist belief in personal freedom is not self-evidently compatible with the idea of community, which might require that society impose upon itself a common set of moral values. But rather than speculating on these problems in the abstract, I should like to sketch a model of market socialism and then ask to what extent it realizes the goals I have identified.

## Why Have Market Socialism?

Consider an economy in which each enterprise is formally constituted as a workers' cooperative, leasing its capital from an outside investment agency. Cooperatives make their own decisions about products, methods of production, prices, and so on, and compete with one another in a free market. Net profits form a pool out of which incomes are paid. Each enterprise is democratically controlled by all who work for it, and among the issues to be decided is the distribution of income within the cooperative.

Let us look a little more closely at what the ground rules of such an economy might be. Enterprises borrow capital from an investment agency at a fixed rate of interest and subject to certain restrictions. They have rights of use in the capital they borrow but not full rights of ownership. This means that the value of their fixed assets must be maintained: Capital cannot be treated as income nor loaned to other enterprises. There must also be bankruptcy rules: Enterprises that cannot provide their members with at least subsistence income must eventually be wound up, with the workers transferring to other cooperatives. Each enterprise must maintain its democratic form. If it wishes to expand, it must take in additional workers as full members with equal voting rights. Subject to that condition, however, it can adopt whatever internal management structure it chooses. Small cooperatives might want to decide most issues by general meeting, larger ones might want to have a more elaborate system of decision making, with executive committees, and so on.

In this model of market socialism, the state would have a significant economic role to play, but it would not attempt to plan the outputs of the economy directly. Its function would rather be to set the parameters of the market in such a way that the economy served broadly egalitarian ends. One important aspect of this function is regulation of investment, which is to be undertaken either by private banks or by public investment agencies (I shall consider later the pros and cons of these options). In either case, the banks' job is to provide capital to both existing and newly formed cooperatives. Investment decisions should take into account not only the commercial viability of each enterprise but also wider considerations—in particular the need to keep the economy competitive, avoiding concentrations of market power, and the need to maintain a regional balance in employment. The investment agencies also have a large role to play in providing information to enterprises about prices, market trends, and so on, and in sponsoring the formation of new cooperatives in industries and areas where the need is greatest. Finally, the state is responsible for establishing a minimum level of income and for supporting members of cooperatives that are unable, in the short-term, to generate this income, so that new product lines can be developed or restructuring take place.

Besides these functions, the state would, of course, continue to carry out many of the tasks it currently performs, for instance, in the area of welfare provision. To advocate market socialism is not to make a fetish of the market. Markets are an effective device for providing a wide range of familiar goods and services, but where the boundaries should be drawn—which goods and services are best provided through the market and which through public agencies—is a matter of practical experience, not of principle. On the other hand, it is a serious error to confuse some possible instrument of socialism, such as the nationalization of basic industries, with the ends of socialism themselves.

The system just outlined is a pure model of market socialism intended to stimulate debate, not a blueprint for a real-world economy. In particular, as we shall shortly see, cooperatives will not always be the best organizational form for every industry. But before considering some practical problems, I want to consider the model in the light of the five basic goals of socialism listed above.

Market socialism sharply retrenches on the first of these goals: the direction of social activities toward conscious purposes. The general framework of the market—the form that enterprises take, investment policy, and so on—is established by deliberate decision; but concrete economic outcomes—what is produced, in what quantities, by whom—are left to the free play of market forces. What is achieved is economic efficiency, in the familiar sense of meeting consumers' needs with the least possible expenditure of resources and labor. Like other market economies, market socialism provides incentives for producers to respond efficiently to consumer demand, but unlike capitalism, it places all workers in this position by linking incomes directly to the net receipts of each enterprise. The microeconomics of a system of this kind have been studied quite extensively now by economists, who can specify the conditions under which it will be efficient in the technical sense. I shall consider some alleged inefficiencies below.

We are forced to abandon, or at least severely curtail, conscious social direction as an aim by our experience of central planning in practice. Economically, it has proved increasingly difficult to coordinate activities through centrally issued directives the more technologically advanced a society becomes; for although the means at the planners' disposal may become more sophisticated, the range of economic activities that have to be coordinated becomes vastly greater. Readers will, I assume, be familiar with the economic difficulties faced in recent years by the communist economies, particularly in the provision of consumer goods, and also with the not-too-impressive record of nationalized industries in the West.

Perhaps more important still, the tension between central direction and democracy that I hinted at earlier has been confirmed in practice. This conflict can occur at two levels. At the national level, it is impossible to envisage effective planning without a bureaucratic machine staffed by experts with access to technical information and therefore always liable to break free from democratic control. Put simply, it is hard to imagine the ordinary citizen being in a position to master sufficient technical detail to challenge a decision of the planning authority. At the level of the local factory or social service unit, central direction will inevitably reduce the scope for direct democracy by preempting major policy decisions. Under full-scale planning, decisions about the nature and volume of production, the pricing of inputs and outputs, and so on, are all made by the central authority, leaving little room for meaningful industrial democracy.

Embracing market socialism also means qualifying, in certain respects, the socialist commitment to community. I do not mean that the commitment should be abandoned—indeed I have argued elsewhere that what continues to distinguish socialists from radical or egalitarian liberals (such as Ronald Dworkin) is their recognition of the importance of communal ties in underpinning collective provision and the redistribution of material resources. What needs to be given up is the vision of an all-embracing monolithic community that leaves no room for social relationships of other kinds. Instead, the market socialist picture is one of a complex society in which elements of community exist at different levels—in neighborhoods, in workplaces, and, above all, in the arenas of politics, where people can act to express their common identity as citizens—but also alongside competitive and other relations. Such a picture rests on a view of human beings as complex creatures both needing and being able to sustain a wide variety of relationships with their fellows.

Whereas market socialism requires some retrenchment on traditional socialist aims of conscious social direction and community, it can be defended fairly robustly by appeal to the values of democracy, equality, and freedom. Market socialism provides the best chance for industrial democracy, which is both valuable in its own right—it's simply a good thing for people to be in control of the environment in which they spend a good part of their waking lives—and important as a training ground and stimulus for democracy on a wider scale. Where the state assumes direct responsibility for economic decision making, there is no real scope for industrial democracy, and I think it hardly needs arguing that capitalist forms of ownership offer little scope for it either, because any delegation of decision making to a company's work force is always provisional and liable to cancellation if the decisions reached affect shareholders' interests adversely.

My second claim is that market socialism embodies a substantial degree of equality, substantial enough, I should argue, to meet the aspirations of most socialists. There is not, of course, complete material equality. The market relies on giving producers material incentives to respond to demand, and although the size of these incentives depends on tax schedules, which are politically determined, I don't want to suggest that they can be reduced to zero. Nor would this be desirable. Pure equality conflicts with the justice of rewarding people according to their productive contribution. The point is that in market socialism all income in the market sector is *earned* income, received as a result of decisions within each cooperative as to how its combined labor is to be deployed. There are no returns to capital as such. Moreover, this income is spread throughout the membership of each enterprise in accordance with whatever schedule has been agreed upon. Particular cooperatives may, of course, strike it lucky, in the sense of finding that their products sell unexpectedly well. But there is no incentive to convert such short-term gains to a long-term position of advantage under the system outlined, since cooperative members will be reluctant to reinvest their profits in what is from each member's point of view a collective asset on which he or she has no individual claim. If what matters in assessing equality is lifetime income, rather than income over some shorter period, it is reasonable to hope that windfall gains will even themselves out. Bear in mind, too, that the guaranteed income proposal provides a secure baseline beneath which no one is allowed to fall. In short, market socialism embodies three forms of equality: an equal minimum income, equal access to the capital allocated by the investment agencies, and a limit to market-generated inequalities by virtue of the cooperative system and social ownership of productive resources.

Finally, market socialism provides substantial and fairly distributed freedom. It provides, in particular, freedoms in the choice of work and in consumption, freedoms that contemporary experience shows to be highly valued. Markets allow people to plan their lives within the limits of the resources available to them, rather than waiting for the decisions of an authority. Existing capitalist markets can rightly be accused of negating this freedom, in the case of most people, by severely limiting the resources to which they have access. The arrangements I have sketched for market socialism aim to avoid this accusation. Access to capital remains crucial, and it is vital that the investment agencies not be able to exercise their powers in a discriminatory way. This is a major reason for wanting to have a plurality of such agencies—for instance, a central coordinating body and a number of regional agencies in charge of investment in their own areas—as I shall argue later. The aim is to dissolve personal power by providing people with a range of partners with whom to deal, so that they are not dependent on the grace and favor of any one official. The market achieves this for consumers, but under market socialism there is no capital market in the conventional sense, and so whatever system of capital allocation is chosen must aim to achieve the same end for producers. With this proviso, freedom under market socialism is secure.

## How Would Market Socialism Work?

That, in outline, is the case that I would offer in support of market socialism: it promises economic efficiency, democracy at work, a high degree of equality, and personal freedom. But a number of critical questions have been raised about how such a system would work in practice, and I shall try now to address the most important of these (I shall avoid technical economic issues).

One set of questions concerns the efficiency of workers' cooperatives as a form of organization. Many existing cooperatives work on a very small scale, and this has led some critics to conclude that they are only appropriate in cottage industries. An alternative explanation, however, is that it is difficult for cooperatives to attract sufficient finance when they are competing with conventional capitalist firms; hence they tend to be concentrated in industries with low capital requirements. Students of cooperative organization suggest that it can work successfully in units of up to about five hundred people. In contemporary capitalism, there are few plants that are larger than this (and moreover, plant sizes have been diminishing quite rapidly, presumably as a result of labor-saving technology). Of course most industrial corporations incorporate many such plants, but the reasons are financial rather than technological; there may be economic advantages in coordinating a complex production process through organization rather than through market relations between separate units. If that is so, then market socialism may miss out on one kind of economy of scale while simultaneously benefiting from an economic structure that is generally more competitive; that is, there will be a larger number of smaller firms, and less tendency to monopoly or oligopoly.

A related worry is that in larger cooperatives an excessive amount of time will be taken up by questions of internal organization, with meetings dragging on endlessly. This is said both to be economically inefficient and contrary to the preferences of the workers themselves, who have a limited appetite for participation (Yugoslavia is sometimes cited as an example where the quest for participation has virtually stalled productive work). In reply, I should reiterate that the only condition imposed by market socialism (in its pure version) is that the employees of each enterprise should retain sovereignty over the affairs of that enterprise and should be subject to market disciplines. They can choose whatever form of day-to-day management best suits their needs (and in larger cooperatives there is a very strong presumption that this would involve a formal management structure). A poor choice would show up in the form of lower incomes for the members, and there would then need to be a trade-off between income and level of participation. Over time, "technocratic" and "participatory" cooperatives might evolve to cater to different preferences. The main lesson to be learned from the Yugoslavian case is that you cannot have a viable system of self-management without exposing workers to the rigors of the market (with bankruptcy the ultimate sanction).

Rather similar comments apply to a related issue, labor discipline. It is sometimes alleged that worker cooperatives are reluctant to set up proper disciplinary mechanisms to deal with lazy or incompetent workers. However, exposure to the market gives workers a strong incentive to put such mechanisms in place, so that each can avoid having his or her income lowered by the recklessness of comrades. Another allegation is that working in a cooperative is uncomfortable, because each employee has an incentive to check that his or her neighbor is not slacking. Clearly these two allegations cancel each other out and perhaps simply reflect different degrees of exposure to market forces. If workers can maintain their incomes while their productivity drops (as appears to be the case in Yugoslavia) then of course discipline is liable to disappear.

On closer inspection, then, most of the charges that are commonly leveled at workers' cooperatives as a form of economic organization fall to the ground. This is not to say that there are no problems for cooperatives.

In an earlier analysis in *Dissent* (Summer 1987)*, Saul Estrin and I pointed out that difficulties were likely to arise in industries subject to rapid technological change, because cooperatives require a relatively stable membership and are ill-equipped to deal with a radical restructuring of their labor force. Difficulties may arise also in industries requiring very high ratios of capital to labor, since cooperatives may be either unable or unwilling to attract the necessary amount of investment. A feasible market socialism ought to be institutionally pluralistic, in the sense that it should allow different forms of enterprise to develop to suit different sectors of the economy—for instance, labor-capital partnerships, firms that operate on the basis of an agreed division of rights, responsibilities, and profits between a labor board and a

---

*Editors' note: See chapter 11, this volume.

capital board might be better suited to capital-intensive industries. This will not undermine the justifying case that I sketched earlier for market socialism provided that the cooperative sector remains the dominant one in the economy, setting employment standards and income norms for the other sectors (think of how relations even within a conventional capitalist firm would change if there were many opportunities for the employees to join workers' cooperatives instead).

The second issue I want to address is that of entrepreneurship. Critics often concede that market socialism solves the problem of incentives under socialism (since under the arrangements sketched, workers' incomes depend on their success in supplying the goods and services that consumers want); but they claim that the system will tend to stagnate, since no one has an incentive to innovate in a bold and risky way. Genuine entrepreneurship, these critics say, is possible only when an individual owner can bear the risks and reap the rewards of his innovations—hence it requires capitalist ownership of the traditional kind.

To evaluate this, we need to be clear about what entrepreneurship consists of. In common usage the "entrepreneur" is often used to designate the person who owns or manages a firm, but clearly these are distinct functions even if often combined in practice. The entrepreneurial function itself consists in perceiving a difference between the future selling price of some good (perhaps a good not yet made) and the cost of the resources (including capital) needed to produce it, and then setting in train a process of production to supply the good. Entrepreneurship is possible because of uncertainty: No one can be sure precisely what the future demand for a good will be at a given price, and because of this it is possible for entrepreneurs to receive a rent over and above the fixed return on the capital they employ.

The most striking entrepreneurial act is the decision to establish a new firm to exploit a market opportunity, but there is no difference in principle between this and the more routine entrepreneurship displayed when an existing firm switches to a new line of production or decides to make its products using a new technique. It then becomes an open question whether in any given economy the entrepreneurial function is mainly discharged by the founding of new firms or by changes in the production schedules of existing firms. Under market socialism there is likely to be a more stable enterprise structure, with less exit and entry of firms, but a greater willingness on the part of firms to adapt to changes in the market and use the skills of their members in new ways. There is still room for entrepreneurship of the first kind. A like-minded group of individuals may simply decide to set up an enterprise to exploit a market opportunity—or, more likely, a group may leave an existing cooperative and establish a new firm.

Perhaps the critics believe that entrepreneurship cannot be exercised collectively, that it always stems from an individual's perception of the state of the market. Now it may be true that bright ideas for new products, say, always crop up first in one person's mind. But even in a capitalist system, would-be entrepreneurs must persuade investors (bankers, shareholders) to advance them capital and workers to join their enterprises; all these people need to be convinced that the entrepreneur's idea is potentially a viable one. Exactly the same is true in a labor-managed economy: a worker with a bright new idea must persuade his or her colleagues to implement it; or failing that, he or she must look around for new colleagues who are convinced by the proposal; and, of course, an investment bank must be induced to put up the capital. The main difference is that the worker in the cooperative system must be prepared to share the returns of his or her entrepreneurial skills with co-workers, in the form of the increased income flows that result. These fellow workers may be willing to give their inventive colleague a bonus—they would be well advised to do so—but there is nothing he or she can do to enforce such a payment while remaining within the cooperative. Capitalist entrepreneurs, on the other hand, can hope to corral all the returns of their entrepreneurship themselves.

The criticism then boils down to the claim that people lack a sufficient incentive to exercise their entrepreneurial talents unless they are able to corral all the proceeds individually. This claim seems a weak one. There is much satisfaction to be gained simply from seeing one's ideas work out in practice (and of course deriving *some* material benefit from this). Notice too that the capitalist system of entrepreneurship is likely to involve an unfair division of risk between the entrepreneur and his or her investors and employees. The former gets the returns of successful entrepreneurship while the latter two groups very largely bear the cost of failure—capital advanced is not fully repaid, workers have to face the considerable costs of finding new jobs, and so on. It is simply not true, as is sometimes alleged, that capitalist property relations allow a mutually agreeable distribution of risk between those who enjoy facing it (entrepreneurs) and those who are risk-averse (rentiers and employees). Everyone is exposed to the uncertainties of the market but not everyone is in a position to respond positively to those uncertainties. Under a market socialist regime, by contrast, all participants in the market sector of the economy have to exercise some degree of entrepreneurship—and bear the gains and losses accordingly—albeit perhaps only in the form of voting to implement X's clever new suggestion for making widgets more cheaply.

New goods and services will typically mean new investment capital, which brings us to the issue of how it should be provided under market socialism. In my initial sketch I assumed, in line with most economic opinion, that cooperatives should be externally financed by means of interest-bearing loans. In order to protect the autonomy of the cooperatives, it seems important that, instead of a single investment agency, there should be several competing sources of funding, so that a cooperative can switch away from an investment agency that tries to dictate the terms of the loan in an unduly narrow way. This could be achieved either by a set of private banks or through a devolved system of public funding—say one in which regional and local banks were made responsible to the tier of government in their area rather than to central government. Private banks might appear to be excluded by the general socialist principle prohibiting private returns from capital, but they could be constituted so that their shares were owned by cooperatives and public authorities in some proportion. The choice between public and private investment banks is a fine one. Private banks—which I assume would aim simply to maximize the return on their investments—would create an orthodox capital market, but perhaps at the cost of neglecting social considerations such as regional levels of employment. Public banks could be instructed to take such considerations into account when setting their investment criteria, but the corresponding danger is that they would become subject to political lobbying, with the result that they might pay too little attention to commercial factors, and, for instance, might prop up ailing enterprises that were large employers of labor in their own area. If public banks are preferred, it seems essential to protect them from such lobbying by granting them a large degree of autonomy—their overall performance might be periodically reviewed by the relevant political body, but not particular investment decisions. Under these conditions, it might not make much difference in practice what formal system of ownership was adopted for the investment banks.

This arm's-length relationship with the state rebuts the charge that investment agencies under market socialism amount to central planning under another guise. The primary function of the banks is to respond to applications for capital investment by cooperatives and other enterprises, and to judge these applications by ordinary commercial criteria. No doubt the banks would act as a source of financial advice to the cooperatives as they often now do to small capitalist firms. Investment banks under market socialism would have a more active role to play in fostering new cooperatives and would probably have special sections devoted to this task, but there would be no question here of any compulsion—the bank would simply play an initiating role in bringing together people seeking new employment, but would hand over the running of the cooperative to the members once it was established. (The best example of a bank's playing such a role is the Caja Laboral Popular at Mondragon in Spain, which has now helped to establish over one hundred co-ops.) The role of central government would be to decide the overall level of investment and to lay down general policy guidelines.

The criticisms I have been addressing are all variants on the theme that you cannot enjoy the virtues of a market economy while instituting a system of social ownership of capital. The final criticism I want to consider comes from a different quarter and has as its target the market element in market socialism. The charge is that because of its extensive reliance on market mechanisms a socialist market economy would suffer from many of the defects of existing capitalist economies, particularly in its effects on the natural environment. Market socialism is driven by the quest for profits; the fact that enterprises are predominantly labor-managed does not alter this fact. Thus, insofar as the quest for profit leads firms to use polluting technology and to destroy natural ecological systems, market socialism holds out little hope for improvement.

In reply I want to make a general point about markets and the environment, and then some specific points about market socialism. There is a tendency to saddle the market economy with environmental effects whose real source is uncoordinated decision-making regardless of economic setting. If one producer (or consumer) releases sulfur dioxide into the atmosphere, little harm is done, but if many do it simultaneously the result is acid rain. This has nothing to do with the market or nonmarket nature of the economy, as we can confirm by observing that the pollution records of centrally planned economies, such as those of East Germany and Czechoslovakia, have been among the worst in Europe.

Whatever the economic system, environmental effects of this kind can only be controlled by collective action. Typically this will mean action by national government (or indeed supranational bodies), although it is worth noting that markets may themselves be responsive to environmental concern by consumers in some cases. We can see this happening in the current race to put environmentally friendly products on supermarket shelves. Where different brand versions of the same product are virtually interchangeable apart from their environmental effects, even a slight degree of green concern on the part of consumers will tip the scales in favor of the friendly brands.

So, although no one in their senses would propose laissez-faire as a recipe for environmental bliss, the relationship between markets and the environment is less one-sided than critics would have us believe. What of market socialism in particular? What difference is the transfer of control to enterprise work forces likely to make to the economy's impact on the environment?

It would clearly be absurd to suggest that no workers' cooperative is ever going to contemplate using polluting technology or destroying natural resources. But three factors make this less likely. First, because profits are shared throughout the enterprise, the economic stakes are lowered. By comparison to a traditional capitalist firm, no one person has much to lose by switching to a more environmentally sound technique of production. Second, the effects of environmental pollution will also be felt more widely among those responsible for making the decisions. This is most obvious where the technology produces toxic wastes that the workers have to handle themselves: it is difficult to believe that the present methods of disposing of wastes at nuclear power plants would have been adopted if those plants had been labor-managed. The point also applies, however, where the pollution takes the form of emissions into the surrounding air, water, or soil. This is very likely to have a direct impact on the lives of at least some of the firm's members, and thus will be resisted fiercely.

Finally, decisions within a workers' cooperative cannot be taken behind closed doors in the way that they usually can in conventional capitalist firms. Every member has the right to be involved, and so unless there is unanimous agreement to conceal a decision, it will become a matter of public knowledge. This means that where environmental legislation is in place, it will be very difficult for a cooperative of any size to pay lip service to the legislation while covertly flouting it.

## Does Market Socialism Have a Chance?

Having now sketched and defended market socialism on general grounds, I should like to conclude with a few remarks about its practical prospects. Market socialism has often been associated in the past with reform movements in the Eastern bloc. This has largely been overtaken by recent events, but in any case there are serious obstacles in the way of a direct move from a central planned economy to market socialism. Some of these can be brought to light by considering Gorbachev's attempt to create a cooperative sector in the Soviet economy as a way of dealing with the worst shortages of consumer goods, especially foodstuffs. Introducing a profit-maximizing institution into an environment characterized by scarcity, administered prices, and an extensive black market has had two main consequences. First, the cooperatives have tended to charge what are in effect black market prices for their products, far in excess of the prices prevailing in the state-controlled shops. Second, given materials shortages in the Soviet Union, many cooperatives have found it more profitable to import manufactured goods from abroad than to produce for themselves. Together these tendencies have created a public image in the Soviet Union of the cooperatives as racketeers and exploiters, and the resulting outcry has obliged the authorities to restrict their activities. But the fault lies with the environment rather than with the co-ops. The lesson is that the market element of market socialism must be in place prior to the socialist element. More generally, the experience of a command economy means that workers are ill-prepared to face the risks and responsibilities of self-management in a market environment. The skills required for cooperative organization need to be learned. Moreover, where wages have long been fixed by bargaining with central authority, the idea of earnings varying according to market success is unfamiliar and hard to take.

Paradoxically, then, market socialist ideas might seem to stand a greater chance of success in well-established market economies, where working under market constraints is a familiar experience, but where many employees find themselves frustrated by the hierarchical structure of the traditional capitalist firm. Paths of transition here might include schemes enabling employees to buy out their own firms, especially as a way of warding off takeover bids; the formation of workers' cooperatives as the natural mode of organization in high-tech industries such as computing, where all or most employees are highly skilled; and various schemes of profit-sharing and codetermination that involve a gradual devolution of responsibility to the shop floor in workplaces of a more traditional kind. None of these initiatives can succeed, however, without substantial political support—in the form not only of enabling legislation but also of financial backing for participatory enterprises—and here we face what is perhaps the most formidable obstacle to market socialism in the West. Consider the position of a society attempting to implement some form of socialism within an international order that remains predominantly capitalist. A society that, for instance, implements a form of self-management or imposes strict environmental controls on manufacturing industry may find that its products cannot compete internationally with those of other countries where capitalist practices remain unmodified. It then faces a stark dilemma: either it restricts trade, with serious economic consequences, including inability to take full advantage of the international division of labor, or it reluctantly reverts to free-market capitalism. We might then face a position where there was substantial support across the advanced societies for social change along lines proposed in this article but where no single nation was prepared to introduce the necessary reforms by itself.

My conclusion is that a strong case can be made for market socialism, in terms of both its congruence with core socialist ideals and its economic feasibility. The major difficulty lies not in the system itself but in finding a path of transition to such an economy either from the collapsing communist economies of the Eastern bloc or from the affluent capitalist economies of the West. Increasing international cooperation may work in favor of such a transition (the European Charter of Social Rights is perhaps a distant harbinger) if there continues to be domestic support for greater economic equality and a more participatory style of work organization. But the path will be a long one, and we ought to think of market socialism as a guiding ideal, not as a platform for the next election.

## COMMENT: Questions about Market Socialism

### by Frank Roosevelt

David Miller's "A Vision of Market Socialism" is a thought-provoking contribution to *Dissent*'s ongoing discussion of this topic. He deserves our appreciation for the way in which he specifies five basic socialist values and then defends his model with reference to these values. Particularly useful are his points (a) that there are *tensions* among the values and (b) that no single model of socialism can express or promote all five values to the same extent. Accordingly, those of us who advocate one or another variant of a socialist market economy must recognize that, in giving priority to such goals as democracy, freedom, efficiency, and consumer satisfaction, we may have to sacrifice to some extent a traditional socialist goal such as "the conscious direction of social activities toward common purposes"—since the achievement of this goal would require consensus and central planning but would reduce the scope for democracy and personal freedom. Similarly, there is a conflict between reliance on competitive markets and traditional socialist conceptions of community. We are faced with difficult choices—and Miller is entirely correct to insist that, in the real world, trade-offs like these are inescapable.

There are numerous other important and helpful points in Miller's article—such as his argument that workers' control is more likely than capitalist enterprise to foster ecologically responsible decision making—and I am in accord with the overall thrust of his project. However, I believe there are several questions that need to be posed regarding the logic, feasibility, and normative power of his model. I hope that raising these issues will be taken as a friendly effort to promote dialogue and enhance progress toward a common goal.

First, Miller's discussion of the *efficiency* of market socialism is incomplete. He focuses on the effectiveness of workers' cooperatives as a way of organizing enterprises in various industries but he does not systematically address the question of how well an economic system made up mainly of workers' cooperatives would be able to allocate resources and achieve macroeconomic objectives such as full employment. He does not mention a problem that has been widely discussed by economists, namely, that workers' cooperatives, because they generally seek to maximize *income per worker,* will tend to employ fewer workers than would comparable capitalist firms. In a recent discussion of the economics of workers' cooperatives, Saul Estrin concludes that a market socialist economy would probably not allocate resources as efficiently as a capitalist economy does.[*] If so, would it not be wiser to concede the point and, after noting that allocative efficiency is not exactly at the top of the list of socialist values, shift the emphasis of our case for market socialism to its other virtues?

Similarly with *entrepreneurship,* Miller offers a sustained argument to counter the oft-repeated charge that market socialism would be inferior to capitalism because it would not provide sufficient incentives to induce entrepreneurs to introduce innovations in production processes and products. This is an important issue, and I found Miller's discussion of it to be imaginative and helpful. However, his solution to the problem—which offers collective entrepreneurship as a substitute for the capitalist kind—remains in the realm of *speculation,* whereas the proponents of capitalist entrepreneurship have numerous

---

[*]Saul Estrin, "Workers' Co-operatives: Their Merits and Their Limitations," in J. Le Grand and S. Estrin, eds., *Market Socialism* (Oxford: Clarendon Press, 1989), pp. 164–92. See esp. p. 179.

case studies to support their view that individual monetary rewards are an effective way of inducing entrepreneurial behavior. Moreover, Miller's discussion of the issue is mainly focused on the differential impact of individual monetary rewards (under capitalism) versus shared rewards (for socialist entrepreneurs). He does not consider other factors such as the possibility that a capitalist environment may be more conducive to entrepreneurship because it provides more scope for—and social approbation of—individual creativity, whereas collective entrepreneurship in a socialist environment may in fact be a more cumbersome and less rewarding activity. If such factors as these (as well as the differences in financial rewards) are indeed operative—and if we assume open borders—we might see potential entrepreneurs emigrating to capitalist countries rather than trying to be socialist entrepreneurs in the way Miller proposes.

Another important issue that Miller takes up is the question of how to provide *capital* (which is not to be owned by individual enterprises or their members) to the workers' cooperatives. The fundamental debate here is over whether the capital-providing mechanism should be in the public sector (and thus democratically accountable through the political process) or whether a market socialist economy would be better off having a set of private banks and ordinary capital markets. Miller adopts a position of neutrality, citing the pros and cons of both options. Although he notes that "private banks might appear to be excluded by the general socialist principle prohibiting private return from capital," he goes on to say that they would be acceptable if "their shares were owned by cooperatives and public authorities in some proportion." What would justify the receipt of—or the benefits derived from—*unearned* income accruing to individuals as members of cooperatives, he does not say.

The more fundamental issue is the question of what criteria will be used to make investment decisions and thus to allocate capital among the various enterprises and localities. Miller notes that there are "social considerations" as well as commercial factors relevant to investment decisions; but, taking into account such factors as the danger that public banks may be unduly influenced by "political lobbying," he ends up on the fence: "The choice between public and private investment banks is a fine one. . . . [I]t might not make much difference in practice what formal system of ownership was adopted for the investment banks."

I must here register a strong disagreement. As Miller himself notes, a system of private banks will allocate capital exclusively on the basis of the rate of return, in order to maximize the banks' profits. This will produce the result—as it does in capitalist countries—that those firms, industries, and regions that are already operating with healthy profits will get most of the new loans—and, hence, the existing inequalities, regional disparities, and other aspects of uneven development will be exacerbated. It seems to me that part of what it means to be a socialist involves being opposed to this particular tendency of a capitalist economy. Given the impact of investment decisions on the future of a country—affecting everything from the energy sources we rely upon to the movement of the population between urban and rural areas to the pattern of wealth and income distribution—it is incumbent upon socialists to make every effort to devise *public* investment mechanisms that can implement democratically determined social priorities without succumbing to the distortions of bureaucratic authority and inappropriate political influence that have been all too prevalent in the Communist countries.

The final question I would like to pose concerns Miller's use of the term and his understanding of *competition*. A reading of his article leaves the impression that he is excessively enamored with the neoclassical economists' model of a "perfectly competitive" economy in which all firms are relatively small; no one firm can influence the price of anything because prices are determined by supply and demand in the larger market; there is free entry into all industries, hence no monopoly; all "factors of production" are paid the equivalent of their marginal contribution to output; and so on.

Miller's commitment to the neoclassical model is evident in the paragraph in which he argues that virtually the entire economy can be made up of worker-controlled firms employing no more than about five hundred people each. He claims that, in most industries, there are no technical factors that require enterprises to be any larger than five hundred person plants and, in a key passage, goes on to say:

Of course most industrial corporations incorporate many such plants, but the reasons are financial rather than technological; there may be economic advantages in coordinating a complex production process through organization rather than through market relations between separate units. If that is so, then market socialism may miss out on one kind of economy of scale while simultaneously benefiting from an economic structure that is generally more competitive; that is, there will be a larger number of smaller firms, and less tendency to monopoly or oligopoly.

There are several problems here. First, in what sense is it true that an economic structure made up of small-scale, worker-controlled firms is *more competitive?* My interpretation is that by "more competitive," Miller really means more like the neoclassical model of "perfect competition." The problem with this is that such an economy —and the firms in it—may not actually be very competitive in the real world. Miller himself concedes this point near the end of his article when he refers to competition in quite a different way: "A society that . . . implements a form of self-management . . . may find that its products cannot compete internationally with those of other countries where capitalist practices remain unmodified."

The issue at stake here is more than a semantic one. Indeed, the sense in which a socialist market economy is or is not competitive is of crucial importance to a strategy for getting from "here" to "there" and, more important, to our understanding of what we mean by "there." Although I do not have the space to deal with all the relevant issues, among the questions we should be considering are the following:

• Is the neoclassical "perfectly competitive" model, with worker-controlled enterprises substituted for capitalist firms, the best available normative standard for socialists?

• If the small-scale, worker-controlled enterprises that Miller proposes are not actually competitive in a world dominated by transnational corporations, by what means should we attempt to bring about a transition from capitalism to market socialism?

• If we establish a market socialist economy in one country but its products are not competitive in international trade, should we restrict trade and move toward autarky?

With regard to the last question, Miller himself mentions—but then quickly retreats from—the idea of restricting international trade and moving toward autarky. It might be useful to recall the argument of John Maynard Keynes in his 1933 *Yale Review* article, "National Self-Sufficiency," that any country wishing to experiment with its social arrangements will have to cut itself off from the world market. Whether or not there is any merit in Keynes's position today, it seems to me that the autarky option constitutes a more logical conclusion to Miller's argument than the rather discouraging speculations with which he ends his article.

I have focused on my disagreements with Miller, but I would not like to end without again expressing my admiration for his bold presentation of the case for market socialism. At a time when a fundamental rethinking of the socialist idea is so obviously necessary, contributions like his are highly valuable.

# 13

# Market Socialism, a Blueprint: How Such an Economy Might Work

## (Fall 1991)

*John Roemer*

Since the fall from power of the ruling parties in Eastern Europe during the amazing events of autumn 1989, most commentators in the West and the East have proclaimed the death of communism. If communism is defined as consisting of the dictatorship of a single party, the administrative and central allocation of most resources and commodities, and the ownership of all firms by the state, then I agree with the diagnosis. The inference that these commentators implicitly make is that socialism, too, is a dead letter. I will argue here for the feasibility of market socialism, a politico-economic system in which firms are publicly owned, the state has considerable control of the "commanding heights" of the economy, and there is democratic control over society's use of its economic surplus.

The failed "communist" experiment was characterized by the following three features:

1. public or state ownership of the means of production,
2. noncompetitive (that is, single-party) politics, and
3. command/administrative allocation of resources and commodities.

The inference that those proclaiming the death of socialism have drawn is that, because (1), (2), and (3) imply economic failure, therefore *all* of (1) through (3) must be negated to achieve a successful economic system. That is bad logic: All we can infer from the failure of (1)+(2)+(3) is that at least one of the three characteristics must be changed to achieve economic success. What I outline below is an economic mechanism in which (2) and (3) are indeed negated—there will be democratic, competitive politics and market allocation of most commodities and resources, but public ownership of the principal means of production is maintained. Put slightly differently, my claim is that markets are necessary to achieve an efficient and vigorous economy but that private ownership is not necessary for the successful operation of markets. It is the failure of both the right and the left to separate the concepts of private ownership and market allocation that has led to the premature obituaries of socialism.

**Components of Market Socialism**

The viability of market socialism depends upon the claim that private ownership of the means of production is unnecessary for the successful operation of a market system. In the blueprint that I shall now sketch, I attempt to support this claim as concretely as possible. We have, as yet, very little empirical evidence that would enable us to evaluate this claim in a rigorous way. So the argument must be, at this point, theoretical.

The market socialism I envisage has these components: firms will be managed by managers whose intention it will be to maximize profits, at going prices. That is, the firm manager will try to hire labor and produce output of such variety and quality as will maximize the long-run profits of the firm. Firm managers will either be elected by workers or appointed by boards of directors, about whose composition I will speak presently. What is important, however, is that managers try to maximize profit. Labor will be hired on labor markets, and wages will be set by supply and demand in the market. Almost all private goods and services will be allocated on markets, and prices will be determined in these markets. The government will continue to provide public goods, financed by taxation of profits and wages. Certain private goods, such as health services, may also be provided gratis to the population—but this is nothing new, even for capitalist countries.

There are two socialist aspects to this economy. The first is that the government will have the power to intervene in the economy to direct the pattern and level of investment. One plank of the platform of a political party in such a society will be the direction that investment would take should the party be elected. The desired investment levels and pattern will not be implemented through a command system but by manipulating the interest rates at which different industrial sectors can borrow funds from state banks. Thus, if the government's intention is to decrease the production of automobiles, it will raise, above the market rate, the interest rate at which the state banks lend to automobile firms. People will thus exercise some collective control, through democratic politics, over the use of savings in society. In this sense there will be public control of the use of the economic surplus, a phrase with a socialist ring. I do not propose that people vote on the composition of investment because of that ring but because I believe we lack the markets that would be necessary for investment to be allocated in a socially desirable way. This is reflected in the extreme volatility of investment in large capitalist economies, which is responsible for the business cycle and therefore, in particular, the rise and fall of unemployment. (What I am saying is less true of small capitalist countries, where the demand for exports can lead the business cycle. But it is substantially the case that the demand for investment goods leads the business cycle in countries like the United States.)

The second socialist aspect of this economy is that the profits of firms will not go to a small fraction of society but will be divided, after taxes, more or less equally among all households, taking a form that Oskar Lange called the social dividend. Thus a citizen will receive income from three sources: wage income, which will vary depending upon the worker's skill and amount of time worked; interest forthcoming from savings, which will also vary across households; and a social dividend that will be, in principle, approximately equal across households. The social dividend will be a form of guaranteed income, or what some European writers have called a universal grant. I prefer not to call it a grant, because it is not a gift (which "grant" connotes). It is that part of the national income which is not distributed as wages or interest but which belongs to the people as owners of the means of production. Of course, a society such as the one I am describing might decide to distribute profits in some other way, such as in proportion to the value of labor that a person expends, but I would oppose that proposal.

What will taxes be used for in this society? All the usual things: public goods that a government provides, income transfers to those unable to work, subsidies to families that cannot earn enough to live decently, and so on. They will also be used to subsidize the government's intervention in the capital market. (If the government encourages the production of refrigerators that do not use chlorofluorocarbons by discounting the interest rate to firms that make them, this will give rise to a deficit in the state banks, which will be financed through taxation.)

Inequality will continue to exist in this society, due primarily to the differential wages that people will earn and also, to some extent, to their differential savings behavior. What will be equalized is that part of income due to corporate profits.

Why do I include as an integral part of this proposal the stipulation that firm managers maximize profits of the firm? Would it not be better to let workers manage the firms directly? My answer is that the firm belongs to everyone, and every household depends upon each firm as a source of part of its income via the social dividend. Workers, in any case, should not be able to appropriate the profits of the firm they work in: that would lead to gross inequalities among workers. We know, from economic theory, that profit maximization under the right conditions (which include a competitive environment for the firm) leads to an efficient allocation of resources—that is the main reason to use profit maximization as a tool. Now, profit maximization will lead to some antisocial behavior, and that will have to be regulated. But we have no example of a large economy that has operated successfully without profit maximization as a goal of firms, and my attempt here is to propose a blueprint that is based, as much as possible, on the successes of capitalism but which deviates from capitalism in certain important ways.

These are the main lines of the blueprint. I shall modify it and fill it in a bit in what follows. If people continue to work about as hard as they do under capitalism, and technological change takes place about as it does under capitalism, then the two major differences between this kind of market socialism and capitalism are the direction of investment by a political process and a more egalitarian income distribution. Funds used under capitalism to finance the consumption of capitalists will here be distributed to all citizens. If capitalists consume a small fraction of national income, as in Norway, then the change in income distribution effected by market socialism would be small. If, as in Brazil, the rich consume 40 percent to 60 percent of national income, then the redistributive effect would be substantial.

## Making the System Work

Will this system work? There are various levels at which the questions can be asked. One is at the level of economic theory. Is it possible for a market system to equilibrate an economy in which profits are distributed as I have described and in which the government intervenes in the investment behavior of the economy by manipulating interest rates if the managers of firms maximize profits, facing market prices, wages, and interest rates? My colleagues Joaquim Silvestre, Ignacio Ortuño, and I have studied this question, and the answer is yes.[1] It is possible for the government to achieve any of a large variety of possible compositions of investment for the economy by the setting of discounts and surcharges on the market interest rate, and prices in all markets will then adjust in such a way that an equilibrium is achieved, in which the demand for each good by consumers is equal to the supply of that good by firms. The social control over investment is achieved without setting ten thousand prices, or one million prices—the figure for the Soviet Union varies, depending upon the source. Nor does the center tell any firm what to produce, or tell firms where to find their inputs and where to ship their outputs. All these millions of decisions, supposedly but impossibly made by the planning system in Soviet-type economies, are left to individuals to arrange through markets. Yet by the adjustment of between five and twenty interest-rate discounts, the economy would realize the composition of investment that its planners aim to achieve.

Thus, I do not think that the lessons of the Communist experience include an admonition against planning as such, against the direction of the economy toward certain ends. The methods of Soviet planning were ineffective and worse because they did not use markets as a way of decentralizing millions of small decisions. Actually, the most effective planning requires the use of markets. What is *not* planned in this vision of market socialism is the composition of output, the prices of goods, or the distribution of labor: just the composition of investment.

Another level at which the can-it-work question may be asked is: Will the managers of firms be *motivated* to maximize profits in an economy where firms are not privately owned by investors? Will entrepreneurial spirit be forthcoming? Will technological innovation take place? This is the level on which most economists are skeptical concerning the feasibility of market socialism.

Let us first take up the question of managerial discipline. Stories abound about corrupt and incompetent management of firms in "socialist" economies: There was the famous *Krokodil* cartoon of the manager of a Soviet nail factory who, to meet a quota of one ton of nails, produces a one-ton nail. It is wrong to conclude from the experience of firms in a command economy what publicly owned firms would be like in a market economy.

Managerial culture in the Soviet Union is demoralized, to say the least: mostly, one can only get the inputs one needs by bribery and barter. This culture would be very different if inputs and outputs could be bought and sold on markets. But this, of course, cannot be the complete answer to the query. "Bourgeois" finance economics maintains that the only reason that managers pursue the interests of shareholders, which require maximizing profits, rather than their own selfish interests, is the threat of losing their jobs. The discipline is provided via the stock market. If a firm is being poorly managed, its profit prospects will darken and its stock price will fall. It will become an attractive target for a takeover by investors who will buy the firm cheaply, put in better management, and return the firm to a profit-maximizing program. The stock market has therefore been called the market for corporate control. It is noteworthy that finance economists believe that private ownership of firms is insufficient to guarantee profit maximization. There must be *highly concentrated* private ownership, they maintain, with a few very large stockholders in whose interests it is to monitor the management closely. It is also large investors who organize takeovers. If this is so, the quandary for market socialism is real: how can an economy whose firms distribute profits diffusely devise a mechanism to monitor firm management?

A clue to a possible answer comes from the experience of Japanese capitalism, where the stock market was relatively unimportant in the economy until recently. Firms are organized into groups, called *keiretsu*. Each *keiretsu* is associated with a main bank, whose responsibility it is to lend to the firms in its group and to monitor the firms' managements. The investment projects proposed by firms are evaluated by the staff of the bank, and in this way the bank is able to monitor the firms' behavior. These main banks also defend firms in their group against takeovers from firms outside the group. This system has been successful, if we take Japanese capitalism to be a successful capitalist variant. But there is no market for corporate control in Japan—at least, it does not take the form that it has in the United States, and capital is not directed to its most profitable uses by the stock market. This last point is worth emphasizing, for another plank of capitalist ideology is that bureaucrats cannot decide how to allocate capital: that is best done by a stock market, where millions of people express their opinions by voting with their dollars. Yet in Japan, apparently, the accountants, economists, and industrial experts working for the big banks are sufficiently savvy to pass good judgment on investment proposals of firms.

Pranab Bardhan, an economist at the University of California, Berkeley, has proposed a system wherein firms in the kind of market socialist economy I outlined above could be organized into groups modeled after the Japanese *keiretsu*.[2] Say firms W, X, Y, and Z are in one group, with bank B. Each firm would own some shares of the other firms in the group, and the bank would also own some shares of each firm. The board of directors of a firm would consist of representatives of its shareholders, that is, of the various firms and the bank in the group. That part of profits of firm W, say, not going to the bank, to the other three firms, or directly to W's own workers would go to the state and would be distributed to all citizens as part of the social dividend. The fraction of firm W's profits going to firms X, Y, and Z by virtue of their ownership of shares of W would constitute a significant other part of the social dividend of the workers of X, Y, and Z.

Thus every worker in the economy would receive his or her social dividend from two sources: a centralized dividend from the government, made up of a small share of profits of all firms in the economy, and a decentralized part, consisting of a fraction of the profits of the other firms in his or her group. The function of this decentralization is to give firms X, Y, and Z an interest in monitoring the behavior of firm W. In particular, if firm X thinks firm W is not profit-maximizing, then it can ask the bank B to buy X's shares of W. This in turn puts pressure on the bank to force W to do better.

Bardhan's proposal is not equivalent to introducing a stock market; it is a mechanism for decentralizing the accountability of firm management to a small number of institutions, in this case other firms and banks, which are capable of monitoring the management. Complete equality in the social dividend received by different households would be compromised in the interests of creating a mechanism for decentralizing the monitoring of firms.

A word about innovation. Again, it would be wrong to conclude from the experience of firms in command economies that firms that are not privately owned will not innovate. I believe that, if there is sufficient competition, innovation will occur in these market socialist firms. To the extent that innovation takes place in organized research and development divisions in large firms anywhere, it can just as well take place in a socialist firm.

It might be said that the kind of innovation that will not occur under market socialism will be that of the lonely inventor who, spurred on by the prospect of becoming a multimillionaire, invents a new kind of computer. Under capitalism, these people exist: if they succeed, they form small firms and are in almost all cases eventually bought out by large firms. I suggest that such private firms be permitted in market socialist economies. They should be nationalized, with proper compensation to the owners, at some given size. The government, instead of IBM, would buy out the small computer firm. Or the publicly owned IBM could buy out the small firm, subject to the usual antitrust considerations, which will be necessary under market socialism as well. This mechanism should provide almost as much incentive to the entrepreneurial spirit as capitalism provides.

To sum up, I think it is possible to use markets to allocate resources in an economy where firms are not privately owned by investors who trade stock in them with the purpose of maximizing their gain, and that the government can intervene in such an economy to influence the level and composition of investment should the people wish to do so. The income distribution will be more equitable than in capitalist countries today.

## Can Justice Exist With Market Socialism?

Will a market socialist society be a just society? Will it maximize the potential for self-realization of its citizens? It is wrong, in my view, to maintain that any market system, with or without capitalists, allocates resources and incomes justly. What perfectly working competitive markets do is pay people according to the evaluation that other people in society put on their "contribution." In a capitalist economy, a person's contribution consists not just of a labor contribution but also of his or her contribution of capital. Leftists have usually attacked the justice of capitalist income distribution on the grounds that capitalists are not the rightful owners of their capital and hence their receipt of profits is an injustice, which, moreover, constitutes exploitation of those to whom the capital should rightly belong. The problem with this argument is that it does not go far enough. For I do not think it is correct to say that a distribution of income in which each is paid the value of his or her labor contribution to the rest of society is just either. For it is surely the case that different people make contributions of very different values to society, owing in large part to their differential training and abilities. (It is wrong to say, as leftists sometimes do, that the contribution of an unskilled worker is just as valuable to society as that of a physician: it could be if, counterfactually, almost no one had the capacity to be an unskilled worker and almost everybody with no training could be a physician. Value must be measured not, as Marx said, just as the labor embodied in producing the thing but in the total real resource cost that people are willing to sacrifice to make the thing available.)

Under market socialism people will receive differential wages, and that will reflect their differential economic value to society. But they will neither *deserve* those wages nor be entitled to them, because I do not believe they deserve or are entitled to returns on their arbitrarily assigned genetic compositions and family and social environments, which largely determine their skills. This is an old Marxist point—in the *Critique of the Gotha Program*, Marx wrote of payment according to the value of one's labor as a "bourgeois right."

I view the differential wages that will accompany a market socialist system as justifiable for only one reason: they are a by-product of using a labor market to allocate labor, and there is no known way to allocate labor more efficiently in a large, complex economy than by use of a labor market. Now there are various ways of decreasing real income differentials of workers that could be used by a market socialist society—to the extent, of course, that a democratically controlled society condones using them. One practice of the social democracies is to tax income sharply and progressively and to redistribute it by providing some goods, such as health services, on an equal basis to all at no fee.

The job of a socialist economist is to design an economic mechanism that would provide each person with sufficient material income to pursue his or her self-realization consistent with an equal degree of opportunity for self-realization provided for others. That's pretty vague, and this is not the place to try and sharpen it up, but the quick statement is that equality of income is a goal, subject to various caveats. So much attention is paid to the *efficient* allocation of resources because, given the present level of technological development and needs of people on the globe, one cannot afford to waste a lot in the process of production and distribution, and because the achievement of efficiency requires some inequality, as, for instance, in the wage differentials of a labor market and in the differential social dividends that would come about in Bardhan's firm-monitoring scheme.

If some inequality is one undesirable feature of market socialism, a second is, as G.A. Cohen has written, that the market "motivates contribution not on the basis of commitment to one's fellow human beings and a desire to serve them while being served by them, but on the basis of impersonal cash reward." Indeed, one should not idealize the behavior of people in a market socialist economy. Firms may advertise deceptively and try, as they do under capitalism, to create in people tastes for goods by exploiting their feelings of insecurity and incompetence. Workers will need unions to protect them from overzealous managers even if they have the power to remove management. More generally, conflicts between different groups of people based upon their different economic interests will continue to exist. Environmentalists and workers in the lumber industry may continue to clash.

## Why Have Market Socialism?

What are the attractive features of market socialism? I have stressed, thus far, income distribution. Profits, that part of the social product that remains after paying wages, interest, and taxes, are to be distributed on a more or less equal basis to citizens. I have also mentioned the planning of investment—but this is neither a necessary part of the blueprint nor something that capitalist countries cannot in principle do, and so it would be wrong to stress it here. What I have not yet discussed is politics, which I believe would be more democratic than in capitalist democracies because a class of capitalists who have the economic power enabling them to affect and to a great extent control state policy, both through the electoral process and by other means, would not exist. One fears, of course, that managers of public firms and banks would become a class, *in loco capitalisti,* and exert political power to maintain their growing empires. I have, thus far, not mentioned an important role for workers' control of firms—a control of which I am somewhat leery as it may impede profit maximization and its concomitant efficiency. But perhaps that danger is small compared to the danger of the growth of a managerial class in itself, and workers' control over the choice of management might be the best form of insurance against the latter.

Suppose that through workers' control of management, or some other kind of checks, no politically powerful managerial class develops. What kind of politics could we expect to see? There will continue to be bourgeois parties—if this society guarantees the kind of civil liberties that the left is committed to, then surely ideological conservatives will organize, not to speak of those who may have historical claims to big chunks of now nationalized wealth. Thus debate will surely continue on all the big issues—war and foreign policy, the level of government transfer payments and public spending, the environment, equality of opportunity, racism, sexism, and so on. I think that the property relations in a system of market socialism will be the basis for a gradual shift to the left in mass politics, and for this reason: there will not be individuals who stand to gain so much from right-wing politics as there are in a capitalist system. Surely the income of citizens will depend upon the profitability of firms—perhaps the social dividend will make up 20 percent of the income of a typical household. There would, however, be no class of citizens with great resources at their command whose incomes would depend *so much* on the profits of firms as the incomes of capitalists do. Consequently, citizens in such a society would be less willing than capitalists to trade off peace, the environment, the welfare of the underprivileged, and so on, for increased corporate profits.

Finally, consider the issue of education. I have stated that socialism does not advocate equality of income as a right. I believe the fundamental goal is equality of opportunity for self-realization, and in a historical era of material scarcity, where for most people more material goods will increase their opportunities for self-realization, equality of income is therefore a corollary goal, though not a postulate. Just as important, perhaps more so, is education; a socialist society must devote resources to rectifying through education, as much as possible, the inequalities of opportunity that children will otherwise face due to their different backgrounds and talents. Will a market socialist society be willing to devote the necessary resources to education? There can be no guarantee that any democratic society will do so, for such a reallocation of resources requires convincing the middle class to subsidize working-class education to a greater degree than it does now. Of course, the education of middle-class children should be improved as well. But if the goal is equalization of opportunity among children, then the greater increase in educational expenditures must be to improve the verbal and mathematical literacy of working-class children, and especially, among these, of minority children. What can be said, I think, is that the influence of the capitalist class on educational policy will be absent, and it will be up to the population at large to decide what fraction of society's resources it is willing to commit to education. Under these circumstances, I believe there would be a gradual increase in the fraction of resources so devoted, although this is surely not a foregone conclusion.

The Bolshevik revolution was, in the beginning, a utopian experiment: its designers inherited from Marx an antipathy toward the market mechanism and believed that they could replace it with a system of central allocation. That was not their most devastating error, but it was bad enough. Worse was the strangulation of all opposition, which made almost impossible the rectification of errors in general. There were advocates of market socialism, in some aspects, throughout Soviet history, from Nikolai Bukharin in the twenties to Leonid Kantorovich (the only Soviet recipient of a Nobel prize in economics) and Evsey Liberman in the sixties and seventies. But by that time, the ideological blinders of the labor theory of value and the physical entrenchment of a class of state and party authorities who derived their power largely from the absence of markets combined to render almost nil the prospects for a transition to market socialism, or, as many would say, to socialism.

What the left must learn from the last seventy-five years is not that socialism is impossible, nor even that planning is unnecessary or harmful, but rather that the transition to socialism will be less dramatic than we had hoped. What some will consider bad news is that socialism, at least for a long time, will require markets. The good news is that markets do not require capitalists, that is, the concentration of economic power and wealth in the hands of a small class. The bad news is that an economic structure based upon markets will make the transition to "the socialist person" a more protracted process than we had hoped. The good news is that without a capitalist class and in a democratic setting, people will be able to think more objectively about, and act in, their true interests than under bourgeois democracy. Marx was a great teacher on the nature of capitalism; he was not competent to instruct us on how to construct socialism, a lesson we must learn from the history, both capitalist and socialist, of the twentieth century.

## Notes

1. Ignacio Ortuño, John Roemer, and Joaquim Silvestre, "Investment planning in market socialism," Department of Economics, University of California, Davis.

2. Pranab Bardhan, "Risk-taking, capital markets, and socialism: A note," Department of Economics, University of California, Berkeley.

## COMMENT

### by Joanne Barkan and David Belkin

Fashioning models for a successful socialist economy is an idiosyncratic inclination these days, but one that we share with John Roemer. He's not willing to concede that the socialist project has been buried irretrievably beneath the wreckage of communism, and neither are we. Working carefully and with an open mind, Roemer has pushed the debate on market socialism forward a good measure. But as we pore over his blueprint, imagining how it would function in three dimensions, it looks seriously flawed.

Roemer begins with some traditional noncapitalist assumptions: state control over the "commanding heights" of the economy, public ownership of enterprises, democratic disposition of society's economic surplus, and income equality. He sets out to show that markets function no less effectively when enterprises are publicly, rather than privately, owned, and that his version of socialism will be as efficient as capitalism. Feature by feature, here's what we found.

### Government Control Over Investment

Roemer's socialist government will arrange the pattern and levels of investment throughout the economy by setting a specific interest rate for each sector's borrowing. Wielding this instrument, the government will control the famous "commanding heights." But how can one partition a complex economy into neat sectors with unambiguous boundaries? Lines based on product groups often cut through firms rather than between them. Most firms, small and large, no longer produce in narrow product niches. Where would General Electric go? Or Du Pont? Or Sony?

As soon as the government attempts to carve up the national product, the lobbying hordes will swoop down, clamoring for their firms or industries to be redefined into a lower interest-rate sector. The system's susceptibility to logrolling and influence peddling will be immense. Firms with good friends in high places—or mass followings below—will wrangle more favorable terms. Not only will these deviations throw off the government's investment plan; they will insinuate soft budget constraints throughout the economy, sabotaging efficiency. (When a firm need not cover costs with earned income because it receives a subsidy of some kind, that firm operates under a soft budget constraint.)

Meanwhile, the government must find a way to make its interest-rate differentials stick. If capital can flow freely from one sector to another, it will naturally seek the highest return. It may well flow in directions not desired by the government, once again foiling the grand plan. So the government will put constraints on the movement of capital—which immediately creates another level of bureaucratic management where lobbyists can congregate. The more successful the lobbying, the less effective the government's plan; but the tighter the controls on capital, the less dynamic the economy.

Roemer argues that this system is both democratic and socialist because citizens, as owners of the means of production, elect their government on the basis of party platforms, each of which includes an investment proposal. So 50 percent plus one of the voters will determine a pattern of interest rates by selecting the one that seems to benefit them most. This may be formally democratic, but is it economically rational? And suppose economic conditions shift dramatically between elections. Are the parties in power locked into a plan that is more detailed than the usual economic program and therefore more inflexible?

If this interest-rate scheme looks so problematic, one wonders how the Japanese pulled off *their* triumph in sectoral planning, which also involved interest-rate manipulation. The answer is that the Japanese version dispensed with democracy. The system is corporatist: a powerful old-boys' network—bankers, industrialists, politicos—called the shots. With vast resources at hand and the likelihood of even greater profits to come, they coordinated long-range plans without the intrusion of democratic procedure.

Furthermore, Japanese industrial policy has always been much less ambitious than what Roemer proposes. A few firms were chosen as industry leaders in several key sectors and favored accordingly. Low-cost capital was provided for research and development, but the state never took on the role of exclusive supplier of credit. Firms often ignored the preferences of the Ministry of International Trade and Industry: they obtained their own financing on their own terms based on their own reading of investment opportunities.

## Public Ownership of the Means of Production

Roemer lays out an economy made up of publicly owned enterprises whose profits after taxes are dispersed to all citizens in the form of a social dividend. He then anticipates the standard and stickiest objection: such enterprises won't operate efficiently even if their managers swear on pain of dismissal to maximize profits. (It's generally agreed that efficiency goes hand in hand with profit maximization.) Economists have discovered—Roemer explains—that even private ownership can't guarantee efficiency unless a few principal owners have a stake in monitoring management.

So Roemer introduces a version of the Japanese *keiretsu* system. State banks would each oversee several clusters of enterprises, deciding on loans and monitoring management. The banks would control shares in each firm, and each firm would in turn control shares in the other firms of the same cluster. After taxes, a portion of a firm's profits would go to its workers and to all its shareholders (the latter also make up the board of directors); the remaining profits would go into the social dividend.

We see several difficulties here. Unable to reconcile profit maximization with public ownership of the means of production and citizen appropriation of economic surplus, Roemer drops some of the socialist features he used to justify his model. First, he actually reintroduces a form of principal ownership with his bank-and-firm clusters, creating a quasi-privatized system. Second, his clusters would inevitably produce substantial variations in wealth and economic power, with some clusters churning out record profits and others barely hanging on. Since Roemer designated income equality as a socialist feature, his model loses another distinguishing characteristic. Gross inequalities would beget the same cruelties in Roemer's society that they do under capitalism. Of course, the government could smooth out sharp differences with progressive taxation—a fine and just solution, but one that's available under capitalism and thus doesn't enhance the socialist nature of Roemer's model.

Third, in order to have principal owners who will monitor efficiency, Roemer must pare down the social dividend—that socialist feature that distributes the economic surplus equally among citizens. Instead, a firm's surplus goes first to its workers and shareholders. Roemer doesn't speculate on how much would be left for the social dividend, but it might not be more than any government could collect with progressive taxes.

Fourth, we wonder if worker-shareholders will really be motivated to monitor management closely. Monitor duty resulting in stronger cluster-firm profits might yield the individual worker no more than a few hundred dollars a year. Workers might find more lucrative (or enjoyable) uses for their time. If workers aren't inclined to oversee management, efficiency throughout the economy will suffer in the long run, and the very rationale for the cluster system falls apart.

When it comes to encouraging risk taking, the cluster system might fail again. By the time profits trickle down to the single worker-shareholder, the potential gain from a gamble might not be hefty enough to induce adventurous investment. Since economists agree that dynamism depends on some high-risk, high-return innovation, a cluster economy could bog down.

Finally, the problem of capital mobility, which cropped up in the interest-rate scheme, surfaces again. Will capital be able to move from a lackluster cluster to a vibrant one? If not, the economy will sink into inefficiency. But if capital is allowed to move freely, the ties between a bank and its firms will be loosened, once again undermining the rationale for the cluster system.

## Workers' Control Over Management

Roemer recognizes a dangerous flaw in his socialist model—the likely evolution of a cryptocapitalist class made up of bankers and managers in the most powerful firms. Sitting atop financial empires, their economic strength would easily slip into political influence. To keep these managers in check, Roemer decides to give the workers of each firm the power to elect and dismiss their bosses. It's not clear whether the new arrangement—workers' control—would be sufficient to counter the power of a managerial class. Roemer simply states that workers' control or some other mechanism might work—which hardly seems an adequate investigation of a serious problem.

Roemer brushes past another difficulty when he mentions being leery of workers' control because it could undermine efficiency. He says no more, but it's worth speculating on what many economists agree could be the results of basing an *entire* economy on workers' control. Worker-shareholders might consistently resist taking on new employees because a larger payroll would shrink profits per worker in the short run. This tendency, rippling throughout an economy, would inhibit labor mobility—and, ultimately, efficiency. Workers might shy away from labor-saving technology in order to preserve their jobs. This, too, would impede efficiency. And workers might prefer taking profits home rather than reinvesting. Over time, innovation as well as efficiency would founder.

## Private Ownership

According to his own standards, Roemer dilutes the socialist nature of his model still further by permitting—reluctantly—private ownership of small firms. He does this to ensure that inventor-entrepreneurs will still play their role as innovators in the economy. When private firms reach a certain size, the government will nationalize them with fair compensation.

Roemer is correct to worry about innovation, but his solution could be a nightmare. Let's say the government takes over firms with more than one hundred employees. Every brisk business with 102 employees would probably badger (or pay off) the bureaucracy for dispensation, monkey around with payroll records, or regularly fire a few hapless workers. And who would make sure that no private business went over the limit? One would need an army of size-investigators to knock on doors all over the country and count heads.

The threat of nationalization would probably ward off foreign investors—as would restrictions on the free flow of capital needed to maintain the cluster system and interest-rate differentials. (Roemer doesn't discuss integration into the international market, but his economy could have big trouble here.) Most problematic of all, inevitable nationalization would discourage entrepreneurs from making long-range plans. They'd be more inclined to take their profits and get out, undercutting innovation in the long run.

## Politics in the Absence of a Capitalist Class

Roemer sees politics shifting left once there is no domineering capitalist class to subordinate the general good to profit making. Unlike capitalists, citizens in his society will think more objectively about their true interests. They'll be more inclined to spend for social benefits like education; they'll be less inclined to sacrifice the environment.

This sounds like wishful thinking—especially since Roemer hasn't demonstrated that his system won't spawn its own domineering elite. But let's suppose that the big bankers and managers are somehow reigned in. Every working person in society now has her or his income directly tied—through the social dividend—to annual profit reports. Roemer speculates that this won't have much effect on political thinking because only a small portion of their income will come from enterprise profits.

We've argued that this small portion might not be enough to encourage workers to monitor management or to jump into risky investments, but it's probably quite enough to shape political behavior. This is because politics in Roemer's system has such a direct and predictable impact on income. The processes that spew out interest-rate differentials, for example, influence the size and distribution not only of the social dividend but of wages as well. How can worker-shareholders not take the deepest personal—that is, factional—interest in these politics?

The serious flaw in Roemer's thinking here is wishing into existence the New Socialist Man and Woman. Rid of the capitalists, suddenly they reveal themselves to be clearheaded, farsighted, and consistently generous.

John Roemer grapples seriously with key issues—democracy, equality, efficiency, innovation—thereby leading anyone interested in market socialism to consider its possible economic mechanisms more closely. But something is wrong. Perhaps because Roemer begins with assumptions that are too global (all enterprises will be publicly owned; the government will direct all investment). Other assumptions implement ideology too rigidly (the people, as owners of the means of production, will democratically select the government's investment plan; all profits will be distributed to the people as owners of the means of production). After setting out these initial propositions, Roemer senses that the boat won't float. So he introduces new devices—again universally applied—such as the cluster system and workers' control. He ends up with an economy potentially mired in bureaucracy and hamstrung by rigid structures. And along the way, the socialist content has been greatly diluted.

What might work better? An economy that begins as a mix of public, private, and worker-controlled enterprises, including banks? Indicative planning for a variable number of sectors? Regulated markets? High quality, universal public services that decommodify human needs by taking them completely out of the market? Not socialist enough! comes the cry. But suppose such a model ends up producing greater socialist substance. . . . Well, whatever the model, it will have to tackle the problems raised here. The debate, we hope, will continue.

## REPLY

### by John Roemer

I will respond to the Barkan and Belkin points seriatim.*

### Government Control Over Investment

There have been, and are, selective credit controls in many capitalist countries, and the "lobbying hordes" that Barkan and Belkin fear have not swept down to sabotage the system. Indeed, the states of the East Asian tigers (particularly, South Korea) have influenced investment through access to credit from state banks. Granted, any system of selective credit controls will induce some rent-seeking activity; but

---

*The author wishes to thank Pranab Bardhan for his important contribution to this comment.

these costs have to be weighed against the substantial benefits of investment planning in the absence of a full set of futures and insurance markets.

Will capital "seek the highest return"? Of course! The point of interest-rate differentials is to make otherwise unprofitable sectors attractive for investment, should society decide that growth of such sectors is socially desirable.

Barkan and Belkin have in mind a rigid and unrealistic conception of democratic politics if they believe that a democratically elected government cannot change its plan should economic conditions so warrant. All actual democratic governments do this, and there is no reason that a market socialist government could not do so as well. It is up to the electorate to decide, at the next election, whether the government responded to changes in the economic environment in a good or bad way.

I am surprised that my critics seem to believe that democracy is incompatible with the implementation of selective credit controls (their comments on Japan). In democratic France, seven of the top ten banks are state owned and are influential in channeling investment. In Germany, the state bank is also important. Of course, Barkan and Belkin might respond that France and Germany are not *really* democratic, because economic policy is heavily influenced by a capitalist class. But then their argument really is that a democracy where people have approximately equal economic power cannot successfully (or efficiently) adjudicate conflicts of interest. This is, of course, a much larger topic than the present comment can discuss, but it may be worth noting the rather nihilistic vision of democracy that their criticism implies.

Finally, I should say that Barkan and Belkin perhaps take my blueprint too literally. It would not be necessary for the government to announce investment subsidies or surcharges for every sector in the economy—perhaps only for a few central ones. And it is not necessarily industrial *sectors* that would be subsidized, but perhaps underdeveloped *areas* of the country. The principal point of my discussion of investment planning is that it is possible for the government to redress the market failures involving investment without direct administrative allocation of investment goods, a system that would be plagued with the inefficiencies that were characteristic of Soviet-type economies. One of the errors of the postmortems of communism has been the identification of central planning with command/administrative allocation systems. These terms are not coextensive; it is only the latter that have been shown not to function.

## Public Ownership of the Means of Production

Perhaps my definition of the social dividend was not sufficiently clear. It is that part of the national income that is left over after wages and interest are paid; it takes the form of profits of firms. Central to my view of market socialism is the claim that a market economy has a great deal of latitude in how to distribute this part of national income—much more latitude, in fact, than it has in the distribution of wages and interest. (It is this claim that is challenged by Hayekian economics, which maintains that profits must be allocated to those entrepreneurs who "create" them, lest profit-creating activities not be brought forth.) In "Blueprint," the share of profits received by a citizen comes from two sources: first, a share of the profits of all firms in the economy, which he or she receives in the form of public services paid for by taxes on firm profits; and second, a direct distribution of a share of profits from the firms in the *keiretsu* in which the citizen is employed. The first part will be more or less equal across citizens (or, in some cases, will be distributed in accordance with need, as in health or education services), while the second part may vary somewhat across citizens, because of the differential profitability of the different industrial groups. This variability, however, will not be extreme, for the government can tax more profitable firms progressively. There must, however, remain some inequality in the second part as an incentive to profit maximization and innovation.

What Barkan and Belkin ignore in their discussion is the important role of bank monitoring: firms are monitored by their boards of directors, which consist of representatives of other firms, other institutional investors (insurance companies, pension funds), and the main bank associated with the industrial group. Bank monitoring of firms has been shown to be a successful alternative to the stock market in Japan and Germany. Of course, the German and Japanese banks are in the main privately owned, and so a legitimate question is: will publicly owned banks monitor firms as well as private banks evidently can?

I believe that, with sufficient legal and institutional safeguards, the answer is yes. Why will banks not soften the budget constraint of failing firms in their group? The key is that these public banks will be in competition to represent, or to induct into their industrial groups, successful firms (including new firms). Thus, a bank wants to build a reputation as a sound financial manager, one that maintains profitability in its group. This will involve efforts to rescue firms that should be rescued but not to prop up firms that should die. It is also important to have legislation insulating banks from government interference in their short- and medium-run activities. Finally, the state must commit itself to a relatively free trade policy (with the exception of infant industry protection). Its firms must be exposed to the brisk winds of international competition, which will weed out the ones that should not survive.*

I see no reason to shy away from the participation of foreign capital in the national economy. The mandate of market socialism is to equalize incomes in the national economy. If the size of the domestic pie can be increased by the participation of foreign capital, so be it. This is "market socialism in one country"; it is not realistic, at this time, to try to plan for an equal distribution of the international pie, desirable though that may be. Again, legal safeguards must prevent international capital from playing an important political role in the country. This may be easier said than done; as in my earlier discussion of rent-seeking, there is a trade-off, and the government must optimize.

## Worker Management

The jury is still out on workers' control over management. Probably the most prudent proposal is for the firm's board of directors and its workers each to have some voice in the selection of management. Economic theory suggests that it may be possible to design the tax

---

*It is interesting to note that Rudolf Meidner, the architect of the Swedish "solidaristic" wage policy, advocated high wages for unskilled workers not just for distributional reasons, but to weed out weak firms that could survive only by paying low wages.

mechanism so that worker-controlled firms maximize profits (see the work of Jacques Dreze), but to date the successful examples involve only small parts of a national economy (there are only 18,000 workers involved in Mondragon). "Blueprint" is distinguished from other proposals of market socialism in the peripheral role played by worker-controlled firms. I would proceed cautiously and experimentally with this institutional form.

### Private ownership

Barkan and Belkin are inventing when they say that I "reluctantly" allow the private ownership of small firms. That was nowhere implied in "Blueprint." The only question concerns private firms that begin as small ones and become large. I suggested that, first, most successful small firms would be naturally taken over by large public firms, as successful small firms are in capitalist economies. Whether to have mandatory nationalization of private firms that grow large and are not absorbed into the public sector is, again, an issue that will require experimentation. It may be desirable not to nationalize large-profit firms, for there is some evidence that public sector managers do a better job if the managerial labor market includes private firms. In France, where managers move freely between the private and public sectors, public firms are reputedly well run; in Belgium, where public sector managers typically do not migrate to the private sector, they are, reputedly, not.*

But even if, for political reasons (that is, to prevent the emergence of a politically powerful capitalist class) the society decides to nationalize large private firms, it need not have the terrible incentive properties that Barkan and Belkin fear. The question is whether the state will pay full value to the private owners. It might be objected that if it does, what's the virtue of nationalizing the firm? After all, its erstwhile owners will walk away with the full value of the firm, if the state sticks to a policy of paying such in order to create good incentives in the private sector. The answer is that citizens with large private wealth in a market socialist society will not have the political

---

*I owe this point to Gerard Roland.

power of citizens with large private wealth in a capitalist economy, for they will not be able to invest that wealth in a way that controls the means of production. While private participation in the "stock market" might not be prohibited, privately held shares would not be given a vote in corporate matters. Again, this practice has been typical in Japan, and has not ruined the capital market. T. Boone Pickens finally sold his 26 percent interest in Koito Manufacturing after his attempts to influence corporate policy were totally rebuffed. The management wouldn't even meet with him! (See *The Washington Post* April 28, 1991.)

**Politics**

Barkan and Belkin are again inventing when they write that my discussion of politics presupposes a New Socialist Person. On the contrary, my intention was to argue that, without the existence of a class of citizens who derive vast incomes from control of the means of production, politics would change. That is, people who derive only a relatively small fraction of their income from profits generally (say 20 percent to 25 percent, which is approximately the share of profits in national income, and would therefore be the share of a citizen's social dividend in his or her income) and an extremely small fraction of their income from any one firm, will have different economic interests from people who derive all of their income from the profits of a single firm, and I rely on that to predict a difference between politics in market socialism and capitalism.

It may be useful to outline the economic argument in more detail. Imagine an economy that has, for simplicity, one large firm that employs all citizens, and produces the one good that they consume. The economy is capitalist: each receives some wage income from the firm, and some profit income, but the shares of profit income are highly unequal. Suppose, now, that the firm's profitability depends on the level of some "public bad," say, the level of pollution that the firm emits. (A public bad is a "bad" that everyone must consume; its existence affects all of society.) A person's welfare in this economy depends upon two things: the level of the private good that she or he consumes and the level of the public bad, which everyone consumes equally.* The trick is that profits increase with the level of the public bad, so that citizens have different interests concerning what the level of the public bad should be, depending upon the fraction of their income that derives from profits. It can be shown that, under reasonable economic conditions, the larger a citizen's share of profits in the firm, the larger the level of the public bad he or she will want. Thus, if the level of the public bad is decided upon by those who own the firm, it will be higher the more powerful the large shareholders in the firm. In particular, in a market-socialist economy, where each citizen receives an equal share of the firm's profits, no one will want the public bad to be produced at as high a level as "capitalists" want it to be.†

I believe this argument has quite widespread application. Besides pollution, consider the following examples: the speed of the assembly line, noxious advertising, investment of the firm in South Africa, and conducting war to lower the price of some imported input used by the firm. Each of these fulfills the requirements of the model described above—it is a public bad that directly reduces the welfare of most citizens (or workers), but increases the profits of the firm and, therefore, of citizens' incomes. The model implies that, were profits of firms equally distributed in a population, these "public bads" would be set at lower levels than they are in a capitalist society. This is not due to the good intention of New Socialist Persons but just to the fact that their *economic interests* differ from those of citizens who receive incomes from firm profits. A citizen who derives but a small fraction of her income from an oil refinery whose profits would soar were a war waged to keep the price of oil low may well find it worthwhile to suffer a fall in that component of her income in return for not going to war; but a citizen whose income may otherwise decline in the hundreds of millions of dollars may well decide to wage the war, despite the fact that he, too, dislikes war.

I suggest, therefore, that we would observe an improvement in the "quality of life" were society's profit income distributed in an egalitar-

---

*Forget about the possibility that the rich can buy houses near the ocean, where pollution is minimal. That only makes my point stronger.

†For the details of this argument, see my as yet unpublished paper, "Would Economic Democracy Decrease the Amount of Public Bads?"

ian fashion, to the extent that quality is synonymous with small levels of public bads that are associated with the profitability of firms. And this conclusion holds given people as they are now, not as they arguably would become after several generations of society without the constant barrage of propaganda meant to win the average citizen over to support the interests of capitalists.

"Blueprint" is purposefully conservative in its proposals. It seeks to redress one of capitalism's main evils—the inequality of the distribution of profit income—by making the smallest possible changes from relatively successful capitalist economies. None of its particular microeconomic features are new: markets, investment planning, bank monitoring of firms, and nonvoting corporate shares are all existing practices and institutions. Nor does it presuppose a new kind of altruistic citizen for its successful implementation. What is new—and I must emphasize that "Blueprint" is not my own creation but the amalgamation of the work of a number of economists to whom I have referred—is the claim that one can separate various characteristics of an economic mechanism that many have believed to be inseparable. To wit, planning is not the same thing as central allocation, and the equal distribution of profits does not entail highly diffuse, and therefore unsuccessful, monitoring of firms. It is not of great import to me whether the firms in "Blueprint" should be denominated as "publicly owned"; they share with the traditional public firm the characteristic that profits are distributed equally to (or finance services that are consumed equally by or according to need by) members of the population, but they differ from the traditional public firm in being controlled by entities that have direct economic interests, as opposed to political interests, in their performance.

# 14

# Challenges to Market Socialism: A Response to Critics

## (Spring 1992)

### Thomas E. Weisskopf

The idea of a market-based form of socialism was first given serious attention in the 1920s, when it was promoted by moderates within the socialist movement as an alternative to the marketless form of socialism identified with Marx's vision of full communism and embraced in principle by the Bolsheviks. The first systematic theoretical exposition of the functioning of a market socialist economy was that of Oskar Lange in the 1930s, who has ever since been recognized as a pioneer of the idea.[1] Since then a great deal of work has been done by advocates of market socialism—many of them economists from or interested in the post–World War II Eastern European countries—seeking to improve upon Lange's model while dealing with various problems raised by critics.[2]

Out of this continuing literature has emerged a variety of different models, but all share the same central goals and the same basic means. Market socialism seeks to promote the traditional socialist goals of equity, democracy, and solidarity while maintaining economic efficiency; it proposes to do so by retaining one major feature of capitalist economies—the market—while replacing another major feature of capitalism—private ownership of the means of production. For at least medium- and large-scale enterprises in most sectors of the economy, market socialists propose some form of social ownership rights; and these socially owned enterprises are expected to operate within a market economy that is regulated—but not displaced—by national government planning.

"Ownership" is a complex concept encompassing a variety of rights, which can potentially be assigned to a variety of different people. For our purposes it will be useful to distinguish two such rights in particular: the right to enterprise *control* and the right to enterprise *income*. The right to control confers the prerogatives and responsibilities of management: those who control the enterprise (or their representatives) make the decisions about how it will be operated, who will work in it and under what conditions, whether or not any aspects of the enterprise are to be expanded, contracted, sold or liquidated, and so on. The right to income confers a claim to the surplus generated by the enterprise—that is, the net (or residual) income after fixed obligations have been paid.[3]

The standard capitalist enterprise is owned by private individuals or shareholders who have (ultimate) control over management according to the nature and the amount of their ownership shares; typically a small number of individuals or shareholders have predominant control. Under market socialism, enterprise control is social rather than private. Control of a market socialist enterprise is held by a community of people, each of which—in principle—has an equal say in management; as a practical matter, this (ultimate) control is usually exercised via appointment of a managerial staff. There are two principal variants of such social control, depending on the nature of the community in which control rights are vested:

• *Public management:* enterprises are run by managers appointed by and accountable to an agency of government (at the national, regional, or local level), which agency represents a corresponding politically constituted community of citizens.[4]

• *Worker self-management:* enterprises are run by managers appointed by and accountable to those who work in them (or their elected representatives), with control rights resting ultimately with the enterprise workers (on a one-person one-vote basis).[5]

In the standard capitalist enterprise, ownership by private individuals or shareholders conveys not only control rights but also income rights—again according to the nature and amount of their ownership shares. Under market socialism, income rights are held socially rather than privately. The surplus of the market socialist enterprise accrues to a community of people in a relatively egalitarian manner. Here again there are two principal variants of such social claims to income:

- *Public surplus appropriation:* the surplus of the enterprise is distributed to an agency of government (at the national, regional, or local level), representing a corresponding community of citizens.[6]

- *Worker surplus appropriation:* the surplus of the enterprise is distributed to enterprise workers.[7]

These two different ways of assigning control rights and income rights under market socialism can generate a matrix of four different possible market socialist models, since there is no *a priori* reason why each set of rights must be assigned in the same way. As it happens, most advocates of market socialism lean primarily in one direction or the other: there is one school favoring what I will label the "public enterprise model," characterized by public management and public surplus appropriation, and a second school favoring the "worker enterprise model," characterized by worker self-management and worker surplus appropriation.[8]

Although the replacement of private with social control and income rights at the enterprise level is what most clearly distinguishes market socialism from (market) capitalism, advocates of market socialism also generally call for a greater degree of government intervention into and/or control of the market than is the norm in capitalist economies. Such control does not typically or primarily take the form of quantitative targets or restrictions, of the kind associated with the discredited system of centrally planned socialism. Instead, it involves more extensive government regulation of enterprises, more extensive government provision of public goods and services, and more extensive use of taxes and subsidies to reflect social costs and benefits that would otherwise be ignored by individual consumers and producers in the market environment. The objective here is to guide rather than to replace the market, so as to bring market price and cost valuations more closely into line with true social benefits and costs.[9] The difference between market socialism and capitalism in this respect is essentially one of degree rather than kind; apart from any control and income rights in enterprises, the economic role of government in a market socialist system differs little from that of government in the more government-regulated (that is, social-democratic) capitalist systems.

Market socialism has been challenged both by those who question the ability of markets to function efficiently in the absence of capitalist private property rights, and by those who question the ability of social ownership forms to meet socialist goals within the context of markets. I will here address the first of these two lines of criticism;[10] and I conclude with a brief discussion of whether there is really any fundamental difference between market socialism and social democracy.

### Markets Without Private Property

Defenders of capitalism have long argued that markets cannot work properly unless they are embedded in a system of property rights that enables private individuals to own, buy, and sell shares in the means of production.[11] Socialists who agree on the desirability of markets must therefore be prepared to defend the proposition that markets can indeed promote efficiency in the absence of capitalist private property rights. To do so, we must meet head-on the following kinds of criticism.

1. *Doesn't the experience of Communist-party-directed socialist economies with market-oriented reforms teach us that market socialism is unviable?[12]*

    This is precisely the lesson that economists such as János Kornai have drawn from the historical experience of those CP-directed socialist countries—notably Yugoslavia and Hungary—that have tried to reform centrally planned socialist economies by introducing a significant role for the market.[13] There can be no question that the market-reformed economies of Eastern Europe have indeed fared very poorly in the last decade; but the evidence on market reform of CP-directed socialist economies is mixed. Both in Yugoslavia (in the 1950s and 1960s) and in Hungary (in the 1970s) the early period of market reform showed considerable economic achievement, and the same appears to be true of China (in the 1980s).[14]

Most important, evidence from any of the CP-directed socialist economies is very limited in relevance to a prospective market socialism in which government is to be democratic rather than authoritarian. The historical experiences of Yugoslavia, Hungary, and China with a form of market socialism have been contaminated by the ubiquitous interference of a powerful Communist party organization—at the workplace, in enterprise management, and in local, regional, and national government. Under these conditions the market has been far from free, enterprises have been far from autonomous, worker self-management has been far from full, and bureaucratic central planners have continued to make many important economic decisions. Regrettably, history offers us no good case study of a democratic market socialist system.[15]

In the absence of decisive historical evidence, many critics of market socialism have raised theoretically grounded arguments designed to show that markets cannot work effectively under socialist forms of ownership of the means of production. Some of these arguments apply only to public enterprises; some apply only to worker enterprises; and some apply to both types. I will consider the more general issues first and then turn to the particular questions most often raised about public and worker enterprises, respectively.

2. *Won't market socialist enterprises suffer from inadequate worker effort in the absence of a serious threat of job loss?*

Market socialists are committed to full employment, whether the economy is characterized primarily by public or by worker enterprises. Critics argue that the assurance of a job will undermine "worker discipline," that is, workers will tend to shirk at the workplace if they don't face a credible threat of joining the unemployed for poor performance.

Note first that job loss is only one of a variety of negative sanctions that can be applied to workers who perform poorly on the job; other such sanctions include not being promoted to better jobs and not being granted pay raises. Furthermore, there are many kinds of positive incentives—involving both material and nonmaterial rewards—which can motivate better work performance. Some of these positive incentives are likely to be more effective in a context of long-term employment relations than in an environment in which job termination is always a credible threat.[16]

Market socialism is likely to provide for greater job stability than capitalism, but workers have no guarantee of retaining their current jobs. Full employment is not to be achieved (as in CP-directed socialist economies) by requiring enterprises to retain or take on additional workers even when this leads to overstaffing and consequent "underemployment." Instead, full employment is to be assured through public programs to retrain and relocate unemployed workers along the lines of Swedish "active labor market policies."[17] Empirical evidence from Sweden suggests that this type of "employment security" (as opposed to "job security") does not impair worker performance at the workplace; retaining one's job remains a significant performance incentive even if the alternative is retraining and relocation to a new job rather than unemployment. A worker with a reputation for performing poorly on the job would face the likelihood of moving to a less satisfying and remunerative job upon re-entering the labor force.

3. *Won't market socialist enterprises suffer from incompetent management in the absence of a "market in corporate control"?*

Managers of conventional capitalist enterprises are liable to lose their jobs if their poor management drives down the stock market value of the firm to the point where major shareholders decide that new management is needed, or to the point where new investors are tempted to buy a controlling share of the firm and install a new management team. The ultimate threat of a hostile takeover is supposed to ensure "management discipline" much like the ultimate threat of job loss is supposed to ensure labor discipline in capitalist enterprises.

Managers of market socialist public or worker enterprises

would have to answer for their management performance to government agencies or workers' councils, just as managers of capitalist firms are answerable to shareholders; here there would seem to be comparable possibilities for success and abuse. However, market socialist enterprises are clearly not subject to hostile takeovers, so their managers don't face the same ultimate threat as managers of capitalist firms. Is this likely to be a systematic source of weaker management performance?

The case is at best a very questionable one. First of all, the threat of a hostile takeover does not exist for privately held companies—many of which have been very successful. Moreover, the threat of hostile takeover of publicly held corporations plays a significant role only in a minority of capitalist economies—notably the United States and Great Britain; and firms from the United States and the United Kingdom have been notably weak in international competition in recent decades. Among the most successful competitors have been Japanese and German firms, in whose economies stock markets play a much smaller role and in which the monitoring of management performance is carried out mainly by large banks.[18]

4. *Won't market socialist enterprises suffer from inadequate entrepreneurship and innovation in the absence of huge individual rewards for success?*

The typical capitalist success story is one in which an individual with a good idea is able to interest venturesome investors in his or her idea, set up a small business to begin operation, watch demand and production grow by leaps and bounds, and end up joining the ranks of self-made millionaires. Such Horatio Alger stories do occur from time to time, and they have certainly exerted a strong influence on public perceptions of the capitalist economic process. By the same token, socialist economies are believed to discourage such entrepreneurship and innovation because they preclude the huge capital gains and individual fortunes associated with success.

But how important is this kind of scenario in the overall innovation process, and how much would it actually be curtailed by smaller rewards to its practitioners? Most research and development in capitalist economies is carried out in large research divisions of large corporations, where individual researchers face constraints and potential rewards very similar to what they could expect in a public or worker enterprise (indeed, some of the most innovative technical research has actually come out of public enterprises—for instance, the old Bell Labs in the United States). As far as cases of individual (basement or backyard) ideas and inventions are concerned, proposals for market socialism typically allow for independent individual and small business private enterprise—allowing thus for considerable individual rewards on a small scale. Only when and if such activities begin to turn into substantial business firms would they have to be socialized as public or worker enterprises; but this too would represent an experience familiar to entrepreneurs in capitalist economies, who often find themselves selling out to a bigger private corporation (with superior production, financing, or marketing potential) after their initial success.

5.  *Won't market socialist enterprises suffer from insufficient availability and inefficient allocation of investment finance in the absence of stock markets?*

Stock markets, in which enterprise ownership shares are bought and sold by private individuals or institutions, are said by enthusiasts of capitalism to serve two important economic functions. First, they should increase the availability of funds for enterprise capital formation by extending the potential sources of such funds beyond internal retained earnings, government grants, and external debt finance to external equity finance—through which potential outside investors can acquire control rights along with income rights in the enterprise. Second, they provide a measure of enterprise performance—that is, the stock market value of its assets—that should help investors determine where capital can be most effectively invested.

Most models of market socialism rule out stock markets, on the grounds that control of enterprises should be vested only in public agencies responsible to citizen constituencies or workers' councils responsible to worker constituencies and that individuals should not be able to reap large capital gains merely by virtue of the appreciation in value of their own property. These *desiderata* do indeed cut off a source of investment finance that would otherwise be available to enterprises; the salience of this problem can be reduced, however, by the development of imaginative forms of external finance that do not carry control rights—for example, "dequity" financial instruments that provide an income return that varies with enterprise performance but confer no control rights.[19] Similarly, it is possible to replace the performance measurement of stock markets with "pseudo-stock markets" in which enterprise shares are traded and valued without actually conferring control rights on the traders.[20]

Finally, for those who believe that such alternatives fall too far short of achieving the putative economic benefits of true capitalist stock markets, there is a version of market socialism that allows for external equity ownership rights and fully functioning stock markets. This is the proposal of Leland Stauber for a "democratic market economy," in which equity ownership and trading is permitted but restricted to public financial institutions and public enterprises.[21] Each local government would have its local investment fund, a publicly controlled (and autonomously managed) financial institution that would buy and sell securities in corporate enterprises, exercising stockholder rights, and so on, seeking to maximize the return on its investments—the net return of which would be turned over to the local government to be used in a way that is democratically accountable to its constituents (operating expenses, public programs, tax reductions, and so on). The essential idea is to maintain all of the efficiency advantages of capital markets while avoiding their usual (vastly unequal) distributive consequences, by restricting participation to public institutions representing large communities of people such as local investment funds, public enterprises, and pension funds. Stauber's model is of course an example of public enterprise market socialism; his proposed public stock markets would be inconsistent with self-managed worker enterprises.

6. *Aren't public enterprises bound to be inefficient because they operate in an environment of "soft budget constraints"?*

Perhaps the most widespread criticism of market socialist models is that public enterprises operate under "soft budget constraints."[22] As East European and Soviet experience has shown all too clearly, government officials responsible for public enterprises are often quite ready to respond to appeals from enterprise managers (and workers) for more funds regardless of firm performance (and indeed especially when firms are failing). This is often attributed to the fact that these officials are dispensing not their own but other people's funds. Public enterprises also depend on appeals to government officials to gain access to external funds for capital formation. Economic efficiency demands that enterprises be subsidized and investment funds be allocated not as an ad hoc response to appeals from firms but only as a matter of general policy designed to support clearly articulated social or economic goals.

To deal with the problem of soft budget constraints, advocates of market socialism have urged that public enterprises be made as autonomous as possible. This requires a system in which enterprise managers are rewarded for success and penalized for failure, and in which they have no special relationship with the government officials to whom they are ultimately responsible. Critics have some grounds for skepticism about achieving these objectives, in the light of historical experience with public enterprises—especially in the East. Yet two important points can be made against the skeptics. First, a democratic political environment—conspicuously absent in the East—can be expected to restrain the ability of government officials and enterprise managers to collude at the expense of the public. Second, pressures by enterprise managers to get special favors from government agencies are hardly unknown in capitalist economies—especially in the case of large and politically powerful private corporations that represent the capitalist counterpart to socialist public enterprises.

Assuring autonomy with respect to government agencies would not appear to be a problem for worker enterprises, whose control in any case is not in the hands of government officials.

In some models of market socialism, however, worker enterprises rely for most of their capital formation on government grants and loans.[23] In such cases they would share with public enterprises both the potential advantages of direct national-level control over the pace and direction of capital formation and the potential efficiency problems associated with direct government allocation of investment funds. In response to this kind of concern, John Roemer and his colleagues have developed an ingenious proposal for indirect government control of investment via the use of variable interest rates (achieved by government taxes and subsidies) within a decentralized system of public banks.[24] This system would allow for some (indirect) national-level control over the pattern of capital formation while reducing the scope for discretionary decision making by potentially collusive government officials.

7. *Won't worker enterprises respond too sluggishly to market signals and fail to provide enough employment opportunities?*

Beginning with a seminal article by Benjamin Ward in the 1950s, economists have undertaken systematic theoretical analyses of the differences between the behavior of capitalist firms and producer cooperatives or worker self-managed firms, where the latter seek to maximize current net income per worker rather than profits per unit of capital.[25] Under the usual simplifying assumptions, these studies tend to show that worker enterprises adjust their output and employment more slowly (if not actually perversely) to fluctuations in the demand for their products. Moreover, because of the self-interest of workers in preserving existing enterprises and the greater difficulty of raising capital to form new enterprises, labor-managed economies tend to discourage the liquidation of (unviable) old enterprises and the formation of (promising) new enterprises.

Although such tendencies are potentially problematic for market socialist systems in which worker enterprises play a prominent role, they are by no means inevitable. First of all, the continuing economic literature on the behavior of labor-managed enterprises has shown that under more realistic assumptions than those made by early scholars such as Ward, or with such institutional innovations as an entrance fee payable by new members of an enterprise, the tendency toward sluggish or perverse output and employment responses is eliminated.[26] To deal with potential problems of insufficient liquidation of old firms or formation of new firms, it may well be necessary to establish a separate entrepreneurial institution with the function of identifying new profitable opportunities, forming new self-managed enterprises to pursue them, and arranging for the liquidation of failing enterprises and the transfer of their workers to more successful enterprises.[27] Finally, it should be noted that even if pure efficiency considerations call for a more rapid process of change in the pattern of enterprises than is likely to be generated under a labor-managed system, the social goals of community and stability might well be better served by a system that is slower to change than capitalism.

8.   *Won't worker enterprises undertake too little capital formation?*

This is probably the most frequently voiced concern about worker enterprises. It is argued that workers tend to underinvest in the enterprises they control because of a "horizon problem": since investment yields returns only to future workers, present workers may prefer to distribute net revenues to themselves as current income rather than invest in long-term capital formation. Even if most workers are relatively young and can reasonably expect to work for many years to come, this kind of horizon problem is potentially serious. For one thing, workers may be legitimately concerned that their enterprise may not survive future hard times; for another, they may wish to have access to their own savings in a time pattern differing from what would be forthcoming as returns to investment.

The horizon problem results from the absence of an identifiable and reasonably liquid capital stake for individual workers corresponding to their own contributions to enterprise capital formation. To overcome the problem, David Ellerman and others have recommended that "internal capital accounts" be established for each worker in the enterprise, to which would be credited in each year an amount representing their share of the retained earnings of the enterprise.[28] These accounts would involve no control rights; they would operate much like external savings accounts, building up individual wealth and generating interest income as if workers had received the retained enterprise revenues due to them and deposited them in a savings account. A further refinement, to deal with the horizon problem as well as other potential capital inefficiencies, is to establish tradable nonvoting equity shares that would be purchased by each worker as he or she joins the enterprise and owned or sold by each worker as he or she leaves the enterprise.[29] Such proposals come close to meeting the standard of an ideal capitalist firm in the efficient use of capital, though they still leave something to be desired regarding the availability of external investment funds as long as potential investors cannot acquire any control rights.

9. *Won't worker enterprises be insufficiently entrepreneurial and innovative?*

Even if some kind of internal accounts or nonvoting equity shares are established to provide workers with a capital stake in their own enterprise, critics are concerned that managers of worker enterprises will be reluctant to take (a desirable degree of) risk since workers will have most—if not all—of their capital assets tied up in their own enterprise. Also, because of this kind of risk, workers might well prefer external savings accounts rather than internal capital accounts.

To overcome problems of risk aversion one could organize horizontal associations of worker enterprises and pool the risks of each enterprise by pooling some fraction of their net revenues with those of other enterprises. In this way exposure to risk would be reduced not by the diversification of individual asset portfolios but by the diversification of enterprise net revenues. A similar effect could be achieved by the creation of holding companies that would hold groups of diversified enterprises, with a substantial part of enterprise profits going to the holding companies in which enterprise workers would have individual capital accounts, and from which retained earnings would be allocated back to the enterprises. Such a plan would trade off some degree of management autonomy at the enterprise level for some degree of reduction in exposure to risk.

10. *Won't worker enterprises be plagued by work shirking and free riding?*

Conventional economic analysis suggests that the more individuals are rewarded according to the collective performance of a whole group—rather than according to their own individual performance—the less incentive individuals will have to perform well and the more likely they will be to shirk work. It follows that worker enterprises will give rise to such problems insofar as there is any sharing of net revenues unrelated to individual performance. Such sharing is in fact very likely—if only because of the ideological commitment to cooperative effort and reward underlying most plans for worker enterprises.

It is questionable, however, whether work shirking will be any more serious in worker enterprises than in more conventional firms in which management is responsible to nonworkers. Measuring individual performance with any precision is difficult in any complex enterprise, and it is often not possible to tailor rewards to individual performance. Thus all kinds of enterprises confront difficult problems of worker motivation of a kind that may best be solved by collective incentives associated with "team spirit" and enterprise goals.

Worker self-managed firms have some important advantages over both conventional capitalist firms and government-controlled public enterprises in stimulating workplace efficiency. When workers themselves exercise control rights, rather than shareholders or public officials, there can be no collective conflict of interest between those in whose interest the enterprise is operating and those who are carrying out the operations of the enterprise. Thus one potentially important problem is removed, with attendant savings in costs of monitoring and compliance. There can still be the classic divergence of interests between the collective of workers and the individual worker—but this is more likely to be reduced through horizontal monitoring among workers themselves when they all are in control of the enterprise.

In summary, advocates of market socialism can provide reasonably satisfactory (and often very ingenious) solutions to each and every one of the potential efficiency problems that have been raised by critics. These solutions tend not to meet fully the efficiency standard of an ideally functioning capitalist economy; but neither in practice do actual capitalist economies. Most of the proposals for promoting efficiency under market socialism share the following characteristic: the more successful they are in obviating the problem posed by critics of market socialism, the more closely the suggested solution resembles the institutional framework of a capitalist market economy. In no case, however, does the suggested solution require the embrace of traditional capitalist property rights in the means of production.

There is one important exception to the generalization that efforts to meet criticism of market socialism on efficiency grounds fall short of capitalist standards of efficiency. To the extent that worker effort and performance are promoted by participation in decision-making, market socialist enterprises with a significant degree of worker self-management promise higher productivity than capitalist firms. This provides a boost to the case for a worker-enterprise variant of market socialism. However, there does remain some trade-off between efficiency gains with respect to labor and efficiency gains with respect to capital: the labor-motivational gains delivered by worker self-management come at the cost of some capital-supply and risk-taking losses.[30]

These considerations raise the larger question of whether enterprise ownership rights in a market socialist society should best be grounded in communities of *citizens* or communities of *workers*. Should control rights—the rights to manage the enterprise—be vested in governmental agencies (democratically accountable to citizens) or in workers' councils (democratically accountable to enterprise workers)? Should income rights accrue to the general public (via government agencies) or to enterprise workers?

Advocates of *public management* stress its advantages vis-à-vis worker self-management with respect to "capital efficiency"—access to capital funds, encouragement of risk-taking, technological progress, and so on. Advocates of *public surplus appropriation* stress its advantages with respect to equity at the societal level: channeling the residual income of enterprises into an aggregate "social dividend" recognizes the interdependence of all production activities, protects workers and citizens against the potential risk and inequity of having their capital income tied to the performance of a particular enterprise (which may do well or do badly for reasons of luck rather than merit), and can distribute society's surplus much more equitably than when individual enterprises retain much of their own surplus.

Advocates of *worker self-management* stress its advantages vis-à-vis

public management in several different respects: (1) "labor efficiency"—motivation of work effort and quality, disciplining of management, organizational improvement, and so on; (2) democracy:
worker self-management at the enterprise level is in and of itself democratic, and may well reinforce democracy at the political level; and
(3) solidarity: through greater participation in workplace and enterprise decision-making, workers may gain a stronger sense of solidarity
with their fellow workers. Advocates of *worker surplus appropriation*
stress its advantages with respect to labor efficiency and solidarity, as
workers' incomes are linked collectively to the performance of their
enterprises.

Clearly there are significant trade-offs here. Different kinds of social control rights are advantageous with respect to different kinds of
efficiency considerations, and different kinds of social income rights
are advantageous with respect to different socialist objectives of equity, democracy, and solidarity. A reasonable solution to the dilemma
of choice—consistent with the overall spirit of compromise inherent in
market socialism—would be to encourage a mixture of public and
worker control and income rights, emphasizing each in the particular
circumstances in which it would do the most good. Such a compromise could take the form of promoting public management in those
industries and enterprises characterized by relatively large economies
of scale or relatively extensive externalities and promoting worker
self-management in industries and enterprises with smaller economies
of scale or less significant externalities. Since income, unlike control,
can easily be shared, it might be best to promote patterns of enterprise
income rights in which there is both a social dividend claim and an
enterprise worker claim.

## Market Socialism and Social Democracy

Advocates of social democracy share the socialist objectives of advocates of market socialism but differ as to the best means to achieve
them. Where market socialism seeks to promote the public interest,
greater equity, democracy, and solidarity primarily by transferring
capitalist ownership rights to communities of citizens or workers, social democracy seeks to do so by government policy measures de-

signed to constrain the behavior of capitalist owners and to empower other market participants. Thus social democrats do not try to do away with either the market or private property ownership; instead, they attempt to create conditions in which the operation of a capitalist market economy will lead to more egalitarian outcomes and encourage more democratic and solidaristic practices than would a conventional capitalist system.

Market socialists have traditionally been highly suspicious of social democracy, on the ground that its failure to attack head-on the source of capitalist power—private ownership of the means of production— would ultimately prevent it from attaining socialist objectives. But as models of market socialism have been refined over the years, the distinction between market socialism and social democracy has been somewhat blurred. Partly because of the problematic experience of East European CP-directed socialist economies with limited market-oriented economic reforms, advocates of market socialism have come to support an increasingly wide scope for markets and increasing autonomy for public or worker enterprises operating within the market environment.[31] While such proposals do not amount to the restoration of full capitalist private property rights, they often do open up opportunities for individuals to receive some forms of capital income.

The elimination of large-scale private property ownership under market socialism certainly leads to a much more equal distribution of income than obtains under conventional capitalism. Both theory and the actual experience of social democracy, however, suggest that government taxation and spending programs can substantially reduce the extent of income and wealth inequalities within a capitalist economy. As far as the pattern of enterprise management is concerned, there is also good reason to question how far market socialism really differs from social democracy. Market socialist enterprise managers, whether accountable to government agencies or to enterprise workers, are expected to operate their enterprises in such a way as to maintain profitability in a market environment; this means that they will typically have only limited leeway to steer the enterprises in a direction much different than would managers accountable to private shareholders.[32] And, indeed, to prevent autonomous public enterprises or worker self-managed firms from acting in their own particular interest, as against the general social interest, it would in all likelihood be necessary for government to regulate them or their markets just as is done by social-democratic governments in a capitalist economy.

At a more fundamental level, market socialism does not dispense with the individual gain incentives and the related inequalities associated with capitalism. Instead, it seeks:

(a) to link differences in rewards more closely to corresponding differentials in actual productive effort (as opposed to differentials in the ownership of various kinds of assets); and
(b) to reduce the extent of differences in individual material rewards associated with differentials in productive effort, so as to reduce (greatly) the resultant distributional inequity without reducing (much) the incentives they generate.[33]

Again, this is precisely what social democracy tries to do—albeit in a different way than market socialism. Social democracy achieves greater egalitarianism via *ex post* government taxes and subsidies, where market socialism does so via *ex ante* changes in patterns of enterprise ownership. As for serving the general social interest, market socialists and social democrats agree that, where the unfettered market will not achieve important social goals, the first option is to try to guide the market toward socially optimal behavior (via appropriate taxes, subsidies, and so on, to internalize externalities by "planning with the market"); where this is not adequate, the second option is to replace price-and-market mechanisms by quantitative controls or direct state operation of enterprises.

On further reflection, one might well ask of market socialists: what compelling reason is there to restrict forms of enterprise ownership to types in which control and income rights accrue to (citizen or worker) communities rather than to private shareholders? Why not simply provide a level market playing field in which all types of enterprises can compete on a truly equal basis? Most contemporary market socialist models in any case allow for individual or small-scale private enterprise. Could not the problems of excessive wealth and power associated with large-scale private enterprise be addressed as easily and successfully via taxation and regulation as via restrictions on private ownership?

To sustain the superiority of the market socialist over the social democratic approach, I would argue as follows. In redefining and reassigning (to workers or communities) rights that form the point of departure for markets, market socialism intervenes into the market system before markets operate—while social democracy intervenes (mainly) after markets operate. This makes social democracy much more vulnerable to weakening or disintegration under political challenge, since tax-and-subsidy schemes and government regulation are much easier to reverse than changes in property rights.[34] Moreover, the maintenance of property-owning capitalists under social democracy assures the presence of a disproportionately powerful class with a continuing interest in challenging social democratic government policies. Under market socialism there may well emerge a kind of managerial class with disproportionate power; but its power will be much less disproportionate because enterprise control rights and personal wealth will be far less concentrated.

## Notes

1. See Oskar Lange, "On the Economic Theory of Socialism," parts 1 and 2, *Review of Economic Studies* 4 (1936–37), and Oskar Lange and Fred Taylor, *On the Economic Theory of Socialism* (Minneapolis: University of Minnesota Press, 1938). Abba Lerner also made seminal contributions to the early literature on market socialism; see his "Economic Theory and Socialist Economy," *Review of Economic Studies* 2 (1934), and "A Note on Socialist Economics," *Review of Economic Studies* 4 (1936).

2. For a brief survey of the history of the idea of market socialism, see Wlodzimierz Brus, "Market Socialism," in John Eatwell, Murray Milgate and Peter Newman, eds., *The New Palgrave: A Dictionary Of Economics* (London: Macmillan, 1987). The most prominent recent contribution to the literature on conceptualizing market socialism was Alec Nove's *The Economics Of Feasible Socialism* (London: Unwin Hyman, 1983); since then Nove has published an updated version of his book, *The Economics Of Feasible Socialism Revisited* (London: HarperCollins Academic, 1991).

3. In this context the enterprise surplus should be defined to include also any capital gains or losses.

4. Examples of recent models of market socialism characterized by public management include those of John Roemer and Leland Stauber; see John Roemer, "Market Socialism: A Blueprint," *Dissent* (Fall 1991) [See chapter 13 in this volume.—Eds.], and Leland Stauber, "A Proposal for a Democratic Market Economy," *Journal of Comparative Economics* 1, no. 3 (1977).

5. Examples of recent models of market socialism featuring worker self-management

include those of David Schweickart and David Ellerman (though in Schweickart's model the national government retains control over net capital formation, and Ellerman does not explicitly use the term "market socialism"); see David Schweickart, *Capitalism or Worker Control?* (New York: Praeger, 1980) and David Ellerman, *The Democratic Worker-Owned Firm* (London: Unwin Hyman, 1990).

6. For example, in Roemer's model of market socialism, (most of the) enterprise surpluses flow back to the national government to be distributed (in large part) to the general public in an equitable manner as a "social dividend"; in Stauber's model, local government agencies receive enterprise capital income *qua* shareholders and either use it for local public purposes or redistribute it to local citizens.

7. For example, in both Schweickart's and Ellerman's models of worker self-management, the enterprise surplus accrues strictly to its workers—though there are taxes and other charges that must first be paid to government.

8. Roemer's and Stauber's models of market socialism represent different kinds of public enterprise models, whereas Ellerman's is a worker enterprise model; Schweickart's is predominantly a worker enterprise model, but includes some characteristics of a public enterprise model—that is, government control over net capital formation.

9. Market valuations are expected to reflect "true" social benefits and costs to a much greater extent under market socialism than under capitalism not only because of the greater degree of internalization of externalities but also because of the more equal distribution of income that results from the socialization of enterprise income rights; thus overall market demand will not disproportionately reflect the demands of a minority of wealthy individuals.

10. In a related paper I respond to critics who question the ability of social ownership forms to meet socialist goals in the context of markets; see Thomas E. Weisskopf, "Toward a Socialism for the Future, in the Wake of the Demise of the Socialism of the Past." Working Paper (University of Michigan, October 1991).

11. This argument goes back to Ludwig von Mises and is associated with Friedrich von Hayek and many other adherents of the "Austrian" school of economics; see Ludwig von Mises, "Economic Calculation in the Socialist Commonwealth," in F. A. Hayek, ed., *Collectivist Economic Planning* (Routledge & Kegan Paul, 1935). For contemporary developments of the Austrian critique, see Don Lavoie, *Rivalry and Central Planning: The Socialist Calculation Debate Reconsidered* (New York: Cambridge University Press, 1985), and many of the readings in Erik Furubotn and Svetozar Pejovich, eds., *The Economics of Property Rights* (Cambridge, MA.: Ballinger, 1974).

12. I will consistently use the term "Communist-party-directed" (or the abbreviated "CP-directed") to describe the kind of socialism that has actually existed in the Soviet Union, Eastern Europe, China, Cuba, Vietnam, and North Korea. There are of course many other adjectives that have been used to characterize this type of socialism—"actually existing," "bureaucratic state," "centrally planned," and so on—and some have even called it a form of (state) capitalism. I prefer "CP-directed" because it underlines in a compact way the authoritarian, hierarchical, and bureaucratic nature of both the political and the economic system.

13. Kornai's negative assessment of the viability of market socialism is set out in many of his recent writings; for a representative example, see János Kornai, "The

Affinity Between Ownership Forms and Coordination Mechanisms: The Common Experience of Reform in Socialist Countries," *Journal of Economic Perspectives* 4, no. 1 (1990).

14. On Yugoslavia's economic progress in the 1950s and 1960s, see Harold Lydall, *Yugoslav Socialism* (New York: Oxford University Press, 1984); on China's experience with market-oriented reforms in the 1980s, see some of the contributions to Peter Van Ness, ed., *Market Reforms in Socialist Societies: Comparing China and Hungary* (Boulder, CO: L. Rienner, 1989).

15. Yugoslavia's version of self-managed market socialism has often been cited as the actual experience coming closest to a desirable model of market socialism, but even Yugoslavia's model is profoundly flawed from a market socialist perspective; see Jaroslav Vanek, "On the Transition from Centrally Planned to Democratic Socialist Economies," *Economic and Industrial Democracy* 11 (1990), pp. 180–82, for a comprehensive list of conditions for "an optimal democratic and self-managing economy"—most of which failed to be realized in Yugoslavia.

16. On this important point, see David Levine and Laura Tyson, "Participation, Productivity and the Firm's Environment," in Alan Blinder, ed., *Paying for Productivity* (Washington, D.C.: Brookings, 1989).

17. There is a vast literature on the Swedish model of and experience with active labor market policies; for a brief summary, see Andrew Zimbalist, Howard Sherman, and Stuart Brown, *Comparing Economic Systems*, second edition (New York: Harcourt Brace Jovanovich, 1989), pp. 72–80.

18. John Roemer and Pranab Bardhan have proposed that independent public holding companies play precisely such a role in a market socialist economy; see Roemer and Bardhan, "Market Socialism: A Case for Rejuvenation," Working Paper No. 91–175 (University of California, July 1991).

19. See David Ellerman, *op. cit.,* pp. 85–89, for a discussion of various forms of variable-income debt instruments that could be used by worker-controlled firms to raise external finance; as Ellerman notes, they operate similarly to conventional capitalist "preferred stock" options.

20. For some ingenious ideas along these lines, see Domenico Mario Nuti, "Financial Innovation Under Market Socialism," Working Paper 87–285 (European University Institute, Florence, 1987).

21. See Leland Stauber, *op. cit.*

22. This term was first coined by János Kornai; see "The Reproduction of Shortage" and " 'Hard' and 'Soft' Budget Constraints," both in Kornai, *Contradictions and Dilemmas: Studies on the Socialist Economy and Society* (Cambridge, MA: MIT Press, 1987).

23. This is the case, for example, with David Schweickart's model; see Schweickart, *op. cit.*

24. See Roemer, *op. cit.,* and Ignacio Ortuño-Ortin, John Roemer, and Joaquim Silvestre, "Investment Planning in Market Socialism," Working Paper (Department of Economics, University of California, Davis, 1991).

25. Benjamin Ward, "The Firm in Illyria: Market Syndicalism," *American Economic Review* 68 (1958). For a useful survey of literature on labor-managed firms and economies, see Louis Putterman, *Division of Labor and Welfare* (New York: Oxford University Press, 1990), chapter 4.

26. For details, see Putterman, *op. cit.*, pp. 165–67.

27. Such a proposal has been advanced by Saul Estrin, "Workers' Co-operatives: Merits and Limitations," in Le Grand and Estrin, eds., *Market Socialism* (Oxford: Clarendon Press, 1989), drawing on the example of the Caja Laboral Popular in the Mondragon cooperative network of Northern Spain.

28. See Ellerman, *op. cit.*, pp. 76–91; Putterman, *op. cit.*, pp. 179–81, notes that the Mondragon cooperative network provides an instructive example of the use of internal capital accounts.

29. See Gregory Dow, "Control Rights, Competitive Management, and the Labor Management Debate," *Journal of Comparative Economics* 10 (1986).

30. See Samuel Bowles and Herbert Gintis, "The Democratic Firm: An Agency-Theoretic Evaluation" (paper presented to the conference on "Microfoundations of Political Economy: Problems of Participation, Democracy and Efficiency," Uppsala, Sweden, 1990), for a persuasive demonstration that no organizational structure can be optimal simultaneously with respect to both labor-efficiency and capital-efficiency considerations.

31. This evolution in the thinking of advocates of market socialism toward an increasing role for markets can be seen very clearly in the work of Wlodzimierz Brus, from *The Market in a Socialist Economy* (London: Routledge & Kegan Paul, 1972) to *From Marx to the Market* (New York: Oxford University Press, 1989) which he wrote with Kazimierz Laski.

32. Some critics of market socialism have argued that a market socialist system is fundamentally unstable, bound to veer back to a form of capitalism under the pressures on enterprises imposed by competition in a market environment. Certainly market competition restricts the scope of viable options for any kind of producing enterprise; but the argument that it obliterates distinctions among enterprise types is based on a very unrealistic economic model of capitalism—one in which mechanically organized firms face no problems of contract enforcement, worker motivation, and so on; only under such restrictive assumptions is there no room at all for discretionary decision making by firm management and is the market all-determining. For a stimulating debate on these issues, see the exchanges between N. Scott Arnold and David Schweickart—beginning with Arnold's "Marx and Disequilibrium in Market Socialist Relations of Production"—in *Economics and Philosophy* 3 (1987).

33. As David Miller puts it in his "Why Markets?" in Julian Le Grand and Saul Estrin, *Market Socialism* (New York: Oxford University Press, 1989), p. 30: "[F]or markets to operate effectively, individuals and enterprises must receive primary profits, but the proportion of those profits that they need to keep as private income depends on how far they require material (as opposed to moral) incentives."

34. The experience of Sweden since the mid-1970s is often cited to show the vulnerability of social democracy to pressures to move toward a more traditional form of capitalism. For informative analyses of the trials of the Swedish model of social democracy in recent years, see Erik Lundberg, "The Rise and Fall of the Swedish Model," *Journal of Economic Literature* 23, no. 1 (1985), and Jonas Pontusson, "Radicalization and Retreat in Swedish Social Democracy," *New Left Review*, no. 165 (1987).

# COMMENT

## by Branko Horvat

Disagreements may arise because of differences in opinion and evaluation or because of differently known and understood facts and logic. I sympathize with the spirit of Thomas Weisskopf's essay but I want to make three specific comments about the second type of disagreement. As I have written extensively elsewhere on the issues raised, I shall confine myself to a brief explanation. Besides, this is not a place to engage in a technical analysis.

Weisskopf writes:

> Although the replacement of private with social control and income rights at the enterprise level is what most clearly distinguishes market socialism from [market] capitalism. . . .

This is neither true nor is the statement exhaustive. Proprietorships and individual farming are completely compatible with socialism. Differing specifics concerning the two systems lie in the social organization of large enterprises that produce about two-thirds of total national output. These enterprises are organized as various sorts of corporations. Proprietorship evolved into the private corporation, and the state enterprise evolves (or will evolve) into a social corporation.

The private corporation is controlled by largely self-appointed management and is privately owned. The latter is taken as an ideological justification for the legalistic fiction that the owners (shareholders) control it.

The social corporation is controlled (somewhat more realistically) by the employees and is socially owned. The latter means that every citizen owns one virtual share of national capital, which cannot be either bought or sold. Therefore, the capital distribution is completely egalitarian and the dividends are expressed in the increasing standard of living.

It is usually not observed that the *basic* control of the two corporations is performed by the market, and therefore the market is important for socialism (that is, an organized and not laissez-faire market). Besides, labor control is somewhat more efficient than control by absentee owners, and therefore a social corporation will be more efficient than a private corporation, as a rule.

Naturally, economic democracy and social relations play an important role, and the organization of firms is bound to influence the organization of the society profoundly. But I restrict myself to purely economic elements, because they are usually not well understood.

Further, Weisskopf contends:

> Defenders of capitalism have long argued that markets cannot work properly unless they are embedded in a system of property rights that enables private individuals to own, buy and sell shares in the means of production.

The statement is based on a widespread confusion. It is true that markets cannot work without clearly defined property rights. That is in fact a tautology. The implication that this necessarily implies private ownership is a non sequitur. In every market economy (capitalist, socialist, or any other), the primary owner is the firm. The firm is registered with the court, engages in all productive, selling, and financial transactions autonomously, hires (and fires) labor and capital, reaps profits, and repays its debts. Who is the owner of the firm is largely irrelevant as far as the market is concerned. The potential owners are private individuals, partners, members of a cooperative, workers in a worker-owned enterprise, state and parastatal entities, or society as a whole. In other words, ownership may be private, collective, state, or social. If we have a well-organized (and also not ideologically dominated) market, it will be advisable to select the most efficient type of ownership by market competition.

In short, market implies ownership but not necessarily a private one. The firm owns property and the firm may be owned by nonprivate entities without jeopardizing the operations of the market, including activities of the capital market. Private dividends are compatible with socialism, as is interest on saving deposits that represents an equivalent exchange of past and present labor time for increasing productivity.

Weisskopf also says that:

market socialist enterprises are clearly not subject to hostile takeovers, so their managers don't face the same ultimate threat as managers of capitalist firms.

Why not? A social corporation has an internal fund of socially owned capital that may be expressed in shares kept by the corporation. If the internally generated surplus is not sufficient for investment undertaken, the corporation may issue external shares (as well as issue bonds or borrow from the bank). If external shares represent more than 50 percent of total capital, a hostile takeover is possible, the incompetent management and individual troublemakers will be fired, the failing firm reorganized, and then the prevailing labor-managed administration re-established in the same way as is done in capitalist firms.

Some sort of hostile turnover is possible when the firm becomes insolvent and the bank or government will not bail it out. But there is also a third possibility, which reflects the greater flexibility of a labor-managed economy. If a firm suffers losses that no longer can be covered out of reserve funds, and workers apply for guaranteed income that no longer can be covered by the firm itself, the firm will be put under receivership, labor management suspended, and a temporary manager appointed by a specialized public agency. Now three possibilities exist: (1) either the firm is reorganized and made profitable again and it regains its autonomy, or (2) the firm is sold ("hostile takeover"), or (3) it is proclaimed bankrupt.

Generally, one may note that a socialist firm is *potentially* more efficient than a capitalist firm. Whether it will be also more efficient in real life depends on cultural factors, including the entire institutional setup. Let me illustrate the problem with a comparison. Probably everybody will agree that capitalism is economically more efficient than slavery. In ancient Rome all essential ingredients of capitalism existed: private ownership and Roman law regulating transactions, market, hired labor, factories, money and credit, foreign exchange and foreign trade. In a sense the market was more universal than the present market because apart from the commodity and money markets there was also a market in human beings. And yet capitalism did not develop; cultural factors and technology were not conducive to it. Are they conducive to socialism today?

# PART V

## Current Debates

# 15

# One or Two Cheers for "The Invisible Hand"

## (Spring 1990)

### James Tobin

Adam Smith's "Invisible Hand"[1] is surely one of the genuine Great Ideas of history, both for its intrinsic intellectual content and for its durable influence on ideologies, politics, and public policies. The proposition that the alchemy of market competition transmutes the dross of personal selfishness into the gold of social welfare is still a powerful message in economics classrooms and in political debates. To be sure, since 1776 the doctrine has experienced ups and downs in popularity. At present, it enjoys one of its strongest and most widespread prosperities.

The symptoms can be seen throughout the world. In almost all the advanced democratic capitalist nations, conservative governments committed to laissez-faire rule the roosts: notably in the United States and Canada, in the United Kingdom and the Federal Republic of Germany, in the other major countries of the European Community (even in France, where the Socialists were forced to fall in step), and in Japan. In the communist countries—China, Eastern Europe, now even the Soviet Union—the new vogue is the promotion of private enterprise and market pricing. The main ideological adversary of the tradition of Adam Smith for the past 140 years, Marxism-Leninism, stands discredited before the world. As a principle for the organization of society and economy, it is a failure. Now it is an admitted failure. Likewise in the "Third World," the success of the economies of Taiwan, Korea, and of other Newly Industrialized Countries (NICs) is attributed largely to free markets and free enterprises, while in contrast stagnation is observed in countries where governments intervene with heavy hands. The official policies of international agencies, the International Monetary Fund (IMF) and the World Bank, make adoption of market-oriented reforms conditions for their aids and credits.

These developments follow and reverse a long period of skepticism and doubt about the Smithian message, even among those who always firmly rejected Marxism and other extreme alternatives. Fifty or sixty years ago the depression in the fortunes of the Invisible Hand was related to the Great Depression of the world economy and then to the pragmatic compromises of market capitalism with social democracy, welfare state institutions, trade unionism, and state planning that flourished before and after World War II. Even governments that by traditional doctrine had eschewed responsibility for fluctuations in economic activity—international, national, regional, sectoral, personal—began to assume more and more responsibilities for them and to be held to account by democratic electorates.

Disenchantment with government interventions spread contagiously in the last twenty years. There were two main reasons. One was the disappointing performance of the world economy in general and of most national economies in the 1970s, in contrast to the quarter century of unparalleled growth, prosperity, and stability before 1973. Whether justifiably or not, the disappointments of the 1970s were blamed on the economic doctrines and policies adopted and often praised during the preceding decades. The other reason was the growing disillusionment and cynicism about politics and governments—legislatures, executives, and bureaucracies—fueled by obvious and perceived failures of policies and their execution and, worse, by endless revelations of venality, hypocrisy, deception, and mendacity.

Professional—shall we say scientific?—economics and the economic ideologies of public and political debate are always intertwined. *The Wealth of Nations* itself was both a tract of political economy and a scientific—or, as the author would have put it, a philosophical—

treatise. The Great Idea has led parallel lives in the two arenas, public and professional. In the professional arena, the Invisible Hand eventually came to be formalized in the basic theorems of welfare economics—that a competitive market equilibrium is Pareto-optimal and that every Pareto-optimal allocation can be supported by a competitive equilibrium with a suitable arbitrary allocation of endowments among agents. This is a very precise and refined distillate of the sweeping conjectures of Smith himself and of hordes of his successors, especially those in the public arena of ideologies. In any event, the appeal of the Invisible Hand within the profession shares the cyclical fluctuations of its popularity in the wider arena. The same dialectic of revolution, counterrevolution, and synthesis has been repeating itself in economic science and in economic politics.

It is not surprising, therefore, that the popularity of the Invisible Hand in our profession has revived strongly in the past fifteen years. The main target has been Keynesian macroeconomics, as it developed in the first twenty-five years after the publication of the *General Theory*.[2] During that time the mainstream consensus of the profession came to support a synthesis of Keynesian macroeconomics and neoclassical microeconomics. Theoretical misgivings about this compromise burst into full-scale counterrevolution in the 1970s, called by its protagonists the New Classical Macroeconomics. This new old macroeconomics, fortified by Rational Expectations theory, extends the pretensions of laissez-faire to macro theory and policy and undermines the case for monetary and fiscal stabilization policies that most economists, even those opposed to microeconomic interventions, had previously come to accept.

On the micro side too the Invisible Hand was gaining professional as well as public adherence. Supply-side economics, fortified by this new label, greatly magnified previous estimates of the dead weight losses attributable to taxes, transfer payments, subsidies, quotas, price controls, tariffs, and regulations of all kinds. Economists, especially theorists, became much readier to take the theoretical optimality of a free-market solution as a reference point, placing the burden of proof on anyone who would defend or propose a government intervention.

These are influential ideas. Given the overhang of regulations and other micro interventions and the vested interests they serve, it is difficult even for conservative free-market governments to dismantle them. Nevertheless, the spirit of the invigorated Invisible Hand certainly makes a difference. And in macroeconomics it has become quite decisive, especially in Western Europe, where established doctrine among policymakers and business and financial leaders is that governments should never actively stimulate aggregate demand, whatever the circumstances of their economies.

## Exaggerations of Exuberant Ideology

Yet there are large divergences of intellectual substance between Adam Smith's Invisible Hand thesis and modern scientific proofs of the optimality of competitive market solutions. Consider several of them:

1. *First, careful economists know that Pareto-optimality, which is all the fundamental theorem of welfare economics can claim for competitive equilibrium, is not necessarily maximization of social welfare.* We know there are trade-offs between "efficiency" and "equality," to mention just one important kind of distributive issue. Maybe real Gross Domestic Product (GDP) could be maximized by allowing free rein and untaxed gain to the enterprising, the talented, the ruthless, and the lucky and by leaving the weak, the ignorant, the shiftless, and the unlucky to their own devices and to private charity. I doubt it. But even if it were true it is an unpleasant caricature of a "good society." A system with zero distortionary fiscal or regulatory interventions is a chimera. The question is always the one Arthur Okun posed so effectively: The bucket carrying goodies from rich to poor is always leaky. How leaky does it have to be before the transfer is not worthwhile?[3]

    Even so good a cause as free trade is, in my opinion, exaggerated when it is argued, as it generally is in public debate even by economists, that free trade is obviously welfare-improving. I am not referring to the slim possibility that a country has some market power in international trade that can be exploited by an "optimum tariff" or by strategic gaming in commercial policy. Assuming that free trade is efficient and maximizes the consumption opportunities of a society as a whole, it still can change—relative to any alternative status quo—the internal distribution of these opportunities, not only among persons, sectors, and regions but also as between broadly defined factors of production, labor, capital, and land.

2. *Smith says, and his latter-day adherents repeat, that selfish motivations and local information suffice to guide individual economic decisions in ways that aggregate into social optima.* Modern theory requires much more: simultaneous clearing of a complete set of markets, including those for future and contingent commodities and globally complete information available to all agents. Economic theorists may take methodological refuge in the assertion that every model, including general equilibrium theory itself, is a simplifying metaphor of reality, to be judged by congruence between its implications and predictions and real-world observations. So far there is no convincing evidence of such congruence, certainly nothing that entitles anyone to accept and assert literally the formal propositions of the model.

3. *The Invisible Hand, especially in the general equilibrium version of formal theory, requires that agents lack market power and take parametrically the prices determined for a predetermined list of commodities.* The looser ideology makes a big logical jump in extending the Invisible Hand proposition to all market structures and to competition in products and other nonprice dimensions. The recent complacency in the United States about mergers and conglomerations, the atrophy of antitrust policy to apply only to overt conspiracy, reflect the broader and looser laissez-faire Zeitgeist.

## Pragmatism in Regulation and Deregulation

These considerations counsel against uncritical acceptance of "free market" and "supply-side" arguments in every application, and suggest that economists adopt more cautious, pragmatic, and discriminating approaches than their ideological and political counterparts.

Of course, a discriminating and pragmatic approach is double-edged. Theory may not be able to prove that a particular intervention is injurious to welfare, but that failure of proof does not justify the intervention. One should be suspicious of advocates of, let us say, lower taxes on capital incomes on grounds of incentives and efficiency when the advocates stand to gain without making any new risky investments. (And likewise of professors who want to raise their own salaries on the grounds that higher pay will attract better talent in the future.) We should be especially suspicious of interventions that seem both inefficient and inequitable, for example, rent controls in New York or Moscow or Mexico City, or price supports and irrigation subsidies benefiting affluent farmers, or low-interest loans to well-heeled students.

I myself think that Invisible Hand theory is mostly irrelevant to macroeconomic stabilization policies. The business fluctuations that give rise to those interventions play no role in the writings of Adam Smith, Leon Walras, and Arrow-Debreu. Whether active counter-cyclical demand management brings better macro performance than stable policies blind to economic conditions is an intellectual empirical question that cannot be settled by pure economic theory.

One thrust of *micro*economic deregulation is justified in almost all countries, the dismantling of institutions that protect privileged individuals from competition. Everybody would like to own a toll booth and grow rich collecting tolls from the multitudes who pass by. As the point is sometimes expressed, people are rent-seekers. Sometimes the bottlenecks and scarcities that yield tolls or rents are natural. Sometimes they are the payoffs of Schumpeterian innovations. Sometimes they arise without government help and are maintained by restraints of trade. Sometimes both the scarcities and the rents are artificial results of government interventions, made to order for political deals and too often irresistible invitations for corruption. In the United States flagrant examples have been on the hit lists of economists in all administrations, liberal and conservative, Democratic and Republican. Even when it can be argued that some deserving low-income persons are beneficiaries of rights to buy or sell at subsidized prices, economists often can show how equal gains could be provided to them in a more efficient manner.

## Government and Financial Markets

Undiscriminating and thoughtless deregulation can misfire. As examples I refer to financial markets and institutions. The epidemic insolvencies of savings and loan associations in the United States are a case in point. In the last ten years, after great political and economic pressure, the regulations of these institutions were substantially relaxed. Originally these were mutual associations attracting savings in the form of "shares" for the purpose of financing mortgages in their communities, but later they were allowed to convert to stock companies managed for profit. In the 1980s they were allowed to broaden their asset menus to compete with commercial banks. They were allowed to convert savings shares into checkable deposits and to pay market interest rates to attract them. They were allowed to seek deposits and lending opportunities nationwide. Their supervisory agency, following the spirit of the times, became less strict and less diligent. Yet their deposits were still federally insured, in principle only up to $100,000 per deposit but in practice 100 percent. Thus the institutions, whether sound or unsound, cautious or reckless, honest or corrupt, solvent or insolvent, could always attract deposits by offering high interest rates. If the deposits were invested in risky loans that went bad, no losses fell on the depositors. Losses were borne in part by other insured institutions, whose insurance premiums would have to be increased to help pay off the depositors, and by federal taxpayers, the ultimate guarantors. The federal budgetary cost is likely to exceed $100 billion. The moral is that you can't apply free-market principles to an industry that deals in contingent obligations of the central government.

The fad of deregulation has led serious economists, as well as exuberant ideologues, to propose free competitive enterprise in the creation of money. The idea that "private money" could supersede government money is a ridiculous one. Someone's IOUs have to be those in which clearings take place among banks and other transactors. Someone's IOUs have to be those the government itself will accept in payment of taxes and other obligations and those the government regards as legal tender in the satisfaction of private debts. Once the government guarantees the value, in the country's unit of account, of any private IOUs, then it cannot allow the private issuers completely free choice as to the assets that stand behind them.

Should government take an "anything goes" attitude toward the financial structure of nonfinancial corporations? At the moment, U.S. corporations are being rapidly, drastically, and spectacularly restructured. Firms whose assets were covered 60 to 100 percent by equity are moving to 10 percent equity, 90 percent debt. Some of this refinancing arises from a reduced assessment of the disadvantages and risks of debt obligations, in part because the tax-deductibility of interest was enhanced in value by the 1986 increase in the effective corporate-profits tax rate. In some respect, the corporation as restructured is simply renaming as "interest" income what formerly was called "profits." The surprising thing is that such restructurings are the immediate sources of such large increases in the value of the assets over the previous market value of the equities, even after the very considerable dead weight losses of the transactions, the fabulous fees of investment bankers and lawyers. Much of the best talent of the country is engaged in transactions of this kind, and their imminence or possibility preoccupies the managers of companies that should be trying to make better mousetraps and compete with Taiwan, Korea, and Japan.

Our federal administration is quite complacent about these activities, and it is indeed hard to see why shareowners of companies with lethargic or inefficient managements should be deprived of the capital gains takeovers might bring them. On the other hand, the wholesale replacement of equity by debt makes companies individually more vulnerable to adverse business developments and the economy collectively more vulnerable to deflationary or recessionary shocks. Monetary policy may be crippled as a result. If the government is going to take responsibility for assuring the survival of nonfinancial companies—individually, like Chrysler and Lockheed, or collectively—then perhaps it should limit their permissible debt/equity ratios, just as it does for financial institutions. As a minimum, of course, the government should make the tax liability of companies neutral with respect to their debt/equity structures.

A disquieting implication of the large premiums in takeover values is to confirm failure of ordinary market prices to reflect long-run fundamental values. The longstanding suspicion of this failure was expressed eloquently by Keynes when he likened the stock market to a beauty contest in which the contestants' prizes depend on voting the same as other contestants. The quest for short-run profits, "day trading," stresses the ability to gauge the immediate impact of news events on other speculators rather than their long-range effects on earnings. In the last ten years, the excess volatility of stock market prices relative to dividends and earnings has been ingeniously documented econometrically by Robert Shiller.[4] Despite their best efforts, the finance intelligentsia who espouse efficient-markets theory have not been able to refute Shiller.

Errors in market valuations have further negative repercussions. Managers of corporations may be shortsighted in their outlooks and investment decisions, believing they get points and bonuses for the performance of their companies' stocks in a quarter, a year, or four years. If the stock market gave them reliable signals of fundamental values, short-horizon managers would be making good decisions. But if the stock market signals are speculative noise, the managers are making bad decisions. Whether the newly structured high-debt firm, in which managers have considerable stakes in highly leveraged shares and stand both to lose much more and to gain much more than under the old structures, will be more efficient remains to be seen. The unrelenting pressure of debt service may force managers to be more efficient, but it might also force resort to short-term expedients to maintain cash flow at the expense of longer-run values.

One way to encourage fundamental investing and to discourage short-horizon speculation is to tax financial transactions. Keynes tentatively suggested this tax, and I favor it today. With international agreement a transfer tax could also, in my opinion, diminish speculation in foreign-exchange markets and allow larger differences among currencies in short-term interest rates, permitting somewhat greater autonomy in national monetary policies.

I think developing and ex-communist countries should go slow in copying the financial institutions and markets of the United States and the United Kingdom, or of Japan for that matter. When I read that Wall Streeters are visiting Beijing to help the People's Republic establish a stock market, I shudder. It is far from clear that the proliferation of financial instruments, markets, arbitrage opportunities, and paper transactions in advanced countries has created social product to justify the high-quality human capital resources it devours. Business schools are beginning to wonder if they shouldn't be teaching students how to make products and manage workers rather than how to shuffle paper. David Halberstam's *The Reckoning* tells how the famous financial "Whiz Kids" of the Ford Motor Company, many years ago, lost the ball game for Ford.

The major purpose of financial markets and institutions is to channel the excess savings of some agents in the economy to the excess real investments other agents are prepared to undertake. There are many ways to organize such flows, and they do not all require speculative markets.

Nor should these countries be in a great hurry to free capital movements into and out of their currencies of all controls and central-bank supervision. Remember that much of the rapid growth of European countries and Japan after World War II occurred before the full dismantling of exchange and capital controls. It is important even for small countries to maintain some degree of autonomy in monetary policy, so that local interest rates are not wholly determined by foreign markets. The foreign-exchange-transactions tax is one way to do that. Third World countries seeking developmental investments from overseas companies should avoid competitive scrambles with each other. Such competition can easily transfer the lion's share of the gains from the investments to the multinational companies, at the expense of the countries themselves. In the United States, states and cities are engaged in unsavory bidding for locations of new business installations, and the result is mutually destructive of their tax bases and other reasonable regulations.

### Where the Invisible Hand Needs a Hand

Intensified confidence in the Invisible Hand—among economists, politicians, and the general public—comes at a time when more and more reasons for doubt are arising. It is not easy to discern how laissez-faire unaided, unguided, and uncontrolled can handle the big new challenges of the twenty-first century. Here are several examples.

1.  At a time when long-range decisions are essential and myopia is especially dangerous, private markets evidently have great difficulty focusing on long horizons. If anything, they seem to be becoming shorter in their orientations. Business managers, especially in the United States, are criticized, even by themselves, for their preoccupation with quick payoffs. Financial markets are untrustworthy guides for managers because they are dominated by speculators. Much activity of financiers and managers is devoted to the thriving markets in whole businesses: takeovers, leveraged buyouts, mergers, break-ups of previous mergers. A disproportionate number of the brightest and most enterprising talent of our youth are devoted to the churning and shuffling of paper, in search of quick wealth rather than production of goods and services.

    Speculative frenzy is not confined to the United States. Consider the fabulous booms in real estate values in Japan, beyond what could be justified by rents, and in related stock market prices as well. These booms generate prices that do not guide allocations of land to economically rational uses.

2.  In the 1970s the world was jolted to a sudden realization that its economies were dependent on exhaustible sources of energy. When oil became plentiful again in the 1980s we seemed to forget the lesson. Energy prices reflect transient demand/supply conditions in disproportion to inevitable future scarcities. Perhaps because capital markets are shortsighted, investments to develop energy resources and to conserve energy use are abandoned or ignored when current prices are low, even though they would be justified by probable future prices. Commodity and capital markets together do not seem to have long enough horizons to give dependable signals. Nevertheless the thrust of energy policy in the United States these past eight years has been to rely wholly on private markets.

3.  Economic theory has always recognized externalities as exceptions to Invisible Hand propositions. Externalities are nonmarket effects of economic activities on other economic activities. When agents receive no price signals to deter them from activities damaging to other agents or to encourage them to engage in activities useful to others, the market by itself fails to allocate resources

optimally among activities. Generators of electricity in Ohio acidify lakes in the northeastern United States and in Canada. Neither the midwest utilities nor their customers consider the acid-rain costs their electricity is imposing on their northeastern neighbors when they decide how much to produce and consume or whether and how much to invest in antipollution technology. Likewise, the driver considering going on to a busy highway or city street thinks of his or her own convenience but not of the extra delays and inconveniences the additional congestion will cause others.

Belatedly, awkwardly, erratically, and often inefficiently, governments have been trying to deal with environmental damage, the health and safety of workers, customers, and neighbors, and other external effects. The affected industries chafe under the regulations and costs imposed upon them. Unfortunately the conservative fashion of deregulation has sometimes been blindly extended to these measures, along with the anticompetitive "toll-booth" interventions that deserve to be dismantled.

Ronald Coase did both Adam Smith and Dr. Pangloss one better by suggesting that the parties to negative externalities on the delivering and receiving sides could and would get together and contract with each other to eliminate or limit them if the social gains were worth the trouble.[5] In the case of positive externalities, similarly, the generators and beneficiaries would bargain to bring them to an optimal level. Thus would externalities be internalized. The Coase theorem seems to be a rationale *for* government rather than against it. It is precisely to handle situations where markets have difficulties reaching agreements and contracts of this kind that societies utilize governments.

Paradoxically, free-market doctrines are more uncritically accepted just when externalities appear to be more serious than ever before. It's hard to maintain the pose of old welfare economics textbooks, that externalities are the exceptions that prove the Invisible Hand rule. Current problems are all the more complex because the adverse effects are cumulative but delayed, and because they are intrinsically difficult to evaluate. Many technologies that are efficient contributors to the welfare of individual consumers today spin off side effects that will be costly or disastrous in the future: ozone depletion, greenhouse effects, toxic and radioactive wastes, receding water tables, and many other environmental and ecological dangers. As my acid rain example illustrates, these hazards do not respect international boundaries.

4. In the background of all our ecological problems is the excessive growth of the world population relative to the sustainable expansion of the planet's capacity to support human life, let alone to support it at standards of living to which all peoples aspire. No market miracle brings population and resources into balance and keeps them there. The only Invisible Hands are the cruel Malthusian checks. The hope of avoiding overpopulation is that fertility will spontaneously decline as standards of living rise. Over the past two centuries this mechanism worked successfully for the now advanced countries. For the poorest countries today the catch is that their rates of natural increase prevent the very progress in living standards that might diminish fertility. Modern medicine can keep people alive longer but it does not add space for them to live or resources to feed them. The rich countries of the world have obligations to help the poorer nations develop, yes even to help the workers of those lands to compete with their own high-paid workers. They are much less likely to offer assistance, markets for products, and privileges of immigration if it appears that the consequences are not to raise living standards but to foster still higher rates of population growth.

5. The Invisible Hand, as exaggerated and glorified in free-market ideology, has several unfortunate social externalities of its own. It is a rationale for unabashed and unmitigated individualistic selfishness. It assures those who seek, above all else, to accumulate material wealth that they are patriots doing Adam Smith's noble work, promotion of the wealth of nations. Indeed, nowadays there are numerous right-wing preachers, "televangelists," telling them they are doing God's work.

One message they get is that their obligations to others are just those specified in the literal language of previous contracts and written laws. All too frequently another one is that disobedience of those rules is worthwhile and even legitimate if the personal benefits exceed the costs. Many ordinary good people do not put quarters in parking meters if they calculate that the probabilities of being ticketed and fined $5.00 are less than one in twenty. That transgression of civic virtue may be innocuous. But if everyone behaves like that in all aspects of life, the social order breaks down. The burdens on police and courts are intolerable; law and litigation absorb the best minds of the society.

Competition is supposed to make self-interest work for the best. But competition itself cannot function without a clement political and legal framework, and competitive markets will not survive the efforts of competitors themselves to eliminate them without the unceasing vigilance of governments. And if governments, elected officials, and civil servants are constantly denounced as wasteful and worthless, as foreign bodies in a utopian organism of private markets, the central institutions and essential infrastructures of economy and society decay and wither away. Taxes are, according to Mr. Justice Oliver Wendell Holmes, the price of civilization.

6. Finally, there are limits to the extremes of inequality that a democracy can tolerate, especially when television incessantly parades the luxurious life styles of the rich before poor youth who can never expect to taste them. Materialism, hardheartedness, and incivility are, according to many observers, byproducts of the Reagan revolution in the United States. President George Bush himself is calling for a kinder, gentler America.

## Notes

1. The famous paragraph containing these words and summarizing the basic thesis of the book occurs in Book IV, chapter II, on page 423 of the Modern Library Edition of Smith's *The Wealth of Nations* (1776), edited by Edwin Cannan and published in 1937.

2. J. M. Keynes, *The General Theory of Employment, Interest and Money* (New York: Harcourt Brace, 1936).

3. Arthur M. Okun, *Equality and Efficiency: The Big Tradeoff* (Washington, D.C.: Brookings Institution, 1975).

4. Robert Shiller, "Do stock prices move too much to be justified by subsequent changes in dividends?" *American Economic Review* 71 (October 1981), pp. 421–36.

5. Ronald Coase, "The problem of social cost," *Journal of Law and Economics* 3 (October 1960) pp. 1–44. See also, R. D. Cooter, "The Coase Theorem," in J. Eatwell, M. Milgate and P. Newman, eds., *The New Palgrave, A Dictionary of Economics* (London: Macmillan, 1987), Vol. I, pp. 457–60.

# 16

# Social Reality and "Free Markets": A Letter to Friends in Eastern Europe

## (Spring 1990)

## *Robert Dahl*

The rapid advance of democratization in Eastern Europe and the Soviet Union, still underway as I write, is surely one of the most extraordinary revolutions in the long history of democracy. Just as no one, to my knowledge, predicted the time or speed of this dramatic transformation, so no one, I believe, can accurately predict the subsequent course of these democratic revolutions. But democrats everywhere are already entitled to rejoice over the enormous vitality of democratic ideas demonstrated by the actions of the people in your countries.

In the midst of our rejoicing over your victories, however, some of us are also concerned, as you must be, over the difficulties that lie ahead. It is not for me to instruct you, who are on the spot and in touch with unfolding events, as to how you might best meet the daily challenges to your efforts to bring about the changes you seek in political life, the economic order, social relations, ideas, and beliefs. But I hope you will permit me to share with you a concern over one of the many issues you confront. This is the question of the place of a market economy in a democratic country.

It is a historical fact that political institutions of the kind you seek and are now engaged in creating—in short, what you and I ordinarily call democracy (that is, actually existing though not ideal democracy)—have existed only in countries with predominantly privately owned, market-oriented economies, or capitalism, if you prefer that name. It is also a historical fact, as I hardly need to remind you, that all "socialist" countries with predominantly state-owned, centrally directed economic orders—command economies—have not enjoyed democratic governments, have in fact been ruled by authoritarian dictatorships. It is also a historical fact that some "capitalist" countries have also been—and are—ruled by authoritarian dictatorships.

To put it more formally, it looks to be the case that market-oriented economies are necessary to democratic institutions, though they are certainly not sufficient. And it looks to be the case that state-owned, centrally directed economic orders are strictly associated with authoritarian regimes, though authoritarianism definitely does not require them. We have something very much like a historical experiment, so it would appear, that leaves these conclusions in no great doubt.

Of course there is an enormous amount of complexity, variation, and qualification packed into my all-too-brief description of the experiment and the conclusions from it. Only metaphorically is history a laboratory; we cannot rerun the experiment at will to sort out all the causal factors. Thus the apparently strict association between dictatorship and the state-owned, centrally directed economic orders of the "socialist" countries is contaminated, so to speak, by Leninism. With its arrogant assignment of the role of vanguard to the Communist Party, which in practice means the hegemony of the party leaders (or leader) in a one-party system, orthodox Leninism denies a place to the political pluralism that a country requires if it is to be democratic. Even during the brief period of the New Economic Policy, Leninist doctrine led directly to the suppression of opposition parties. In short, independently of a state-owned, centrally directed economy, Leninist political views would no doubt have been sufficient to bring about the suppression of oppositions and the creation of authoritarian regimes.

If the historical experiment is not as clear-cut as it looks, there are nonetheless good reasons for thinking that a predominantly state-owned, centrally directed economy will prove to be incompatible with democracy in the not-so-long run. For such an economic order places enormous resources in the hands of leaders—resources for persuasion, inducement, corruption, and coercion. As far as I know, the only instances in democratic countries of a centrally directed economy (though not widespread state ownership) were the comparatively brief experiences of Britain and the United States in the Second World War, when the need to mobilize all possible resources for the war effort led to the creation of systems of centralized allocations and price fixing. Although these systems performed magnificently in achieving their limited purposes, in both countries they were rapidly dismantled after the war ended—in part because the public would no longer tolerate the restrictions they imposed. Had they endured, I shudder to think of the effects they could have had on American and British political life. In this country, even a scrupulous president would have found it hard to resist the temptation to use his power over the economy to discourage opposition. An unscrupulous president—Richard Nixon comes immediately to mind—might well have used that power in far more sinister ways.

Therefore even if systems of state ownership and centralized direction of the economy had not proved themselves inefficient in meeting the needs of relatively modern, well-developed countries—as they clearly have—you would be wise to reject them on the separate ground that they pose a standing danger to democratic institutions. I realize, of course, that to rid your countries of these systems will require a hard, tough, and probably protracted battle; for the changes will be resisted by many people, not only office upon office of bureaucrats but others whose security, income, status, careers, and indifferent work habits depend on the continued existence of these obsolete systems. Conceivably, that task may be so difficult that what I am about to say will seem to you to be almost irrelevant to the immediate situation you face.

Nevertheless, I want to suggest that your path lies somewhere between the economic system you are rightly rejecting and full reliance on a market economy. In urging these considerations, I am reminded of a book published nearly half a century ago that bears rereading today—*The Great Transformation* by Karl Polanyi. Polanyi argued that the visible failures of state intervention in England from the 1790s to the 1830s, particularly the disastrous consequences of the Poor Laws, profoundly influenced the thinking of several generations of important thinkers, from Bentham, Burke, and Malthus to Ricardo, Marx, Mill, Darwin, and Spencer. The lesson many liberal thinkers of the time drew was that state intervention, even for humane ends like the care of the rural poor, was likely to cause far more harm than good. The alternative they should support instead, they concluded, was a full market economy with self-regulating markets in land, labor, capital, and money. And with the passage of Poor Law Reform in 1834, a self-regulating market economy seemed finally to have arrived.

Yet no sooner had it arrived than discontent with its consequences began to bring about state intervention to regulate markets—efforts so successful that Herbert Spencer, an advocate of unregulated market capitalism, lamented the long list of regulatory actions he could compile by 1884: regulations governing food and drink, penalizing the employment in mines of boys under twelve not attending schools and unable to read and write, empowering Poor-Law officials to enforce vaccination, extending compulsory vaccination to Scotland and Ireland, punishing chimney sweepers who compelled boys to sweep chimneys so narrow that the boys often suffered injuries and sometimes death, providing controls for contagious diseases, empowering local officials to set up public libraries at public expense, and so on. The list extended for several pages. And since 1884 it has lengthened. Even in the United States, which is often thought of as the very citadel of laissez-faire capitalism, to describe briefly all the ways in which governments—national, state, municipal, regional, district, and so on—regulate, supplement, displace, or otherwise alter the operation of markets would take a small library.

Polanyi's account is consistent with a much broader range of historical experiences in the countries where today we find the most advanced and successful market economies: in Europe, North America, Japan, and the Pacific. From the experiences of these countries—to whose political and economic institutions you may now be looking in search of feasible solutions for your own problems—we can, I think, draw the following conclusions.

1. *Many of the criticisms of capitalism advanced by socialists were*
   *essentially correct.*

   Capitalism is persistently at odds with values of equity, fairness, political equality among all citizens, and democracy. Where many socialists went badly wrong was in believing that the evils they saw could best be solved by abolishing markets, competition among economic enterprises, and the seeming "anarchy" of the price system, and by transferring the ownership and direct control of the economy to "the public," or "society," as represented by the state. In Western Europe, however, socialists discovered that they could not achieve these goals; they were unable to replace capitalism with the centralized state socialism many of them believed to be ideally preferable; and they turned their political efforts instead to finding specific solutions to the concrete problems that a market economy inevitably gives rise to. Thus while they never achieved "socialism" in the sense they commonly thought, they did help to make their economies more decent, humane, and just than was the capitalism of Marx's time.

2. *In making their economies more humane, socialist, labor, and social democratic parties contributed to—though they were not the sole authors of—the development of the mixed economies that exist in advanced countries today.*

   If these mixed economies are a far cry from the centralized systems you wish to dismantle, they are also very far from the classic liberal model of a self-regulating market economy. If you wish to look to the most advanced economies for guidance, then, you should not allow yourselves to be misled by dogma about "free markets." Although the economies of these countries are often described as "free market" systems, they are not. Instead, all the world's most advanced and successful economies are mixtures of markets (themselves of enormous variety) and deliberately imposed government interventions in the market (also of incredible variety).

3. *In addition, a century or more of efforts to arrive at a feasible and politically acceptable mix of market and nonmarket elements has not produced a definitive, stable, or uniform solution.*

   There is not the slightest reason to think that the search for the best mix has anywhere come to an end. In the United States, for example, we are now harvesting the consequences of eight years of the Reagan administration, during which deregulation and wor-

ship of the beneficent effects of the market dominated the thinking, and to some extent the policies, of that administration. We
are now engaged in discovering—or rather rediscovering—how
much damage can occur if public policies are based on the simple-minded assumption that everything, or almost everything, can
be entrusted to the marketplace. In the United States, laissez-faire
has been dead in practice for a long time; even eight years of
Reaganism have not restored it to life. So we continue to be
engaged, as we have been for generations, in attempts to find a
more acceptable balance between market and nonmarket arrangements. I strongly doubt, however, whether we Americans, or people in any other democratic country, will ever manage to arrive at
a point where market and nonmarket forces are all at a stable
equilibrium, politically speaking. Our society, including the economy, is too dynamic to allow for permanence in public policies.

4. *The experience of the democratic countries with the most ad-*
   *vanced economies also tells us that no single pattern, or even a*
   *dominant one, has emerged; and what has emerged is a product of*
   *the special characteristics and the unique history of each country.*
   Thus the Scandinavian countries, Austria, Germany, and the
   Netherlands, among others, have developed what are sometimes
   called systems of democratic corporatism. The expression *demo-*
   *cratic corporatism* is used because economic policies of exceptional consequence are made, more or less beyond the reach of
   parliament, by agreements among the major corporate entities, in
   particular the trade unions and employers' associations, sometimes
   together with organizations representing consumers or farmers.
   Yet not only do the patterns of *democratic corporatism* differ
   greatly among these countries, but in others, such as Britain and
   the United States, "corporatist" structures are comparatively weak,
   in part because unions and employers' associations are much less
   inclusive, more fragmented, and more decentralized. The point is
   that you do not have a single model of relatively satisfactory "market economies" to consider for possible emulation in your countries; instead, you have many models. Each country's pattern to
   some extent reflects the country's unique, or, at any rate, far from

general, conditions and history. Attractive as you may find the Swedish model, for example, you should not assume that it can be transferred to your country, where the necessary conditions may not exist now or in the foreseeable future.

5. *Actual practices in the advanced democratic countries are, then, far too diverse and complex to be captured by ideologies.*

Thirty-five years ago, Charles E. Lindblom and I argued that it had become increasingly difficult for thoughtful persons to find meaningful alternatives posed in the traditional choices between socialism and capitalism, planning and the free market, regulation and laissez-faire. Economic organization, we insisted then, poses knotty problems that can be solved only by painstaking attention to technical details. I believe that experience since then strongly confirms this judgment. It does not necessarily mean "the end of ideology." But it does mean that no sensible person should expect an ideology to provide solutions to concrete problems. Probably more often than not, an ideology is not very helpful even as a general guide. To take one example, questions about property and the most suitable forms of ownership admit of no simple answers. "Public versus private ownership and control of the means of production" is no more than a simplistic slogan. Not only do "public" and "private" mask an almost infinite variety of possibilities, but no reasonable person—or society—would, after carefully examining the concrete possibilities in specific situations, conclude that any single form of ownership and control would invariably be superior to all others. Likewise to pose the issue as "planning versus the market" is, in the light of the experiences of advanced democratic countries, simply silly. A good deal of "central planning" exists in these countries, particularly in the form of fiscal, budgetary, and monetary controls. Yugoslavia, by contrast, furnishes an example of a "socialist" country where the absence or weakness of these instruments for central influence over the economy has led to disastrous economic consequences.

6. *It seems obvious, then, that the search for solutions to the problems generated by a predominantly privately owned, market-*

*oriented society has been and will continue to be a major element in the political agenda of every democratic country.*

As in the past, the search will take place amidst political controversy. And it should. For even if solutions often depend on technical knowledge, rarely, if ever, is technical knowledge enough. Alternative solutions invariably engage important values as well—equity, equality of opportunity, liberty, security, progress, and community, among others.

7. *Because intelligent choices of public policies require both technical understanding and sensitivity to the values involved, in modern democratic countries a form of specialized intellectual activity has evolved that tends to combine both aspects of policy.*

And a rather new type of intellectual has developed to engage in this activity: the policy specialist. Although the locations and functions of policy specialists vary among the democratic countries, in the United States policy specialists are now located in major institutions of all kinds, not only in the executive branches of government at every level—national, state, and local—but in the Congress and the state legislatures and municipal councils, in the political parties, business firms, trade unions, lobbying organizations, independent research centers, and universities. Their numbers, variety, and differences in perspectives and institutional loyalties tend to ensure that expertise is not monopolized by any single group, such as the White House or a Congressional committee.

To keep technical knowledge in your countries from becoming the monopoly of any particular group, you will probably need to create and maintain a considerable measure of pluralism among organizations engaged in the analysis of public policies and you will need a supply of well-trained specialists to staff them. For this task, neither ideological perspectives, such as a belief in the need for democracy and a market economy, nor technical knowledge bearing on the specific problem at hand, whether that of economists, engineers, scientists, or whatever, will, by itself, be sufficient.

It is no simple or easy task to manage a market-oriented economy in such a way as to maximize its advantages, which are great, and to minimize its disadvantages, which are also great. How best to do so is, and surely will continue to be, a subject of continuing debate and political struggle. In your own political struggles, the experiences of democratic countries with advanced economies may be helpful to you. But I urge you to avoid the mistake of the classical liberals whose ideas were formed in reaction to the failures of mercantilism and the Poor Laws. Reacting to the failures of state ownership and central direction of the economy, you may be tempted to conclude that the best alternative for your countries is to turn everything over to unregulated markets. Not only would this be a misreading of the experience of the advanced democratic countries; it would be a misfortune for your countries.

# 17

# Virtues and Vices of the Market: Balanced Correctives to a Current Craze

## (Summer 1990)

### Ernest Erber

Not since they encountered it in nursery rhymes have references to the market so intruded into the consciousness of Americans as in recent months. There is now a virtual consensus that the market is the natural state of economic affairs, and its creation in nations not yet blessed with it is the prescription for every economic ailment. This makes vague good sense to most Americans, for whom the market has long since come to determine their tastes and values, their very lives.

This new consciousness of the market reflects, of course, the events triggered by Gorbachev's announcement that the Soviet system, having sinned against the market and God (in that order of importance), requires restructuring on the basis of the market—with a tip of the hat to God.

Meanwhile, infatuation with the market seems most pronounced in Eastern Europe, where the people get just enough of a glimpse to be smitten by its allure but remain maddeningly unable to embrace it. For most Soviets, the market is still too distant to be a realistic prospect. Most West Europeans accept the market with sophisticated reservations: alert to possible failing but overwhelmed by evidence of success and increasingly drawn to American-style consumerism.

Democratic socialists—above all, European social democrats—increasingly accept the market as the only realistic basis for economic growth, increased wages, and social reform. And now they seem also to believe that the market can accommodate the transformations necessary to achieve social democracy's most far-reaching goals.

This worldwide consensus would not exist if it did not reflect a body of evidence that links the market with economic growth, increased productivity, and improved living standards. That this historical progress has been facilitated by the market's competitive and entrepreneurial incentives cannot be contested. Neither can the beliefs that the market's function as a pricing mechanism has historically contributed to economic stability conducive to growth, even if plagued by a persistent tendency toward inflation in recent years, nor that the market's negative, even self-destructive, side effects have been largely diminished by state intervention through regulation, credit-budget-tax policies, price supports, and social welfare programs.

But does this frequently cited evidence suffice to sustain the view that the market has proved itself to be the most feasible—if not the only—economic institution for the optimum development of productivity and, above all, for the most rational allocation of goods and services? And, with respect to the future, does the evidence prove that the market is a mechanism for social change that can go beyond capitalist property relations to accommodate the progressive transformation identified as democratic socialism?

These questions lead to asking which areas of evidence were not probed, but should have been, in establishing the consensus view of the market. Let me glance at three major areas of inquiry:

1. The identification of the market's distinctive historical role, examined apart from such related phenomena as (a) the Industrial Revolution and subsequent technological progress, (b) the rise of capitalist production methods, and (c) the economic role of the state as "jump-starter" and crutch.
2. The intrinsic negative side effects of the market and the questionable effectiveness of political intervention in overcoming them.

3. The limits of the market's susceptibility to goal-oriented social policy.

## Nature of the Market

Let me first set down a few concepts on the nature of the market. The market of modern times cannot be understood if perceived simply as the continuity of barter, trade, commerce, and so on that served organized societies throughout history. The market as we know it today is the historically specific product of industrial capitalism and can only be understood if perceived as such. Integral to capitalist society, it permeates its every aspect. Referring to this historically unique institution by capitalizing it as a proper noun (a practice recently initiated by Robert Heilbroner) enhances clarity.

The Market is, essentially, an economic decision-making process that determines the allocation of society's resources by deciding what and how much is produced and how and to whom it is distributed. Those who participate in this process are buyers and sellers who "meet" in the "marketplace," though they are not only individuals, since buyers and sellers also include businesses of all sizes, farmers and professionals as groups, and governments at all levels.

As an alternative to the Market, society's resources can also be directly allocated by political decisions of government (that is, by "command"). Government can also act deliberately to influence directly how the Market functions indirectly. Those who determine a government's economic role are citizens, governing officials, and administrators (including, sometimes, planners, though every governmental impact upon the economy should not be called "planning" and, in the United States, it almost never is that). Within capitalist economies, the purpose of governmental intervention in the Market is two-fold: (1) to facilitate the functioning of the Market by protecting it from its shortcomings, including tendencies toward self-destructiveness; (2) to supplement the Market by providing those goods and services that the Market has no incentive to supply because they do not entail a profit (public schools, social welfare, low-cost housing, infrastructure, and so on).

The extent to which government should influence the economy is an issue that has been fought over for a very long time. Charles E. Lindblom begins his definitive *Politics and Markets* by observing that "the greatest distinction between one government and another is in the degree to which market replaces government or government replaces market. Both Adam Smith and Karl Marx knew this."

The word "degree" is used by Lindblom deliberately, for neither the Market nor government replaces the other completely. Thus all economies are a mix of the Market and political decision-making. Even the totally mad Stalinist effort to eliminate the Market in Soviet-type societies fell short of complete success, for these societies had to tolerate market operations in corners of the economy, either by compromise, as in permitted sales from garden plots of collective farmers and *kolkhoz* "surplus" production, or through black market sales of scarce commodities, tolerated because they were considered helpful to the economy.

Another variant of madness, though largely rhetorical, is the Thatcherite and Reaganite pronouncements about getting government out of the economy and "letting the market decide." After a decade of such huffing and puffing, the role of government vis-à-vis the economy, both in Great Britain and in the United States, remains essentially unchanged, some privatizations not withstanding.

The Market as a decision-making process acts somewhat like the neurotransmitters of the brain, sending messages that trigger decisions, serving as a link among the economy's leading actors: capital, labor, and consumers. It triggers action in response to supply and demand, offers and orders, and incentives that provide opportunity. (That is why "the market process" as used by its theorists/apologists in the Adam Smith-von Mises-Hayek tradition is, perhaps, more accurate than the term "the market," which tends to suggest an actual place.)

The mass of consumers who make their "buy" decisions through the Market process (so-called consumer sovereignty) exert unequal economic weight and consequently have unequal impact. They include the Pentagon, businesses from General Motors to a Mom-and-Pop store, individuals and households buying stocks, bread, oil, transportation, bombs, dynamos, ranches, bonds, Bibles, pornography, steel mills, clothing, you name it.

The Market exists subject to the power of government: the right to buy/sell and produce/develop prevails within the constraints of laws enacted to serve policy objectives. Now that politics has come to dominate the economy, it also dominates the Market. And although government appears to be loosening its grip on the economy within most ex-Communist nations, it continues to tighten its grip in the capitalist world, for instance, in the planned emergence in 1992 of a new and more advanced stage of the European common market with a common currency and central European bank.

The Market shapes the economy—and society as a whole—by virtue of its impact upon production rather than, as widely supposed, upon distribution. For in a Market-dominated society, what can be sold determines what is produced. In turn, what is produced determines the allocation of capital and the employment of labor. It follows that the Market process is but the buy/sell linkage of the economy's three functional markets: the capital market, the labor market, and the goods/services market. (In a Market-based economy, capital and labor are treated, for the first time in the history of economic institutions, as commodities—and bought and sold accordingly.) The Market shapes societal development by determining where and how capital is utilized (that is, invested) and, consequently, employment by volume and type, land use, and population distribution, as well as a myriad of other economic, social, cultural, ecological, and political trends.

## The Market's Historical Context

The Market took shape when the Industrial Revolution transformed mercantile capitalism, which existed marginally in late feudal society, into industrial capitalism. We owe our understanding of the historical uniqueness of the Market largely to the work of Karl Polanyi, especially his *The Great Transformation*. In an essay written shortly after World War II, Polanyi observes that

> the birth of laissez faire administered a shock to civilized man's view of himself, from the effects of which he never quite recovered. Only very gradually are we realizing what happened to us as recently as a century ago.... A chain-reaction was started—what before was merely isolated markets was transmuted into a self-regulating *system* of markets. And with the new economy, a new society sprang into being.

Its basis was the transformation of land and labor into commodities, to be bought and sold in the marketplace, whereas all previous societies had

> restricted markets to commodities in the proper sense of the term, with land and labor subject to public regulation or self-regulation (as with the guilds).
>
> Aristotle was right: man is not an economic, but a social being. Man's economy is, as a rule, submerged in his social relations. The change from this to a society which was, on the contrary, submerged in the economic system was an entirely novel development.

The Market, therefore, originated with the Industrial Revolution and the capitalist mode of production. To what extent was it a contingent relationship? It might be argued with considerable evidence that the rapidity with which the Industrial Revolution developed and spread was due to the Market and the capitalist mode. But it cannot be reasonably argued that the Industrial Revolution would not have taken place in the absence of the Market and capitalism. The Industrial Revolution was the product of the growth of scientific knowledge and technological invention, in the first place, and only secondarily a product of socioeconomic phenomena. (There is also the evidence of Soviet industrialization, which was neither a product of the Market nor of the capitalist mode.)

But of a higher order of significance is the question as to whether the Market-driven development of the Industrial Revolution could have occurred without the capitalist mode of production. This question is relevant to the future of Eastern Europe and the Soviet Union and is at the heart of the controversy now being joined there, as the Market is featured with its ties to the capitalist mode obfuscated.

Insofar as this question also encompasses the issue of "market socialism"—that is, market relations without capitalist relations—its significance includes all of Europe and, ultimately, the industrial world. This is likely to be the question of the twenty-first century.

A final aspect of the Market's historical context is the largely forgotten role played by the state in getting market-based economies off the ground in various parts of the world. Japan, Prussia, and Czarist Russia are outstanding examples of the state's role in "jump starting" both capitalist production and market relations through generous credit, subsidies, enactment of special rights, licenses, and so on. Government construction of infrastructure often played a key role.

What we can conclude is that the prevailing view that attributes the material progress of human societies during the last century or two *solely* to the Market is fallacious because the Market's contribution cannot be sufficiently separated from that of the Industrial Revolution, the capitalist mode of production, or the nourishing role of the state. To the extent that references to the Market are euphemistic in order to advocate capitalism under another name, there is an implied admission that the Market cannot be separated from capitalism, that is, private property in the means of production, labor as a commodity, unearned income, accumulation, and so forth. But insofar as there now exists an effort to utilize the Market's virtues while straining out its vices, in order to serve the common welfare, an assessment of its feasibility cannot be made until we have clearer insights into how it would resolve a number of contradictions that seem to make this objective unworkable.

## The Market's Side Effects and Political Remedies

The following descriptions of the Market's side effects are valid, on the whole, though in some cases not entirely separable from other causes. The rationale of the Market is competition—for survival and gain. It pits each against all in social Darwinian "survival of the fittest": worker against worker and entrepreneur against entrepreneur, capital against labor and producer against consumer. The weak are eliminated and the strong survive, resulting in the trend toward concentration and monopolies. Businesses live by the "bottom line," with an incentive toward price gouging, adulteration, misrepresentation, and environmental degradation. Product or service promotion caters to every human weakness. Advertising seduces consumers to develop endless wants. The central effect is to subvert human solidarity and civic responsibility.

The multitudinous buy/sell decisions that drive the market process are made in total ignorance of their collective impact, as expressed in Adam Smith's now hoary "unseen hand." Its social impact causes

society to "fly blind," as when millions of individually bought automobiles collectively spell traffic gridlock and death-dealing air pollution. Government seeks to overcome these destructive results by
regulating the manufacture of automobiles and gasoline. If this fails,
as is likely, government will have to turn to long-range planning of
alternate transportation, replacing private automobile trips with public
conveyances. This will be a political decision to allocate resources
from the private sector's automobile solution to the public sector's rail
and bus solution. This is only one example of the choices between
decisions by the Market and by the political process (made with or
without planning).

The nineteenth-century laissez-faire market process, almost total
economic determination by consumer demand, eventually proved unworkable. This was capitalism as Karl Marx knew it, and unworkable
as he had predicted. During the course of the twentieth century, laissez-faire gave way to large-scale political intervention resulting in
state-guided and, increasingly, state-managed capitalism, with the
state's control of money flow through central banks (Federal Reserve
in the United States), credit control, tariffs and quotas, subsidies, tax
policy, industrial and agricultural loans, price supports, wages policy,
loan guarantees, savings incentives, marketing assistance, stockpiling,
and various regulatory controls. This continuing transformation of
market-based economies, which has come to be known as the Keynesian Revolution, is likely to be viewed by historians as of greater significance than the Soviet Revolution.

The proportions of market vs. political decision-making in economic affairs do not necessarily reflect the proportions of private vs.
state ownership of the economy. State-owned industries in countries
such as Austria, Italy, and France, where they form a high proportion
of the economy, are largely indistinguishable from the private sector
in operating by the rules of the Market to produce in response to
consumer demand. On the other hand, despite a relatively small nationalized sector, the state in Sweden is omnipresent in managing
economic affairs. *The current widespread tilt toward privatization
does not, therefore, diminish the trend toward an increased role of the
state in economic affairs.*

The Market process demands that those who wish to participate pay admission. Those who cannot afford to get in—or who drop out—fall through the cracks, if lucky, into a social safety net. As the burden increased beyond private charities' resources, government was forced to assume it and the twentieth century's "welfare state" emerged. Its "transfer" programs of public goods and services exist outside the Market for those who cannot make it within.

The insecurity of various categories of entrepreneurs (such as farmers, oil drillers, ship owners, owners of small businesses, bank depositors), caused by the instability and unpredictability of the market process, led these entrepreneurs to use their political power to seek public assistance through subsidies, loans, insurance, "bailouts," and so forth, eventually becoming entitlements. The latter, together with welfare state transfer payments, proliferated and grew enormously, in part because they reflected the universal transition within affluent societies from satisfying needs to meeting wants. Adding these to the cost of traditional categories of public goods and services (such as national defense, public schools, parks, libraries, streets and roads) resulted in ballooning governmental budgets and the diversion through taxation of increasing proportions of the GNPs of industrial nations to their public sectors.

This had the effect of cutting into the availability of accumulated capital for investment in direct wealth-producing enterprise. Government response differed sharply, depending upon whether it followed a national economic policy or relied upon the Market. Sweden, an example of the former, tapped its Supplementary Pension Program to create the so-called fourth fund for targeted industrial investment, creating and sustaining employment that yielded a flow of payroll deductions back into the fund. The United States, on the other hand, permitted Market forces to drive up interest rates, bringing an inflow of foreign capital and an outflow of dividends and interest.

But, regardless of how the problem is managed, there are political limits to the diversion of funds from the private sector to the public sector via taxation. This can be seen in the "tax revolts" in Europe and the United States in the last two decades, which also had repercussions in the Scandinavian countries, including Sweden. This diversion also triggered the resurgence of laissez-faire ideology and right-wing politics.

Even for those countries in which the Market successfully accumulates the "wealth of nations," there results a lopsided inequality of distribution within the population, resulting in recurring economic instability and social confrontation. (Brazil, a country with the eighth largest Market-based economy in the world, leads all others in polarization between rich and poor.) The Market process generates cyclical and chronic unemployment, bankruptcies, mass layoffs, over- and underproduction, strikes and lockouts, and many other kinds of economic warfare and social tension. There is good reason to believe that the sharp shift in income from earned to unearned during the 1980s will be reflected in rising class conflict in the 1990s.

The Market is not a surefire prescription for the "wealth of nations" because its acclaimed incentives, acting as a spur to economic development, are also historically specific. Just because eighteenth-century England used the Market process to turn itself into a "nation of shopkeepers" and nineteenth century England used it to lead the way in the Industrial Revolution to become the "world's workshop," there is no assurance that, at any other time in history, people of any other culture and level of development can similarly use the Market to the same end—notwithstanding the examples of Western Europe, the United States, Canada, and Japan. (South Korea and Taiwan, judged by their per capita incomes, have not yet made it.)

Internationally, the Market has resulted in a hierarchical ranking of nations by wealth, grouping a fortunate few as the rich nations and the rest as relatively or absolutely poor. Market-process relations between the industrially developed nations and the rest take the form of the developed responding to the consumer-driven demands of the underdeveloped for investments, loans, goods, and services, thereby aggravating their dependency and frustrating their ability to accumulate enough capital to significantly improve their productivity (Argentina, Brazil, Mexico, Egypt, India, to name some).

In summarizing the Market's negative side effects we have noted that it flies blindly; that its growth becomes destructive of communitarian values and institutions and of the natural environment; that its "work ethic" becomes exploitation, even of children (child labor is again on the rise in the United States according to the Department of

Labor); that it reduces the cost of production but also triggers inflation; that it produces a cornucopia of goods but also mountains of waste; that its pharmaceutical research lengthens lifespans, but its chemicals (pesticides and herbicides) shorten them; that it makes feverish use of humankind's growing power over nature, born of scientific and technological progress, but puts profits above ecology and market share above the need to conserve natural resources; that it provides conveniences, comforts, and luxuries for an increasing number but shows no ability to close the widening gap between haves and have nots, neither within nor between nations. But, above all, the Market, despite Keynesianism, operates in cycles of boom and bust, victimizing businesses, large and small, farmers, professionals, and wage workers. Left to its own devices, the Market is inherently self-destructive.

Though the Market's negative side effects can be countered through government intervention and largely have been, such countering tends to be ameliorative rather than curative and often raises new problems requiring additional intervention, thus reinforcing the overall tendency for the state to backstop the Market. But, despite this, Market economies still move blindly, though increasingly within broad channels marked out by government. The Market economy still overheats and runs out of fuel, but government now acts to cool it and then to fuel it (and even attempts to "fine tune" it). Will it prove a viable arrangement in the long-term for government to treat the Market as if it were an elemental force of nature?

The people seem to want the benefits of the Market but look to government to minimize the dreadful side effects that come with it. But one person's "dreadful side effects" are another person's sweet accumulation of capital. Translated into social relations, this conflict of interests expresses itself as interest-group confrontations and social-class struggles. And as decision-making in economic affairs continues to shift from the Market to the political process, an ever fiercer political resistance is mounted by the interest groups and classes whose power is far greater and more direct in the Market than in the political arena—for instance, the resurgence of the new right in waging ideological and political warfare on behalf of laissez-faire policies.

## The Market's Thrust vs. Societal Guidance

Understanding the direction in which the Market is likely to move in the next few decades is critically important to an assessment of its capacity to accommodate solutions for outstanding problems. In the past, especially since World War II, the Market's contribution to easing the great problems of civilization has been in the form of economic growth. The nature of the problems that now loom, however, makes them less subject to solution through economic growth. The rising tide that once raised all boats now leaves many stuck on muddy bottoms.

Market-based growth has not demonstrated an ability to reduce the glaring inequality in living standards and in educational/cultural levels within and between nations. In the United States during the last decade the gap between the bottom and the top income quintiles has widened. And growth solutions now generate new problems: the degradation of the natural environment on earth and in space; the exhaustion of natural resources; the emergence of *social* limits to growth, caused by the level at which acquisition of goods, services, and facilities by enough people spoils the advantages of possessing them; the puzzle of insatiable wants after basic needs have been satisfied (when is enough enough?). There are also the growth of private affluence and public squalor; an individualistic society's reluctance to resort to collective solutions (national health care) before first going through the agony of postponing the inevitable; and other looming problems sensed but seemingly too elusively complex to articulate. These problems join a long list of old problems that go unsolved to become a leaden weight on progress.

Is there reason to believe that the Market's failure to cope with these problems will (or can) be remedied in the future? Is there anything in the nature and function of the Market that is likely to redirect its performance to be able to solve these problems? Are any of its negative side effects going to be eliminated, except insofar as governmentally applied correctives can curb them without altering the overall thrust of the Market? Left to its own devices, the Market's current trends are likely to expand and exacerbate problems. Are any countervailing forces in view? Yes.

One is the sharpening competition in the world market. The latter is being badly misread. True, a coded message on a computer or fax machine can transfer billions of dollars overseas at the end of the business day and retrieve it first thing in the morning—with earnings added. True, multinationals no longer fly a single flag. But national interests are as sharply defined as ever. And waging war with economic weapons has not reduced competitiveness and aggressiveness. The competitors are dividing into several major blocs: North America (the United States plus Canada and Mexico), Japan (plus the Asian rim countries), and a united Europe. The goal: market share. As Japan has shown (and also Europe to a lesser extent), this warfare requires maximum mobilization of economic resources: capital, management, knowledge-industry, and labor. Japan has shown that the way to bring these together is by making them all part of the corporate state. The power of Japan, Inc. is recognized in all American boardrooms, though a much smaller nation, Sweden, has also used the corporate strategy brilliantly. The striking similarity of Japanese and Swedish economic strategies, though for different social ends, is largely overlooked because the former is dominated by corporations and the latter by organized labor acting through the Social Democratic Party.

The corporate state strategy has antimarket overtones. Rather than letting the market decide, it operates through strategic planning and a national industrial (investment) policy. If global market share is the goal, the nation's consumers had better not be permitted to decide on the allocation of resources. Laissez-faire America illustrates why not. The consumers opt for second homes, third cars, snowmobiles, Jacuzzis, and Torneau watches, thereby shortchanging education at all levels, skill retraining of the labor force, housing, and health care—all essential ingredients in mobilizing resources to fight for market share.

The last thing any nation needs or will ever want after the debacle of the Stalinist model is an administrative-command economy (misnamed "planning"). Let the Market process determine the number, style, size, and color of shoes. And similarly for other basic needs and reasonable wants. But the nation also has collective needs, and the polity should determine the allocation of resources to supply them. Because this cannot be determined by the blind outcomes of the Market, the latter must be subordinated to strategically planned priorities designed to serve an overriding common purpose.

If coping with the major problems facing humankind in both its social and natural environments requires societal guidance, it necessitates setting goals and choosing strategies to achieve them; in short, strategic planning. This calls for conscious, deliberate, and coordinated measures to mobilize a nation's resources. The American people with its Market-instilled value system is decidedly averse to this (except in time of war, when by political decision a goal-oriented government controlled wages, employment, prices, profits, manufacturing, and construction).

The twenty-first is not likely to be an American Century. Clinging to the Market, the negation of societal guidance, we might not even come in second. More likely we will be third, after a united Europe and an Asian-rim dominant Japan operating with strategic planning. Americans are more likely to be content with nursery reveries of

*To market, to market, to buy a fat pig,*
*Home again, home again, to dance a fast jig.*

# 18

# "Market Socialism" and "Free Economy": A Discussion of Alternatives

## (Fall 1990)

### Alec Nove

An attack on "market socialism" is now coming from a number of East European economists, converts to free-market ideology, who usually express regret at their own "naive" illusions of earlier times about the "reformability" of Soviet-type "socialism." A leading exponent of these ideas is János Kornai. He expresses his views systematically and cogently in *The Road to a Free Economy* (W.W. Norton & Co., New York, 1990). (The original Hungarian title was "A Passionate Pamphlet in the Cause of Economic Transition.") Its basic argument is that there is *no* "third way," no viable alternative to Western capitalism in one of its several forms, once one rejects Soviet-type "socialism." The experience of Hungary shows particularly clearly the failure of attempts to combine public ownership and marketization. So anything like "market socialism" is, in his view, a chimera. It cannot work. True, he points out that the Western model comes in many varieties: Sweden, the United States, and Japan differ in many ways. However, for him they share the characteristic that the bulk of the means of production is in private hands, and the market plays a dominant (though of course not an exclusive) role. No doubt echoing the views of many in his country, he declares that "following a number of decades in which a maximal state prevailed, it is now time to take great steps in the direction of a minimal state. Perhaps later generations will be able to envisage a more moderate mid-way."

I agree at once that the Hungarian halfway house—with state enterprises still subject to various instructions, benefiting from subsidies, "soft budget constraints," and lack of effective competition—was very unsatisfactory. Also that what he calls "freedom requirements" for private enterprise should certainly exist: there should be no discrimination in respect of supplies, taxes, access to foreign markets and foreign exchange, no need to apply for permits and licenses (though the need to register, if only to ensure that taxes are paid, is not an unreasonable requirement). I raised earlier the question whether, to qualify as "socialist," a society needs to impose some upper limit on the size of private activities. This is not a question that concerns Kornai, and this is, of course, an important difference. More important still is Kornai's emphasis on correcting (overcorrecting?) for the Communist regime's ideology of egalitarianism and negative attitudes toward "unearned" income, that is, income from property ownership, stock exchange or commodity deals, and the like, as well as income from other kinds of entrepreneurship. "Private production can be increased, modernized and raised to the level of successful modern large firms only if a considerable accumulation of private wealth takes place." He is so concerned with providing incentives for private enterprise that he even opposes progressive taxation.

Here our paths do diverge. But I can see why. He is understandably concerned with legitimizing private acquisitiveness in a social setting in which it was denigrated when it was not actively repressed. To take a Soviet example, suppose there were apples in Krasnodar and no apples in Kharkov. An enterprising would-be trader could make a lot of money by buying them cheap in Krasnodar and selling them at a much higher price in Kharkov. Most of his fellow citizens, as well as the law enforcement agencies, would regard such activities as illegitimate speculation, the apple merchant as "greedy" and a scoundrel. Clearly, all this must change. The way to prevent fortunes from being made in such ways is by encouraging free entry into the apple merchandising business; competition should quickly eliminate the excess profit. This is indeed much, much better than to send the successful merchant to jail, or to subject him to a 90 percent tax rate. On this I agree entirely with Kornai. But an inhabitant of Thatcherite Britain could be excused for wishing to stress the undesirability of extremes of inequality, much of it based on inheritance, or on what have to be characterized as unproductive activities. To me an entrepreneur is one who devises some new product or method, produces goods and services, thereby enriching not only her- or himself but society. He (or she) *works,* indeed works very hard and responsibly. This is not quite the same as pocketing an enormous commission for placing privatization issues on the stock market, or buying land needed for housing in order to resell it at a large profit, or the "work" of corporate raiders, whose takeover is followed not by installing a more efficient management but by a break-up and sell-off. The many American company executives who award themselves annual incomes of $1 million and more surely do so because of their position at the top of the company's *nomenklatura* rather than through successful entrepreneurship or exceptional marginal productivity!

Kornai rightly states that "the critical deficiency of socialist state property consists in the impersonalization of ownership." Therefore I, too, would welcome the emergence of real owners who take personal care of their business. But does he not know that in French a company or corporation is known as a *societé anonyme*? It is on record that this characteristic of the limited liability company caused concern to Adam Smith. We now have institutional investors who acquire large packages of shares with other people's money and sell them again maybe a few weeks later. Or the "owner" is an indifferent absentee, his fortune administered for him as he basks in the sun in Bermuda. There is quite a sizable theoretical literature on the relationship of principal and agent, the formal owner(s) and working management. Sometimes the "owner" is an Arab sheik's bank, totally remote from the actual concerns of the firm, ready to be "satisficed" if things do not go badly. For all these reasons I connect my vision of a flourishing private sector with the concept that "small is beautiful," with owners that do relate directly with what they own. I do not conclude from this that absentee owners should be expropriated, or limited liability com-

panies abolished in the real Western world in which we live. But in
envisaging a transition from Soviet-type "socialism" to something
more acceptable, we should not consciously aim to reproduce some of
the less desirable features of Western society, and by "less desirable" I
mean also those that contribute negatively to economic efficiency and
welfare. True, Kornai shows himself well aware of the fact that private-sector operators can "greedily want to make money . . . cheat
customers . . . defraud the state . . . forgo productive investment," and
so on. Customer choice, "the dissolution of the shortage economy,"
competition, should act as a cure.

Yes, it should. But should it not also act as a cure to inefficiency of
publicly owned or cooperative enterprises? Of course a nationalized
monopoly facing a queue of customers in a sellers' market will often
fail to perform adequately. But must public-sector enterprises necessarily operate amid shortage? Yes, Kornai himself wrote in *Economics
of Shortage,* in which he demonstrated that the generation of shortage
was, so to speak, systematic. Let us accept that it is indeed a built-in
characteristic of Soviet-type planning. But we are not speaking of a
Soviet-type economy. Such economies also, with barely any exception, were polluters of the atmosphere and underfunded medicine. Is
this then a necessary characteristic of any variety of economy containing a large public or socially owned sector?

Kornai himself would no doubt agree that competition, customer
choice, makes a vital difference to productive efficiency, to producer
motivation to satisfy demand. Would he also argue that Soviet and
Hungarian experience proves that publicly owned enterprises are of
their very nature incapable of competition? To the example of Moscow theaters, which undoubtedly compete for spectators, I could add
Soviet literary journals such as *Novyi mir, Znamya, Nash Sovre-
mennik,* and many others. Under conditions of *glasnost,* they seek with
the utmost vigor to attract subscribers, while pursuing a variety of
editorial policies. Kornai may point to the danger of censorship, to the
possibility of sacking independent-minded editors, and I naturally
agree that there should not be an imposed state monopoly in publishing. However, the world knows of many cases of censorship being
imposed on privately owned papers, and such owners as Rupert
Murdoch are not averse to sacking editors and imposing their political

line. In Budapest there are (and have long been) restaurants that are the property of the state, or are leased, or cooperative, or private. Can one discern a correlation between forms of ownership and the quality of the cooking or service? Is it not the fact of competition, the absence of queues, of chronic shortage, that really matters? And in some areas of life the sense of public service matters, too. One thinks of the quality contrast between American commercial television channels and the BBC, the tradition (where it has survived commercial pressures) of punctual postal deliveries, and the like.

Is there not a case for much more research into which publicly owned enterprises perform well and which badly, and where, and why?

*Electricité de France,* the Dutch railways, Norwegian coastal shipping, American airports, Swiss postal buses, Swedish telephones, even Budapest's own municipal transport system could be contrasted with examples of wasteful or unsuccessful "public" activities, which exist also. Must Kornai also not study the many cases where the state- or municipally-owned enterprise is subjected to a hard budget constraint? The world is full of complaints that public-sector expenditures of all kinds have been repeatedly cut, so it seems obvious that governments can resist pressures, and can close down the unsuccessful, if determined to do so.

And what of the role of the state as provider or financer of health, education, public parks, roads and other infrastructure, old-age pensions, a better environment, low-rent housing? Do such things lead us along "the road to serfdom"? Kornai does seek minimum social provision, but his attitude toward taxation and his emphasis on private gain and individual welfare seem to leave few resources for social purposes. It is not as if Eastern Europe under Communist rule provided adequately for such things. On the contrary. In which case it seems wrong to stress private affluence to such a degree. He may rely on private-sector provision. But take just one example: housing. He is all for decontrol, for market forces to operate. But he must know that in Budapest, as in London, New York, Paris, and so on, the market rent exceeds the total earnings of a high proportion of teachers, postal workers, cleaners, hospital staff members. Nor is this a passing, transitional phenomenon. As for infrastructure, even in affluent America the individualist tax-cutting ideology has led to a dangerous backlog of repairs to roads and bridges. The USSR, Poland, and Hungary need large-scale infrastructural investment of a kind typically financed by the state in all countries.

Inflation, says Kornai, "is not a natural disaster, it is created by governments or the political powers behind them." An oddly Friedmanite formulation. In Britain, despite the government's commitment to combating inflation *and* a budget surplus, inflation has been fueled by unrestrained credits and loans granted by deregulated private financial institutions.

Lastly, a word on structurally significant investment and the related question of the functioning of a capital market. I would simply refer to the ideas of Richardson,* and also to the quite considerable literature on the behavior of Wall Street and the City [of London], the struggle of theorists to comprehend the gyrations of stock prices (and exchange rates too). Of course one needs to provide a means to acquire capital, to market shares, and this in turn requires the emergence of a stratum of market intermediaries, dealers. It is the diversion of so much energy and talent to what Keynes called "the casino" that causes concern to those who wish capitalism to prosper. In Britain, at least, the stock exchange is not a significant source of venture capital, or of resources for real investment. We have low savings, of which a large part goes into the purchase of foreign assets; high interest rates maintain a high value for the pound while discouraging productive investment; and the government believes in laissez-faire and even cuts scientific research budgets. All this hardly suggests changes in the structure of the British economy, which are urgently needed to cope with record trade deficits and industrial decline. Hungary, too, has inherited a number of structural distortions. I imagine Kornai's reply: Yes, and these distortions were due to state control, state intervention, state investments, so why should the remedy involve more of the same? To which one can only reply: The state also neglected the environment and achieved record levels of pollution, but it still remains the task of the state to clean up the mess. To clean it up in association with private business, private capital, including foreign capital, is most certainly needed to finance

---

*G.B. Richardson showed that perfect competition provides no basis for investment decisions, since the profitable opportunity is seen by all one's competitors.

necessary investments. Yes, it is necessary to incorporate a small country like Hungary into world markets, especially into Western Europe. But Western Europe too will be contemplating its own investment strategy, involving energy, fish stocks, steelworks. It also proposes a Social Charter, much disliked by Thatcher and apparently also by Kornai, since he emphasizes that wage bargains must be a matter left solely to free negotiation between employer and employee (other than in the state sector, where he advocates tight wage control).

Kornai is, after all, not Hayek or Friedman. He does recognize a role for the state beyond that of a "night watchman." He would agree that industrial zoning, preservation of architectural ensembles, policies designed to restrict megalopolises (Mexico City now has over twenty million inhabitants!) are necessary areas of public policy, and that public parks provide more human freedom than would their sell-off to private individuals. Nor does he oppose the "safety-net" concept of a welfare state, and he favors action to protect the environment. If I understand him aright, he wishes to give emphasis to private wealth creation, so that, in due course, social democrats could demand and obtain more for social purposes. Indeed, he may then even join them himself. Of course his ideas are deeply influenced both by East European experience and by the urgent need to compensate (even overcompensate) for the distortions imposed by state and party under Communist rule. He stresses that he is concerned with immediate remedies for countries such as Hungary, and not with describing the sort of society he prefers. I imagine that if he were a British citizen in the year 1990 his emphases would be different, as mine are. For one thing he would be conscious of the fact that Thatcherite laissez-faire has *not* had a positive effect on the real wealth-creating sectors of the British economy.

Which leaves us both far from "socialism" in any variant of that ill-defined word. Perhaps we would both settle for a kind of welfare-capitalism-with-a-human-face, not easy to distinguish from a "socialism" with a big role for private capital and individual entrepreneurs? Much may depend in the end on the stability of the international system that the East Europeans are now so keen to join. What if it founders under a mountain of debt and cumulative trade-and-payments disequilibria? As far as I am concerned, *not* devoutly to be wished. But who can say that it is impossible?

# 19

# Remaking Our Economy: New Strategies for Structural Reform

## (Spring 1993)

### *Fred Block*

Across the political spectrum, there is an absence of serious and persuasive ideas for reviving and rebuilding the U.S. economy. Bill Clinton's advocacy of extensive federal investment in infrastructure, training, and education is a vast improvement over anything else on the horizon, but it represents only a first step. The economy needs reforms on the scale of the New Deal, but Roosevelt and his Brain Trust were able to draw on a rich vein of bold reform ideas that had previously been advanced by progressive and socialist reformers and intellectuals. Today's left has failed to produce a comparable body of ideas.

This essay is intended as part of a broader effort to make up this deficit. It seeks to sketch out a series of structural reforms that could contribute to both a stronger economy and increased democracy and equality. But first it is necessary to reconsider some of the intellectual assumptions that shape our thinking about the economy and our vision of the good society.

Many on the left continue to hold on to a vestigial Marxism that sees the economic realm as somehow "more real" than everything else; with all kinds of subtle qualifications, they retain the idea that the economy is determinant in the last instance. However, the economy does not have a necessary logic of its own; it is only a set of practices that appears to be coherent because we share certain cultural beliefs. The claim, for example, that the broad outlines of the society are determined by the search for corporate profit is unpersuasive on two grounds. First, there are many different strategies by which corporations can attempt to increase their profits—sweating workers and smashing unions is only one of a range of options now being pursued. Second, the calculations of what is profit and of how much profit is enough are themselves the products of prior assumptions that vary significantly across countries.

Yet this same argument also points to a radically different conclusion. Although the economy is not determinant in bourgeois society or any other society, economic ideology does play an extraordinarily central role in market societies. When we ask why we cannot have more democracy or more protection of the environment, the inevitable answer is that it would interfere with the efficient workings of the market. Similarly, when we ask why women cannot be paid the same as men or why we cannot spend more money to combat the AIDS epidemic, the answer is that as a society we simply "cannot afford" to do these things. In short, when social movements of the left demand institutional changes, resistance to those changes is based on the claim that they would be economically irrational.

Winning gains for these movements rests—in part—on their ability to challenge this dominant economic ideology. The movements need to show that these assertions about what we cannot afford or what would be economically irrational are rooted in "claims of false necessity," which are intellectually incoherent and empirically unsustainable.

The left should devote a portion of its energies to this critique of economic ideology. Yet critique without some sense of alternative is ultimately empty. Hence, the next step is to move beyond the false dichotomy of plan versus market to imagine the broad range of possible institutional structures for organizing the economic dimension of society.

The left's suspicion of markets is rooted in the romantic critique of commodification and an underlying nostalgia for feudalism. Yet these traditions mislead because there is nothing inherently wrong with buying and selling things at prices determined by a market. To be sure, not everything should be sold on the market—human beings, medical care, and the attention of politicians are some of the obvious exceptions. However, the task is not to eliminate markets but to block certain types of socially undesirable exchanges while regulating those that are organized through markets. To be sure, market participants sometimes exercise coercive power over others, but effective regulation can limit the extent of coercion in markets.

Contrary to the utopianism of both classical liberalism and classical Marxism, the idea is not to make all allocation dependent on either the market or "the plan," but rather to combine markets with various forms of regulation to achieve desired ends. Across the developed market economies, there are distinctly different institutional arrangements for providing health care, for organizing scientific research, and so on. We can draw on these experiences to imagine new institutional arrangements that could assure a highly productive economy without compromising democracy, equality, and the protection of the environment.

The last step is to move beyond broad visions of alternatives to imagine the specific institutional arrangements of a new kind of society. Our insistence that claims of necessity are false rests on the argument that there is a *better* way to do things in which we would not have to engage in one of the false choices—for example, protecting jobs or having a clean environment—that defenders of the present system insist are inevitable. It is not until we have imagined the institutional framework of a better kind of society and have persuaded millions of people that ours is an attractive vision that we can expect any radical social change.

To be sure, this process of designing blueprints forces us to confront the danger of totalitarianism—the risk that even a well-intentioned vision of a good society could degenerate into dictatorship. It is for this reason that the blueprints must be thoroughly pluralist. This means retaining many of the inherited techniques for avoiding the concentration of power while also inventing new ones. It involves, as well, rejecting the implicitly totalitarian dream of a New Socialist Man or Woman in favor of a multiplicity of visions of what it is to be human.

The blueprint must be based on reformist principles, so that the bounds of what is possible within the existing society are being pushed forward step-by-step. While this does not eliminate hard choices about political priorities, it eliminates the radical separation between the present and the future that troubled the Marxist tradition.

## An Alternative Vision

In constructing an alternative economic vision, it is necessary to establish some principles of design—what do we want this new institutional structure to do? My own starting point is to combine a highly productive advanced economy with institutions that would give much broader scope to democracy, equality, personal liberty and autonomy, and environmental protection than existing arrangements.

But why can't we have more democracy, more equality, more liberty, and a healthier environment within our present institutions? The classic answers of the left—the anarchy of the market, private ownership of the means of production—are no longer adequate because they flow from a vision of a socialist alternative that is now empty of content. A somewhat different answer is that the central flaw in our current institutions is the exercise of class power by those who own and control most of the society's productive wealth. It is this exercise of class power that restricts and narrows the range of democratic politics. Not only are major structural reforms kept off the political agenda, but even minor reforms—higher corporate taxes, tighter environmental regulation, labor law reforms—are rarely advanced because capitalist interests insist that they will have dire economic consequences.

This restriction in the scope of democratic politics exacerbates each of the other problems. Institutional reforms to create more equality—across class, gender, and racial lines—are made far more difficult by the obstacles to measures that would redistribute resources from the rich to everyone else. The environmental regulations that we have are not the result of a broad democratic debate but rather those that people have the courage to support in the face of economic blackmail—the threat that tighter regulations will lead to a disappearance of jobs and economic opportunities. Even in the sphere of personal liberty, our ability to support reproductive freedom or to eliminate the stigmas on gay lifestyles are limited by resource constraints that are, in turn, linked to the exercise of class power.

If rich people simply had one vote like everybody else, there would be no problem. They would make their arguments for less redistributive taxation, for fewer rights for employees, and for less environmental regulation, and they would likely lose every vote. The problem, of course, is that they exert disproportionate influence over politicians through campaign finance and through their control over the economy. Although the former channel of undue influence has been closed in some democratic societies through legal reforms, the latter remains a potent weapon to limit democracy.

In this exercise of power, we encounter again our old friend—the prevailing economic ideology. People of wealth do not simply say, "Please do not increase taxes on our incomes and on the corporations because we do not like it." They insist instead that higher taxation will damage the overall economy; it will lead to inflation, higher unemployment, or trade deficits. But the most important point is that if they happen to lose this battle, and their taxes are raised despite their warnings, they usually have the ability to make their predictions come true. By slashing new investment, they can push up unemployment or they can raise prices faster than they previously planned to increase the rate of inflation. Then they can go back and say, "We told you so," and the likely result is that they will win the next round. The strategy works even if the logic of their economic arguments is deeply flawed.

Are there institutional reforms that could eliminate this systematic exercise of class power? The four reforms proposed below would leave many of our existing institutions untouched, but they could radically diminish the exercise of class power by the wealthy. They could broaden the sphere of democratic politics and create a terrain on which struggles for equality, for the environment, and for liberty would have far broader opportunities for success.*

---

*These reforms would also contribute to the kind of highly productive economy that I analyze in *Postindustrial Possibilities: A Critique of Economic Discourse* (Berkeley: University of California Press, 1990). For a fuller discussion of these reforms, see "Capitalism Without Class Power," *Politics & Society,* September 1992.

## Campaign and Registration Reform

This is familiar territory. The modest post-Watergate campaign reforms in the United States have been a total failure. Political Action
Committee (PAC) money from corporations and business associations
has corrupted the Congress, and loopholes in the law allow substantial
flows of "sewer money"—large contributions by individuals directly
to the political parties to finance presidential campaigns. Public funding for all federal offices, the elimination of PACs, free time for
candidates on television and radio, and a $100 contribution limit could
help restore an even playing field. At the same time, universal voter
registration and Sunday elections would help to overcome the current
class bias in electoral participation.

## Restructuring the Corporate Form

The U.S. corporation is one of the last bastions of dictatorship on
earth. A board of directors that is—in theory—chosen by the shareholders appoints a chief executive officer (CEO) who has virtually
absolute power over the firm. A CEO is often able to stack the board
with friends and supporters, eliminating the last legal barrier to unlimited power. Even when the board is not in the CEO's pocket, the
CEO's power is still formidable. The CEO decides on the fate of the
firm's managers; any of them can be thrown overboard for crossing
the big boss. The CEO also decides which of the firm's divisions are
sold off, which are exploited as "cash cows," and which are targeted
for future growth.

   This dictatorial form makes it far easier for corporations to exert
economic blackmail. If the CEO is persuaded that a particular government initiative—increased regulations or higher taxes—is undesirable,
he or she acting alone has the power to cut back the firm's investment
plans. If fifty of the CEOs of the largest firms reach the same conclusion, they can put a powerful brake on the entire economy.

   Since the message of the revolutions of 1989 is that dictatorship is
inferior to democracy, it is time this lesson was also learned in corporate boardrooms across North America. The most reliable means to
transform the firm from dictatorship to democracy is to restructure the

corporate board to make it represent a variety of different constituencies. This could be done by requiring all corporations above a minimal size to incorporate at the federal level, and the federal statute would mandate a board chosen as follows: 35 percent of the board members by the shareholders, another 35 percent by the employees, and the remainder by other constituencies—bondholders, creditors, suppliers, consumers, and advocates for the natural environment.

With no single constituency able to dominate the board, the firm's direction would be shaped by an open process of debate. Since employees would also need open political debate to choose their representatives, discussions among employees would interact with debates within the board. The result would be that CEOs would be much more like democratic leaders than dictators; they would have to develop convincing rationales for their choices. This broader debate and discussion should measurably improve the quality of executive decision making.

On issues of central concern, the CEO would no longer be able to decide unilaterally to slash the firm's planned investments in response to what he or she perceived as an unfavorable business environment. The board would consider such cutbacks long and hard, and it would be likely to question the rationale behind economic blackmail. For example, why should the firm cut back its investment plans just because of higher taxes on rich people? The board might well decide that this is precisely the time to increase investment so as to gain market share from competitors who might reduce the size of their investments.

### New Banking Institutions

Though our democratized firms would be willing to invest at high levels, the commercial and investment banks that provide them with capital might be unwilling to lend. This is another important way in which class power is exercised: those who control the flow of money engage in "strategic nonlending"—the refusal to make capital available for certain activities in certain political circumstances. It is well known, for example, that employee-owned firms often find it extremely difficult to borrow money even when they have good collateral and good prospects. By their reluctance to finance "deviant" organizations, the bankers reinforce the idea that the dictatorial corporate firm is the only way to do business. Moreover, bankers as a group are even more effective at exercising economic blackmail. When the major commercial and investment banks start cutting back sharply on loans and new underwritings in response to government policies that they do not like, they also have the power to bring the economy to a halt.

The solution here is to make the banking industry more competitive so as to reduce the opportunities for the collusive behavior that underlies strategic nonlending. The federal government can do this by launching ten new commercial banks and ten new investment banks that would operate as semipublic entities. These banks would be insulated from partisan interference, but they would be subject to government oversight to assure that they fulfill their mandate to lend money in the public interest. The government would provide the banks with their initial capital, and they would compete with private banks to raise money on the capital markets and to find customers in need of finance.

From the start, these new banks would be oriented toward long-term results and sustained cooperative relations with their clients. In our current financial institutions, money managers are rewarded for their successes in producing high quarterly returns on their portfolios. In these new banks, money managers would be rewarded for nurturing productive enterprises over five to ten years. In short, these new banks would play a role that is similar to the role of banks in the German and Japanese economies.

Although this proposal could have significant economic benefits, the greatest payoff would be in reducing the possibilities of economic blackmail. If private banks reduce their lending activities, the public banks could be expected to step in aggressively to steal those clients. This would make it far more difficult to launch an investment strike against government policies. Moreover, the public banks would be less likely to discriminate against "deviant" borrowers such as employee cooperatives and local governments engaged in productive investment.

## Capital Controls

Even with all of these steps, wealthholders and firms would still be able to sabotage the economy through capital flight. Here again, they have the power to make their prophecies self-fulfilling. They argue that if the government pursues its redistributive course, it will damage the investment climate and lead to a huge shift of capital abroad. And if the government persists, lo and behold, the predicted capital exodus takes place. The resulting balance of payments crisis is usually enough to force governments back into line.

For this reason, it is essential to eliminate this weapon from the arsenal of wealthholders. This can be done by a system of internationally negotiated stand-by controls on capital flight that require countries to return capital that has moved abroad in violation of a nation's laws. Since such returned funds would be confiscated if the owner was convicted of illegal capital exports, such an internationally sanctioned system would provide a powerful deterrent. It is significant that the early drafts for the IMF (International Monetary Fund) agreement written in the Roosevelt administration contained provisions for precisely these measures to assure the return of illegal flight capital.

Still, objections to capital controls might be raised on grounds of economic efficiency, liberty, and practicality. The efficiency argument is that in an integrated world economy, capital must be able to flow across international lines in response to market signals. However, it is possible to have open and vigorous international trade including complex networks of cooperation among international firms operating in different countries without huge and continuing capital flows. If IBM wants to build a new facility within the boundaries of the European Economic Community, it can borrow the needed money in Europe, and the same goes for Japanese or European-based firms. Moreover, requiring that such investments be financed with locally raised capital will help to preserve the ability of national or regional monetary authorities to use interest-rate policies for macroeconomic stabilization.

It is only for investment in less developed countries and the former Soviet bloc that these restrictions on capital export would significantly interfere with commerce. However, the experience of market-mediated capital flows to the Third World has been disastrous. Third World countries in the aggregate have been net exporters of capital. This shows that the market mechanism cannot assure that finance flows to the regions where it is most needed. To assure positive capital transfers to poorer regions requires reducing the role of market flows and reorienting the activities of international development agencies. In short, a new regime governing international capital flows could be developed that combined reduced mobility for private capital and new mechanisms for assuring real capital transfers to developing areas.

The argument from liberty is that taking away someone's ability to shift $100 million of wealth from dollars to deutsche marks interferes with basic rights. However, rights and liberty are rooted in political communities, and such communities must be able to keep their members from engaging in behavior destructive of the social fabric. If the costs to the larger community of allowing full capital mobility are too high, there is every reason to restrict the exercise of that right.

The practicality arguments assert that such capital flows cannot possibly be controlled and that an international agreement to establish such controls is highly unlikely. The first argument rests on the idea that if technology has made something easy to do, then it cannot possibly be regulated. Since new technologies make it easy to shift a billion dollars from one country to another in a few seconds by typing on a keyboard, then it is impossible to prevent people from carrying out such electronic shifts of capital. However, the technological ease makes it all the more important that such flows be carefully monitored by regulatory authorities.

This was, after all, the lesson of the Bank for Commerce and Credit International (BCCI) scandal. The new technologies meant that thieves operating in the cracks between national banking regulations could steal billions. The looting that occurred in the United States in the savings and loan scandal that was made possible by lax regulation will continue to happen internationally on an even larger scale if national authorities do not cooperate to regulate international capital flows. In a word, international electronic fund transfers make more oversight a necessity, and with that increased oversight, the range of legitimate capital transfers could be narrowed.

But what of the prospects of international agreement? The reality is that U.S. enthusiasm for international laissez-faire is not shared by many in Europe and Japan, or by much of the Third World. The dangers of the free international movement of capital are understood abroad much better than they are in the U.S. If the U.S. position on international capital mobility were to shift, the prospects would be good for negotiating a new international regime governing capital movements. Such a regime would be resisted by nations or islands that have built their economies as tax and banking havens, but the risks to the world economy of unregulated banks operating in such locales are now so great that the resistance could be overcome.

I leave it to others to judge whether these four reforms could be implemented in the foreseeable future. The critical point is that if we imagine a society that had made these four reforms, its politics would be radically different from our acquired conceptions of both "socialism" and "capitalism." There would still be private ownership of the means of production, but the degree of "privateness" of control over corporate property would be greatly diminished by the need to create effective governing coalitions out of different constituencies. At the same time, the ability of private wealthholders to prevail in political conflicts would be greatly diminished because they could no longer credibly threaten to pick up their marbles and go home. All of this could be accomplished without centralizing control over investment decisions in the hands of the state.

In this new political space, a democratic citizenry would have far more freedom to shape the economy as it wished. The decision as to how much emphasis to place on the protection of the environment could be made without a threat of economic blackmail. People would no longer have to see the amount of leisure time or the quality of the jobs in the economy as factors over which they had no control. Tradeoffs would remain; increasing leisure time or cleaner air might mean diminished output. But the citizenry would gain the ability to decide how much of one variable to trade against the other. That they would make the right choices is certainly not assured, but that danger is inherent in democratic government. After all, the great virtue of democracy is that it gives us the capacity to learn from mistakes.

# Index